THE IRWIN SERIES IN ECONOMICS

CONSULTING EDITOR

LLOYD G. REYNOLDS

YALE UNIVERSITY

BOOKS IN THE IRWIN SERIES IN ECONOMICS

ANDERSON, GITLOW, & DIAMOND (Editors) *General Economics: A Book of Readings* rev. ed.
BALASSA *The Theory of Economic Integration*
BEAL & WICKERSHAM *The Practice of Collective Bargaining* rev. ed.
BLAUG *Economic Theory in Retrospect*
BORNSTEIN & FUSFELD *The Soviet Economy: A Book of Readings*
BRANDIS *Economics: Principles and Policy* rev. ed.
BUCHANAN *The Public Finances*
BUSHAW & CLOWER *Introduction to Mathematical Economics*
CARTTER *Theory of Wages and Employment*
DAVIDSON, SMITH, & WILEY *Economics: An Analytical Approach* rev. ed.
DAVIS, HUGHES, & MCDOUGALL *American Economic History: The Development of a National Economy*
DUE *Government Finance: An Economic Analysis* 3d ed.
DUE & CLOWER *Intermediate Economic Analysis* 4th ed.
DUNLOP & HEALY *Collective Bargaining: Principles and Cases* rev. ed.
GAMBS & WERTIMER *Economics and Man*
GORDON *The Investment Financing and Valuation of the Corporation*
GRAMPP & WEILER (Editors) *Economic Policy: Readings in Political Economy* 3d ed.
GROSSMAN, HANSEN, HENDRIKSEN, MCALLISTER, OKUDA, & WOLMAN (Editors) *Readings in Current Economics* rev. ed.
GUTHRIE *Economics* rev. ed.
HAGEN (Editor) *Planning Economic Development*
HALM *Economics of Money and Banking* rev. ed.
HARRISS *The American Economy: Principles, Practices, and Policies* 4th ed.
HIGGINS *United Nations and U.S. Foreign Economic Policy*
JOME *Principles of Money and Banking*
KINDLEBERGER *International Economics* 3d ed.
KUHLMAN & SKINNER *The Economic System* rev. ed.
LEE *Macroeconomics: Fluctuations, Growth, and Stability* 3d ed.
LOCKLIN *Economics of Transportation* 5th ed.
MEYERS *Economics of Labor Relations*
PEGRUM *Public Regulation of Business*
PEGRUM *Transportation: Economics and Public Policy*
REDDAWAY *The Development of the Indian Economy*
REYNOLDS *Economics: A General Introduction*
SCITOVSKY *Welfare and Competition: The Economics of a Fully Employed Economy*
SHAW *Money, Income, and Monetary Policy*
SIEGEL *Aggregate Economics and Public Policy*
SIRKIN *Introduction to Macroeconomic Theory*
SNIDER *Introduction to International Economics* rev. ed.
SPENCER, CLARK, & HOGUET *Business and Economic Forecasting: An Econometric Approach*
SPENCER & SIEGELMAN *Managerial Economics: Decision Making and Forward Planning*
VANEK *International Trade: Theory and Economic Policy*
WILCOX *Public Policies Toward Business* rev. ed.

AMERICAN ECONOMIC HISTORY

The Development of a National Economy

AMERICAN ECONOMIC HISTORY

The Development of a National Economy

LANCE E. DAVIS

JONATHAN R. T. HUGHES

Both of the Department of Economics
Purdue University
and

DUNCAN M. McDOUGALL

Carleton University

REVISED EDITION · 1965

RICHARD D. IRWIN, INC.

HOMEWOOD, ILLINOIS

Revised Edition

First Printing, April, 1965

PRINTED IN THE UNITED STATES OF AMERICA

Library of Congress Catalog Card No. 65–17697

PREFACE

Our objectives in writing this book are varied. In the first place, we want to place the study of American economic history back into the core of the study of economics. Largely because of the lack of rigor and coherence in many standard textbooks, economic history has increasingly become marginal to the undergraduate study of economics. We hope to correct this situation. We have tried to make possible a more general use of the materials of economic history by relying upon the use of simple economic analysis to explain the main patterns of America's economic development since the early nineteenth century. At the same time, however, we mean this book to provide an empirical foundation upon which students can base their subsequent work in economics. To do all this we have gone far afield from the standard textbook in economic history. We have tried to ask economists' questions of the historical materials.

Nor does our break with tradition end here. We advocate that this book be used as the basis of the first course in economics. Ideally such a course should *precede* a really rigorous Principles course. For pedagogical reasons it appears to us that the historical materials in this book belong at the very beginning of a student's study of economics. For several years we have experienced the disheartening problems of teaching economic history to students who have no knowledge of theory, and of teaching "principles" to students with little or no institutional information at their disposal. We believe that these problems are solved most readily by providing institutional material first; but in so doing we will, of necessity, introduce the students to the basic tools of economic theory. This book could then provide a suitable terminal course in "principles." Certainly it is apparent that the teacher of this book will need somewhat more sophistication in both the worlds of history and economics than is required by many economic history textbooks.

Since ours is a relatively new approach to the study of American economic development, several difficult and novel problems have arisen in our attempt to write the "new" history. First, we have found it necessary to avoid (as irrelevant to our purpose) many of the traditional discussions of social and political movements of the past. Second, we eschew any treatment of the Colonial period and the years up to the end of the Napoleonic Wars. Admittedly, this change of emphasis eliminates many exciting and familiar episodes in our nation's past. However, our analysis is most appropriate to an independent political unit engaging in international trade, and generating a rising per capita output; and neither conceptually nor in terms of available data would our system of organization and analysis do justice to the interesting but different problems of the earlier American and Colonial economy. Third, we have no intention that this book should be viewed as a complete economic history of the United States even after 1820. This book is a teaching vehicle. We are concerned with specific economic phenomena subject to economic analysis. Reference can therefore be made to the literature or to standard works to supplement our specialized treatment if the instructor so desires.

If the result of our labors is a sharp break with tradition, we can only say that, as teachers of economics as well as of economic history, tradition has not served us well. We hope that the reader who is familiar with the traditional treatment of American economic development will find enough new material incorporated into this study to outweigh the loss of those parts of American history we have omitted. We believe that the approach adopted in this book offers the best hope both of reviving the study of economic history and of enriching the economics curriculum with the experience of the nation's past. "History" is many things to many people; it is, among other things, the laboratory of Economic Science.

The authors are gratified by the response to the first edition of this text. Bearing in mind the suggestions made by critics, we have revised the materials, bringing the book up to date, and we have added new materials, including new chapters. While this revised edition therefore exhibits the usual vice of revision—growth—we have not allowed the size of the book to change in order of magnitude, nor has the fundamental conceptual framework been altered in spite of some rearrangement of chapters. This book was written for a special kind of use, one we, and our adopters, have found satisfactory. We offer the revised edition to those who believe, as we do, that this initial approach to the study of economic phenomena is a good one.

L.E.D.
J.R.T.H.
D.McD.

ACKNOWLEDGEMENTS

Acknowledgements are due to the following authors and publishers for permission to quote: A. F. Burns and W. C. Mitchell, *Measuring Business Cycles*, National Bureau of Economic Research; J. Frederic Dewhurst and Associates, *America's Needs and Resources: A New Survey*, The Twentieth Century Fund; R. W. Goldsmith, *Financial Intermediaries in the American Economy Since 1900*, National Bureau of Economic Research and The Princeton University Press; S. Kuznets, ed., *Income and Wealth, Series II*, The Johns Hopkins Press; S. Kuznets, *Economic Change*, W. W. Norton and Company; W. C. Mitchell, *Business Cycles: The Problem and Its Setting*, National Bureau of Economic Research; W. Owen, *The Metropolitan Transportation Problem*, The Brookings Institution; S. H. Queen and D. B. Carpenter, *The American City*, McGraw-Hill Book Company, Inc.; A. M. Schlesinger Jr., *The Age of Roosevelt, Vol. I*, Houghton Mifflin Company; B. Thomas, *Migration and Economic Growth*, N.I.E.S.R. No. 12, Cambridge University Press.

Acknowledgement is also due the following journal for permission to quote: S. Kuznets, "Quantitative Aspects of the Growth of Nations," *Economic Development and Cultural Change*.

ACKNOWLEDGEMENTS

Acknowledgements are due to the following authors and publishers for permission to quote: A. F. Burns and W. C. Mitchell, *Measuring Business Cycles,* National Bureau of Economic Research; J. Frederic Dewhurst and Associates, *America's Needs and Resources: A New Survey,* The Twentieth Century Fund; R. W. Goldsmith, *Financial Intermediaries in the American Economy Since 1900,* National Bureau of Economic Research and The Princeton University Press; S. Kuznets, ed., *Income and Wealth, Series II,* The Johns Hopkins Press; S. Kuznets, *Economic Change,* W. W. Norton and Company; W. C. Mitchell, *Business Cycles: The Problem and Its Setting,* National Bureau of Economic Research; W. Owen, *The Metropolitan Transportation Problem,* The Brookings Institution; S. H. Queen and D. B. Carpenter, *The American City,* McGraw-Hill Book Company, Inc.; A. M. Schlesinger Jr., *The Age of Roosevelt, Vol. I,* Houghton Mifflin Company; B. Thomas, *Migration and Economic Growth,* N.I.E.S.R. No. 12, Cambridge University Press.

Acknowledgement is also due the following journal for permission to quote: S. Kuznets, "Quantitative Aspects of the Growth of Nations," *Economic Development and Cultural Change.*

TABLE OF CONTENTS

III. The Public Economy

IV. The Accumulation of Capital and the Mobilization of Resources

V. The Expanding Dimensions of the American Economy

INTRODUCTION

Much of economic history merely chronicles events that can be said to have an economic focus, that is, events that influence man's efforts to achieve the maximum quantity of useful output from his environment.

This book, while economic history, is not simply a chronicle of economic events. We conceive the past as the social scientist's laboratory where hypotheses are tested and, if necessary, revised. In this book we have attempted to analyze America's economic past on the basis of a model (or system of ordering permitting deduction) cast in terms of the process of economic growth and development.

A moment's reflection on the vast number of economic events that have occurred in the United States in the past 200 years makes it perfectly clear that one could not write a chronicle with any hope of success. Those writers who attempt to record what has happened must have in mind a model, perhaps a very simple one, of what constitutes an economic event. In addition, they also have in mind a rule distinguishing a relevant from a nonrelevant economic event.

The Model

In popular discussion there is a marked tendency to talk of economic growth and development without specifying clearly what is meant by the two terms. A nation is sometimes said to be growing economically if it is becoming larger in terms of gross national product, or steel production, or automobile output, but we would prefer not to use the term "growth" if the increases in size are achieved by a mere increase in the quantity of resources applied to the processes of production. Instead, to us, economic growth and development involve changes in the processes of production themselves: a combining of resources in new and more productive ways to increase output. To put the matter in a different, and perhaps more concrete, way, consider the following example. Country A has established political control over an uninhabited island in the South Seas. Persons emigrate from country A to the island and establish a farming community. As subsequent waves of immigrants settle on the island, the farming frontier is pushed back; but farming remains an individual enterprise, each unit remaining sufficient unto itself. As settlement continues until the island is occupied, the island economy will grow in terms of output, but there is no reason to believe that output per capita will change. If the immigrants are of equal efficiency, the land of equal fertility, and farming methods unchanged over time, the last independent farm settlement will be just as well off as the first. That is, output per capita (assuming equal family size) will remain constant over time, and economic growth and development will not have occurred.

Suppose now, using the same illustration, we make some changes in the assumptions. The first immigrants to arrive on the island set about the process of establishing their community by concentrating first on the problem of providing a food supply and elementary shelter. As new immigrants arrive and the island market increases in size, the possibility of labor specialization opens up so that some workers on the island begin to concentrate on the production of agricultural implements, house furnishings, and so on. These craftsmen then trade the products of their labor for the agricultural surplus of the farm population. This domestic trade permits workers to concentrate on those activities in which they have a comparative advantage. In this way the output of both agricultural products and tools is increased.

When workers begin to concentrate it is highly probable that new ideas will be born. Craftsmen will see ways in which machines and techniques can be improved, and the new methods of production will yield a higher output per unit of input than the old methods. This increase in efficiency will be further stimulated if there is effective cross-fertilization of ideas, so that the ideas of one man or group of men are made freely available to all others. Any attempt to hide new discoveries will be an effective barrier to further progress.

There is no reason to believe that these new techniques of production will necessarily involve any large capital expenditure. All too often when one thinks of the industrial revolution the emphasis is upon impressive new machines, such as the steam engine. There were, however, a vast number of minor improvements in production operations whose cumulative effect upon output was equally important. While such improvements have important effects upon efficiency, it is nonetheless true that the effects are limited and that new large-scale technical breakthroughs are necessary for continued progress. Such technical breakthroughs are likely to involve heavy investments because, in general, increasing efficiency in the transformation of inputs into outputs requires more powerful sources of energy. If the island economy is to embark on programs involving substantial capital investments, an extension of the economy's market would be a wise move. Entry into foreign trade would permit increased specialization of the economy's resources and provide a source of capital for development. Increased specialization would result in a higher real output and therefore increased capacity to invest in durable capital goods. Investment in the island economy by foreigners would permit the economy to take advantage of investment opportunity beyond the current means of the economy. Repayment of the investment would be possible out of the increased real output produced by the capital put in place with the aid of the foreign savings.

As the island economy begins to take advantage of these opportunities, it begins to grow and develop. The output of the economy is growing as the population increases; and the economy is developing as specialization, trade, and technological improvements increase the output per worker. Once the economy has begun to develop economically, it is likely to continue to do so, at least for some time. Given a continuously vigorous labor force, the application of new techniques of production, a sufficient resource base (either in terms of a raw material, a power source, or specialized labor skills), and barring a natural or man-made catastrophe, the island will continue to develop. A spurt of development frequently grows into a self-sustaining process. As the labor force becomes more productive and an increasingly large surplus is generated, it is possible to support inventive inquiry leading to new efficiencies and even greater output per worker. If the population is willing to accept change and if resources are able to move into their most profitable use freely, then an environment is created within which development can easily take place.

Once the island economy has started on the process of development, is there a necessary way it must proceed? We are accustomed to talk of the nonindustrialized countries of the world as being synonymous with the underdeveloped countries. While it is true that all underdeveloped countries of the world are nonindustrial, it is not true that all nonindustrial countries are underdeveloped. New Zealand and Denmark can be called nonindustrial, but it would be manifestly untrue to call them underdeveloped. Those countries are parts of the modern specialized world market but are earning their livelihood at occupations other than factory production. Other countries, such as Australia, Canada, and Argentina, may also be placed in the commercialized but nonindustrialized category. Building a factory is not a precondition for development; unfortunately many new countries make the mistake of believing that it is. Resources that can be ill-afforded are squandered in an attempt to construct the trappings of the wealthy industrial countries. It is true that machines have only begun to be used in production throughout the world, but they can frequently be used in agriculture, fishing, and the provision of services more effectively than they can in factories. The comparative advantage of the island economy we have been discussing might, for example, lie in agriculture. It would then be a mistake, from an economic point of view, to concentrate heavily in the production of manufactured articles.

Patterns in American Development

Although the salient features of American development resemble in many respects those of the island economy, many aspects of that nation's development cannot be examined in the framework of the hypothetical economy we have been discussing. In this section we will summarize the main patterns in the history of American development, as we see them. These factors, will, of course, be examined in greater detail later in the book.

It would be well at this point to make explicit two matters that lie implicitly behind the historical analysis of this book. First, we have to a large extent ignored the chronological ordering of events so dear to the hearts of many of those who write history. Our model, although useful in analyzing economic events, is still a very blunt instrument and does not provide us with the means for setting down exact temporal relationships between variables. Thus, while in many cases we are able to see that economic events have succeeded one another in time, it is not possible yet to say that the observed ordering is a necessary one. Second, while the model is crude, the information used to illustrate (test) the model is in many cases even cruder. There are, therefore, vast gaps in our knowledge of the development of the American economy; and much patient research effort must still be expended if we are ultimately to fit together a complete picture of the economic development of the United States.

We begin our discussion of American development with an analysis of the population variable. There is a basic and very obvious reason for this choice. Without people the American economy would neither have grown nor developed. In addition, the development of the American economy was greatly facilitated by the fact that population increased rapidly, but not so rapidly that it outstripped the growth of the resource base.

There are still other dimensions of the population variable that have been very important to American economic development. The people that populated this country brought with them, or developed in the American environment, characteristics of mobility and adaptability that played a significant role in economic development. However, it must be remembered that the population also gave a peculiar cast to American economic development that may, at least in its outward respects, be quite unique. It may, for example, be a mistake for underdeveloped countries to attempt to imitate the American economy in much detail.

Before examining the characteristics of American population that appear to be of particular relevance in terms of American development, it might be useful to recall that America was not uninhabited when the Europeans landed. Although there are conflicting estimates, it appears probable that the native population of what is now the United States was something in the neighborhood of 1 million persons. Moreover, from what we can tell, population was probably not growing, and with no change in technology it is extremely unlikely that the population would ever have reached two million. Clearly, therefore, it was not the existence of people themselves that made development possible.

The factors that contribute to the characteristics of a population group are fantastically complex and only imperfectly understood. In the popular mind the distinction between racial and ethnic groups is frequently clear and indisputable, and the same type of superficial distinction is generally given to national groups as well. For example, Americans are characterized abroad as loud, softhearted, and naïve. Such generalizations are completely untenable. But as soon as one begins to explore beneath the surface there is a danger of being swamped in diversity. However, for our limited purpose of the study of American development, it is possible to give in broad terms those characteristics of the American population that facilitated the process of development.

The Western Europeans who colonized the United States were the products of a civilization that had passed through a period of intense intellectual ferment. It is difficult for us today to realize to what extent the Renaissance and the Reformation had reformulated the character of European man. Their product was a man who was independent, inquisitive, and acquisitive—a man impatient of authority exercised from above, inquisitive about the world around him and his place in it; a man who saw nothing immoral in attempting to do all in his power to make his stay on earth as pleasant or comfortable as possible. For such people, America was a promised land. Here was room to grow, room to be independent, and a wealth of resources available for exploitation. In such an environment the dynamics of Western man were let loose with truly impressive results. The dynamic characteristics of the American population were maintained throughout the nineteenth century and into the twentieth century. Recently, however, some observers of the American scene have pointed to the increasing size of the central government and the formation of power blocs within the economy as evidence that the dynamic element of the American people has died. Whether this is in fact the case, or whether modern complex industrial societies require a form of group dynamics to function and develop, we consider an open question.

However one wishes to describe the current American population, the evidence suggests that, in the past, the population was remarkably mobile. There was geographic mobility; settlement flowed west across the continent. There was occupational mobility; labor moved (willingly or unwillingly) from less attractive to more attractive occupations. There was class mobility; wealth was relatively easy to acquire and no rigid barriers prevented people moving from lower positions on the class scale to the upper positions of power and prestige.

It was this mobility that contributed most to the dynamics of the American population. We do not mean to imply that everybody was on the move at all times. All that was necessary was that there be sufficient mobility at the margin to equalize economic returns in various occupations and areas. The mobility of the population implies, of course, that there were places to move to. In the United States the movement was something more than a geographic shift.

The American people were moving westward, but they were reshaping the whole economy at the same time. It was in the reshaping of the economy that the rational, acquisitive nature of the American people played such an important role. These characteristics permitted them to develop new methods of production, adapt the techniques of Europe for application to the American environment, and reorganize the focus of productive effort as opportunities changed over time.

We have placed a great deal of emphasis on the role of population in economic development. We feel that many studies have concentrated too much on the measurable results of human activity rather than upon the humans themselves. This bias is, no doubt, due to the fact that many of the characteristics of populations we have been discussing are not quantifiable and therefore it is very difficult to say anything concrete about the role of population in development.

The institutional organizations developed in the United States played a significant part in the development of the economy. The formation of a federal government with the power—given to it by the Constitution or by court decisions—to encourage and regulate economic behavior, was of far-reaching importance. Imagine the chaos if the separate states were permitted to restrict interstate trade, to coin their own currency, to set weights and measures, or to establish their own law of contract and property. The people also gave the federal government both a taxing power to implement its decisions and, significantly, the ownership of unsettled lands. The existence of these public lands gave the federal government a tremendous prestige and power in determining the rate of development of the nation's economy. Federal government surveyors moved out in advance of settlement, marking trails and exploring the new country. As settlement began, the surveyors marked out the land, and the army provided protection and attempted (in most cases) to police the treaties by which the federal government tried to pacify the frontier. All levels of government participated heavily in the transportation systems that tied the economy together and made the large-scale internal market a reality. The tariff policy implemented by the federal government contained provisions that determined the growth of important segments of the economy. In some cases the people, through their government, decided to leave areas unregulated; such decisions also had far-reaching economic effects. It was not until the 1890's that any laws were passed regulating the inflow of migrants, and not until the 1920's that such regulation was effectively enforced. Although many of the operations of business were regulated under the common law, it was not until the end of the nineteenth century that the government felt it necessary to enter into extensive regulation of business practice where such practice clearly contravened the social good. Similarly, labor as an organized group in the economy was controlled and regulated under common and statute law until the 1930's, when its rightful role in the economy was finally recognized and its position vis-à-vis other groups was regularized. Finally, in the field of banking, centralized regulation has never been important in the United States and there were long periods when even state regulation was almost nonexistent.

We have talked at length about the mobility of population and the role such mobility played in the economic development of the United States. Capital mobility also played a vitally important role in development. The phrase "capital mobility" is used here to cover a number of topics. First, before a community can devote current productive effort to capital formation there must be saving, either voluntary or involuntary. The people must be able and willing, presumably under some sort of inducement, to forego consuming their total current output. Second, some institutional framework must exist whereby the savings of the community can be channeled from the net savers of the community to those willing to use the released command over resources for investment purposes. The banks, insurance companies, stock exchanges, and investment funds are examples of the type of business that provides the institutional framework for the capital market. Such institutions should, ideally, be quite sophisticated. They should be diligent in bringing together the savings of all groups in the community, and impartial in allocating these funds among investors. All too frequently the savings of small units in the economy were ignored and regional prejudice or ignorance barred investors interested in new geographic or industrial areas from access to the available pool of savings. Admittedly, to expect such sophistication from the financial institutions of nineteenth-century America would be unrealistic when many of these same charges can be leveled against American financial institutions today. The development over time of more sophisticated institutions has been an important element of American economic development. Third, capital mobility implies the existence of a body of entrepreneurs farsighted and dynamic enough to recognize the existence of profitable opportunities. Not all societies develop men with the necessary optimism and willingness to accept risks that successful capital formation requires. While some very large socially necessary projects can never be financed entirely by private entrepreneurs, too extensive government involvement in capital formation is quite likely to result in large-scale inefficiencies.

Foreign savings were also an important source of funds for capital formation. When the United States was unable to match its purchases from abroad by exporting goods and services, the difference was made up by foreign savings. The nineteenth century was a particularly happy time for the foreign borrower, and America was certainly a favored outlet for foreign savings. In the nineteenth century, the continental investor—and especially the English investor (because of the rapid development in London of specialized financial institutions)—appears to have been incurably optimistic about the profitability of the "new lands." In spite of periodic financial panics and defaults, money flowed in surprising volume out of Europe. America was a favored recipient because it was relatively close and well known, and perhaps also because of the "press agentry" of the American promoters. The myth of great wealth lying ready for the taking on the American continent was widely believed in Europe well into the nineteenth century. The Irish immigrants who expected to find the streets of New York paved with gold had their only slightly more sophisticated counterparts in the financial houses of London.

These, then, are some of the salient features of the American economic environment. The result of the development that occurred within this environment during the 175 years after the British relinquished this portion of their colonial empire is a nation of over 190 million souls that is generally conceded to be the most well-off economically in the history of the world. How did we achieve this status? That growth is the subject of the next twenty-five chapters.

The Tradition. Before we go on, it will be well to note briefly our objections to the traditional method of writing textbooks for courses in American economic history, since the organization of this book is different from that which generally prevails. In the following three chapters the student is provided the basic logical equipment to use in the study of American economic history. Why did prices move as they did over time? To what extent did prices reflect changes in technology, secular demand, or both? How did savings habits, consumption, international trade, and investment change over time? What were the effects of these, together with population movements, upon economic growth? These are some of the questions for which we are going to seek answers in the historical materials.

The information is arranged according to special topics arising from the basic economic questions we ask. This approach to the subject, although it has advantages for the student, does not follow tradition. Let us consider the tradition a moment. American economic history has long been a part of the curriculum at the better colleges and universities. It has been taught by both economics and history departments. More often than not the subject matter has been largely a derivative of American political history. The main categories for study have been viewed as descriptive and passive, while the primary dynamic element has been simply the passage of time. Thus the study of the nation's economic development has been organized primarily according to the fancies of the professional historian, who thinks in terms of politics, international affairs, and—mainly—war.

The traditional organization has been simply to divide the nation's history into five parts: roughly (1) from the Jamestown Settlement (1607) to the Revolutionary War (1775–1783), (2) from the Constitution (1789) to the Civil War (1861–65), (3) from the Civil War to World War I (1914), (4) from 1918 to World War II (1939–45), and (5) from the Japanese surrender to the present. Sometimes the last part of the organization simply runs from 1918 to the present. Such a scheme has the merit of ease and convenience. We all learn about our nation's major wars, and the dates of those wars become a convenient set of pegs upon which to hang the facts of the country's economic advance. Moreover, insofar as war leaves a permanent deposit of economic change, there is some *analytical* legitimacy in this traditional organization of our economic history. The relevant question is "how much change did the war make?" It is, alas, not answered, or really even asked by writers of textbooks organized on the traditional basis.

If we look at the major subdivisions that flow between the dates of peace agreements and declarations of new wars (Diagram A) in the major textbooks, we see that, in fact, war has had little to do with those primary characteristics of economic change which have attracted the attentions of writers of textbooks. One might reasonably conclude that economic historians who write textbooks have largely been military and political historians in disguise, their thinking basically committed to a traditional chronology of military effort and political achievement, with the history of economic achievement merely a series of descriptive slices sandwiched in between the really important historical events.

There is a good case, of course, for considering America from 1607 to the Revolution in a mainly political compartment. The basic fact of American economic life before 1775, and one which intrudes into everything, is British colonial policy. The thirteen seaboard

DIAGRAM A

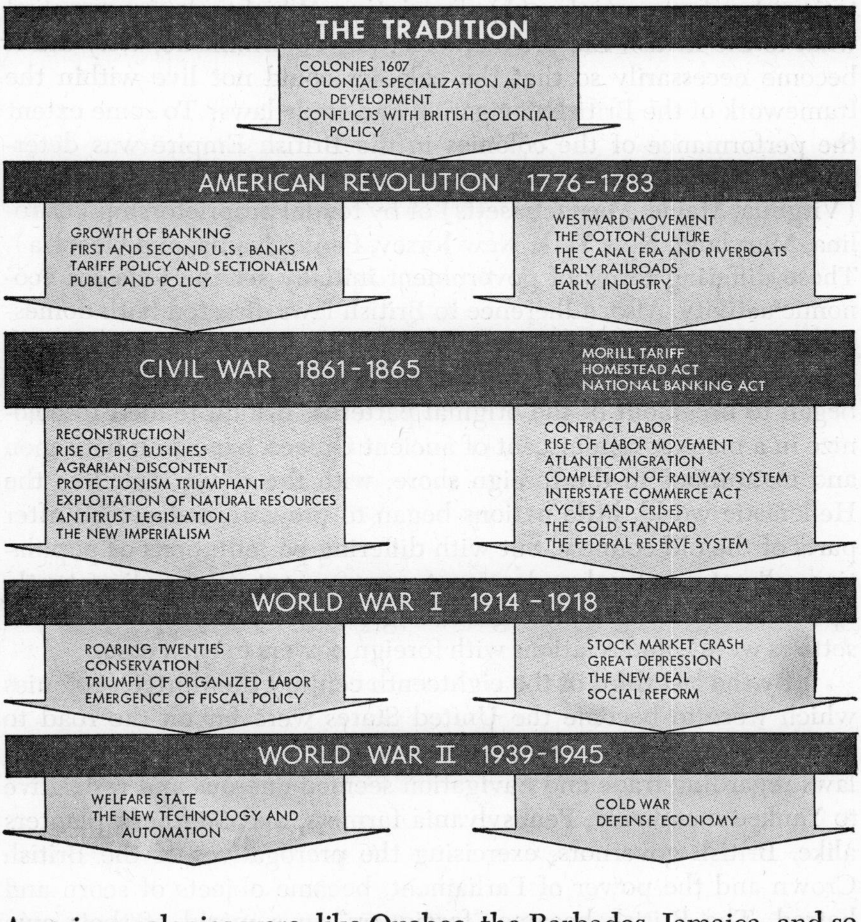

American colonies were, like Quebec, the Barbados, Jamaica, and so forth, objects of a governmental policy explicitly designed to enhance the welfare of the United Kingdom. Indeed, the colonies were originally little bits and pieces of Britain overseas, offshoots of British domestic affairs. Under the early Stuarts, the Commonwealth, the later Stuarts, Queen Anne and the Hanoverian dynasty, these overseas settlements were established, controlled, and defended as disconnected parts of the mother country. Except where the Americans ignored the colonial laws and regulations promulgated by their British cousins (which in London looked increasingly like the majority of the time as the decades marched toward 1776) economic life in what became the United States was largely a frontier reflection of metropolitan Britain.

Accordingly, treatment of colonial America by economic historians has been mainly: (1) descriptive, Which colonies supplied what to the British Empire markets?; (2) deterministic, Why did it become necessarily so that the colonies could not live within the framework of the British navigation and trade laws? To some extent the performance of the colonies in the British Empire was determined by the nature of the original settlement, whether by charter (Virginia, Maine, Massachusetts) or by feudal proprietorship (Carolina, Maryland, New York, New Jersey, Pennsylvania, and Georgia). These differing forms of government initially set the tone for economic activity. Also, adherence to British laws directed both domestic development and foreign trade into distinct molds. But gradually, with a force accelerating in the eighteenth century, the colonies began to break out of the original patterns. Britain tended to colonize in a manner reminiscent of ancient Greece, exporting both men and institutions to the foreign shore, with the result that, like the Hellenistic world, little nations began to grow abroad copied after parts of the old country, but with differing permutations of population, climate, natural endowment, government (depending partly upon the original grants of governing powers, partly upon *who* the settlers were), and relations with foreign powers in each case.

By the last third of the eighteenth century the thirteen colonies which were to become the United States were far on the road to economic and political separation from the mother country. British laws regarding trade and navigation seemed onerous and restrictive to Yankee merchants, Pennsylvania farmers, and Southern planters alike. British governors, exercising the prerogatives of the British Crown and the power of Parliament, became objects of scorn and hatred. The British became "foreigners" in a world of their own creation.

After the long years of the American Revolution the new nation followed an independent course. The Revolutionary War did mark a major departure in American economic development, if for no other reason than the simple one that the success of the Revolution produced a fundamental change in institutions. Major Alexander Hamilton, who fought with Washington to free the American colonies from the system of British mercantilism, lived long enough to draw up a plan for a systematic kind of American mercantilism before he was killed by the pistol of Aaron Burr at the age of only forty-seven. A ubiquitous change in institutions on a national scale came that quickly. From the settlement of Jamestown Colony to the Declaration of Independence had been 169 years. By the speed of change alone the first conventional line of demarcation in American economic history, the Revolution, would seem to be justified.

But from the Constitutional Convention (1789) onward the political divisions of American economic history are far more artificial. Unless wars significantly change either the institutional framework of the economy or the order of magnitude of the economic data, it is difficult to see why a war should have been considered as a more important bench mark than, say, a great boom in economic activity, or a deep depression—both of which usually left significant deposits of economic and even demographic change.

Let us consider some of the major examples of the peculiar "twist" given to the interpretation of our economic history by political divisions. A major theme in the period 1789–1865 is the movement of the population across the Appalachian Barrier to the Pacific Coast. This is usually called something like "Westward Expansion." The major territorial acquisitions, the Louisiana Purchase (1803), the Mexican territories (1848), the Gadsden purchase (1853), and the Oregon settlement (1846) did all come before 1860. But the process of filling these vast areas with people, farms, and factories was a continuing phenomenon—it still is—and the westward expansion of a functioning economy accelerated mightily after 1865. It is curious to place a set of economic and demographic facts, a continuing process in time, only by its chronological beginning.

American commercial policy toward foreign governments is usually given a chapter under the title "The Tariff Question," and it later appears as something like "Protectionism Triumphant," or perhaps as parts of chapters dealing with "Economic Imperialism," "The Age of Big Business," or what have you. This makes a rigid stick figure out of a continuous, changing, and important thread in the total fabric. Tariffs, originally as sources of revenue, and later as protection and as foreign policy weapons (reciprocity) have risen and fallen according to all sorts of influences, including even the consequences of the business cycle. The element of "protection" in the arguments favoring tariffs was there from the beginning, and importantly so after the 1820's. Yet tariffs were reduced periodically, in the 1840's and 1850's, again in 1914, under the terms of reciprocity policies in the 1930's, and today in our dealings with foreign nations. The heights of protection reached in the various periods, like the Morrill Tariff (1861), the McKinley Tariff (1890), or the Smoot-Hawley Tariff (1930), represented phases of a continuing relationship between American economic development and her foreign customers, and not once-over changes, as is implied by such colorful phrases as "Protectionism Triumphant." As a logical division in American tariff history, the Civil War is difficult to justify.

The development of the nation's agricultural economy has, similarly, experienced several distinct phases. The primary long-term characteristic has been a steadily mounting volume of production, an increasing ability to feed more people, while the proportions, and then the numbers, of people employed in agriculture fell. This pattern of development has proved to be typical of agriculture in industrial economies. American agriculture, except for its extraordinary productiveness, thus follows a path trodden by others. Certain events, like technological change, the opening of new tracts of agricultural land, federal legislation, and the application of science to agriculture have had great and lasting effects—more so, certainly, than the sequence of wars. The present problems of surplus production find an echo as far back as the "Populist Revolt" and the "Greenback" movement. The successive commercialization of agricultural life goes back to the opening of the Erie Canal and beyond. This continuous history is robbed of its own rationale if it is considered merely as a series of interludes between wars.

Similarly, the development of the American financial system has been an unfolding panorama, and the wars we have fought, except for special problems, such as those related to their finances, were not themselves more important in forming the financial institutions than were less dramatic episodes. The Suffolk Banking System was a forerunner of the present Federal Reserve System. The New York Safety Fund System was a forerunner of the Federal Deposit Insurance Corporation. The present system of "unit banking" is mainly an outcome of a long evolution of state banking. The investment banks are descendents of ante-bellum merchant banking, and so forth. The Civil War brought bank reform, but that reform was not of a magnitude different from those episodes already mentioned. The other wars resulted in no significant institutional changes in the banking structure. The present American financial system is the residue of a long history and is best understood if that history is weighed and balanced according to its own qualities. Wars were mainly interludes in that history, not the other way around.

Finally, the political division of industrial growth is one of the most ambiguous consequences of the tradition. Those who write and teach that the growth of large-scale industry in the fifty years after the Civil War was directly a consequence of that great disaster have their work cut out for them, especially in view of the large-scale enterprises developed in New England textiles decades before the Civil War, and the fact that scale of operations depended so much upon technology and the gradual development of markets. Such labels as "The Age of Trust," the era of "Monopoly Capitalism," and the like, applied to American industry in 1870–1900 and so dear to the heart of the tradition, describe nothing dependent upon the Civil War. Similarly, the "Rise of the Welfare State" can hardly be considered to be a product of either world war. As we will try to show in succeeding chapters, the growth and development of American industry is a history which owes little except profits to wars.

Thus the tradition in the organization of American economic history, while it has certain merits, also has the great drawback of unjustifiably confining our economy's development within the narrow limits of a political framework which is largely inappropriate to the subject matter. We therefore think that the topical and analytical method used in succeeding chapters ought to be an improvement in many ways and should make the study of the American economy's development a logical and meaningful exercise for the student.

I

Theoretical Background to the Study of Economic Development

Chapter 1 THE FREE-ENTERPRISE SYSTEM AND THE ALLOCATION OF RESOURCES

1–1. *Economic Problems and the Nature of the Economic System*

If there were no scarcity, every person could have all of every commodity that he desired, and questions relating to the best use of resources or products would be meaningless. In fact, however, our world is characterized by an infinite number of human wants and a finite number of goods and services capable of satisfying these wants. Given this divergence between wants and the goods required for their satisfaction, every economy is faced with the problem of allocating scarce resources among many possible alternative uses. In short, it is the function of the economic system to decide what is to be produced, what combination of inputs is to be used in their production, and which persons are to be given claims on these final products. Let us examine these three questions in more detail.

The resources available to society at any point in time can be used to produce many different commodities, but they are insufficient to produce all commodities in quantities sufficient to satisfy all wants. Which commodities and how much of each should be produced? Again, most commodities can be produced using various resource combinations. A comparison of agriculture in the United States and Europe, for example, indicates that in the United States relatively little labor in combination with relatively more land and capital is used to produce the same products produced in Europe with less land and capital and more labor. Each economy must decide which of the various resource combinations available to it should be chosen. (It should be obvious that the use of capital-intensive harvesters and combines was not a choice that faced the agricultural economy of medieval Europe.) Finally, the output of society must be distributed among its members, but how much should each receive? Workers have contributed their labor, landowners their land, capitalists their capital, and entrepreneurs their organizational ability. What fraction of the output should accrue to each?

These problems are not peculiar to the industrialized world, or the capitalistic world, or the Western world, but face every economy characterized by resources insufficient to satisfy all wants; in short, every economy yet known by man. There are, however, a multitude of possible ways of solving the three problems. Primitive tribes, for example, frequently let custom and tradition provide the answers. In the modern world, decisions are at times made by central direction, and at times made by the individuals and businesses of the economy interacting through a system of prices and markets. (An economy utilizing the latter structure is termed a free-enterprise economy.) Although there are no modern examples of either absolute central direction or perfect free enterprise, most modern economic systems lie somewhere between these two extremes; and it is common to characterize them on the basis of their position on the decision-making spectrum. Thus, we do not hesitate to say that the Soviet economy is largely centrally directed, although some elements of free enterprise do exist; and few people would refuse to call the American economy a free-enterprise system, although the government plays an important role in economic life.

It should be noted, however, that the distinction between types of economic systems used in this book is based solely on the location of economic decision-making power and implies nothing of the political structures of the economies under consideration. Free enterprise is not synonymous with democracy, nor is central direction necessarily associated with totalitarianism. (Britain, in the late eighteenth and early nineteenth centuries, was hardly a democracy but was certainly largely a free-enterprise system. Today, India is certainly a democracy, but its economy depends heavily upon central direction.)

Since the American economy (the subject of this book) lies closer to the free-enterprise end of the decision-making spectrum, it will be useful to examine the workings of a theoretical free-enterprise system in more detail. This model can help us understand the operation of the American economy and provide us with a standard against which the economy's performance may be measured. A centrally directed economy, with decision-making power effectively centralized, is easily imagined (although ease of conceptualization does not imply ease of operation); but a free-enterprise economy, with decision-making power spread between millions of consumers and thousands of business enterprises, is not so simple. How, then, does this system operate?

The operation of a modern free-enterprise economy would be difficult indeed to understand if one were faced with the entire complex agglomeration at once. However, the use of simplified economic models permits us to examine the various relationships within the economy in isolation, and later we can place these simplified relationships together into the complex model that more closely approximates reality. Thus, through abstraction and simplification, we are able to understand a complex organism that otherwise would defy analysis. Economic theory provides us with a logical model that, because it has been simplified and abstracted from reality, does not describe reality but does help us to understand it.

For the moment, let us abstract from reality and assume that our theoretical economy has no government and no foreign trade. It is an economic agglomeration of individuals who sell their services, or the services of things they own (land and capital), and buy the things they need; and of businesses who buy the services sold by the individuals and produce and sell the products demanded by the public. Let us further assume that no artificial or legal barriers exist to prevent any exchange, and that both individuals and firms are free to enter or exit from any business or market as they choose.

1–2. *The Mechanism of Market Adjustment and the Function of Prices as Commodity Rationers*

Within the framework of a free-enterprise system, the question of "what to produce" is answered by the consumers. Each consumer is assumed to have some ordering of preferences (that is, he can say, "I prefer cars to pie, and pie to tomatoes"), a certain stock of money, and a knowledge of the products available to him and their prices. The consumer can maximize his satisfaction by purchasing each commodity until the satisfaction he derives from spending his last penny would be the same, regardless of what commodity he chooses to spend it on (or, more precisely, until the ratio of the satisfaction derived from the last unit of any commodity to its price is equal for all commodities within the consumer's preference ordering). Let us examine this selection process in more detail.

The amount of any commodity the consumer chooses to buy can be related to a number of factors, including (1) the price of the commodity, (2) the price of other commodities, (3) the consumer's tastes, and (4) his income. A change in any of these factors may cause the consumer to alter his purchase decisions. In what manner do these factors affect the consumer's market decisions and how do these decisions affect the markets for commodities? For the moment, we will assume that the output of the commodity under consideration is fixed, and we will see how consumer demand interacts with the supply on the market to produce a price that just clears the market, a price that supplies those persons whose demands are most intense (i.e., those willing to pay the highest price) and rations out those whose demands are less intense. We have already seen that the quantity of a commodity demanded is a function of many things, but, for simplicity, let us first assume that only the commodity's price changes. What, then, is the effect of a change in price on the quantity demanded? Since every consumer has a limited income and a finite stock of assets (although these limits may be quite large), more of any commodity can be purchased only if the purchase of other commodities is restricted. Thus, the real cost of purchasing an extra unit of any commodity is the satisfaction that would have been derived from the other commodities that can no longer be purchased. Therefore, one would expect (other things being equal) that, as the price of a commodity increased, a consumer would tend to buy less of that commodity, since each price increase would force him to forego increasing quantities of other goods. A consumer's theoretical reaction to a price change is illustrated in Figure 1–1. This figure shows a schedule of the quantities of a commodity demanded at a list of prices, all other things being equal. Economists call this construct a *demand curve.*

Figure 1–1 indicates that a consumer is willing to increase his purchases of the commodity as its price falls, since the cost of the extra units, in terms of foregone commodities, has declined. If the price were *Oa,* the consumer would buy none of the product; if the price declined to *Ob,* he buys *OB;* and, if it falls to *Oc,* he increases his purchases to *OC*. The actual shape of the curve *DD* (it is drawn as a straight line only for convenience) depends, of course, on the other *determinants of demand* (taste, income, and other prices). In general, however, it can be said that the more necessary the commodity, the steeper will be the demand curve; and the more substitutes there are for a commodity, the flatter it will be (for any given scaler of the ordinate and abscissa and for any given price and quantity). Thus, the demand for insulin by a diabetic might be almost vertical (limited only by his income constraint), while the demand for any particular brand of cigarettes may be almost horizontal (despite the claims of Madison Avenue, one cigarette is, after all, much like another).

If we add the individual demand curves together, we get a market demand curve (Figure 1–2). The quantity available for sale is indicated on the same figure by the vertical line SS (we have assumed a certain quantity and no more is available for sale). As the figure indicates, at any price above *Oa* (*Ob*, for example), the quantity demanded is less than the quantity available (quantity *OB*

FIGURE 1–1

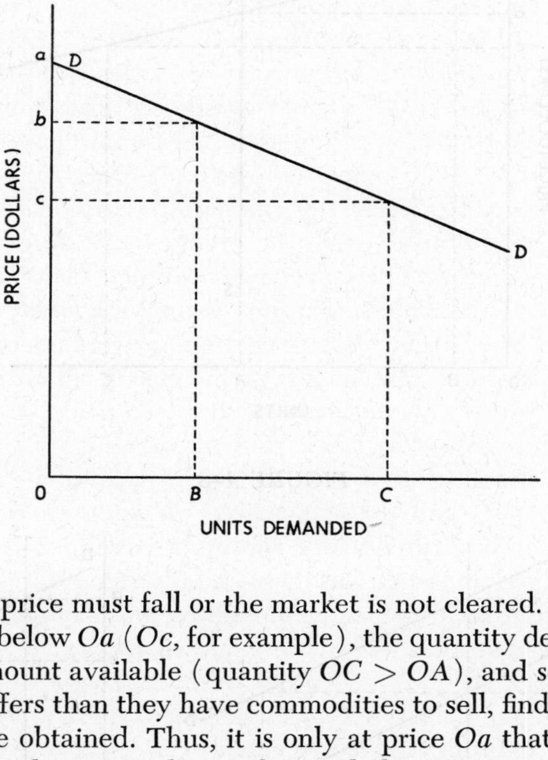

$<$ *OA*) and price must fall or the market is not cleared. Conversely, at any price below *Oa* (*Oc*, for example), the quantity demanded exceeds the amount available (quantity *OC* $>$ *OA*), and sellers, faced with more offers than they have commodities to sell, find that higher prices can be obtained. Thus, it is only at price *Oa* that there is no tendency for change in the market and the entire output is sold. The price *Oa*, then, serves to exclude all demanders willing to pay only prices lower than *Oa* and permits the demands of those willing to pay the highest price to be met.

Figure 1–3a illustrates the effects of changes in one of the other determinants of demand on price in the market; and Figure 1–3b illustrates the effects of an increase in the quantity of the commodity available. In Figure 1–3a, we see the effect of a change in consumer tastes (people now desire more of the commodity at every price than they did before). At the old price, *Oa*, the quantity demanded is now in excess of the amount available ($OX > OA$). As a result, sellers, faced with more offers than units to sell, feel free to raise the price, and these increases will continue until offers and the quantity

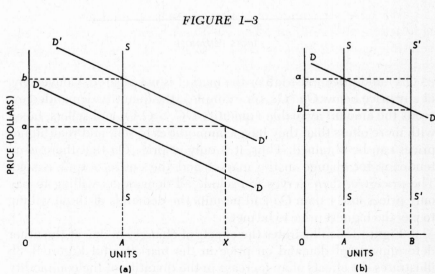

FIGURE 1–2

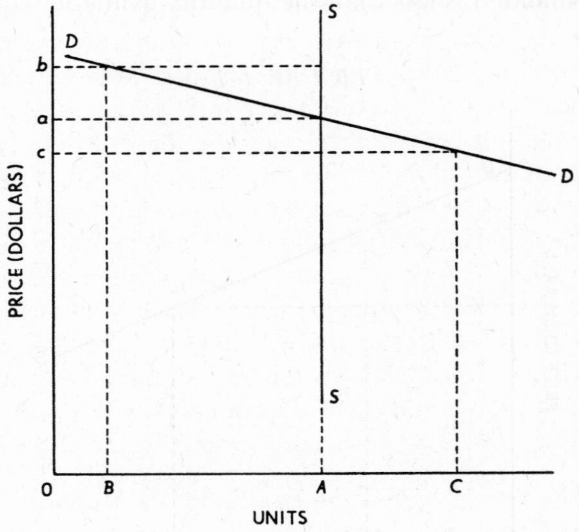

FIGURE 1–3

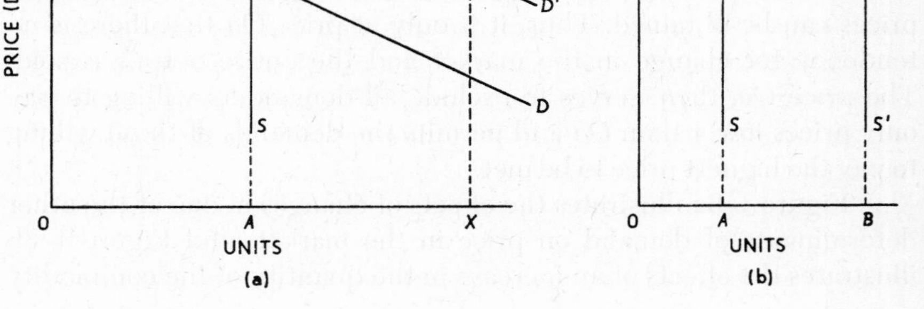

available for sale are just equal (at price *Ob*).[1] In Figure 1–3b, an increase in the quantity available for sale is indicated by the shift from SS to S′S′. After the increase, the amount now supplied at the old price (*Oa*) is considerably in excess of the amount demanded at that price ($OB > OA$), and sellers, faced with unsold commodities, would be forced to reduce price to *Ob*, where offers and the amount available are again equal.

Since we assume that consumers are attempting to maximize their satisfaction, it follows that they will set their consumption patterns so that the last penny they spend on any commodity will yield as much satisfaction as it would had it been spent on any other commodity. If this condition were not met, the individual could make himself better off by reducing his consumption of those commodities that yield the least satisfaction in relation to their costs, and increasing his consumption of those yielding higher satisfaction per penny spent. Moreover, it follows that, should any determinants of demand or the supply of any commodity change, the consumer (if he wants to maximize his satisfaction) should alter his consumption pattern in line with the new conditions. Thus, the free market permits each consumer to choose those commodities he wants to purchase and to select the quantities of each he desires. (Always, of course, within the limitations established by his income.)

1–3. *The Entrepreneur, the Firm, and the Response to Consumer Choice*

We have seen how consumers, in their attempts to maximize satisfaction, allocate their income between competing products, and how the market adjusts to these consumer decisions. But how are consumer desires transformed into new products? As the auto replaced the buggy in consumers' tastes, what guaranteed that the free-enterprise system would reduce the supply of buggies and expand the supply of automobiles? The moving force, then as now, was the entrepreneur. The businessman, in search of profits, watches for changes in consumer behavior and adjusts his production in accord with these changes. An increase in consumer demand results, as we have seen, in an increase in price. The businessman finds that he can increase his profits by increasing production. As a result, the increase in demand is met by an increase in the quantity of the product supplied. Before we examine this adjustment process in

[1] Although the illustration chosen deals with changes in tastes, the effects of changes in any determinant of consumer demand can be shown in a similar fashion.

more detail, let us restate our assumptions about the nature of the business world in our model. If a competitive free-enterprise system is to operate efficiently, it is necessary that each industry be made up of a sufficiently large number of relatively small firms, so that no one firm by itself can affect price and so that no barriers exist to prevent new firms from entering, or old firms from leaving, the industry.

Since the businessman is interested in making profits, he is interested not only in the price he can receive for his product but also in the amount it costs him to produce it. His costs, in turn, depend on two sets of factors: the prices of the land, labor, and capital required to produce the product; and the technological relationships that relate these inputs to the outputs (product) he will sell. Ignoring the first of these relationships for the moment (since the individual firm has been assumed to be quite small, the price of its inputs lies outside its area of control), let us examine the latter. We can say nothing general about the specific form of the relationship between inputs and outputs (called the *production function*), since these depend upon the individual technological relationships and vary from industry to industry. We can, however, say something about the general form of these relationships in the short run, at least. In any short period of time, a firm can increase output by hiring more of a certain kind of input, but lack of time prevents them from acquiring more of certain other inputs. For example, more labor can be employed rather quickly, but the time required to build a new plant may prohibit increases in that input in the near future. For analysis, it is convenient to divide inputs into two categories: variable (those that can be changed in the short run), and fixed (those that cannot be altered except over relatively long periods of time). Since the fixed and variable factors are not perfect substitutes for each other, any short-run adjustment to an increase in the quantity demanded must involve an increasingly intensive use of fixed inputs. Any attempt to combine more and more of the variable inputs with a set amount of the fixed inputs will ultimately result in a decline in the output attributable to the last unit of the variable input factor (the *marginal product* of the variable input). This relationship between physical inputs and physical outputs with certain inputs held fixed is known as the "law of diminishing returns."[2] For

[2] The law can be precisely stated in the following manner: "If the quantity of one productive service is increased in equal increments, the quantities of other productive services remaining fixed, the resulting increments of product will decrease after a certain point." George Stigler, *The Theory of Price* (New York: Macmillan Co., 1949), p. 116.

example, if we attempted to increase output by adding more labor to a fixed quantity of machines and plants, we might get the result illustrated in Table 1–1.

TABLE 1–1

Units of Labor	*Units of Output*	*Output Attributable to the Last Input*
0	0	
1	50	50
2	250	200
3	425	175
4	575	150
5	650	75
6	685	35
7	710	25

At first, successive equal increases in the quantity of labor add successively greater increments to output; but after some point (two workers) diminishing returns set in, and each further increment of input adds successively less. If we were to graph the relationship

FIGURE 1–4

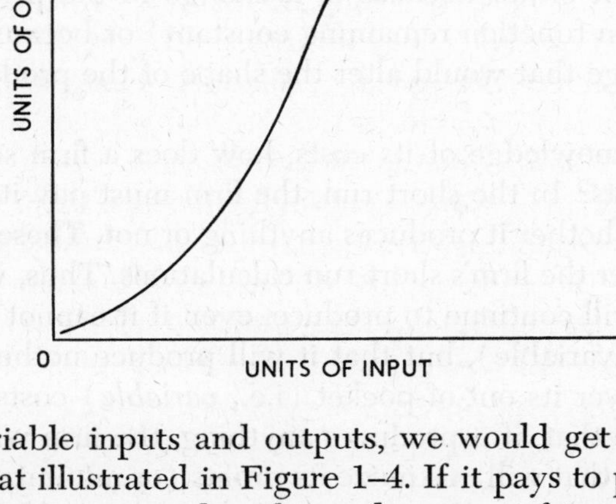

between variable inputs and outputs, we would get a relationship similar to that illustrated in Figure 1–4. If it pays to produce at all, it will usually pay to produce beyond an area of increasing returns (0 to 2 workers); therefore, production usually occurs in the area of diminishing returns. If the output of any worker can be sold at a profit, it follows that when an additional worker can contribute more than his predecessor (barring certain peculiar circumstances) he should be hired, since his output can be sold even more profitably.[3] The exact number of workers employed will, of course, depend on the prices of the inputs and the prices of the final products.

The businessman translates his technological data (shown by the production function) into cost data, to determine his most profitable output. Likely, he would be interested in two types of costs: average and marginal. Average cost is merely the mean cost per unit incurred in producing some specified level of output. Precisely,

$$\text{Average cost} = \frac{\text{fixed costs} + \text{variable costs}}{\text{output}}$$

However, since fixed costs do not change in the short run, the cost of producing an extra unit (the *marginal cost*) involves only changes in the variable component. Precisely,

$$\text{Marginal cost of the } A^{\text{th}} \text{ unit} = \text{Total cost of } A - \text{Total cost of } (A - 1)$$

The production function can be readily converted into a *cost curve* by changing inputs in physical terms into dollars of cost, and relating these costs to output. After the conversion, the decline in output per unit of input attributable to diminishing returns shows up as an increase in costs per unit of output (it now takes more units of input to produce an increment to output). These cost curves, since they are based both on the production function and the cost of inputs, can shift either because of a change in the price of inputs (the production function remaining constant) or because of a technological change that would alter the shape of the production function itself.

Given a knowledge of its costs, how does a firm set output to maximize profits? In the short run, the firm must pay its *fixed costs* regardless of whether it produces anything or not. These costs, then, should not enter the firm's short-run calculations. Thus, we conclude that the firm will continue to produce, even if it cannot cover all its costs (fixed + variable), but that it will produce nothing if it cannot at least cover its out-of-pocket (i.e., *variable*) costs. Moreover, we can assume that, if it produces anything, the firm will select the level of output that will maximize its profits (or minimize its losses).

[3] Indivisibility in the fixed factor or market imperfections might occasionally make it profitable to produce in the area of increasing returns.

At any point, a calculation of marginal cost will tell a businessman how much it would cost him to produce an additional unit of output. If the marginal cost is less than the price he can receive for the product, the firm can increase its profits (or reduce its losses) by producing that extra unit. Thus, the firm will continue to expand production if marginal costs are below price, and will reduce output if price is less than marginal cost. In general, we can conclude that a firm will maximize its profits (or minimize its losses) if it produces

FIGURE 1–5

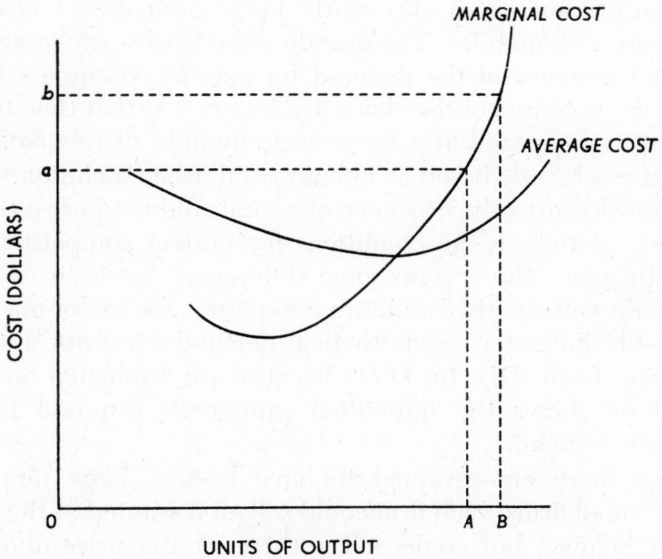

where marginal cost equals price (assuming that it at least covers its out-of-pocket costs; otherwise, it would produce nothing). Figure 1–5 illustrates this point. If the price that faces the firm is *Oa*, then the firm will maximize its profits by producing quantity *OA;* but if market price rises to *Ob,* then the firm should increase its output to *OB,* in order to maximize its profits. At the original price, *Oa,* profits could be increased by increasing output from any quantity less than *OA,* and by reducing output from any quantity greater than *OA*. After the price increase, however, profits could be increased by increasing output from any quantity less than *OB*. Beyond *OB,* however, it costs more to produce a unit than it brings on the market, and so profits could be increased by a reduction in output to *OB*.

Since the portion of the marginal cost curve that lies above the variable cost curve relates prices to the quantities the firm will produce, it can be looked at as a *supply curve* for the firm (that is, a schedule of quantities that will be supplied at a schedule of prices, assuming that technology and factor prices do not change).[4] By adding the supply curves for all firms in an industry (in a manner identical with our earlier demand summation), we can construct an industry supply curve.[5]

Let us see how a firm reacts to changes in market conditions. During the period from 1915 to 1925, the American consumer underwent a substantial (and apparently fairly permanent) change in taste toward automobiles. The decade after 1915 was characterized by a rapid increase in the demand for cars as consumers became aware of the potential of the "horseless buggy." At that time the auto industry was composed of a fairly large number of relatively small firms, and was largely based on already established techniques (thus, lack of knowledge or the existence of patents did not pose a threat to expansion). Although the conditions for perfect competition were not exactly met (there were some differences between cars), the industry was sufficiently competitive to permit the use of our model. Figure 1–6b illustrates a hypothetical demand curve for autos that has shifted from *DD* to *D′D′* because of a change in tastes. Figure 1–6a shows the individual producers' response to these changes in demand.

Since there are assumed to have been a large number of relatively small firms, each firm could sell all it wanted at the market price (or below), but could sell nothing at any price above that established in the market (the consumers would merely buy from another firm). Thus, each firm would assume that the demand for its product was a straight line at the market price (lines *dd* and *d′d′* in Figure 1–6a).

If each firm was originally producing output *OA′* (the output that would maximize their profits, given the price *Oa*), the shift in consumer demand would cause each firm to increase its output to *OB′* (the output that would maximize profits at the new price *Ob*). The total increase in the quantity supplied (*AB*) is equal to the sum

[4] If a firm cannot at least cover its out-of-pocket (variable) costs, it would pay it to produce nothing. Thus the quantity supplied at all prices below the variable cost curve would be zero.

[5] If there are any industry effects (price changes that occur if all firms alter output that would not occur when only one firm changes its output), the industry supply curve will not be exactly equal to the sum of the firm's supply curve.

of the increases in the output of the firms in the industry. In short, the businessman's search for profits led him to increase his production of those items that the consumers wanted the most (i.e., were willing to pay the most for). Moreover, if the increase in preference for cars was accompanied by an increasing distaste for buggies, an opposite reaction would have led to a decline in the quantity of buggies supplied.

FIGURE 1–6

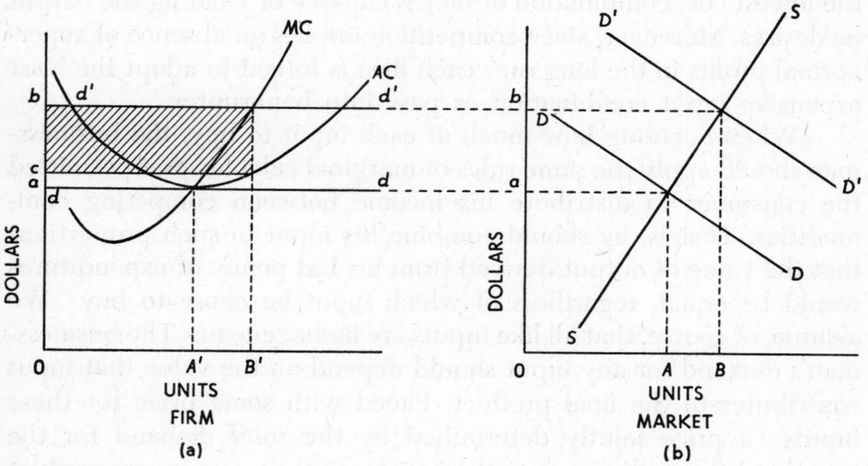

We have thus far traced the economy's short-run adjustment to a change in demand; but the process is not yet complete. The new price permits the existing firms to earn super-large profits (costs are assumed to include normal profits, and so extra-normal profits show up as an excess of revenue over cost: $ac \times OB'$); and these high profits attract new firms into the industry. As new firms enter, the industry supply curve shifts to the right (there are now more marginal cost curves to sum, more cars are supplied at every price), and prices begin to decline. This decline will continue as long as extra-high profits exist (new firms continue to enter the industry until profits are no higher there than elsewhere in the economy). As a result, in the long run, although the industry's output has increased, competition has eliminated extra profits and has forced each firm to produce at its most efficient point (the lowest point on its average cost curve). At any price above the lowest point on the average cost curve, super-normal profits would continue to exist, and there would be continued incentive for new firms to enter.

1–4. Efficient Input Choice and Factor Income Determination

Within the context of a free-enterprise system, the question of what to produce was answered by the consumers, and the relevant production decisions were effected by the businessman. Although a single commodity can frequently be produced by a myriad of different processes, the system can also answer the question, "how." The same search for profits that directed resources into the production of those items most in demand leads the businessman to select the lowest cost combination of inputs capable of yielding the output he desires. Moreover, since competition implies an absence of supernormal profits in the long run, each firm is forced to adopt the least expensive input combination or pass into bankruptcy.

When deciding how much of each input to buy, the businessman should apply the same rules of marginal calculus that permitted the consumer to distribute his income between competing commodities. That is, he should combine his input in such proportions that the value of output derived from his last penny of expenditures would be equal, regardless of which input he chose to buy.[6] We assume, of course, that all like inputs are homogeneous. The businessman's demand for any input should depend on the value that input contributes to the final product. Faced with some price for these inputs (a price jointly determined by the *total* demand for the input and the willingness of the inputs, or their owners, to work at various prices), the businessman should continue to hire any factor as long as it contributes more than its costs, or, more precisely, until the amount contributed by the last factor employed just equals its cost. Figure 1–7 illustrates this situation. Figure 1–7b shows how the market price is established by the interaction of total factor demand with the factor's supply considerations; and Figure 1–7a shows the individual firm's adjustment to the market price. The firm's demand curve is shown by the line *MVP* (called *marginal value product*) and represents the contribution made to revenue by the last factor hired. The industry supply curve *SS* depends upon the willingness of factors to work (or of their owner to let them work) at various prices; its upward slope implies that higher factor payments will bring greater numbers of factors into the market. Since each firm is assumed to be small, relative to the market, the firm's supply curve (*ss*) reflects its ability to buy any amount at the

[6] Or, precisely, until the ratio of the value of the output contributed by the last unit of each input employed to its price is equal for all types of inputs.

market price. The industry demand curve (ΣMVP) is the sum of the individual firms' demands.[7]

At price Oa (the price that clears the market), each firm would hire OA', and all firms together would hire OA. At employment levels less than OA', the firm could increase its profits by hiring more of the input (since extra units contribute more than they cost); but at levels beyond OA', profit maximization could dictate a reduction in the quantity of the inputs employed.

FIGURE 1–7

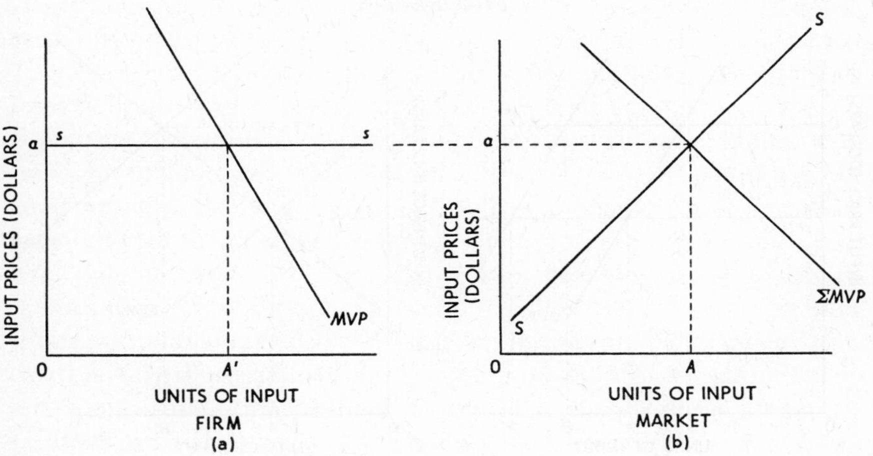

It follows that the incomes accruing to the inputs are determined by the same forces that underlie the pricing and output decisions in the product market. Moreover, the business firm's response to price changes is reflected in the input market, as well as in the product market. Let us return to our automobile example, and trace the effects of the change in tastes on employment and input income. In the first instance, as the price of the firm's products rose, the contribution of the inputs increased. (Remember that the demand for an input depends on the incremental product of that input multiplied by the sale price of the product produced; and, although the physical productivity of the factor has not changed in this example, the value of its output has.) This situation is illustrated in Figure 1–8. As each firm's demand for inputs increased from MVP to MVP', the total industry demand increased from ΣMVP to $\Sigma MVP'$. And, as a result, input prices rose from Oa to Ob. In the absence of the price in-

[7] The greek letter Σ is used to denote sum.

crease (but an increase that was necessary to call forth the additional inputs), each individual firm would have increased employment from *OA′* to *OA″*; but, in the face of an increase in factor prices, the firms only increased employment to *OB′*. Thus, in the short run, higher prices have called forth the extra inputs required to produce the additional products demanded by the consumer. But, like the product market, these short-run adjustments do not complete the process. In the long run, inputs employed in other industries become aware of the extraordinary high returns in the auto industry,

FIGURE 1–8

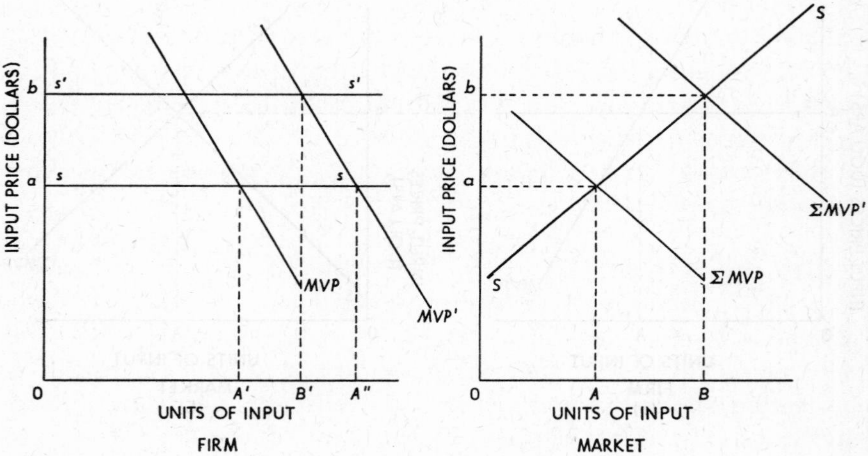

and begin to transfer out of their old employment. As more inputs become available, the curve showing the supply of input to the industry shifts to the right, and the input payments necessary to maintain employment drop from *Ob* to *Oa*. Finally (in the absence of any artificial or natural barriers), sufficient transfers will result that the earnings of inputs will be no higher in the newly expanded industry than in any other.[8] Thus, in the same manner that competition between firms removed monopoly profits, competition between inputs remove abnormally high input prices, in the long run. The incomes of the inputs are, of course, determined by the payments they receive for services rendered.

Because of the interaction of firms and individuals on the

[8] An unwillingness of inputs to move geographically or a refusal of unions to let new workers into an industry are examples of barriers that might interfere with the long-run adjustment process.

market, the free-enterprise system has been able to achieve a theoretical equilibrium that, while perhaps not the "best" in some abstract social welfare sense, is the "best" that can be obtained in an economic sense. No one is yet capable of making interpersonal comparisons of welfare; that is, we cannot say with any certainty that a transfer of $1.00 from one individual to another will actually increase, or decrease, total welfare. Thus, the strongest conditions for a "best" allocation of resources we can establish say only that, with this particular allocation, no individual can be made better off without someone being made worse off. The free-enterprise competitive economy produces such an allocation. Each consumer has been allowed to purchase the market basket that maximizes his satisfaction. Each firm has set its output where its profits are highest; has hired factors in proportions that minimize expenses per unit of output; has, in the long run, set production at the most efficient point; and has been prevented from accruing any monopoly profits. Each input is permitted to maximize its income by moving to the most lucrative employment.

1–5. *Possible Deviations from the Optimal Equilibrium*

The competitive free-enterprise system can produce a "best" allocation of resources. However, this optimal state can be reached only when the conditions that underlie our model (many firms, perfect knowledge, perfect markets, and absence of barriers to entry and exit) exist. What happens to our "best" allocation when these conditions are violated?

If any barriers to entry or exit exist in the product market, they will result in greater long-run profits or losses than those permitted by the perfectly free system. Similarly, impediments to mobility in the input market can result in input prices remaining higher or lower in a particular industry than those paid for similar contributions elsewhere in the economy. If, for some reason (the existence of a patent, for example), new firms are not permitted to enter an expanding industry, the existing firms may receive extra-normal profits for an abnormally long period of time. Likewise, a labor union or professional organization that maintains both a closed shop and a closed union could maintain wage levels above those that would exist in the absence of barriers. (The building trades and medical profession provide us with present-day examples of the effects of artificial barriers to entry.) In the first instance, income is distorted toward the workers; in the latter case, toward the businessman. In both cases, it is the consumer who pays the bill (he gets a smaller share of the output than he otherwise would receive). Barriers to exit can also cause a misallocation of resources. The government's persistent refusal to permit the railroads to abandon passenger service, even in the face of extra-normal losses in the industry, has caused a redistribution of income from the stock owners and freight shippers to the consumers of passenger service.

Moreover, when there are barriers to entry, there are no longer any competitive pressures to force the firms to adopt the most efficient production techniques. Even more important, it is highly unlikely that, in the absence of competition, the firms will be willing to assume the risks of innovating techniques. If an industry has so few firms that each feels it can affect the market by its own output decisions, the result is also a distortion of the allocation of resources. If a firm is a monopolist (the only seller of a product), it can maximize its profits at a lower level of output and a higher price than can a competitive firm. Since it is the only firm in the market, its demand curve is the market demand curve. Thus, since additional units can be sold only at a lower price, the change in the firm's total revenue (*marginal revenue*) resulting from the sale of one more item will be less than the price it receives for that item (in order to sell the extra unit, the firm is forced to take a lower price for all other units sold). This situation is illustrated in Figure 1–9. Under competition, the industry would produce output *OC* and charge price *Oc;* but if that industry were monopolized by a single firm, the most profitable output would be only *OM,* and the price a much higher *Om.* (If the industry were neither competitive nor monopolistic, the quantity produced and the prices charged would, in the long run, lie somewhere between the two limits.) Thus, the consumers pay more for and receive less of the industry's output than they would under competition. Moreover, since the demand curve for a noncompetitive firm is not a horizontal line (his actions can affect price), no amount of entry can ever leave such a firm producing at the lowest point of its average costs curve. An absence of competition in the market for inputs (either on the buyers' or sellers' side) will have similar misallocative effects.

With these simple ideas in mind, let us turn briefly to American economic history and see what types of problems our framework helps us to analyze. The increasing movement toward monopoly and trustification that occurred during the last quarter of the nineteenth century can probably be fruitfully examined with our theoretical apparatus. Our model suggests that such a deviation from competition should have resulted in higher prices and lower outputs than would otherwise have been the case, and it should have also induced a redistribution of income from consumers to the owners of business enterprises. Evidence of monopolistic pricing and output decisions and income redistribution exist, but, in the absence of our model, we would not have known where to look to assess the economic effects of monopolization.

FIGURE 1–9

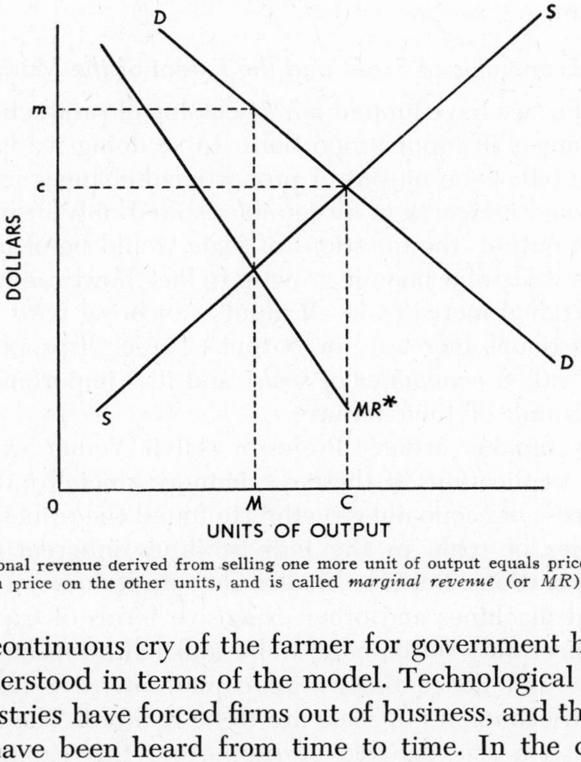

* Additional revenue derived from selling one more unit of output equals price received minus the reduction in price on the other units, and is called *marginal revenue* (or *MR*).

The continuous cry of the farmer for government help can be better understood in terms of the model. Technological changes in other industries have forced firms out of business, and their appeals for help have been heard from time to time. In the case of the farmer, however, these cries have continued for the better part of a century. Why don't the farmers follow the example of other firms faced with technological unprofitability, and exit from the industry? The model suggests that we look for some barrier to exit, and indeed we find almost insurmountable barriers in the farmer's cultural attachments to farm life, and in the relatively greater difficulty that characterizes transfer from farm to nonfarm jobs than that which marks the movement between industries in the nonfarm sector.

It is difficult to assess the contribution of the railroads to American development until one views them as a technological improvement that resulted in a fall in the delivered cost of products. Then their contribution becomes clear. The falling prices that characterized the economy during the latter half of the nineteenth century are also a puzzle until they are related through the model to the technological improvements of the period. In short, our model, although it does not describe the world, helps us to better understand it. And throughout this book we will frequently make use of supply-and-demand analysis to help us understand the process of American development.

1–6. *Economies of Scale and the Extent of the Market*

Thus far, we have limited our discussion of production to questions of changes in input proportions. In so doing we have all but ignored the effects on output of proportional changes in all inputs. If proportional increases in all inputs resulted only in proportional increases in output, the questions of scale would be of little importance to the study of economic growth. In fact, however, it is possible that proportional increases in all inputs can bring with them more than proportional increases in output. These disproportional increases are called *economies of scale*, and it is important to understand something of their nature.

In his famous article, Professor Allyn Young explored the causes and implications of these economy-producing indivisibilities for the process of economic growth.[9] He found the principal sources of economies of scale in the indivisibilities inherent in capital-intensive operations. Because small-scale output does not lead to the use of great machines and other expensive forms of capital equipment, it is necessary for demand to be sufficient to make large-scale production—and hence the use of capital-intensive technology—profitable, if economies of scale are to be realized. The ability of a firm to reach a size capable of supporting this capital-intensive technology depends to a large extent on the size of the market. The larger the market, the more likely it is that techniques based upon the use of machinery can be profitably introduced and costs cut. If all inputs were perfectly divisible, it would be possible to apply capital-intensive technology to the manufacture of even a few items. However, in the present state of technology, perfect divisibility does

[9] Allyn Young, "Increasing Returns and Economic Progress," *Economic Journal*, Vol. XXXVIII (December, 1928), pp. 527–42.

not exist and the benefits of economies of scale are restricted to those industries that can tap large market areas.

In addition to the advantages accruing from a more highly capitalistic technology, economies characterized by large market areas can also gain from a greater division of labor among industries. Thus, the growth of markets could result in the vertical disintegration of existing firms and the growth of more highly-specialized businesses. These developments could result in a higher degree of specialization in management and a better geographical distribution of industrial operations. The attainment of the economies of scale inherent in large-scale enterprise is not necessarily costless to society. We have already seen that, if the competitive free-enterprise system is to achieve an optimal allocation of resources, each industry must be characterized by a very large number of relatively small firms. It is certainly possible that, in cases where the minimum size of the efficient units is quite large, the existence of economies of scale will lead to some noncompetitive market form. Such reasoning has, for example, frequently been used to explain the prevalence in American manufacturing of industries characterized by a few large firms. If economies of scale do lead to noncompetitive market forms, the public must balance between the benefits they derive from the economies and the costs of these benefits in terms of the breakdown of the competitive system.[10]

1–7. *Interregional and International Trade and Specialization*

Within a country with a large market area and differing factor endowments among its regions, efficient production takes the form of regional specialization. That is, each region specializes in the production of those things it does best (e.g., Indiana produces corn and pigs, while lumber is produced in Oregon) and then trades with other regions for those commodities that it needs but does not produce. At the same time, since labor and capital are free to flow between regions, inputs should move to the most lucrative employments, and, in the long run, interregional equality of factor prices should result. (The argument here is analogous with the case for interindustry income equality, previously discussed.) Of course, if

[10] It is also possible that there are certain diseconomies of scale. Particularly, management may not be divisible, and difficulties ensue when the firm gets too large. These diseconomies may explain the existence of industries dominated by several firms rather than monopolized by a single enterprise.

inputs do not move to the most lucrative positions, permanent factor price differentials may result (e.g., the southern farmer appears to be relatively immobile, despite much better economic alternatives elsewhere. The result has been lower than average incomes in southern agriculture).

However, because of political and cultural barriers (to say nothing of the economic costs of transfer), this same factor mobility does not exist on an international scale. Factor immobility can prevent international equalization of factor prices, but they should not prevent even those countries with small market areas from reaping the benefits of specialization. That is, these countries can attain the benefits of specialization by substituting international for interregional trade. What are the benefits of trade? If one country is unable to produce some desired commodity at any cost, the benefits of trade are obvious. Thus, it is not surprising that almost no one argues that the United States should not trade for Bolivian and Malayan tin. Moreover, if certain commodities can be produced domestically only at a much higher cost (in terms of resources used) than they can be produced abroad, and if the less efficient country can produce other commodities more cheaply than can its foreign neighbors, the case for trade again makes intuitive sense. It is easy to see that both countries could be made better off (in terms of having higher total incomes) if each would specialize in the production of those things it does best and trade for those commodities its neighbors produce most efficiently. Finally, it can be shown that, even if one country can produce everything more cheaply than its neighbors, it still will pay that country to specialize and trade if it produces some things relatively more cheaply than others.

Since this latter principle (termed the *law of comparative advantage*) is intuitively more difficult to understand than the previously cited cases of absolute advantage, let us examine it in more detail. At one time, a famous night club impressario also held the world's typing championship. Did it, then, pay this versatile man to type his own correspondence? The answer obviously is no. He was both a better typist and a better showman than most others, but, relative to others, he was a much better showman than typist. Thus it paid him to specialize in producing shows, and trade for the typing services he needed. Less interesting but perhaps more relevant illustrations of the law can be found in international trade. For simplicity, let us assume only two countries and two commodities (although the analysis can be expanded to include more countries and commodities). For illustration, let the two countries be England and the United States and the two commodities autos and lathes. Moreover, let us further assume that, in the United States, one unit of input (land, labor, and capital) can produce ten cars if devoted to auto production, or two hundred lathes if used in the machine-tool industry. In England, the same unit of resources can yield two cars or one hundred lathes. Although the United States is more efficient in the production of both commodities, would it pay that country to specialize and trade? The answer is yes. At any exchange ratio (price) between one car for twenty lathes and one car for fifty lathes, both countries can increase their total income if each specializes in that which it can do relatively better (cars in the U.S. and lathes in England), and trades for the other commodity.

This then, is the case for free trade. During the 170 years of our history we have frequently interfered (through government action) with the free flow of commodities across national boundaries. Although there may have been political and social reasons for these restrictions, the economic result (despite frequent pseudo-economic arguments in favor of tariffs) has been a reduction in income in the country below what it otherwise would have been. The tariffs have interfered with the process of international specialization and have forced us to produce commodities that could have been produced more cheaply abroad. Luckily, the United States has a large internal market area, and, as a result, the costs of tariffs may have been lower than they would have been had our geographic expansion been halted at the Appalachians.

This chapter has dealt with those portions of economic theory that implicitly assume full employment and a static economy. In the next chapter, we will consider economic models applicable to periods of less or over-full employment, and, in the subsequent chapter, with an economy characterized by a growing population and capital stock.

Chapter 2 INCOME ACCOUNTING AND INCOME DETERMINATION

2–1. *Introduction*

In Chapter 1 we discussed the economic problem of resource allocation. Beginning with a set of assumptions about the economic environment, we deduced rules of behavior for the individual decision makers within the economic system. In this chapter we will examine the economic behavior of groups of decision makers, such as consumers and businessmen. If the study of economic behavior were a tidy discipline, like the study of the chemical behavior of elements, there would be no need to deal separately with the behavior patterns of groups of individuals. The principles of the behavior of groups of individuals would then be the algebraic sum of the behavior of the individuals making up the group. But as in many other aspects of human behavior, the whole is not the sum of the parts. While this problem of aggregation is at times a source of frustration, it is also one of the most intriguing aspects of social studies.

2–2. *Income Accounting*

The gross national product (GNP) account is a convenient starting point for a study of aggregate or macroeconomics. The term GNP has become very familiar because of the publicity given the concept by politicians and the press. The GNP of the United States for the year 1964, for example, has been estimated at about $620 billion. This total of $620 billion is the total market value of goods and services produced for final use by the American economy during the calendar year 1964. Three things should be noted about this definition. First, the definition has been stated in terms of market prices. This means that the current output of the economy is valued in terms of the prices existing in 1964. Because prices do not remain constant from year to year, this measure of GNP for 1964 is not strictly comparable to the similar measure for 1950 (or for any other year). Frequently, the measure of GNP is given in constant prices (sometimes called "in real terms") to enable comparisons across time. Thus, for example, if one wished to compare GNP in 1950 and 1964, one would value output in 1964 not in terms of 1964 prices but in terms of 1950 prices. By using a constant price base, such as 1950, it is possible to compare changes in the physical volume of output because the effects of price changes have been removed.

Second, it should be noted that only goods and services produced for final use are counted as part of GNP. Goods produced during the year that are then transformed by further production before being sold to the final user are not considered part of GNP. In fact, to count such goods (called intermediate goods) as part of GNP would be to count them more than once. Perhaps a simple illustration will help to clarify this point. Consider for a moment the case of wheat which is produced in 1964, ground into flour used to bake bread, and then sold as bread to the housewife—all in 1964. Clearly, the price of the bread includes the value of the wheat produced and the value of the grinding process by which the wheat was transformed into flour. Thus, to count the value of the wheat, the flour, and the bread, all in GNP, would involve counting the value of the intermediate products more than once.

We dated the steps in this bread example for a particular reason. It is obvious that production is a continuing process which does not complete itself and start anew to conform to the particular dating of the national accounting period. When the GNP accounts were closed on December 31, 1964, some flour produced in 1964 was held by bakeries. Such flour must, for the purposes of the accounts, be considered as part of the production of the year 1964; and its value must be included as part of GNP. To count this flour held in inventories does not represent double counting, since the bakery was the final user at the time the accounts were closed. Inventories included in GNP are not, however, limited to intermediate products, but also include some final products produced but not yet sold. Some bread, for example, might be produced in 1964 and yet not sold until 1965. Such bread would also be counted as part of the product by 1964 and would be included as an increase in inventory of the bakery.

The third point to notice about the definition of GNP is the word "produced." At first glance the word seems to be unambiguous, and yet one can become confused about its meaning in this context.

One has no difficulty deciding that a loaf of bread, or an automobile, or a chair has been produced; and a moment's reflection is sufficient to realize that the word "production" covers the provision of services by a barber, a doctor, or a lawyer. But suppose somebody builds a chair in his basement as a hobby, or a father cuts his son's hair—is such activity considered production and should the value of the output be included in GNP? The answer is no. Such activity takes place outside the market economy; it is, in a sense, leisure-time activity, and its value is not included in GNP. There are many human activities that are not considered productive in an economic sense and therefore are excluded from GNP. The output of the housewife is excluded. Thus, while the product of restaurants is included, the meals prepared in the household are excluded, largely because of the difficulty of measuring the value of such activity.

To limit the area of economic activity, for the purpose of measuring GNP, primarily to those activities that take place through the market economy makes the problem of international comparison of GNP very difficult. The market economy, for example, obviously includes a larger part of economic activity in the United States than it does in India. Thus, because of the differences in the economic organization between the two countries, the GNP measured on the same basis for both of them is not exactly a comparable measure. Comparisons by means of GNP between countries at widely different stages of economic development must be handled carefully.

There is yet a further point about the use of the term "production" that needs clarification. While it is true that production implies a change in value, the reverse is not always the case. It is possible for the value of things to change without there being any production. The value of a common stock may increase, for example, as a result of speculation; but, because the increase in value did not arise from production, it is not counted as part of GNP. Also, there are transfers of income that, unlike wages and salaries for example, do not arise from current production. Relief payments and gifts of money between individuals represent income payments that are excluded from GNP because they are not associated with any current productive effort.

2–3. *The GNP Account*

The theory underlying a GNP account is a simple one. The basis of the account is the distinction we have just drawn between an income payment and the production of goods and services.

Let us begin with the simple case of a single firm producing a single product. In the process of production, economic resources, usually divided into land (including raw materials), labor, and capital, are combined under the direction of the businessman to produce a product to be sold. Thus the productive process has two sides: the input of resources, and the output of goods. There are at the same time equivalent streams of money. The firm sells the product for money and, from the flow of money thus generated, the inputs receive their income payments in the form of rent, wages, interest, and profits. These two flows of money must be equal, and this equality permits one to draw up an income and product account

TABLE 2–1

NATIONAL INCOME AND PRODUCT ACCOUNT
(Billions of Dollars)

Wages	$341	Consumption expenditures	$375
Rent	12	Government expenditures	123
Interest	24	Gross private domestic investment	82
Profit	102	Net foreign balance	4
National income	$479		
Indirect business taxes	56		
Depreciation	49		
Gross national product	$584	Gross national product	$584

Source: The figures used in this table are drawn from the gross national product account of the United States for the year 1963 in U.S. Department of Commerce, *Survey of Current Business,* July, 1964 (Washington, D.C.: U.S. Government Printing Office, 1964), Tables 1 and 2, p. 12.

listing the flows of income through the firm in the accounting period. The GNP account for a nation is exactly the same type of income account. On one side is recorded the value of the flow of goods and services produced during a year, and on the other side is recorded the corresponding flows of income payments to the factors participating in production. A GNP account (based on the American account for the year 1963) is presented in Table 2–1.

Listed on the right-hand side of the account are the values of goods and services produced and their distribution among four sectors. Consumers purchased $375 billion worth of goods and services, businesses purchased $82 billion, all levels of government purchased $123 billion, and the net foreign balance was $4 billion.

The purchases by business of $82 billion of goods and services should not be confused with the purchase of intermediate products (such as flour by the bakery). The $82 billion represents the purchase of goods (called investment goods) that are not resold by business but are used in the process of production, such as machines, trucks, buildings, and so on. In this category also is placed the inventory item, goods produced for sale but not sold during the accounting period.

The investment category of final product does present a problem. While it is true that a firm will buy a machine as a final good, the machine is purchased to be used in production, and in the process of use the machine will be worn out. The part of the machine worn out during the year is quite as much an intermediate product as the flour used by the bakery. Strictly, therefore, the GNP account should not include that part of the current production of investment goods used to replace the capital stock worn out or depreciated during the present period. There are, however, insurmountable problems in measuring the actual value (at current prices) of the capital worn out. Therefore, the GNP account includes in the flow of final product the output of investment goods used for replacement purposes; and this fact is signified by the use of the word "gross" investment, i.e., the investment figure includes the production of investment goods for replacement. A measure (quite imperfect) of depreciation must then be added to the left-hand side of the account to insure balance. Were it possible to get a true measure of depreciation, that amount could be subtracted from both sides of the account and we would have a measure of the net production of new investment goods, i.e., the actual amount by which the capital stock of the economy grew as a result of current production. In that case we would have a net rather than a gross investment figure, and the account itself would be called the net national product account.

We have yet to explain the net foreign balance item in the flow of final product. The United States produces goods that are sold abroad, and buys goods produced by foreigners. The goods and services produced by Americans and sold abroad generate a flow of income that is recorded on the left-hand side of the account, and this total must therefore be balanced by recording the value of these goods and services on the right-hand side. From this total is subtracted the flow of goods and services purchased from foreigners. This is necessary because the purchases by consumers (or any other sector) include purchases of foreign goods whose production was not balanced by a flow of income to American resources.

On the left-hand side of the account is recorded the flow of income earned by the factors contributing to the output of final product. The total of these income flows is called national income at factor cost, or more simply, national income. The sum of factor payments is, however, less than GNP. We have already explained the reason for the depreciation item. The final item is indirect business taxes, and its inclusion needs further explanation. Indirect business taxes represent taxes collected by the government directly from businesses engaged in the production of goods and services. In the case of income taxes, wages are earned and paid and then income taxes are taken (perhaps by withholding), and the wages item includes taxes to be paid. An indirect business tax, such as the excise tax, is a different matter. When a consumer pays twenty-five cents for a package of cigarettes, eighteen cents may represent tax. Thus, the producer received only seven cents for the cigarettes, out of which the income payments were made. Thus consumption expenditure on the right-hand side totals twenty-five cents, but the flow of income on the left-hand side is only seven cents. The difference of eighteen cents must therefore be added to the left-hand side of the account to insure balance. If it were possible to measure depreciation accurately, and if the government did not collect excise taxes, the national income at factor cost would equal net national product.

While the GNP account as just presented is the most familiar form of the national account, other ways of presenting the same information are frequently very useful for analytical purposes. In particular, a breakdown of income payments by industry of origin is a very useful device in analyzing economic development because it indicates the relative importance of the industrial sectors of the economy in the production of goods and services. Such an account can be constructed by entering under each industrial classification the income payments made by the industry during the year. A nine-industry breakdown of national income (based on the United States accounts for 1962) is presented in Table 2–2.

The industries listed in the table can be broadly divided into two main groups. The first four are commodity-producing industries and the last five are noncommodity-producing (roughly service) industries. It is interesting to note that, while manufacturing is the largest single industrial source of national income, the commodity-producing sector as a whole generated only about 39 per cent of total national income. It is useful to bear in mind that the provision of services is more important (as measured in this way) in the present American economy than is the production of goods.

Before leaving the GNP accounts, a few words of caution are

in order. We have already indicated two problems. First, the problem of correcting for price changes over time; and second, the problem of measuring GNP on a basis that would give meaning to comparisons between countries with widely different economic institutions and systems. There are also other problems that are particularly important when GNP is used as a measure of an economy's performance over time. Consider the problem of developing comparable measures of GNP for the United States over the period from 1870 to 1964. In part, the problem is much like the problem raised by an attempt to compare the GNP of the United States and,

TABLE 2–2

NATIONAL INCOME BY INDUSTRY

(Billions of Dollars)

Agriculture, forestry, and fisheries	$ 19
Mining	5
Contract construction	25
Manufacturing	137
Trade, finance, insurance, and real estate	126
Transportation, communication, and public utilities	40
Services	60
Government	64
Rest of the world	3
National income	$479

Source: The figures in this table are drawn from the U.S. Department of Commerce, *Survey of Current Business,* July, 1964 (Washington, D.C.: U.S. Government Printing Office, 1964), Table 7, p. 13.

say, India, in 1964. The American economy in 1870 was much less involved in market transactions than it is today, and, therefore, there is the question of the comparability of measurements over the ninety-year period. There are still additional problems that must be considered when dealing with product estimates covering long periods of time. Some goods that were produced in large quantities in 1870 are no longer a significant part of the present economy, and some items that are important today were not produced in the earlier era. Take, for example, wagons and harnesses that have given way to automobiles and trucks. If we want a comparable measure of GNP, we must use constant prices; and yet the value of GNP clearly depends on the year we chose to establish as a price base. What year should we choose so that prices will give a "proper" weighting to both wagons and automobiles? Moreover, even if these problems can be adequately solved, we still must remember that even today our data are far from perfect. It is for reasons such as these that we urge caution in the use of GNP statistics.

Before we leave this section on accounting there is yet one further account that is extremely useful in the study of economic history. This account is the one detailing the relationships between a country and the rest of the world. It is from such an account that the information is gathered that is included as the net foreign balance in the GNP account.

Our transactions with other countries, like our transactions at home, consist of more than just the payment of money for commodities. We purchase services from them (as, for example, when a tourist flies to Europe on Air France), and they from us. Moreover, we lend money abroad, borrow from foreigners, make grants of funds, Americans of foreign origin send money to the "old country" to relatives, we purchase goods and services abroad for our armed

TABLE 2–3

HYPOTHETICAL BALANCE-OF-PAYMENTS ACCOUNT

Merchandise exports	100
Merchandise imports	−80
Net trade	20
Less interest payment	−20
Less immigrant remittance	−25
Current account	−25
Rise in foreign holdings of dollar assets	25

forces stationed in foreign countries, foreigners buy United States government securities, and we pay them interest. The total of all these transactions in financial exchanges, grants, services, commodities, and so forth is called our *balance of payments.* The total is divided (in some cases quite arbitrarily) into two parts: (1) the current account, and (2) the capital account. In the most general way, this division divides transactions between current payments for goods and services, and straight transfers, loans, and credits of various sorts. Consider the following example. Our sales of goods to foreigners equal 100 and their sales to us equal 80; we pay 20 as interest on money they lent us some time ago (which we have not paid back as yet); and some citizens send a check for 25 to their aged parents in Scotland. Table 2–3 presents the current and capital account computed from these items.

In this case we end up the year with a negative figure, −25, or a "current-account deficit" of that amount. But the old people in Scotland have got a check, a claim on us for 25 which matches the size of the "deficit." Thus we have a current-account deficit even though we have a trade "surplus" (our exports of merchandise exceed our imports). Since in trade the value of purchases equals sales, or, put another way, expenditures equal receipts, our total accounts "balance." The capital account (the rise in claims of 25 in the example above) balances the deficit on current account. This is why it is known as the "balance" of payments—it always balances, by definition.

Now let us complicate our example a bit to make it slightly more realistic (and useful to us later on). Suppose that this time the interest payment is only 5, the government gives the dictator of some foreign country a grant of 80, and we pay the British 5 for letting us ship goods on their ships. The immigrant remittance is assumed to be the same, except that the old folks in Scotland spend 10 of their check and their bankers use the 10 to buy gold from the U.S. Treasury. The new account is shown in Table 2–4.

TABLE 2–4

HYPOTHETICAL BALANCE-OF-PAYMENTS ACCOUNT

Merchandise exports	100
Merchandise imports	−80
Net trade	20
Less interest payment	−5
Less government grant	−80
Less services (British shipping)	−5
Less immigrant remittance	−25
Current account	−95
Net rise in foreign holdings of dollar assets	85
Net rise in foreign gold holdings	10

Note that in this case the balance was achieved by a rise in foreign holdings of claims on us and a loss by the U.S.A. of 10 in gold, which appears here as a rise of 10 in foreign gold holdings. Even though we had a surplus in trade, our combined payments overseas for services, gifts, and grants necessitated a loss of gold in order to achieve "balance" in our international payments. Moreover, we must stand ready to pay off the other 85 as it is demanded in the future. If, however, we had ended with a current-account surplus (for simplicity, just reverse all the signs in the example) then we would have increased our claims on foreigners, and, had we demanded gold, we would have experienced a rise in our gold stock.

2–4. *Income Determination*

The concept of the circular flow of economic activity developed in the discussion of the GNP accounts is a useful point from which to begin the theory of income determination. We have seen how the value of the output of goods and services and the flows of income are in essence two sides of the same process. The value of goods produced is determined primarily by the level of expenditure (aggregate demand) for those goods. If the economy produces more goods than can be sold, the surplus piles up in inventories and the likely result is a subsequent reduction of production. To reduce the level of production is to reduce the flow of income to factors, because fewer factors are employed.

Let us concentrate for a moment on an economy that has only two sectors: households and businesses. In such an economy there are only two types of expenditures: for consumption goods and for investment goods, and the sum of the two represents aggregate demand. In any accounting period the flow of income to households will be equal to the value of aggregate demand (remembering that inventories represent part of final output). Part of the income households receive they use to buy consumer goods, and the remainder of their income they save. The amount of household saving therefore must be equal to the amount of investment. If, for example, $400 billion of goods are produced and consumers spend only $350 billion, $50 billion must represent both saving by consumers and the production of investment goods, and perhaps an accumulation of inventories.

It is generally assumed that the level of consumption expenditures is determined by the level of income. This relationship is shown in Figure 2–1. In that figure we have graphed consumption expenditure as a function of income. The consumption function is drawn as a straight line with a slope of less than one. Also shown on the diagram is a 45-degree line. Any point on this line is equidistant from the two axes and therefore the horizontal distance along the income axis to any point is equal to the distance from that point to the 45-degree line. The consumption function intersects the 45-degree line at *b*. At that point (level of income *Oa*), consumers' expenditure (*ab*) is equal to income—i.e., savings are zero. At any higher level of income (*Oc* for example), consumers spend a portion of their income (*cd* in this case) and save the rest (*de*). If the level of income *Oc* is to be maintained, therefore, businessmen must be willing to invest an amount equal to *de* so that aggregate demand *cd* plus *de* is equal to the level of income *ce* (equals *Oc*). Given the community's consumption function and the quantity of investment expenditure businessmen are prepared to make, we can determine the level of income. The given volume of investment expenditure "plugs the gap" between a level of consumption and a level of income, and, together with that level of consumption expenditure, determines the level of income. Consumers spend some part of this income (again shown by the consumption function) and save the remainder. The level of savings must, therefore, always be equal to the level of investment. As long as the level of investment expenditure remains unchanged, the level of income will remain unchanged (we make the assumption that the consumption function does not change). We have an equilibrium level of income; a level of income

FIGURE 2–1

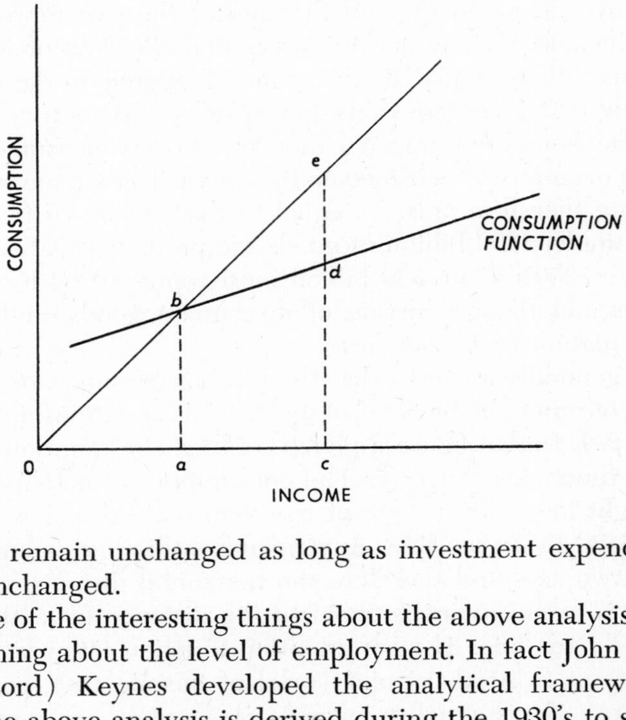

that will remain unchanged as long as investment expenditure remains unchanged.

One of the interesting things about the above analysis is that it says nothing about the level of employment. In fact John Maynard (later Lord) Keynes developed the analytical framework from which the above analysis is derived during the 1930's to show that an equilibrium level of income is not necessarily a full-employment level of income. Thus, an economy does not necessarily move to a level of full employment by its own volition but must frequently be helped to attain that goal. That is, the level of income *oc* shown in Figure 2–1 is an equilibrium level of income, but unemployment can certainly exist at that level of income.

In terms of the analysis above, a depression would result from a level of aggregate demand insufficient to employ all the economy's resources. Since the consumption function is assumed fixed, insufficient aggregate demand implies an insufficiency of investment demand. Therefore, to stop a depression in such an economy it is necessary to find a policy that will increase investment expenditure. To implement this policy, we must first find out what it is that determines the willingness of businessmen to invest. Businessmen are likely to invest more willingly when they are optimistic about the future than when they are pessimistic; however, an optimistic attitude is a very difficult thing to engender when the economy is depressed. Furthermore, businessmen are more likely to invest when they see a possibility for large profits. Since investments yield their return over a period of time, money must be committed to the venture now, to be returned only over some number of years. The cost of borrowing money—the interest rate—represents therefore a cost that must be deducted from the return yielded by the investment. The lower the interest rate, the smaller the cost of borrowing and the more profitable a given investment will be, other things being equal.

It is at this point that the banks enter the picture. We have mentioned that households save and businessmen invest. The banks are the institutions through which the savings of households are transferred to businesses. However, the process is more complicated than a simple transfer. When money is deposited in a bank, the bank does not just store the money in its vaults until it is withdrawn. A small portion of the money is held in reserve and the rest is loaned out, because banks have found that people transact the largest part of their business by check instead of with cash. In fact, people look on a check as money. Thus banks need only keep a small reserve on hand, in case withdrawals of cash exceed deposits.

The fact that banks need to keep in reserve only a fraction of the total money deposited with them, and the fact that people treat their bank deposits and checks as money, opens up the possibility that the banking system can change the total supply of deposit money in the economy. This is demonstrated in Table 2–5 with simple accounts for two banks. In these accounts only the relevant entries are shown and only changes resulting from the transactions under discussion are entered.

Step 1: Suppose an individual deposits in Bank A $100 in cash that he has been hiding in his cookie jar. Bank A credits the individual's checking account (a liability of the bank) with $100, and adds $100 to its assets. If the bank keeps a cash reserve of 10 per cent

TABLE 2–5

MULTIPLE EXPANSION OF BANK DEPOSITS*

Bank A				Bank B			
Assets		*Liabilities*		*Assets*		*Liabilities*	
Cash and Reserves	+100 (1)	Demand Deposits	+100 (1)	Cash and Reserves	+90 (3)	Demand Deposits	+90 (3)
	− 90 (3)		+ 90 (2)				+81 (4)
Loans	+ 90 (2)		− 90 (3)		+81 (4)		

* The numbers in parentheses refer to the sequence of transactions explained in the text.

of its deposit liabilities, then it will need to keep only $10 as a reserve and $90 will be a free cash reserve.

Step 2: The $90 it now holds as a free cash reserve will not be permitted to lie idle, in normal circumstances, but will be loaned out, for example, to a businessman who requires credit to purchase inventory. The bank will answer the businessman's request for a loan by crediting his deposit account with $90, and accepting from him in exchange a promissory note which it will add to its assets. The bank's account now balances at a total of $190.

Step 3: When the businessman receives his new inventory he will send his supplier a check for $90 which the supplier will deposit in his Bank B. Bank B will then send the check to Bank A for payment and Bank A will reduce the businessman's deposits by $90, and send $90 out of its free cash reserves to Bank B. Bank A now has a deposit liability of $100, $10 in cash reserves, and a promissory note for $90.

Step 4: Bank B will add $9 to its cash reserve (10 per cent of the new deposit of $90), and will have a free cash reserve of $81 which it will be able to loan out by creating a new deposit of $81 and accepting a promissory note in exchange. Bank B's account now balances at $171. This new deposit of $81 in Bank B can be transferred by check to Bank C (not shown) creating free cash reserves and thus adding to Bank C's ability to create loans.

This process of expansion can continue, each time the new loan being created amounting to 90 per cent of the new deposit, until no further loan creation is possible. Note that no one bank can be said to have created any money because each bank only granted a loan equal to its free cash reserve. However, the banks as a group did expand the supply of deposit credit. This apparent contradiction can be explained by the fact that each new loan was granted on the basis of a loan already granted. In effect the original free reserve of $90 received by Bank A is loaned over and over again although each time the sum loaned is 10 per cent less than the previous loan.

The process just described is generally called the multiple expansion of bank credit. The amount of expansion clearly depends upon the proportion of each new deposit that the banks add to their cash reserves, and on the fact that people are willing to accept loans and payments in the form of a check. If the businessman who had borrowed $90 from Bank A had taken his loan in cash and had put the money in his cookie jar, no multiple expansion would have taken place.

Finally, it should be noted that the process just described is reversible so that if currency is removed from the banking system a multiple contraction of bank credit can take place. Alternatively, if the banks decide to hold a larger proportion of their deposit liabilities in the form of cash reserves, a multiple contraction of deposits will result.

The banks, through their ability to loan, have therefore the power to expand the money available to the economy. In a period when investment demand is lagging the banks, if they have free cash reserves, can encourage investment spending by lowering the interest rate and encouraging businesses to borrow. Unfortunately, however, banks are businesses and they are in business, just like everybody else, to make money. In a period of depression they are unlikely to expand loans. In fact, they are more likely to restrict their loan activities to their very best customers; a perfectly rational policy, but one that does nothing to ease the depression. We need, therefore, an institution to act in an "irrational" way if we are to make headway against the depression and to decrease the volume of unemployment. It is at this point that we expand our model economy to include a government sector.

Government antidepression policies can be divided into two broad categories. The first is termed "monetary policy." In this group are included those policies designed primarily to affect the money supply and the rate of interest. We have seen that the depression has resulted because of a lack of spending. The main purpose of monetary policy is to influence the level of spending through changes in the money supply. Through the Federal Reserve System, to which most of the nation's banks belong, action can be taken to stimulate lending by changing the reserves the banks that are members of the System are required to hold. We have seen that banks keep some proportion of their deposits in the form of cash. The proportion they are required to keep is determined by the Federal Reserve System. During a depression the System can reduce the required reserve percentage, thus releasing cash the banks can then use to increase their loans (presumably by lowering the interest rate). The Federal Reserve System can also increase the supply of money by buying government bonds held by the banks and the public. The Federal Reserve System increases the quantity of money available, and therefore presumably encourages spending, by giving people money for their bonds. We say "presumably encourages spending," because there is nothing to prevent the receivers of the money from not spending it, and the purchase of the bonds (or indeed the lowering of the required reserve percentage) may have no effect upon the level of spending.

The second general group of policies that the government can use to cure the depression are included under the heading of "fiscal policy." While monetary policy is aimed at the supply of money, fiscal policies are directed toward manipulation of the level of the receipts and expenditures of government. Because the depression was caused by a lack of spending, the government can move directly to cure it by spending money. Public-works projects are the usual means by which the government attempts to stimulate the economy directly. However, it could also increase the level of unemployment benefits and other forms of direct payments to members of the community. Alternatively (or as an added measure), the government could reduce its receipts (taxes). When the income of the community falls, tax receipts are automatically reduced; but an additional reduction in taxes that leaves taxpayers with more money may be an effective way to encourage increased expenditures. A government that pursues such antidepression policies—and all enlightened governments do—will find that a period of depression is a period of rising government debt. An increase in the government's debt is, however, a small price to pay if it results in a reduction of unemployment.

So far we have discussed the problem of depression. What about the opposite problem of "over-full" employment, or inflation? Inflation arises when the money people spend for goods and services increases more rapidly than the output of goods and services can be expanded. Clearly, the government should act to reduce the volume of expenditure. In the field of monetary policy, required reserve percentages should be increased so that the banks have less money to lend, and the Federal Reserve System should sell its government bonds to the public to "mop up" money. In the field of fiscal policy, government expenditures should be reduced and taxes increased perhaps, to remove additional buying power from the community. In effect, then, the government would be running a surplus. Hopefully, the surplus would be sufficient to cover the deficit to be expected if the economy moves back into a period of less than full employment.

Finally, we should consider the possibility that the fourth sector of the GNP accounts, the net foreign balance, can be utilized to affect the level of business activity in an economy. It would appear at first sight that if the American economy is experiencing a lack of aggregate demand, a conscious policy of stimulating exports and discouraging imports would be a worthwhile policy. America might, for example, subsidize export goods so they would be cheaper abroad than formerly, and at the same time raise tariff barriers against imported goods to make them more expensive in America. While this sounds like a fine policy for the United States, think for a moment of how the policy will be viewed by other countries. From their point of view, America is engaging in a conscious policy aimed at reducing the output of their export industries and, therefore, at increasing their unemployment. America is in effect "exporting" her unemployment. The natural reaction of the foreigners would be to subsidize their exports and raise tariffs. The end result of such actions by the countries of the world is likely to be a very drastic reduction of world trade, and no net gain in employment.

Chapter 3 INTRODUCTION TO ECONOMIC GROWTH: THEORY AND PROBLEMS

3–1. *Allocation of Resources in a Static State v. Changes in the Patterns of Allocation*

Thus far we have discussed the formal logic (theory) of resource allocation in a society characterized by the existence of free markets. The main assumptions of this body of theory relate to an essentially timeless and, in any given period, changeless state of economic affairs (in the same way the classical laws of physics relate to objects *in vacuo*). Hence, we call such economic theory "static." The severity of the assumptions limits to some extent the usefulness of static theory to a study of economic growth: a process which involves incessant changes in factor combinations, in their qualities, in consumer tastes, and in technology. But these limitations of static theory should not be exaggerated; it can be "dynamized" to a great extent without doing too much violence to its essential forms. Nevertheless, the problems of economic change have always provided a challenge for the development of a more "dynamic" economics: one involving time. A long history of attempts by economists to meet this challenge is treated briefly below. In recent years, the problems of creating a dynamic economics have developed an urgency that has brought economists in large numbers to the job of improving that part of economic theory. The urgency has come in part from dangerous political instability in the new nations of the world that are economically underdeveloped. The specter of economic underdevelopment has introduced a pressing need for dynamic economics to include a theory of economic development—involving not only time but changes in all of the elements assumed to be fixed in static theory. We have, as a result, become interested in something beyond the allocation of resources in advanced economies through time. The presence of economic underdevelopment has forced us to consider "the *mobilization* of resources in all states of development" for economic growth.[1] Our thinking about economic problems of growth involves us in the very unwieldy problems of factor improvement, mobilization, and technological change.

But if the need for a dynamic theory of economic development has been forced upon us by current economic and political pressures, the perfection of such a theory is equally important to us as a means of understanding our own past more completely. This is true because we, like other countries, developed our economy from primitive beginnings. The dynamic theory of economic development that we need is not yet in sight. But perhaps we have the elements out of which such a body of logic eventually can be developed.

The elements of a potential theory of economic development at our disposal stem essentially from two separate discussions in the history of economic thought: the "classical" discussion of income distribution, and the Neo-Keynesian mathematical formulations of models of economic expansion. Together these two discussions treat both the problems of population growth and the rates of net capital formation required through time to achieve given rates of economic expansion. In combination it would seem possible to find the conditions of economic expansion which, given population increases, would achieve rising output per capita—the condition the economist usually has in mind when he uses the phrase "economic growth." But this still leaves untouched the vexing problems of "human capital" and technological change, both of which are germane to any realistic plan for economic growth. We will treat the population and capital formation problems first, and then turn to the problems of human resources and technological change.

3–2. *The Classical Dynamics and the Neo-Keynesian Growth Models*

Assuming away any problems relating to natural endowment, the basic content of a comprehensive theory of economic development would need to be compounded from at least five parts: (1) the element of population growth; (2) a statement of the effects of the "technical" relationships of the productive system upon each other through time without fundamental technological change; (3) a synthesis of (1) and (2); (4) a method of accounting for changes in the quality (age distribution, savings habits, education,

[1] Ragnar Nurkse, "International Trade Theory and Development Policy," Paper Number 9, *Roundtable of the International Economics Association,* August, 1957.

technical skills, and so on) of the population; and (5) the effects upon the technical relationships of technological change. To some extent we have information regarding all these elements. We certainly have enough information to give us a rough general understanding of the processes of economic development sufficient to aid us materially in our studies of the development of the American economy.

A basic ingredient in any country's economic development is the change in population. This factor was at the root of notions about economic growth in the systems of the early British economists. Although the early nineteenth-century British economists were not primarily concerned with economic growth per se, certain growth problems entered into their discussions because of the Malthusian analysis of population growth. That economics has been known throughout modern history as "the dismal science" is probably due to the influence of the Reverend Thomas Malthus (1766–1834). It was his legacy to mankind, *An Essay on the Principles of Population* (1798), that confronted the human species with the specter of "overpopulation." He argued that population tends to press continuously against the food supply; that population increase was limited only by "positive checks": famine, war, and pestilence. An improvement in the standard of living, from whatever source, would, by removing the checks, allow population to increase. Since men could increase more rapidly than the food supply could be raised, famine would soon reimpose a check upon further population expansion.

In their studies of the economic system of early British capitalism, the "classical" economists—David Ricardo (1772–1823), J. R. M'Culloch (1789–1864), James Mill (1773–1836), and Nassau Senior (1790–1864)—dealt with this problem. They were not in agreement on many points, but, as Professor William Baumol has recently shown,[2] their theories can be roughed together into a general synthesis which embraces the Malthusian formulation of population increase.

The synthesis can be stated very simply. Assume that output (income) is divided into rent, profit, and wages. The wages of labor are determined by the amount of product necessary to maintain laborers at a subsistence level. Rent is a payment to the owners of land. Because diminishing returns exist in agriculture (i.e., costs rise as agricultural output is expanded), the owners of fertile land

[2] *Economic Dynamics* (New York: Macmillan Co., 1951), pp. 11–19.

(those with low costs) earn a rent which is the difference between the price of agricultural output (determined by the high-cost producers) and the costs of production. Profit represents the return to the capitalists who have invested in machinery and is the residual of the total output after wages and rent have been paid. There is an additional assumption that constant returns to scale prevail in manufacturing.

Suppose now that capitalists decide to save an additional amount of income to invest. This means that funds are available to increase wages. The Malthusian demon now takes over and the population expands. The expansion of the population means an increase in the output of food. Because of diminishing returns in agriculture, the cost of food rises and rents also rise. The manufacturer is then faced with the following situation. His wage bill has increased because, although the subsistence wage eventually reasserts itself, there are now more laborers. At the same time, because constant returns prevail in manufacturing and because the price of any commodity is determined by the resources that produced it, the prices of manufactured commodities have remained unchanged. The manufacturer therefore finds that after he has paid his wages his profit residual has been reduced. Profit will eventually return to zero and the process of expansion ceases. A new cycle may begin, but inevitably population expansion will bring the economy to a halt.

Such a *simpliste* notion of economic life might strike the modern reader as being incredibly shortsighted and narrow. And yet, as one can easily see in the cases of those underdeveloped countries that suffer from "overpopulation," the crude classical theory seems to be relevant. We might leap ahead of ourselves for a moment and note that continuous, or rapidly recurring, increases in output per worker would radically modify the classical model; today such increases would of course result from innovation and technological improvement. But the classical economists were primarily interested in explaining progress only to a point of normal or equilibrium activity. They were not interested in change for its own sake.[3] For

[3] An economist of the nineteenth century who was interested in change for its own sake in "historical development" was Karl Marx. Since his system does not lead us to modern growth theory, or toward a useful theory of economic development, we will not concern ourselves with Marx at this point. The interested reader might consult Paul Sweezy's *Theory of Capitalist Development* (London: Dobson, 1946), or Joan Robinson's *An Essay in Marxian Economics* (London: Macmillan & Co., Ltd., 1942) for discussions about Marx's notions of economic change.

that we must turn to the two primary Neo-Keynesian growth theories.

If a nation is to achieve economic growth there must be an accumulation of capital; that is, the instruments of production must be supplied year by year out of national product over and above the supply of consumer goods. The net (net of depreciation) addition to a nation's capital stock, if it isn't borrowed from abroad, must be the result of nonconsumption of national product. The output not consumed is the nation's investment output. It may take the form of plant and equipment, "social-overhead" investment, or just inventories. This output is "freed" from consumption, voluntarily or involuntarily, by saving. The temptation is strong to see here, as many have before us, certain "obvious" relationships that can easily lead to fallacious extremes. We could become zealots for high rates of saving at all levels of employment to "free" output for investment, or for high rates of consumption at all levels of employment to encourage greater investment. Let us examine briefly these two "obvious" positions before going on to explore the complexities of growth.

If it were assumed that no "market problem" existed—that is, if all output could instantaneously find profitable end uses—then it would seem that the greater the rate of saving the faster would output grow, because the investment output "freed" by saving would add to the capital stock. Since the capital stock is always (assumed to be) profitably employed, the faster the nation's stock of capital grew the more rapidly would income expand. Hence, the key to economic growth would seem to be simply a high rate of saving, or nonconsumption of output. But the market problem does exist, and output must be absorbed by consumption and capital formation if resources are to be freed for any kind of "investment" except unsold inventories. The latter, of course, would actually deter investment. Here we are at a dead end. Why invest in, or produce commodities for, an economy that currently absorbs only a part of the output, leaving the rest to pile up in profitless inventories? Since investment is not self-perpetuating, evidently we need more consumption.

Let us try the other extreme. If there is to be a stimulus for investment, such a stimulus must come from a market that absorbs all (except for "normal" inventories) of the current output of consumers' goods. This would justify an expansion of capital stock to increase the rate of output of consumer's goods in answer to a flourishing demand for such goods. Hence, a high rate of consumption would seem to be the key to economic growth. But it is also apparent that, once men and resources are fully employed, rising consumption could use up too high a proportion of output. None would be available to create the new capital goods justified by the high levels of consumption. Further increases in investment with full employment prevailing could only take place by raising the prices of the factors of production to lure them away from consumption goods output. Here we are at another dead end.

We can't have it all the way either way; and we can't have it both ways. It is perhaps paradoxical that economic growth is a complex problem of a compensating balance over time between the growth of consumption and investment, and hence savings. Moreover, we must take into account not only actual but "potential" output at all times.

The problem of capital accumulation has long vexed economic thinkers, but the logic of its study did not appear until after J. M. Keynes developed the static theory of national income determination. Using the Keynesian analysis, two economists developed independently theories of economic expansion that are quite similar. Roy Harrod,[4] a British economist, and Evsey Domar,[5] an American economist, used the savings-investment analysis to develop models of economic growth. We will rely mainly on Domar's model, because of the use of the notion of productive capacity: ". . . total output (of an economy) when its labor force is fully employed in some conventional sense."[6] We can see from a brief examination of the main outlines of Domar's model how precarious is the balance between consumption and savings in a growing economy.

Let us set up a simple model of an economy without any government or foreign trade. In such an economy, the total demand for output is composed of two parts: the demand for consumer's goods and the demand for investment goods. We have seen that national output is determined by the aggregate demand for that output. The supply of output is determined by the employment of the available resources and the level of techniques. In Chapter 2 we ex-

[4] R. F. Harrod, "An Essay in Dynamic Theory," *The Economic Journal,* March 1939, pp. 14–33; reprinted in *Economic Essays* (New York: Harcourt, Brace & Co., 1952).

[5] E. D. Domar, "Expansion and Employment," *The American Economic Review,* March 1947, pp. 34–55; reprinted in *Essays in the Theory of Economic Growth* (New York: Oxford University Press, Inc., 1957).

[6] *Ibid.,* p. 71.

plained that aggregate demand and supply could be equal and yet there could be unemployed resources at the same time. There was, however, one level of income at which demand would be equal to *full-employment supply*. The question that Harrod and Domar asked themselves was: what are the conditions under which this full-employment level of income can be maintained over time? Clearly, the same level of real income maintained over time will lead to a situation in which there is increasing underutilization of the capital stock. While a continuing level of investment expenditure will maintain a given level of income, the investment expenditure increases the productive capacity of the economy at the same time. Thus, while investment in one period will maintain a full-employment level of income in that period, the same investment insures that the supply of output will increase in the next period. Thus, if there is not to be excess capacity in the next period, demand must increase to absorb the increased supply. The conclusion is, therefore, that to maintain an equilibrium income over time both aggregate demand and supply must increase at the same rate—a rate determined by the productivity of investment and the quantity of investment expenditure per time unit.

Thus, steady, untrammelled economic growth would be difficult to achieve even if there were no problems relating to the quality of the labor force or to the growth of population. But in fact, these last two problems are now, and have been, part and parcel of the overall process of growth. We must take them into account. We can first use the classical population-growth model and the Harrod-Domar model to see the complexities we face. What we need to do is to achieve a rough synthesis between the classical model of expansion with population growth and the Neo-Keynesian growth models. This will give us a general schema of economic expansion involving both the magnitudes of the labor and nonlabor factors of production. The device for this rough synthesis is the notion of the "capital/output ratio." How much capital equipment is needed to make how much final output? The stock of capital at any time relative to net output (national income) in that period gives us the answer. This simple concept is useful at this stage of our discussion, when we want merely to speak of changes in population and national income (the ratio is not as useful as the ratio of capital to labor force when we speak of the "quality" of that population in producing output).

In point of fact, efforts to measure the capital/output ratio in various countries have not yielded indisputable results. There is, however, strong agreement about the ratio when land, natural resources, and foreign assets are excluded from such computations. It is agreed that, on this kind of calculation, the capital/output ratio in economically developed countries (and perhaps in others) lies somewhere generally between 3:1 and 4:1. In terms of growth, this means that it takes from 3 to 4 per cent of national income devoted to (net) investment to make income grow at 1 per cent per year. Similarly, net investment must be from 6 to 8 per cent per year to make national income increase 2 per cent per year, from 9 to 12 per cent for 3 per cent, and so forth.

Since we generally define "economic growth" as rising output per capita, it is clear that the investment-capacity problem in the Neo-Keynesian growth models must also be attuned to population growth for there to be growth of income per capita as well as undisturbed expansion of income. If income is growing fast enough to absorb current capacity but not as rapidly as population, then we shall not have economic growth but rather falling per-capita output. This can lead to unemployment of labor, with serious social and economic consequences.

For a nation like the United States, these problems have presented no insurmountable barriers to growth. We will treat these problems at some length in later chapters; suffice it to say at this point that, except for cyclical disruptions (depressions) of short duration, we have been able throughout our history to devote more than enough of our national output to investment to maintain a growth of national income that exceeded our population growth. We have rarely had a population growing at more than 3 per cent per year, and net investment, as a proportion of national income, has usually been higher than the 9 to 12 per cent necessary—with a capital/output ratio of 3:1 to 4:1—to give us rising output per capita over time.

What would our country be like if that hadn't been the case? We can illustrate the point by digressing a moment to revisit the "Malthusian Specter" as it applies to a modern problem. In the so-called "underdeveloped" nations today, it is difficult to get economic growth, or even just to maintain the *status quo*. It is not difficult for advanced countries to devote 12 to 15 per cent of national income to investment and to get annual income growth of 3 to 4 per cent with a population growth of less than 3 per cent. Clearly, success breeds success here. But in the underdeveloped nations of the world, 5 per cent is a high percentage of investment of any year's national income. This yields little more than a 1 per cent annual increase in income, and in most of these countries population is increasing at a more rapid rate. They thus face stagnation, at least, and if they can't raise their rate of growth they will clearly face the Malthusian catastrophe. It is no wonder that in many of these countries political authorities dispair of solving the problem without direct government intervention in the economies. Remember that, given the 3:1 to 4:1 capital/output ratio, if the population should grow annually at 3 per cent the investment proportion of national income must be 9 to 12 per cent just to *maintain* the current rate of production of income per capita. In some underdeveloped countries, the population increase is not so rapid. India, for example, has a large population but it is growing relatively slowly, just over 1 per cent per year. Here a level of investment of from 3 to 4 per cent of national income can hold the line, and anything above that could contribute to a rise in per capita output. But what is to be done with the annual 3.5 per cent growth of population in Ceylon? Ceylon has little hope of achieving an investment ratio high enough to offset such a figure without a rigorous saving program. A most tragic consideration here is that consumption per capita would doubtless need to be reduced below the pitiful levels already ruling, in order to raise the rate of investment. Even if income grows rapidly enough to avoid this drastic measure, there certainly isn't much hope for an immediate rise in consumption standards if population is increasing rapidly.

In our own history we have managed to stay away from the Malthusian extreme. There have been short periods of depression when unemployment was due to falling income (we will treat this at some length in a later chapter). But this is not the same sort of crisis we would face if, over the long run, we could not maintain a level of investment that would keep our growth of output moving ahead of population. We have been one of the successful societies in this regard. The history of economic development in the United States is one in which the conditions for economic growth in the investment-capacity model have been met, in one way or another, so as to avoid any Malthusian problem. We have in fact had the opposite; with output growing sufficiently rapidly our large and growing population has been our great asset.

Part of this success story has been due to the steady improvement in the productive capacity of our population, a consequence of flexibility of what we might term the "sociological framework"; and partly success has been due to technological advance. We will discuss these two factors in a very broad way to see how they fit into our general schema of economic growth. Armed with these tools, together with the theoretical knowledge derived from Chapters 1 and 2, we can examine in detail the history of American economic development.

3–3. *Significance of the American Sociological Framework: Population and Technological Change*

In later chapters we will examine in detail some characteristics of social mobility in American history and the importance, as the national economy developed, of our flexible and liberal social system. In general, the great contribution a growing population makes to its own economic development comes in both the initiation of and response to change. The application of science to technology and resources, which can raise output per capita, would come to nought if the work force of a country did not accommodate itself to such advances and alter its skills, work patterns, and geographical distribution according to the requirements of progressive change. As we noted earlier, in the classical model of population growth, continuous increases in productivity brought about by technological advance could maintain the growth of population above the subsistence level. Moreover, since technological change creates obsolescence, it is a force which causes old productive capacity to be "junked" and creates conditions conducive to further investment and rising income. Economic growth thus breeds on itself, so long as excess capacity is absorbed or eliminated.

To do all this, the social system within which a population lives needs to provide the means for a ceaseless change in the structure of skills (and therefore incomes) of labor as the composition of output of goods and services is transformed over time. All this seems simple enough to a modern American. We have successfully adapted ourselves to such changes so that, for example, in modern times the scientist and engineer could have the income and status required to call forth the supply of those skills our society requires. In the process, incomes and status of others have declined either relatively or absolutely within the overall hierarchy of incomes and status that we call our social system. These are typical characteristics of a dynamic society.

But suppose we had not made such changes; it is clear we

would then have been stuck with the less-efficient methods of grandfather's time. As our population grew we would have needed more and more of the national income just to satisfy consumption requirements, and investment would have been choked off. Put another way, resources could not have been freed from consumption to supply the needs of capital accumulation.

In general, one might imagine a whole society sunk in this morass, living by horse-and-buggy methods in the twentieth century. A rigid system of social classes could produce such a system; a caste society based upon religious belief and/or land ownership could create such a system. Parts of Southeast Asia and Europe spring to mind as baleful examples of such societies.

The growth of a "dual economy" is another way in which development might have been forestalled. The notion of the dual economy is easily understood. If the adoption of new methods in commerce and industry had been restricted to a few areas and there had been no widespread acceptance of change—no thoroughgoing permeation of new ideas throughout the country—we would have developed two virtually separate economies. One, a backward and "traditional" economy, based primarily upon primitive agriculture and home manufacturing, would have existed alongside the advancing industrial sectors. The latter would have doubtless been dependent largely upon foreign trade to find markets where increased production matched its own and made trade possible. But the backward sector of such an economy is usually not completely independent of the "modern" sector. It is to some extent attuned to the modern sector, if only for famine relief, medical aid, and as an outlet for the more ambitious of its population. In this way, population expansion has occurred in history, and does in dual economies today, beyond that which would have been possible with no economic advance at all. From the primitive sector, however, the modern sector gets little aid and is thus constrained in its own development.

In many countries of Africa, Asia, and Latin America, such dual economies exist. In fact, except for the remotest Eskimo tribes and other such totally isolated groups, economic underdevelopment typically takes the form of the dual economy. For whatever reason, there were, and are, social obstacles to the wide permeation of modern industrial, commercial, and financial methods. The modern sector is created usually by world demand for exports of some primary commodities, and modernization and development are carried no further. The Cadillac of the oil-rich sheik rolls down an unpaved road beside the donkey trains. The success of the modern sector cannot compensate for the squalor and misery of the primitive sector. The dual economy of Peru is a neat illustration of the point. There is a large population living in conditions that have scarcely changed since the Incas, alongside the modern economy based upon export-oriented extractive industries. The recent catastrophe of the Congo provides a further timely, if tragic, illustration. Beside the glass and stainless-steel society of Leopoldville and the industrial areas, there continued to live millions of Congolese—ignorant, superstitious, diseased, and captives of their traditional tribal systems. When the developed sector ceased to produce during the political chaos of 1960 and early 1961, the population of the modern sector was impoverished. But so were the primitive tribesmen who could no longer exist without the marginal contribution of the modern sector. Both sectors fell into famine and anarchy.

The dead end of the dual economy threatens any society subject to the revolutionary impact of technological change. The dual economy is a peril to be avoided at nearly any cost. Until recently, the plight of the American Indians represented the dual economy in the United States. Efforts have recently been made to bring them more fully into the modern economy. Backward agricultural regions in the South represent the threat of the dual economy, as do the masses of ignorant and untrained peoples in the festering slums of our great cities. But we can hope to meet the challenge. Technological change displaces men and skills, but it also opens new possibilities for the employment of men. Indeed, in our economic history technological change has been the heart of progress; it has created vastly more jobs than it destroyed. Fortunately for us, American society has a tradition of change, almost for its own sake, and our social system has not only generated technological advance but has for the most part adapted itself rapidly to the revolutionary implications of such advance. The resulting change in the "quality" of our population, that is, its changing skills and economic habits, has thus been of fundamental importance in our economic development. A nation cannot be better than its people. We have, and have had, the advantage of a labor force that both initiates and accepts the consequences of technological progress. The consequence has been rising productivity. As a result, we have, thus far, managed to achieve the conditions of economic development set out in the schema of growth earlier in this chapter.

Finally, it might be useful to remind the reader at this point that the "real world" is infinitely more complex than is the theory we have touched upon—and so is our historical disquisition in the chapters which follow. But the theory we have advanced is the intellectual springboard for our studies in the history of American economic development, and it will repay the reader to master the contents of the first three chapters of this book and refer back to them from time to time as he proceeds through the following chapters. The factual content will not be burdensome if the reader remains aware of the simple underlying principles of economic analysis presented thus far.

II
The Demographic Variable

Chapter 4 INCREASING NATIONAL ENDOWMENTS: NEW LANDS AND RESOURCES

4–1. *Some Theoretical Considerations*

If one takes output per worker as a measure of economic well-being, it follows that increases in the stock of natural resources or capital (if they lead to an increase in total output) contribute to the health of the economy. The American economy has benefited from increased stocks of both capital and natural resources. Since resources either do or do not exist, one might conclude that a nation's stock of resources can never change. In a sense that conclusion may be true, but if we define a *resource* as something that is *economically* useful and the *stock of resources* as the supply of these items that are available to the economy, the statement is not true. In the first place, it is certainly possible to discover additional stocks of resources. In the middle of the nineteenth century, for example, it was generally known that iron ore was a valuable resource, but most experts thought that the continental United States was deficient in this important metal. The discovery of the Great Lakes fields, however, increased the U.S. supply of known resources beyond those of any other country in the world. In the second place, resources may be known, but because no efficient transportation routes exist, they may be of no economic value. The timber of the Northwest had been known since Gray's voyages of discovery; however, it had no economic impact until transportation routes had been built to link that area with the rest of the economy. In the third place, technical developments can turn known stocks of valueless items into valuable resources (or, as an economist might say, "resources are a function of technology"). The earliest settlers (to say nothing of the Indians before them) knew that oil existed in western Pennsylvania, but it was not until the development of a satisfactory kerosene lamp and the innovation of an adequate refining process that petroleum became a valuable economic resource.

One other consideration should be kept in mind. Resources can be known and available, but they do not serve to increase an economy's output unless they are used. (Of course, this is not to argue that they should be overused.) In some parts of the world, the stock of resources has been concentrated in a few hands, and their owners, for their own reasons, have failed to make productive use of them. In the case of the United States, public policy (particularly policy relating to the distribution of western lands) has tended to encourage the rapid exploitation of our natural resources. As a result, although this policy has given rise to periodic complaints about the wasting of our resources, it has tended to make them available to the economy.

4–2. *Land Policy and American Development*

Historically, many Americans have believed that frontier land should be made available free to bona fide settlers and kept out of the hands of land speculators. At times this belief has been used as a criterion for evaluating the success of American land policy. Viewed by these standards, large parts of our public land policy were failures. From an economic (as opposed to a social) point of view, however, this criterion does not appear to be particularly relevant. More reasonable, perhaps, would be an index of the speed with which new lands were opened and the size of the increases in agricultural productivity that were a function of these new lands. In terms of these latter standards, American land policy comes off much better. Certainly the policy could have been better designed for the area west of the 100th meridian, but, with this exception, it is hard to visualize how the West could have been opened any more rapidly. Certainly, in contrast with land policy elsewhere in the world, American policy was almost revolutionary. The low agricultural productivity and the cries for land reform in the underdeveloped world today reflect the results of other land policies.

The roots of American policy lie in the original debates over confederation. Representatives of the state of Maryland demanded that states cede their western lands to the central government. In 1781 the cessions were effected, and the public domain was created. At that time it included most of the Northwest Territory, the portion of Minnesota east of the Mississippi River, and the parts of Alabama and Mississippi north of the thirty-first parallel. Gradually more lands were added. With the exception of parcels already under private claim, the lands added by the Louisiana Purchase

(1803), the Florida purchase (1819), the Mexican cession (1848), the Oregon treaty (1846), the Texas purchase (1850), the Gadsden purchase (1854), and the Alaska purchase (1867) all became part of the public domain. Altogether over 2.8 million square miles of land were included at one time or another.

Early legislative acts also set administrative precedents for land policy. In particular, the Ordinance of 1785 provided for survey before settlement, and the Act of 1787 set standards for incorporating the public domain into the political life of the country. Although these ordinances dealt specifically with the land acquired by the cession, the same principles were applied to later additions. From an economic viewpoint, it was the opening of the western lands that was important; however, the shape of land policy was largely due to political pressure. Some lands were given to veterans as military bounties. Some were sold for federal revenues. Some were given free for political reasons. Some were granted as subsidies for internal improvements. Occasionally some titles were granted as payments for land improvement.

The first distributions of western lands antedated the cessions. A number of states offered land warrants to their soldiers during the Revolutionary War, and these were valid even within the ceded areas. Later wars brought further bounties, and over the first half of the century military payments accounted for a small but significant proportion of the total lands passing out of the public domain. During the War of 1812, veterans were offered 160 acres of land in Michigan, Illinois, or Arkansas. Since these areas were then on the far frontier and the warrants would not be transferred, the impact of this offer was small. Grants made to veterans of the Mexican War were more significant. These warrants entitled the holder to from 40 to 160 acres of land, and they were transferable. A regular market existed (prices ranged from \$.70 to \$1.10 an acre) and the land bonus did open new lands to settlement.

The government's need for funds encouraged rapid disvestment of the public domain. Since revenues were derived almost entirely from import duties and land sales, it was important that lands be sold. Until 1820 the price of land was \$2.00 an acre but credit terms were easy (up to four years to pay). In that year, however, while the price was reduced to \$1.25 an acre, the government demanded immediate payment. These prices were certainly sufficient to ration some prospective settlers out of the market (and the demand for immediate payment may have also worked in this direction). However, the price was still low enough to encourage sales to eastern farmers and immigrants who had some resources. Moreover, since speculators were required to pay cash, they were under real economic pressure to sell their land as quickly as possible.

Not all land was worth $1.25 an acre, and some land remained unsold. In 1854 the Graduation Act was passed and previously unclaimed land was sold for less than $1.25 an acre. In general, although one can argue that the price credit and minimum acreage policies prevented some deserving people from taking up land, the land policies of the period did result in the rapid extension of agriculture across the Old Northwest Territory and the new South during the ante-bellum decades.

The federal government was also desirous of promoting investment in social overhead capital. Since the government's major asset was the public domain, it is not surprising that their subsidies most often took the form of land grants. Nor is it surprising that the firms that received the grants should want to dispose of their holdings as quickly as possible. The railroad and canal companies frequently needed additional finance to complete construction, and, perhaps more important, they needed settlers along their right of ways. Therefore, the companies typically spent considerable money and effort encouraging settlers, and they tended to price their land attractively. Before the Civil War the Illinois Central (one of the first railroads to receive a federal grant) encouraged immigrants from the East and from Europe. Although their land prices were fairly high (they ranged from $6.00 to $10.00 an acre), their terms were very attractive to poor settlers. A typical contract required a down payment of 4 per cent, no further payments for two years, and seven years to complete. Since it took only two good crops to clear a mortgage, these lands were quickly claimed by new settlers. After the war, the western roads were equally anxious to sell their land. The Northern Pacific, for example, launched an almost world-wide advertising campaign for lands in the Red River Valley. The railroad normally charged $5.00 an acre for this fertile wheat land, but this price was discounted $2.50 to anybody who would farm it. Moreover, their terms were nothing down and ten years to pay.

The free land ideal was finally achieved in 1862 and the largest portion of the public domain (although by no means the best land) was given almost free to prospective farmers. The demand for free land, as we have seen, can be traced far back into American history. In the early period, however, its advocates met with determined resistance in the South and East. If the government had continued to sell land on easy credit terms after 1820, the pressure for free land might well have been less. As it was, the insistence on cash sales generated a rising political demand from those unable to pay and this demand was further intensified as the number of squatters preempting land ahead of survey increased. Throughout the 1820's and '30's there was a continual pressure for a preemption law that would legalize squatter claims. A series of acts passed in 1832, 1834, 1838, and 1840 granted partial preemption rights, and the Act of 1841 permitted general preemption (i.e., allowed the squatter the right to purchase the land he had farmed). In effect, the act granted a free loan to the settler from the date of preemption until the date of the official land sale.

In 1862 the principle of free land was explicitly recognized in the Homestead Act. That act granted any citizen (or alien who had declared his intention of becoming a citizen) the right to take up 160 acres of land upon payment of a nominal filing fee. The title officially passed to the homesteader without further cost when he had lived on and farmed the land for five years. Moreover, if he chose, after six months of residence the homesteader was permitted to acquire clear title by paying the standard $1.25 per acre price.

The Act of 1862 has been frequently criticized. Certainly, much of the best land in the public domain had been sold before the act was passed, and even after passage, railroad land grants removed some of the most desirable lands from the rolls. Moreover, although 160 acres had proven itself more than adequate in the Old Northwest and probably adequate in the area immediately across the Mississippi, it was woefully inadequate in the dry lands west of the 100th meridian. Still, the fact remains that in the period from 1862 until 1922 title to almost 214 million acres was transferred from the government to homesteaders.

Military bounties, sales for revenue, grants for internal improvements, and the Homestead Act accounted for most of the transfers out of the public domain; however, some land was settled as a result of legislative attempts to improve the quality of the land. In 1873 an act granted 160 acres of land west of the 100th meridian to anyone who would agree to plant 40 acres (later reduced to 10) in trees. For a twenty-five cent per acre down payment, the Desert Land Act of 1876 granted any settler who would agree to irrigate the land the use of 640 acres. Final patent rested upon successful irrigation and payment of an additional $1.00 an acre, but the settler had three years to complete the contract. Although few new lands were irrigated, cattlemen found that eight cents per year was cheap rent and some new lands were added to the agricultural sector.

4–3. *Power*

Although the rise of a manufacturing sector is not necessarily a precondition for economic growth, in the United States the process of commercialization was closely tied to the growth of manufacturing. Manufacturing can, of course, be carried on on a handicraft basis, but the great increases in productivity are usually the result of the substitution of machines for tools. A tool is nothing but the extension of a man's hand, but a machine applies nonhuman power to the task. For machines to operate, however, it is necessary to have power, and the growth of the manufacturing sector in the United States was to a large measure dependent upon the successful exploitation of our power resources. In some activities (particularly agriculture and local transportation), animals furnished the bulk of the power throughout the nineteenth century. Animals could not, however, supply economical power to manufacturing, nor could they provide inexpensive motive power for interregional transport. Instead, development in these sectors awaited the effective harnessing of steam and water power. To harness this power, however, new techniques were required.

a) ***Water Power.*** The United States (particularly the eastern part) was well endowed with a number of swiftly flowing streams. To make the power potential of these rivers usable, however, the water power had to be transformed into mechanical power. Water wheels had been used for centuries for this purpose, but the traditional undershot wheel was quite inefficient (even the best were only about 40 per cent efficient). The development of the breast type pitch-back wheel improved the situation considerably. The new wheel was driven by both the momentum and the weight of the water, and it was as much as 75 per cent efficient. In the 1840's, the development of the turbine further increased the amount of water power that was available. With vertical shafts and powered by falling water, the turbines were at times as much as 90 per cent efficient.

To generate power was not enough. If it was to be used, power also had to be transmitted to the work head. For stationary power, reliance was placed upon copies of English cog and gear systems, but they were not well suited to the United States. With higher labor costs, there was a greater need for faster machine operation, and cog and gear drives did not operate well at high speeds. Moreover, the machine-tool industry was not well developed and the copies of the complicated gearing mechanisms that they produced did not work as well as the British originals. In 1828 Kirk Boot innovated a belt drive in a new textile mill and the results were almost revolutionary. The new principle permitted much higher speeds, yielded higher operating efficiencies, and made it easier (although not easy) to operate a number of machines from a single power source. As a result, the drive was widely innovated throughout the manufacturing sector.

b) ***Coal.*** Despite improvements in the design of water wheels and the invention of the turbine, direct water power was not ideal. Not only did it depend upon a constant supply of water (even the largest mills were frequently forced to close in the summer when the stream ran dry), but despite the improvements in transmission, water power was definitely not portable. As a result, transportation equipment remained animal-powered, and as the demand for industrial power rose, the price of mill sites also went up.

The idea of generating energy by the combustion of coal is not new. For centuries, coal had been consumed for heat, and far back in antiquity Hero had developed a simple steam engine. In the early 18th century both Newcommen and Savery had developed primitive, but useful engines, and in the second half of the century Watt had begun to produce a very good low-pressure engine. Their impact on the American economy was, however, quite small. In the first decade of the nineteenth century, Oliver Evans designed a high pressure engine that was small relative to the power it developed and also many times more efficient than Watt's. It was upon the Evans model that American innovation was based.

But given a technically satisfactory engine, steam power did not immediately replace the water wheel in industrial uses. Because of its availability in the early years, the cost of water power was only about one fifth the cost of steam power, given the best steam engine. In addition, because of the primitive state of the American metallurgical and machine tool industries, the early engines were not the best. In markets where steam engines competed with the water wheel, the latter usually won. In transport, however, the engine quickly replaced the horse.

In the second decade of the nineteenth century, steam was successfully innovated on the inland waterways. On the western rivers alone, some 3,500 steamships had been built by the Civil War, and as late as 1838 almost 60 per cent of the nation's steam engines were used to power river steamers. Steam engines also underlaid the development of the railroad system. Although there had been many experiments with horse-drawn railroads, it was only after the application of steam that the roads provided a viable form of interregional transportation.

As time passed, the technical problems that had made steam engines expensive in industrial applications began to be solved. Changes in design made some contribution, but most important were parallel changes in the metallurgical and machine-tool industries. With the developments in these complementary industries, the prices of steam power began to fall. By the middle of the century, although the water wheel still provided the cheapest form of power, the gap was narrowing. Then, however, the gradual development of available mill sites and the shift of industry toward the Midwest (where there were relatively few fast-flowing, year-round rivers) began to increase the costs of water power. At the same time, increases in the supply of coal caused prices to fall and added additional incentive to shift from water to steam. As a result, by the 1870's steam had become the most important source of industrial power.

In the early years, most of the nation's steam engines were fired by wood, but as the forests were cut the cost of wood rose. Since the price of coal was falling, business began to substitute it for the more expensive fuel. By the 1850's coal was generally used in the eastern railroads, and by the time of the Civil War it also served the bulk of the midwestern roads.

The nineteenth century saw few improvements in coal-mining techniques, but new discoveries greatly increased the nation's reserves. Although Pennsylvania remained the leader, that century saw the opening of important new fields in the Midwest (particularly in southern Illinois) and in the South, and less important fields in the Rocky Mountains. As a result, the relative price of coal fell throughout most of the century. This downward trend continued in the early decades of the present century, not because of new discoveries, but because the application of electricity and compressed air to mining permitted much greater mechanization in the cutting and hauling operations. Thus, technical change in the manufacture of steam engines coupled with a change in the relative price of fuels resulted in the substitution of steam for water power.

At about the time coal began to be used as an important source of power, it also began to be used as a source of heat energy in the metallurgical industry. Traditionally, charcoal had been used to smelt iron ore, but that fuel was very expensive. Not only was the charcoal manufacture a labor-intensive process, but also the price of timber tended to rise rapidly as the forests were cut down. Great Britain had been faced with rising charcoal prices over a century earlier than the Americans. In early experiments, it was discovered that coal would not pass the blast of air needed to heat the iron. In the early eighteenth century, however, Abraham Darby successfully substituted coked coal for wood and the basis for the modern iron industry was laid.

In the United States, where timber prices were low and the demand for iron was small, it was economically feasible to continue charcoal production well into the nineteenth century. Ultimately, however, rising charcoal prices coupled with falling coal prices induced a substitution of mineral for vegetable fuels.

c) ***Electric Power.*** By 1870 steam had proven itself superior to water power, but it still was not an ideal energy source. The shift from water to steam left unused the vast energy potential of the nation's rivers. Moreover, while steam-driven machines were not tied to their energy sources in the same way that the old wheel-drive factories had been, the system was still not very flexible. Since there were important economies of scale in the use of steam engines, it paid to have a single prime mover in a factory. Given a single power source, however, it was difficult (even with complicated belt and pulley arrangements) to operate machines at different speeds and divisions at different tempos. What was needed was a system that would divorce power use from power generation.

In the 1830's Faraday had shown that a dynamo could generate electricity, and even before that it was known that electricity could run a motor. Despite these developments, no one was able to build a commercially satisfactory dynamo, and electricity remained a laboratory plaything until the 1870's. At that time several satisfactory dynamos were developed, and thereafter the industry progressed much faster. At first electricity was used only to transmit the energy inherent in water power to an industrial site some distance away. A water-driven dynamo would be used to generate electricity which, in turn, would be used to operate a single prime mover in a nearby factory. In the 1890's Sidney Paine, a General Electric salesman, saw that it was senseless to tie an entire factory to a single prime mover when electricity could be used to operate any number of motors at any number of speeds. The complicated systems of belts and pulleys that had been so eagerly innovated sixty years before became obsolete, and by World War I flexible electric power had been widely innovated throughout the manufacturing sector.

Nor was the indirect production of power through the intermediary of electricity to be limited to the energy potential of water. The first generating systems used simple adaptations of the traditional water turbines to drive the dynamos, but the invention of the steam turbine in the 1890's made it possible also to use the energy in coal. This invention was so successful that by the mid-'90's over half of the nation's electric power came from steam turbines, and today the proportion is almost 80 per cent.

The technical problems were not all in generation. Generating facilities were subject to increasing returns over a substantial range of outputs but when direct current was transmitted more than a few miles, the power loss became prohibitively high. The loss in the line is equal to the product of the resistance of the line times the square of the current carried on the line. Since the resistance was a function of length, the size of the market was limited and industry was unable to achieve the economies of scale that would otherwise have been available. Alternating current provided a solution to this problem. The voltage could be stepped up through a transformer and at higher voltages less current had to be transmitted. With lower power losses, it was possible to support region-wide electric networks. The battle between alternating and direct current raged over a decade, and Edison's stubbornness held back widespread innovation. The success of the Niagara Falls system, however, proved that AC was superior, and the growth of electric power industry in the twentieth century has been almost entirely associated with alternating current. As a postscript, it is interesting to note that recently the Russians have apparently succeeded in solving the technical problems inherent in the long-range transmission of direct current.

Electricity itself is not a source of power. It does, however, represent a very efficient method of transmitting and distributing the energy potential of steam and water power. Today, electricity is used to transmit and distribute about one fifth of the total energy produced in the United States.

d) ***Oil.*** The development of petroleum into an important energy source clearly demonstrates the close relationship between resources and technology. The oil discoveries in Titusville in the 1850's did not produce a new product. Oil had been widely known for years, but despite a few attempts to produce inflammatives and lubricants, it was generally assumed to be useless. In fact, the original consortium that had combined to send "Colonel" Drake to Oil Creek expected to use the petroleum as a patent medicine base. The pressures of the growing industrial economy had, however, increased the demand for lubricants beyond those that could easily be supplied from plants and animals. Moreover, the success of the coal-oil lamp had suggested a ready market for another successful illuminant. The technology of the 1840's could not, however, support the production of illuminants and lubricants from petroleum.

No new inventions were needed, but some inspired innovation was. The application of drilling techniques long used in water wells and distillation techniques well known in the production of coal oil turned the nearly useless petroleum into a valuable resource. In the years after 1860, the new wells and refineries supplied from the heavy distillates a lubricant superior to natural substitutes and from the middleweight distillates (particularly kerosene) the energy source for a significant fraction of the world's artificial light. Later, the development of the internal combustion engine and its successful application to land transport turned the lightweight distillates (gasoline and diesel fuel) that had heretofore been considered dangerous nuisances into yet other valuable resources. Thus petroleum, which had contributed nothing to the nation's energy supply in 1850, rose to supply about 5 per cent of the total in 1900. Since then the increase has been even more rapid, and by the middle of the present century it contributed well over a third of the total.

The increase in the relative contribution of petroleum reflects not only new demands but also further technical change and the discoveries of new reserves on the supply side. Although some technical gains were realized in drilling and exploration, until recently most of the improvements have been in refining and transportation. New refinery designs dating back to the 1870's greatly reduced refining costs; and in transportation, the development of the pipeline, the railroad tank car, and the ocean-going tanker (all introduced in the last quarter of the nineteenth century) helped to reduce the delivered price of the refined product. Moreover, the two interacted. The new refining technology was subject to increasing returns to scale over significant ranges of output, and declining transport costs greatly increased the size of the market and permitted these returns to be realized.

The original boom had been centered in western Pennsylvania, but in the 1880's new fields were discovered in northwestern Ohio and eastern Indiana. By the 1890's this region had taken the lead in production, but the day of "Lima crude" was short-lived. About the turn of the century major new fields were located in California, and a few years later discoveries in Texas, Louisiana, and Oklahoma caused the center of production to shift into the Southwest. More recently, new discoveries elsewhere in the world, coupled with the relatively high cost of exploiting the shale deposits in the United States, have increased our demands for foreign petroleum. In the absence of trade restrictions, it is likely that today we would seek the major portion of our requirements outside the continental United States.

e) ***Gas.*** Today one quarter of the total nonanimal energy consumed in the United States comes from gas. Since most of it is used in heating (it has been estimated that if we utilized every bit of hydroelectric energy that is available we could heat only one home in twenty-five) it is easy to overlook its importance.

In the 1880's it was discovered that a natural illuminant could easily be manufactured as a by-product of the coke-making process. Many producers discovered that the by-product was more profitable than the coke itself, and production expanded rapidly. It was this man-made gas that provided the first central lighting systems for American cities. Artificial gas was inferior to natural gas, and natural gas was known. Why then was the inferior product used? The answer lay in the high cost of transportation. Unless natural gas reserves were nearby, the transport costs were prohibitive. Pipelines, however, were able to provide low-cost transport. The first pipelines were local and had little impact on the national market. Gradually, longer lines were built, and the consumer was able to purchase natural gas at prices below those of the artificial product. In the 1920's a market area of 250 miles was considered large. Soon thereafter, however, companies like Panhandle Eastern built lines linking the cities of the Midwest with the gas fields of Texas and Oklahoma; and during World War II these fields were joined with the East. Since that time, developments have continued, and new fields in the four corners area and in western Canada have been linked to the American market.

f) ***Atomic Energy.*** The examples thus far cited might lead the reader to believe that there is an almost magical relationship between technology and energy resources. In each instance technology has made it economically feasible to exploit some new body of resources. The history of atomic energy, however, suggests that required technological changes are not always forthcoming. No sooner had the world recovered from the shock of Hiroshima than scientists began to explore peacetime uses of atomic power. To many, it seemed obvious that a vast new energy source had become available, and some believed that the day of almost free power was close at hand. Since 1945 the United States, Great Britain, and Russia have all poured large amounts of scientific resources into the atomic power area, and each country has built and operated at least one atomic-electric power plant. Despite the resources devoted to the task by both the public and private sectors, no one has yet been able to generate power at a price competitive even with steam generation. In 1950 the officers of several of the country's largest utilities announced that atomic power was just a few years away. The past fifteen years, however, have seen few advances; and today these same officials are much less hopeful. Nor has the failure been entirely an American one. Russia (a nation probably even more concerned with low-cost power) has also been unable to produce competitive atomic power and recently they have even closed down one of their experimental stations. At all times and places, resources remain a function of technology and conversely, technology can keep potential resources unavailable.

4–4. *Minerals*

It is possible to fill volumes with a recapitulation of the discovery of American mineral wealth, but we will limit ourselves to a brief discussion of three minerals: iron, copper, and sulfur.

a) ***Iron.*** Not all our resources have been opened by technology. Some were discovered in the ordinary way. Before the middle of the nineteenth century, the center of the nation's iron industry was eastern Pennsylvania. As late as 1850 the nation's iron production was concentrated in Pennsylvania with some peripheral production in the Ohio and Cumberland valleys. Even these meager resources showed signs of running out, and the nation's iron masters were looking for additional ore in northern Alabama and Missouri. Taken together, these areas would probably have been sufficient for the nation's demands given the technology of the period. However, they would never have produced enough ore to support a steel-based manufacturing sector.

In the 1850's, however, the first of the Lake Superior iron ranges were discovered (the Marquette, the Gogebic, and the Menominee), and with the opening of the St. Mary's canal these ores began to flow to the blast furnaces of western Pennsylvania. By 1860, although the Superior fields accounted for only 10 per cent of total production, Michigan was already the fourth leading iron producer. After the war, however, further discoveries dwarfed the first Great Lake fields. In the 1870's the Vermillion Range near Duluth was opened, and a decade later mining began in the Mesabi. While the southern Great Lakes ores were hard and could only be mined from underground, the new ores were soft and crumbly and lent themselves to strip mining. As a result the cost of ore fell.

By 1900 Minnesota was second to Michigan, and Alabama (despite the fact that its ores could not be used for Bessemer steel) had taken over third place among the nation's leading producers. Pennsylvania had fallen to fifth position, and its production barely exceeded its 1850 output. The concentration of output in the new ranges continued during the first decades of the twentieth century, and by the end of World War I, 70 per cent of the ore produced in the Great Lakes region came from the Mesabi. The contribution of the Great Lakes ranges is readily apparent if one examines the trend in total iron output in the United States. In 1860 the economy produced less than 2 million tons of ore, by 1880 the lower Great Lakes ranges had pushed output to 10 million tons, but the opening of the Mesabi underwrote an even larger increase after 1890—an increase that led to totals of 42 million tons in 1905 and 79 million tons in 1917. Thereafter, with no new major discoveries, the nation's output began to level off.

Thus the history of iron ore in the nineteenth century is largely a history of new discoveries. More recently, however, technical problems have become important. Although the Great Lakes region still possesses large reserves of high-grade ores, there is some long-run concern. Miners have first mined those deposits that were most accessible, and in particular those that could be mined by open-pit and wash techniques. As reserves have been depleted it has become necessary to push into the higher cost ores, and as a result there has been an increase in costs. Today the greatest untapped deposits are the low-grade taconite fields (25 to 40 per cent iron), but it is still uneconomic to use them. Because it takes about three tons of taconite to produce as much ore as a ton of high grade and because the diffusion of the iron through the ore requires an extra agglomeration process, the cost of mining taconite is about three times the cost of high-grade ore. If, however, new mining and agglomeration techniques were discovered, the price of taconite might become competitive; and once again the nation would possess almost immeasurable iron reserves.

b) ***Copper.*** Because copper alloys (particularly brass and bronze) are fairly strong, capable of rolling, and rust-resistant, copper has always been a valuable resource. However, in the past hundred years the rise of the electric industry has greatly increased the importance of that metal. In the nineteenth century the growth of our stock of ore was largely a function of discovery, but about the turn of the century a technical breakthrough in separation added additional millions of tons to our reserves.

In the early decades of the nineteenth century, known reserves were small and widely scattered. Rich fields were discovered in Michigan in the 1840's, but shortages of capital and inadequate transportation delayed their exploitation. As a result the Tennessee-Georgia border area supplied most of the new demands, but Michigan ores began to appear on the market in the 1850's. In the latter part of that decade, eastern capital poured into the Michigan mines, and the midwest railway network reached the mining area. So swift was the rise of the Michigan centers that by the outbreak of the Civil War that state was producing about 75 per cent of the nation's total, and it was a rapidly growing total indeed (output increased about 400 per cent in the years from 1860 to 1880).

In the 1870's a series of new discoveries altered the geographic structure of the industry. The Anaconda Copper Company discovered a very rich vein near Butte, and with the arrival of the transcontinental railroad, Montana's production increased rapidly. By the 1880's that state's output was equal to Michigan's, and thereafter it forged ahead. In the 1890's discoveries in Arizona matched those in Montana, and by the first decades of the twentieth century the southwestern state had surpassed Montana and relegated Michigan to a distant third. The impact of these vast new reserves was reflected in the trend in copper prices. Despite the increase in the demand for electrical copper, the 1880's saw copper price decline by over half. As the output of the western mines began to appear on the market, prices fell from about twenty-three cents a pound to less than ten cents.

The new areas would have been insufficient to supply the growing electric industry, but technological change again increased our stock of usable resources. The Michigan, Montana, and Arizona deposits were of high-grade ore that was amenable to traditional concentration techniques (stamping and washing). As the best ores were mined, however, it became necessary to work poorer and poorer deposits and the recovery process became more and more expensive. It was, in fact, not profitable to mine ores of less than 7 per cent copper unless they also contained some precious metals. Large deposits of porphyry ore were discovered in the West, but these were less than 3 per cent copper. Innovation of the strip-mining techniques that had been profitably employed in the Mesabi reduced costs of mining. More important, the discovery of the oil flotation process made it economically feasible to concentrate these low-grade ores. As a result, by World War I porphyry ores accounted for about a third of total production, and since then their proportion has continued to increase. Total copper output did, of course, increase tremendously. Production rose from 30,000 tons in 1880 to 445,000 tons in 1905 and to over a million tons a decade later.

Thereafter, however, there have been no significant additions to our copper reserves. Despite the growth of the electrical industry, the production achieved in 1916 was not reached again until 1942 and not until 1956 in a peacetime year. As a result, copper prices have tended to rise, and by the 1950's they reached forty cents a pound (an increase of some 500 per cent over the low of the 1930's). As prices rose, copper users sought substitutes, and in aluminum they found a fairly adequate one. Although larger wires were needed (aluminum is an inferior conductor and a greater cross-section area is needed to attain the same low resistance), its total weight was no more and its lower price meant that the additional requirements could be met and costs still kept below the cost of copper wire. Throughout the late '50's and early '60's copper faced increasing competition from aluminum, and the end of the substitution is still not in sight.

c) ***Sulfur.*** Heavy manufacturing (particularly the petroleum and fertilizer industries) consumes large quantities of acid. Pyrites can be used as a basis for an industrial acid, but the nation's pyrite resources are meager and the acid is inferior to sulfuric acid. In the nineteenth century we imported the raw products for most of our industrial acids from Spain and Portugal, but the rising industrial demand put such products at a premium. Ultimately, through discovery, technical progress, and the rise of certain complementary industries, we began to exploit our own sulfur resources.

Vast new sulfur beds were discovered in Texas and Louisiana in the later years of the nineteenth century. Since these beds were located far underground, they could not be exploited economically.

In the first years of the twentieth century Frasch developed a new hot-water pumping technique that could be used to bring the sulfur to the surface, but the process required a great deal of heat to keep the water boiling, and it was not economical. Soon thereafter, however, oil was discovered in adjacent fields, and these fields supplied the needed low-cost fuel. Sulfur production began immediately and continued to increase at a phenomenal rate. Production that had never exceeded 5,000 tons before 1900 reached 200,000 tons in 1905, 1 million tons in 1916, 2 million tons in 1923, 4 million tons in 1947, and 6 million tons in 1956.

4–5. Conclusion

There can be little question that the United States has been among the world's most favored nations in terms of its natural endowments. Endowments, however, are not the whole story. Professor Kuznets has shown that many of the underdeveloped countries not only have relatively poor endowments but do not even make efficient use of what they have. In the case of the United States, our transportation system developed so that bodies of resources located far from markets could be economically utilized, our technology changed to turn otherwise valueless items into valuable resources, and public policy (although, perhaps, failing to encourage adequate conservation) was designed to effect the rapid exploitation of the nation's resources. These resources, in turn, helped to feed the economic engine during the periods of our most rapid growth.

Chapter 5 POPULATION

5–1. *Introduction*

The rate at which a nation's population grows is an important determinant of the rate at which the output of the nation will grow. We do not mean to imply by this that a growing population induces a growing per-capital product. The underdeveloped countries today provide ample evidence that no such relationship is necessary. At the same time, a population growing within the framework of expanding resources and a dynamic technology provides perhaps the most effective environment for economic development. It is the purpose of this chapter to examine some of the characteristics of available information of population growth, with particular reference to the United States.

5–2. *Population Growth in the Past*

The rates of population growth that the Western world has become accustomed to and that in underdeveloped countries are now called the "population explosion" are, in terms of even human history, of recent origin. Estimates have been made of the population of the various regions of the world back to the year 1000. The rates of growth per decade derived from these estimates are very instructive in terms of the long-run trends. If we take the period between the years 1000 and 1650, Europe (including Asiatic Russia) shows a rate of population growth of 1.4 per cent per decade, the Americas show a decline, and Asia and Africa show a rate of 0.9 per cent. For the world as a whole, the rate of growth was 0.9 per cent a decade over the 650-year period. Although such a rate of growth can be caused by many factors, from other knowledge we have we can reconstruct in broad terms the factors that must have been at work.

We know from historical records of wars, famines, and plagues that the death rates of the population prior to 1650 must have been high. In some plagues, for example, we are told that as many as one third of the population of a city perished. The inefficient state of agricultural technology and the poor transportation systems aggravated the problems of periodic spells of bad weather, so that famine was a relatively common and perhaps regular occurrence. On top of this, frequent armed conflicts added to general misery, not so much through direct mortality but as a result of the disease and economic dislocation following in the train of medieval armies.

If this was, in fact, the mortality experience, then it is clear that the birth rate must have been high as well. In some periods, in fact, the birth rate must have been substantially above the death rate to offset the periodic calamities that decimated populations.

With such a picture in mind, it is possible to infer other things. We have stressed the role of capital formation in economic development. How could capital formation occur in such a society (except for brief bright instances) when the expectation of life was so short that immediate consumption far outweighed any anticipation of future returns? In those brief periods of wealth and prosperity that did occur, as for example in some of the Italian city-states, it is no wonder that many of the capital expenditures took the form of buildings and *objets d'art,* rather than roads. The "eat, drink, and be merry, for tomorrow we die" philosophy must have been widely accepted. The almost pathological obsession with religion and the concentration of the meager resources available upon the construction of churches is understandable in a society living in constant fear of death.

Technology, the application of new ideas to production, would be nonexistent. Such things as tools, plows, carriages, and construction equipment in 1650 were very similar to those of the year 1000. Even if there had been any time or resources available for evolving new techniques, there was almost no way in which the information could have been disseminated or passed on to following generations. The art of making stained-glass windows, which one would expect to be a jealously guarded technique, was lost and has hardly been duplicated since.

One gets the impression of a society locked in a vicious circle, held down by a very low productivity that left little surplus or incentive for the kind of activity that could have led to a cumulative breakthrough to higher standards of living. Communities were bounded by a time horizon that allowed little more than a daily struggle for existence. Modern American corporations think nothing of planning twenty-five years in advance. The medieval European merchant took a far greater risk investing in a three-year trading voyage to the Orient.

5–3. Recent Population Growth

It is impossible to date the various developments that caused the radical changes in the population experience of the world. The changes have not yet taken place even today in some regions of the world. For a large part of the world's population, they are of very recent origin. In Western Europe and some of its colonial offshoots, it is possible to trace a substantial change from the seventeenth and eighteenth centuries. Many factors contributed to the changes in Western Europe. The spirit of scientific inquiry that seems to have originated from trading wealth in Italy, and that eventually spread across Western Europe, led finally to substantial changes in the techniques of agricultural production and released the population from the regular fear of famine. Advancing medical knowledge and concern for public health eventually had a great effect upon mortality. The slow consolidation of political power in the hands of sovereign states and the desire to increase this power led to improvements in public safety, internal communications, and the freeing of internal trade from the control of local power groups. The effects upon population growth were tremendous. For Western Europe (including Asiatic Russia) the rate of population growth between 1650 and 1950 was 5.7 per cent per decade, and between 1750 and 1950 was 6.9 per cent per decade. From 1650 to 1950, the Americas grew at the compound rate of 12.7 per cent per decade, and for the period 1750 to 1950 at a compound rate of 18.5 per cent per decade. For the world as a whole, the growth rate from 1650–1950 was 5.2 per cent, and from 1750–1950, 6.0 per cent per decade.

Again, the significance of these rates of growth lies in what can be inferred about the conditions of the population. We know that the main cause of the increase in the rates in the recent period was a decline in the death rate. This means in effect an increase in average life expectancies of the population. As people's time horizons expanded, both their outlook on life and their place in it also changed. For many groups, the old philosophies changed radically and were given new names; others evolved from the old to meet the new condition. The restless search for the new and more efficient and the accumulation and dissemination of knowledge became powerful forces as Western society struggled out of the restricted life of the past into a system of experiences that rapidly proved unique in human history.

5–4. Population Growth and Industrialization

Information on birth and death rates for the eighteenth and nineteenth centuries is very crude and not very reliable. Almost no information is available for the United States, but enough material exists for some European countries, especially England, to give the general trends that occurred during the period of European industrialization. It appears that the growth of population observed in this early period resulted primarily from a fall in death rates. Furthermore, the death rates did not fall uniformly in time in all parts of Europe. There seems to be a correlation between the rate of industrialization and the fall in the death rate and, hence, the increase in population. From the information available, England was the first country to experience the fall in the death rate that eventually spread to the rest of Europe and, in our century, around the world. The fall apparently occurred between about 1780 and 1810, when the death rate fell from a crude rate of 30 deaths per 1000 population per year to a crude rate of 20 deaths per 1000 population per year. The significance of this fall can be explained by the following example. If the crude birth rate is 40 per 1000 and the crude death rate 30 per 1000, the natural increase in the population is 10 per thousand, or (excluding immigration and emigration) the population is growing at a compound rate of 1 per cent per year. If the death rate falls to 20 per 1000, the birth rate remaining at 40 per 1000, the natural increase in the population is 20 per 1000 or (again ignoring migration) the population is growing at a compound rate of 2 per cent per year. As we shall see shortly, this example very nearly describes the situation in England during most of the nineteenth century.

What factors caused the death rate to fall in England about the end of the eighteenth century? Two sets of factors, one economic and the other medical, appear to have been the cause of the change. The main economic factor was undoubtedly the improvement in agricultural techniques. New knowledge of seeds, fertilizer, crop rotation, and stock breeding made relatively tremendous improvements in agricultural output. The desire to implement the new ideas helped to stimulate the breakup of the old manorial system of agriculture in which all families in a village had control over different types of land spread about in the surrounding area—one man might have a strip of river-bottom land, another strip on the hillside, another on sandy soil, and yet another on relatively infertile land. While this strip system may have been an equitable method of allocating a scarce resource among the families of the village, it was a positive hindrance to the development of scientific farming. The strips were not fenced off and all harvesting of a crop was done at the same time by the whole village. It did not pay a man to drain his own land unless his neighbors drained theirs. Scientific stock breeding was an impossibility when animals were allowed to roam almost at will. Merely walking from one strip to another was a time-wasting process. There was no room, in effect, for individual initiative. With the enclosure of land, each family that had held land under the old system received a consolidated farm. Within his own farm, a man with initiative could innovate as he saw fit, in an attempt to improve his output. The resulting increase in food supply had a positive effect upon lowering the death rate.

While agricultural output was increasing so were employment, output, and real wage per laborer in other sectors of the economy. This had a beneficial effect upon diets, as more nutritious foods were added to the consumer's budget. For example, the increasing use of tea, as a result of increasing incomes, helped end the widespread consumption of gin with its deleterious effects so well portrayed by Hogarth.

While the practice of medicine was not yet a very advanced science, sufficient observation had been made of conditions in hospitals to show that elementary precautions of sanitation could work wonders in reducing deaths. The effects were particularly noticeable in the very young age groups and, because this group was such a large proportion of the population, the sanitation measures had a proportionately great effect on the crude death rate.

The effects upon the death rate of both the increase in the food supply and the rudimentary improvements in medical knowledge are even more impressive when one considers that the period of 1780–1810 in England was one of the increasing urbanization associated with the process of industrialization. Cities have always been killers, and this was particularly true in the early period. Age group by age group, death rates in cities have been above, and in some periods substantially above, rural death rates.

After reaching a level of about 20 per 1000 around 1810, death rates in England apparently stayed almost constant until about 1880, when they dropped again; today they are roughly 10 per

1000. The constancy of the rate during the greater part of the nineteenth century is probably explained by the growth of cities. It was not until the science of bacteriology was developed that any significant attack could be made upon the control of disease in urban areas, and it took some time before large-scale advances could be made in the problems of urban sanitation.

The crude birth rate in England apparently moved downward very slowly from about 35 per 1000 in 1800, to a level about 30 per 1000 at the end of the nineteenth century, when it began to decline along with, but at a faster rate than, the death rate. The fact that the birth rate declined slowly is slightly puzzling. The population was becoming healthier and, in particular, childhood diseases that frequently have a direct bearing on fertility in later years were being controlled more effectively. Furthermore, people were to some extent better off and therefore in a position to enter into marriage at an earlier age. Under the old system of land tenure associated with the manorial system, a male heir frequently had to wait until his father died before he could get married because the only livelihood for many was agriculture and there was no new land available. The same set of circumstances is said to exist in parts of Eire today. With the coming of the factory system and the general increase in well-being, alternative opportunities were open to the rural population. The increase in health and economic opportunity would tend to cause the birth rate to rise. On the other hand, factors tending to cause a reduction in birth rates were at work. The first was probably a result of the fall in the death rate that, remember, was largest among the young age groups. As fewer children die, fewer need be born to attain a desired family size. The concept of a desired family size is one that has changed over time. However, in the nineteenth century the concept had developed over centuries of high child mortality and it is probable that the desired size was a known and constant figure. The second tendency operating to reduce the birth rate was the general economic change occurring in England in the nineteenth century. Opportunities existed for men to attain positions of wealth and power, and such men are likely to feel that their ability to compete is restricted by a large family that, whatever joys it may provide, is nonetheless a time-consuming project. Also, industrialization was accompanied by a vast growth of cities that absorbed a greater proportion of the population, and the birth rate in cities has always been lower than in rural areas.

The population growth of England during the nineteenth

century, while greater than that recorded for any previous century, did not constitute a "population explosion," as that term is used currently. The fall in the death rate was not great enough to outpace the growth of resources so that per-capita incomes rose over the period. By the end of the century, when medical science had advanced to the point where substantial cuts could be made in the death rate, the birth rate also fell as families made adjustments to the new economic and medical environment. By 1860, 63 per cent of English families had four or more children. By 1925, only 20 per cent had four or more children.

We mentioned earlier that England was the first country to experience what we might call the modern population pattern. Other European countries also had approximately the same experience as their development followed the English example. Thus, the death rate in Scandinavia appears to have begun to fall sometime about 1820, roughly by the same amount as the earlier English fall. In the case of Germany, the same fall, although this time at a more rapid rate, appears to have begun about 1860, coinciding with German unification and industrialization. The more rapid fall in Germany can be attributed to the fact that she had access to the medical and scientific knowledge discovered in England. All Western European countries entered on the period of falling death and birth rates at the end of the nineteenth century at roughly the same time.

We have been dealing with trends in birth and death rates for European countries because we have more information about events in those countries. In the United States, there are only very scattered pieces of information about population trends in the nineteenth century. It is generally assumed that in the early part of the period the birth rate may have been as high as 55 per 1000, largely as a result of a plentiful food supply and the rural living of the majority of the population. The birth rate gradually fell throughout the century until it had reached a level of approximately 30 per 1000. Then the birth rate in the United States apparently went through the same sharp fall that characterized the European experience. As to the death rate, again all we have is only limited information. The death rate in the United States was probably not as high as in Europe, again because of better economic conditions. It may, in fact, have been throughout the nineteenth century lower than the rate of 20 per 1000 recorded for England. The death rate seems to have been fairly constant throughout the century, perhaps with a slight decline, until at the end of the century the medical advances previously noted for Europe brought a sharp decline.

To sum up the above discussion, consider the rates of natural increase of the populations implied by the birth- and death-rate trends we have been discussing. In Europe, the fall in the death rate at the beginning of the nineteenth century with the birth rate remaining unchanged caused a sharp increase in the rate of population increase. Throughout the century, when the birth rate and death rate remained constant the rate of increase was also constant. In the United States, the constantly falling birth rate, with a constant death rate, implies a constant, although moderate, fall in the rate of population increase. In both Europe and America, the sharp decline in the birth rate around the end of the century and the somewhat slower decline in the death rate imply a decrease in the rate of population growth.

The trends in birth and death rates we have been discussing have been described in terms of changes in economic and medical conditions. In the United States, the sharp break in both measures that occurred about 1900 continued into the 1930's, when the birth rate fell below 20 per 1000 and the death rate was about 10 per 1000. This means, therefore, that the rate of increase of the population (ignoring immigration and emigration) was less than 1 per cent per year compound. The extremely low birth rate recorded for the 1930's was no doubt due in part to the severity of the depression. On the other hand, it appeared at the time to be an extension of the trend. The decline that occurred during the 1920's has been associated with many things. It is known that high-income families have fewer children on the average than low-income families and that urban families have fewer children on the average than rural families. In the 1920's, America was becoming wealthier and more urbanized. Also, the status of women was changing. More women were working, and for many women the home played a smaller part in their mode of life than it had previously. These signs pointed to a situation of very limited population increase for the future.

The population forecasters who projected such trends into the 1950's were confounded by events. While the death rate remained at 10 per 1000, the birth rate jumped above 25 per 1000 in the 1940's, and has stayed there. At first it was felt that this upsurge in the birth rate was a result both of wartime conditions and of the desire of families to reach a projected family size after the bad times of the

1930's that had restricted the birth rate. But the birth rate has remained high and, while it may eventually fall, a new situation may perhaps have established itself.[1] Perhaps suburban living has caused a change in desired family size, or perhaps larger families are becoming socially acceptable again. Whatever the reason, it augurs well for the American economy. There is a dynamism in a growing population in a country like ours that acts as a general stimulant to business and makes a whole community optimistic about the future. In America, where the existence of social and occupational mobility, both up and down, is a generally accepted belief, a growing population keeps supplying the human talents necessary if new projects are to be undertaken and new technological areas opened. Without such mobility a society tends to stagnate, with those in power maintaining their position on the basis of what is frequently an outmoded system of techniques.

These movements we have been observing in the birth and death rates have had powerful effects upon the age distribution of the population. In 1850, 2.6 per cent of the American population were 65 years of age and over, and 41.4 per cent were under 15 years; by 1900, 4.1 per cent were 65 and over, and 34.5 per cent were under 15; in 1940, 6.8 per cent were 65 and over, and 25 per cent were under 15. Consider for a moment the ratio of these dependent age groups to the productive age group between 15 and 64 years. The aging of the population (in 1850 the median age was about 19; in 1960 it was about 30) has increased the proportion of the population in the productive age groups. For every person in the dependent age groups in 1850 there were 1.3 persons between 15 and 64. By 1940, there were 2 persons 15–64 for every nonproductive person. The increase in the birth rate had reduced this to 1.5 by 1960.

Chart 5–1 presents a population pyramid for the total population by ten-year age groups for the two years 1850 and 1960. By placing the pyramids side by side, a striking picture can be gained of the changes in distribution over the period. Notice that, for 1850, the lower age groups have a proportionately much heavier weight in the distribution than in 1960, where the aging of the population is clearly visible in the heavier proportions in the upper age groups.

[1] The estimated birth rate has been falling slowly from its 1957 peak of 25.3 per thousand; in 1962 it was estimated to be 22.4 per thousand. It is too early to tell whether this movement will continue. The death rate has been holding at roughly 9.5 per thousand.

Notice also the startling manner in which the effects of the depression decade of the 1930's shows up in the pyramid for 1960. The low birth rate in that decade is reflected in the small percentage of those 20–29 years of age in 1960.

Changes in other characteristics of the population, although not directly related to birth and death rates, are relevant for this study. The changing technology in Western countries has led to a shift in

CHART 5–1

AGE DISTRIBUTION OF AMERICAN POPULATION, 1850 AND 1960

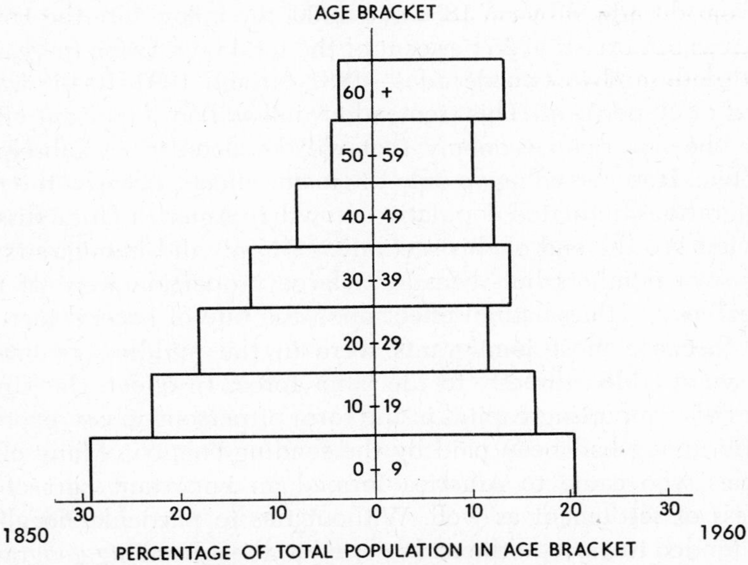

Sources: 1850: *Historical Statistics, 1960,* Series A71–85, p. 10; 1960: *Statistical Abstract, 1963,* Table 18, p. 26.

the proportion of rural to urban inhabitants. In 1800, only about 6 per cent of the American population resided in urban areas; by 1900, the proportion was roughly 40 per cent. By 1920, more people lived in urban than in rural areas; and by 1960, almost 70 per cent of the population lived in urban areas. The new technology, with its concentration of production and increases in the average size of manufacturing operations, led to growing cities that fed upon themselves as new industries gravitated to urban areas to take advantage of the existing labor force and the available facilities.

Throughout the period there was a steady movement from the rural areas that had a higher birth rate than the cities, and after the close of the frontier the large flood of immigrants ended in cities.

5–5. Migration of Peoples

One of the most interesting aspects of the population experience of the North Atlantic community in the nineteenth and early twentieth centuries was the migration of peoples. In no other period of human history have voluntary migrations of such magnitude taken place. Although there were flows both ways across the Atlantic, the main migration stream was toward the Americas from Europe. In every decade between 1850 and 1920, the inflow into the United States was in excess of 25 per cent of the total population increase in the decade and in two decades—1881–90 and 1901–10—it was in excess of 40 per cent. This tremendous inflow had important effects upon the American economy that will be detailed in subsequent chapters. Here we will give only the major effects. Clearly, the mass immigration stimulated population growth in America (for a dissenting view see the end of this section). Not only did immigrants add their own numbers but, because a large proportion were of marriageable age, they had an effect upon the rate of natural increase. Also, because most immigrants were in the middle age groups, they were added directly to the labor force. In effect, the United States was importing capital in the form of persons whose expenses of upbringing had been paid by the sending country. Many of the peoples who came to America formed an important part of the process of settlement as well. Without ties to particular localities, they tended to move in the early period to the advancing geographic frontiers and in the later period to the growing industrial areas of the new country.

The expanding American population provided a widening market for the output of the nation and, as incomes rose over time, a deepening of the market in the sense of the amounts and kinds of goods demanded. As the size of the market expanded and as the transportation network improved, it became possible to concentrate production into a relatively few larger-scale units to take advantage of economies of large-scale production. There is some evidence also that the mechanization of production was accelerated by the inflow of unskilled labor from abroad and the necessity of simplifying the processes of production to fit the unskilled labor force. There is a clear association between the growth of population and the growth of product in America. In periods of rapidly growing population, total product also grew rapidly. But as we have stressed before, this was something more than a one-to-one relationship. An expanding population encouraged investment in machines and larger-scale processes of production; and as scale increased the search for and use of more powerful sources of energy was accelerated. The productivity of the American labor force increased as population growth increased, and tended to slow down as population growth slowed down.

These swings in the growth of American population and total product have been related by Professor Brinley Thomas to swings in the economic growth of the other regions of the North Atlantic community. The broader picture gives an understanding of the rhythms of resource movements that accompanied the early stages of the growth of America.

There is evidence of a birth cycle in European countries in those records we have stretching far enough back in time. Twenty to twenty-five years after a peak in the population-growth cycle there would be a bulge in the population pyramid in the young, vigorous, productive age groups. If this bulge occurred at a time when the country was passing through the dislocations associated with the introduction of the new techniques of the industrial revolution, an outflow of people to America, the land of opportunity, would occur. This inflow into the United States would induce an expansion in the American economy. The expansion, which frequently took the form of opening new regions for settlement, called for an inflow of capital from abroad. Britain, as the leading lender, provided the bulk of these funds. As the emigration from Europe slowed down when the initial cause no longer existed, American growth slowed also. Thus, in the formative years of American development there was a rhythm in the process of growth, with the North Atlantic community acting as a whole.

In the above analysis emigration is a "safety-valve" movement. During the process of industrialization of a nation, the changing production functions and the new combinations of factors required as the new technology is substituted for the old cause a substantial dislocation of the accustomed patterns of production. These dislocations of factors mean that some parts of the labor force, particularly those on the land, are displaced from their accustomed occupations. The process of change is accelerated because those displaced or bypassed by the process of change had an outlet in the virgin lands of the Americas. Thus, the settlement of the Americas was accomplished by the free movement of people from Europe who, finding their position in the new order of Europe intolerable, moved to America. One can almost trace the movement of the new technology across Europe in the record of the source of immigrants into the Americas. The movement started from the British Isles and then moved eastward across Europe, ending with the inflows of southern and southeastern Europeans in the first decade of the twentieth century.

World War I brought an end to the large-scale immigration from Europe. The ability of the nation to move to wartime production without a continuing inflow of people added support to labor's contention that continued immigration was not essential to maintain a viable American economy. The labor movement had been trying for a long time to restrict immigration, to maintain labor standards. This movement was supported after the war by public opinion that feared a flood of undesirable immigrants fleeing from war-torn Europe. In 1921, a law was passed restricting immigration, except from most of North and South America, to 360,000 per year. When this law lapsed in 1924, it was replaced by one restricting immigration to 165,000, with a provision that quotas under the act be recalculated in such a way that over the years the total would gradually fall as the foreign-born element of the population diminished in size. A now discredited argument was also advanced that immigration did not in fact increase the size of the population but only changed the proportion of native-born to foreign-born. The argument was that at any time there was a given population that could exist in the United States and that an immigrant merely displaced a native-born, so that the total population remained unchanged.

5–6. *Population Growth and Economics*

The study of population growth has been an integral part of the study of economics since Adam Smith. For Smith, a growing population was an important aspect of economic development. A growing population provided a market for goods and a labor force that permitted increasing specialization and, therefore, productivity. Smith's optimism was followed by the pessimism of Malthus who saw a growing population as an inevitable, but not attractive, prospect. For Malthus, human populations, like many animal populations, can and will grow at a rate that outstrips the ability of the land to provide them with food. Thus, humans are forever doomed to a life of struggle at a subsistence level. The dismal predictions of Malthus have not appeared in the Western world where the more optimistic predictions of Smith seem to be closer to the truth. In the Western world, the application of a new technology has enabled men to increase their per-capita product, and, as we have indicated, to increase it at a rate that eventually persuaded people to lower the birth rate. Man's ability to control the power of nature has increased tremendously his ability to extract from his environment the things he desires. As we have intimated, it may in fact be that the dynamics of a rapidly growing, increasingly healthy population have provided the incentives that have created the conditions under which men have been willing and able to extract useful goods from nature. In addition, a growing population is generally characterized by a high degree of social and occupational mobility, a desirable feature if the changes associated with growth are to be effected smoothly. If the relation is a symmetrical one, then a slowly growing or declining population may be a stagnant one.

The problem of economic stagnation came to the fore in the United States in the 1930's. The constantly declining birth rate and the immigration barriers erected in the early 1920's seemed to portend an American population growing ever more slowly until it stabilized. Professor Alvin Hansen, in a famous article, after analyzing the causes of the rapid growth in America up to World War I, predicted a secular (long-term) stagnation for the American economy. He pointed to three factors as prime movers in the early American growth: rapid population growth, the frontier, and ever-expanding outlets for American investment.

The nineteenth and early twentieth centuries were periods of impressive growth of the American economy. We have already seen that population grew rapidly and that total output grew at an even faster pace, so that per-capita product also increased. Hansen placed the rate of population growth at the foundation of his explanation of American economic development. The frontier was an integral part of the rate of population growth because it was the existence of unsettled land that induced the large-scale immigration into America and the high rate of natural increase that characterized the period.

The rapid population growth and the settlement of new territories were important in the development process because they provided an investment outlet for the large volume of savings generated by America's rapidly rising per-capita income. The opening up of a new region to settlement and the expansion of population in a settled region involved large investments in houses, schools, roads, railways, and all the other social overhead and business capital required by modern living. This continual outlet for savings insured that the economy operated in the long run at rates that made full use of the available resources.

The settlement of the geographic frontier, the ending of large-scale immigration, and the reduced rate of natural increase due to a falling birth rate meant that these powerful forces of rapid development no longer existed in the American economy. A slowly growing population does not require the continual investment expenditures in social or business capital that a rapidly growing population does. Moreover, the American population is, as we have seen, an aging population that does not require the same expenditure—e.g., houses—that a young population does.

Hansen pointed to a further factor at work in reducing the investment outlets in the American economy. There is a tendency, he said, for modern technology to develop capital-saving rather than capital-using techniques. Thus, the railroad with its heavy fixed investment has been replaced by the airplane, a mode of transportation whose fixed investment is almost independent of the distance traveled. Finally, Hansen pointed to the fact that as incomes increase to high levels, a larger and larger proportion of consumer expenditure goes for personal services such as education, dry cleaning, and health. The provision of such services does not require as large a capital investment as would the same expenditure for manufactured commodities.

Hansen foresaw that the lack of privately generated investment outlets would inevitably lead to a chronically depressed economy unless the government stepped in and provided investment outlets in the form of slum-clearance projects, highway building, and so on. Since Hansen wrote, we have been through a period of over twenty years marked by war or preparation for war in which the federal government has played a large part in the American economy. This fact can be pointed to as support for Hansen's contention but, as is inevitable in the social sciences, we cannot point to proof because we do not know what would have happened had it been possible for the federal government to withdraw from large-scale involvement in the economy. Also, of course, the trend of population growth as projected by Hansen has not occurred in practice. The declining birth rate reached a low point in the 1930's, but it has risen since and remained at a high level.

Quite apart from these conditions, however, is it true that a dynamic economy requires a rapidly growing population as Hansen has suggested? In the period of rapid American development, population growth and the frontier played a large part. The process of development was essentially one of continuing expansion of simple techniques over new territories. The techniques were familiar ones and essentially they were repeated over and over again. This made growth relatively easy and, given favorable conditions, very rapid indeed. But this is not to say that the development process requires a rapid rate of population growth. It is quite possible to picture a nation showing only a moderately growing population and nevertheless a rapid rise in per-capita income.

The dynamics of the early period of American development resulted from expansion into a geographic frontier. The same type of dynamics can result from expansion into technological frontiers. Hansen's answer to such a suggestion was that new techniques tend to be capital saving and thus less useful as means of balancing the savings leakages. But he wrote before the advent of atomic energy, electronics, space technology, and all the other discoveries of what has been called the second industrial revolution. There seems to be no a priori reason why these new technological breakthroughs should not provide all the investment outlets needed to absorb the resources released for capital expenditure by the community's decision to save. Furthermore, if past experience is any guide, it seems to be the case that as nations attain a relatively high standard of living increasing attention is paid to the less fortunate members of society. While it is true that many community projects of a social nature are proposed as a means of combating unemployment, unemployment is clearly still one of the greatest evils of a rich society. But there are many other projects—health insurance, old-age and disability pensions, slum-clearance programs, aid to education, and so forth—that are aimed at other specific evils but that can help solve the problem of unemployment. The prospect, in fact, is not a lack of investment opportunities but a lack of savings capacity to fill the many needs.

5–7. Conclusion

The underdeveloped countries today are faced with the tremendous problem of an exploding population. There can be no denying that in such countries as Egypt, population is currently expanding at a rate that threatens to drag the whole nation down to a level of misery. The Malthusian specter is very real in such situations. On the other hand, in the new countries of the world with plentiful resources, such as Canada and the United States, no known rate of population growth has been sufficient to prevent an increasing standard of living. Clearly then, it is not the rate of population growth *per se* that is terrifying but rather the availability of resources to feed, house, and clothe the population. If the advanced countries of the world are willing to aid the underdeveloped countries to the limit of their ability, there is no reason why, through education and increased standards of living, the rate of natural increase of the underdeveloped countries should not decline. Once a certain standard of living has been attained for all, there is then no reason why the world—armed with ever more powerful techniques—should not look forward with the greatest confidence to population expansion and the dynamics that such an expansion involves.

Suggested Readings

CARR-SAUNDERS, A. M. *World Population, Past Growth and Present Trends.* Oxford: Clarendon Press, 1937.

FERENCZI, IMRE. *International Migrations.* New York: National Bureau of Economic Research, 1929.

HANSEN, A. H. "Economic Progress and Declining Population Growth," *American Economic Review*, 1939.

MALTHUS, T. R. *An Essay on Population.* London: J. M. Dent, 1952.

SMITH, A. *An Inquiry into the Nature and Causes of the Wealth of Nations.* ED. E. CANAAN. London: Methuen, 1925.

THOMAS, BRINLEY. *Migration and Economic Growth.* Cambridge: Cambridge University Press, 1954.

Chapter 6 THE AMERICAN LABOR FORCE

6–1. *The Changing Labor Force over Time*

In many respects, people are a nation's most valuable resource. Many countries with widely differing natural resource bases have attained similar standards of living because of the energy and resourcefulness of their human resources. The purpose of this section is to examine the nature of the American labor force and the economic characteristics of this particular segment of the population.

The crudest measure of the utilization of human resources is given in Table 6–1, where the proportion of the total population in the labor force is given by decades from 1820. Unfortunately for purposes of analysis, the figures are not strictly comparable over time. Because of differences in definition all that can really be said is that the total labor-force participation rate in the United States has not shown any significant change over time. The very careful studies that have been done on shorter segments of the period substantiate the constancy of the labor-force participation rate over time.

The constancy of the participation rate for the total population has been the result of fairly substantial but offsetting changes in the participation rates for certain segments of the population. As the standard of living in the United States has advanced over time, various groups have reduced their participation and other groups have increased their participation.

The changing sex composition of the labor force has perhaps been the most impressive change that has occurred. In 1870, roughly one out of every seven workers was female; by 1950, one worker out of four was female. In 1870, 13 per cent of all females ten years of age and over listed a gainful occupation; by 1950, 29 per cent of all females ten years of age and over were working. In appraising these changes it must be remembered that being a housewife or helping part-time on the family farm or in the family business does not constitute a gainful occupation under the census definition.

The reasons advanced to explain this increasing participation of women in the labor force are many and varied; and frankly, no one of them appears to contribute a significant part of the explanation. First, it is asserted that women now have less to do at home and therefore they have the opportunity to spend time working outside the home. In the last chapter it was pointed out that the average family size has decreased over time and thus, with fewer children to care for, housewives are freer than in previous

TABLE 6–1

Labor Force as a Percentage of Total Resident Population, 1820–1960

1820	32.6
1830	32.6
1840	33.1
1850	35.5
1860	35.3
1870	32.4
1880	34.6
1890	37.0
1900	37.4
1910	39.9
1920	39.2
1930	39.6
1940	42.4
1950	42.6
1960	40.6

Source: Resident population, *Historical Statistics, 1960,* Series A1, p. 7, and *Statistical abstract, 1963,* Table 2, p. 50. Labor force, Stanley Lebergott, *Manpower in Economic Growth,* Table A1, p. 510, and Table A3, p. 512.

periods. Also, it is pointed out that great advances have been made in wife-saving machinery—washers, dryers, stoves, vacuum cleaners, and so forth, that reduce the effort required to keep house. Second, the emancipation of women is pointed to as increasing the opportunity for wives to spend their spare time in earning income to support the household. While there is still considerable prejudice against women in certain occupations, there is no longer the same social stigma against working women that there was at one time. Furthermore, with equal educational opportunities women now have the ability to handle jobs that were previously closed to them while, at the same time, the reduction in average working hours and the increasing mechanization of jobs have opened up opportunities that did not exist before. Third, it is suggested that as incomes have increased over time, more and more household operations have become commercialized so that many women find it profitable to work and pay others to perform many household chores. Associated with this point is the increasing urbanization of the population. Women living in cities have more job opportunities than those living in rural areas and it is in the cities that the greatest commercialization of household services has taken place.

All these factors probably contribute some part of the answer to the question of increased female labor-force participation. It is impossible, however, to point to any one as being a major factor, or, in fact, to another as being unimportant. All that can be said is that the factors above probably reacted together to induce an increasing proportion of females to seek gainful employment.

With the participation rate for females increasing over time but the participation rate for the population remaining almost constant, it is clear that some other group in America must have reduced its participation in the labor force. The reduction in labor-force participation has come mainly from two groups: those under twenty years of age and those over sixty-five.

In 1890, roughly two thirds of all persons sixty-five and over were in the labor force; but by 1950, the proportion had fallen below one half. A number of factors have operated in favor of reduced participation rates by elders. As incomes have increased over time it has become possible for families to contribute to the support of the elderly, enabling them to retire instead of continuing at a job. Also, social security benefits, meager as they are, and private pension plans have done much to ease the fear of retirement. There is evidence also that the elderly have been pushed out of the labor force: institutional factors such as compulsory retirement have helped to force retirement. But more important has been the entrance of trained women into the labor force. The elderly person who graduated from school (if he attended at all) forty years ago cannot compete in many areas with the recently graduated young male or female job seeker. There may well be, therefore, a direct connection between the increasing participation of females in the labor force and the decreasing participation of the elderly.

A greater change has occurred in the participation of the young, and within this group the sharpest change has been among those in the early teens. The participation rate for boys and girls between the ages of ten and fifteen increased from 1870 (when the statistics begin) to 1900, but declined thereafter—very sharply after 1920. In 1900, 26 per cent of the boys and 10 per cent of the girls between ten and fifteen years were listed as gainfully occupied. By 1930, only 6 per cent of the boys and 3 per cent of the girls were listed as gainfully occupied. The censuses after 1930 did not even count children under fourteen in the labor force. Some part of the decline in the participation of the very young has been due to the declining relative importance of agriculture, where most of them were employed. More important has been the changed public attitude toward the employment of the young, as expressed in legislation forbidding child employment and requiring compulsory school attendance. The participation of the age group between ages fifteen and twenty has also decreased, although not as impressively as the rate for the very young. Between the ages of twenty and twenty-four, the participation rate for males has declined, but for females it has increased. The downward trends are almost wholly the result of the fact that an increased proportion of these groups are taking more years of schooling than did their parents.

In the previous chapter we mentioned the role of the immigrant as a resource input of the American economy. Because the majority of immigrants to the United States in the period before 1914 were males in the productive age groups, they contributed more to the American labor than the same number of native-born. In addition, in the early period the labor-force participation rate of the foreign-born was higher for each age and sex group. The rates have declined over time until they are now roughly equal for both groups. The higher participation rate in the early period is explained by eagerness of the foreign-born to accumulate sufficient wealth and status to find acceptance in the new community. The decline over time is probably explained by the ending of discrimination against the foreign-born. As their job opportunities and their incomes have increased, they have adopted the working habits of the native-born. The same explanation probably accounts for the decrease in the participation rate of the Negroes. As job opportunities have increased, the Negro has been able to approach the income of the native whites, quite rapidly in recent years, and he has been able to enjoy a higher standard of living with reduced labor-force participation.

6–2. *Short-Run Changes in the Labor Force*

The American economy has not been uniformly successful in fully utilizing the productive capacities of the labor force. It is extremely unlikely that there will ever be a period of zero unemployment. Even in late 1944, at the peak of the war effort, there were never less than 400,000 persons unemployed. We do not subscribe to the notion that there exists a hard core of unemployables in the sense of people able to work who are such social misfits that they cannot find any employment. The impossibility of reducing unemployment to zero results from the fact that in an economy such as the United States there will always be those who are moving from one job to another, those whose jobs are of a seasonal character, or those who find themselves between jobs for no fault of their own. In fact, the transfer of labor resources from job to job provides an element of mobility that is a very useful feature of the American economic system. The fact that there are always some people who are willing to move to new opportunities breaks down sectional exploitation of labor and provides a welcome flexibility to the American economy. Government employment agencies, by advertising vacancies and persons available, and government unemployment benefits that help to finance mobility, are very useful programs in stimulating shifts of labor resources.

The problem of those who find themselves out of work as a result of change is a particularly perplexing one in a dynamic economy. A man may find his job ended as a result of regional concentration, as a result of the decline in demand for the product he helps make, or because a new machine is invented that supersedes his skill. In such cases it is useless to try to pin responsibility upon the cause of the unemployment and force the culprit to pay the cost of retraining and/or relocating the displaced worker. In heavily unionized industries the unions have been able, by "featherbedding" clauses, to force the company and eventually the customer to absorb the cost. While such action protects the worker involved, it also has the regrettable effect of retarding technological advance by making the new method absorb the cost of displaced workers, and makes the competitive position of those industries faced with a declining demand even worse. Society is eventually coming around to the realization that this type of unemployment is a social problem and enlightened governments (probably the federal) will doubtless be forced to deal with the costs of retaining and relocating such workers.

The cost of unemployment is great. In purely economic terms, the product that could have been produced by an unemployed worker has been lost forever. It has been estimated that the cost to the United States in terms of lost production during the 1930's amounted to $300 billion. But the pure economic costs of unemployment are only a small part of the total social costs. The readers of this book have no doubt seen personally the emotional scars left on persons whose productive life span encompasses the 1930's. At any time, unemployment means reduced family income, perhaps lost school opportunities for the children, and certainly, if prolonged enough, a descent into that condition of life in which it is very difficult for a family head to provide for the health, education, and welfare of his dependents.

Although the labor-force participation rate for those over fourteen years of age has remained essentially stable over the long run, World War II offers an interesting example of the changes that can occur in the rate in the short run. In the summer of 1940, there were roughly 46 million employed (8 million unemployed) in the civilian labor force, and less than 0.5 million in the armed forces. By the summer of 1944, there were 55 million employed in the civilian labor force and close to 12 million in the armed services. Thus, in four years the civilian employed plus the armed forces increased by approximately 20 million persons. This increase was made up in the following way. The 8 million unemployed in 1940 were absorbed, there were 4 million normal additions to the labor force, and 8 million emergency workers. Our interest centers on this latter group. Of these 8 million emergency workers, roughly half come from the teen-age groups who would normally be attending school, a further quarter of the total represented women engaged in war work who would not normally be in the labor force, and the final quarter came from retired persons called back to jobs and marginal workers who would customarily drift in and out of the labor force. These reserves of labor contributed about 12 per cent of the total (civilian and military) employed in the peak year 1944. For the nation as a whole in 1944, 62 per cent of those fourteen years of age and over were employed, against the normal long-run participation rate of 55 per cent. By 1946, there were only 1 million of the 8 million emergency workers left in the labor force, representing those (such as married women) never previously in the labor force who decided to stay plus a few previously marginal workers attempting to retain their positions.

The mere increase in the number of persons in the labor force does not tell the full increase in labor effort. During the decade of the 1930's, part-time employment was common. As the war effort accelerated, part-time gave way to full-time, which in turn gave way to overtime. The full-time equivalent labor force, therefore, increased by more than just the increase in the number of workers. The increase in employment and production during the period 1940–1944 was tremendous, and the crucial role of government in the process was evident to all.

6–3. *Productivity of the American Labor Force*

Although the American economy has been faced at various times with periods of wasting labor resources, there has been a continuing increase in the efficiency of the employed. The impressive part of the American experience is that the increases in output per unit of labor input are so much higher than in the United Kingdom, also a highly industrialized economy. In the post–World War II period, numerous studies were made of the productivities of industrial labor in the two countries. These studies indicate that the productivity of labor in American industry is over twice as great per man as productivity in British industry. These studies also showed that some obvious factors have no effect upon the difference. For example, the average age of machinery, the horsepower available per man, the size of the market, and the size of plants (except in the case of automobiles) can all be rejected as explaining the difference. The factors these studies indicated as important were the following. First, the greater degree of standardization and specialization in American than in Britain. Second, American industry was characterized by better planning and supervision of production. The need to economize labor in America has led to a greater engineering effort in plant layout and the organization of plant operations. Also, in America there is better cost accounting, a greater use of scientific time and motion studies aimed at increasing labor efficiency, and a greater use of supervisory personnel to insure that jobs are performed and to watch continually for possible improvements in production. Finally, the American worker seems to be more productive because of his attitude toward his job. American workers are more interested in their jobs and seem in general to be more willing workers than workers in the United Kingdom. Some part of the explanation of the willingness of American workers to perform may be a result of the fact that the American worker identifies his own interest with job performance. Worker performance in America has been rewarded with better conditions on the job and, over time, by a more relaxed atmosphere between labor and supervisory personnel. A reduced work week has also been a result of increased productivity, and workers may see hopes for further leisure resulting from further increases in productivity.

In their struggle for improvement, American workers have attempted to consolidate and extend their gains from processes just described, through organization.

6–4. *History of Organized Labor in the United States*

Although the question of union organization is only incidentally important to a study of economic growth (e.g., through its effects upon productivity and labor mobility), it has recently become so important politically that the reader should have some idea of the historical background of the current controversy. Much has been written about the development of "bread and butter" (i.e., economic) unionism in the United States, and about the marked contrast between it and the political unionism of the rest of the world. In fact, however, the American trade-union movement has not always been economically oriented; instead, it has several times changed its basic orientation. To a large extent, the history of the movement can be discussed in terms of three court decisions: (1) the Philadelphia Cordwainers case in 1806, (2) *Commonwealth* v. *Hunt* (1842), and (3) *The Jones and Laughlin Steel Company* v. *The National Labor Relations Board* (1937). Between the first and second, the union movement vacillated between economic, political, and idealistic unionism. Between the second and third, economic unionism faced severe challenges from political unionism; and it has only been since the third that economic domination of union philosophy has gone relatively unchallenged.

NB

To fully understand the nature of the American labor movement, it is necessary to be aware of the forces in the economy that have affected the shape of that movement. First, throughout most of its history this country has been characterized by a high degree of class fluidity. Thus, since upward mobility was always possible (if not for the worker, at least for his sons), a working-class consciousness has never developed to the extent common elsewhere in the world. Second, the United States has always been a nation with a plethora of land resources; thus it has been possible to achieve economic development and, at the same time, maintain tolerable living standards among the workers. Third, even though the frontier, in fact, actually attracted few workers, its existence probably tended to increase labor's share of industrial income, since the threat of movement into agriculture always existed. Fourth, the growth of a national market made union organization much more difficult. Since unionization can be effective only if the entire market is organized, the larger the market area the more difficult is organization. Fifth, the stream of immigrants that flooded the United States during the nineteenth century came from a wide variety of ethnic and cultural backgrounds. As a result, the labor force drawn from this pool was extremely heterogeneous and lacked the common background that unified the labor forces in the countries of Western Europe. Sixth, and finally, the social, political, and legal environment also helped shape American unionism. The typical American has always considered himself a member of the middle class; and, like his counterparts elsewhere, has tended, most of the time, to be biased toward business and against labor. In addition, the federal system and judicial supremacy together have made it almost impossible for the union movement to operate politically.

Although workers may have organized from time to time to accomplish some particular end, there were no permanent trade unions in the United States before the 1790's. Apparently the first permanent union was the Philadelphia Society of Journeymen Cordwainers, organized in 1792; but during the next decade unionism gradually spread among the skilled workers in the larger cities. These early unions, like their modern counterparts, were primarily concerned with the enforcement of apprenticeship requirements (the curtailing of supply), union security (the closed shop), and minimum-wage (or piece) rates. As they grew, the early unions developed bargaining techniques closely akin to those used by unions today. In 1802, the Philadelphia Cordwainers demanded a single set of rules (a contract) to cover all workers. In 1809, the New York printers and their employers settled their differences through collective bargaining; bargaining done in a manner very similar (including the give-and-take) to that used today.

The union movement (at least among the skilled trades) might have developed rapidly from these rather impressive beginnings had it not been for a series of court decisions. In the Philadelphia Cordwainers case (1806), the court (basing its ruling on the conspiracy doctrine of English common law) held that unions per se were an illegal conspiracy. Three years later, a New York court tempered this decision only slightly by ruling that union organization in itself was not an illegal conspiracy, but that if the union members took any joint action that injured either workers (through work restrictions) or consumers (through higher prices) their action was an illegal conspiracy. Unions did continue to exist in the face of the court decision, and even attempted from time to time to use economic weapons in pursuit of their goals (e.g., the early 1820's were marked by a series of strikes over the ten-hour day). The threat of court action, however, certainly slowed the rate of union growth and frequently forced the workers to look for other (noneconomic) ways of achieving their objectives.

During the late 1820's, for example, because of the conspiracy doctrine and depressed economic conditions, the workers largely abandoned economic weapons and goals and turned to political action. Political parties were organized by labor in New York, Philadelphia, and Boston. In New York, the labor party was almost successful in electing its mayoralty candidate. In Philadelphia they held the balance of power between the established parties; thus they were able to bargain for many of their objectives. Although prosperity and the presidential election were directly responsible for the defeat of the labor parties in 1832, inept leadership, the tendency of established parties to absorb popular issues into their own platforms, and the suspicion of the middle class would probably have spelled defeat of the labor parties in any case. The movement did, however, prove that the growth of industry and the extension of male suffrage had given the American worker a political voice. Moreover, it also appeared to indicate that the established political parties were more than willing to implement most of the workers' demands and that separate parties, therefore, made little sense. Within a few years, laws providing free education and mechanics' liens had been enacted, and the laws requiring imprisonment for debt and compulsory militia service had been repealed, as the established parties incorporated labor demands in their platforms.

After a short revival of economic unionism during the 1830's (a period that saw renewed agitation for the ten-hour day and the birth of the first city labor federation), depressed economic conditions and renewed union prosecution under the conspiracy doctrine combined to again turn labor away from economic weapons. With the failure of political action still fresh in their minds, the workers looked to the nation's intellectuals for leadership. As a result, they cast their support to a group of socioeconomic schemes espoused by these intellectual leaders. Three schemes (presented to the workers as panaceas) drew most of their attention. First, associationism offered the workers a new planned and idealistic society. All of the economy, argued the plan's supporters, should be restructured into self-sufficient producing units of about 400 families. In the new society, the workers were to receive two thirds of their output. Several of these economic units (called phalanxes) were actually organized. However, despite the support of labor and several national figures (e.g., Horace Greeley), the experiments were almost uniformly unsuccessful.

Second, the workers were told that cooperation would solve their problems. As a result, the workers began to organize producing, banking, and distributing cooperatives. These co-ops were supposed to increase the workers' real wages, by cutting out the entrepreneur's and middlemen's profits. The cooperatives were, however, only slightly more successful than the phalanxes. The inability of the cooperatives to compete with private firms, coupled with rather poor management, forced most of the enterprises to close their doors within a few years. Aside from a few building and loan associations that can trace their lineage back to the 1840's, little is left to show for the resources the workers devoted to their cooperative schemes.

Finally, the lure of the frontier proved strong enough to induce labor to support George Henry Evans' plan to distribute the western lands to the people. There was nothing fundamentally unsound about Evans' scheme; in fact, a similar plan was finally passed in 1862 (the Homestead Act). During the 1840's, however, when worker agitation was at its height, little headway was made; and even after the Homestead Act was passed, few city workers benefited directly from its provisions.

One indirect benefit probably did accrue to labor from the experiments of the 1840's. The workers learned to distrust the leadership of the intellectuals; and, with few exceptions, the men that have since formulated labor policy have been workers themselves.

Despite the enthusiasm aroused by such schemes, the event of the 1840's that was to affect labor most profoundly had nothing to do with either the intellectuals or their pie-in-the-sky schemes.

In 1842, the Massachusetts Supreme Court held that the English conspiracy doctrine did not apply in the United States. Thus, they ruled that the actions of unions were not illegal unless either their intent or the means they used was illegal. It should be noted, however, that the decision in this case (*Commonwealth* v. *Hunt*), while holding that unions were not illegal, did not say they were legal. Thus, for almost the next century American unions existed in a limbo between legality and illegality. Moreover, the decision greatly increased the power of the court in labor disputes since that institution alone was charged with the task of deciding on the legality of particular means and ends. Still, the decision did immeasurably strengthen labor's economic weapons and permitted the movement to turn once more to economic goals. Thus, from the 1850's, with few exceptions, economic goals and policies have dominated American labor philosophy.

Very Important

Effects of the Hunt decision were visible as early as the 1850's. In that decade the first national unions were organized (the Moulders in 1856, and the International Typographical Union the following year) and total union membership began to increase. Once started, economic unionism continued to gain strength (excluding the war years) until the panic of 1873. Moreover, in 1869 the Knights of Labor was organized; for the first time a national union, reaching across craft lines and including both skilled and unskilled workers, began to recruit members. Although the Knights occasionally were swept up in idealistic schemes (e.g., the cooperative movement), they were essentially an economically oriented group and it was in this role that they scored most of their successes.

Until the advent of the Knights, organization had been limited to skilled groups who possessed a common bond (their skill) and a certain amount of monopoly power. The Knights, however, substituting the mysticism of a fraternal organization for the bonds of skill, accepted all gainfully employed workers. The Knights differed in one other respect from earlier unions. Although national unions had existed, almost all power had been concentrated at the local level. In the organization of the Knights of Labor, however, power was concentrated at the national level.

Although the union movement did suffer from the depression that began in 1873, the Knights began to pick up strength soon afterward. By 1886, when, after a successful strike against one of Jay Gould's railroads, membership reached 600,000, the union had become the largest in the history of the nation. Within a few years, however, inept leadership, combined with the weaknesses inherent in any combination of skilled and unskilled workers and competition from the American Federation of Labor, practically destroyed the organization. The Knights had, however, demonstrated the potential of unionism in the emerging industrial economy; and it had shown that unskilled and semiskilled workers also desired the benefits of unionization.

As unions grew, so also did management resistance, and the latter part of the nineteenth century was marked by frequent outbursts of labor violence. The railroad strikes of the 1870's had induced the government to call out federal troops. The Pittsburgh steel strike almost resulted in civil war; the Molly McGuires kept the coal field ablaze for the better part of a decade; and the 1886 general strike for an eight-hour day led to the infamous Haymarket massacre.

The death of the Knights of Labor and the explosion of labor violence followed by swift government retribution did nothing to further the cause of organized labor. The 1880's did, however, witness the birth of the first permanent, national, intercraft federation, the American Federation of Labor (AFL). The founders of the federation, Otto Strasser and Samuel Gompers (both cigarmakers—one of the most skilled trades), had early been advocates of Marxian socialism. As they examined the American scene, however, both came to realize that, given the sociopolitical structure of the country, workers had little to gain from political unionism. The founders also concluded that, since there was little class consciousness among the American workers, a successful union must be based on craft bonds. Therefore, they argued, each craft should remain almost autonomous within the federation, and the federation should be given little power over its constituent unions. Table 6–2 shows the federation's rapid growth; and, although some strength was lost during the depression of 1892, the AFL became the first national intercraft organization to survive a major recession.

Although the success of the AFL assured the domination of economic unionism, the philosophy did not remain unchallenged. Since unions were still not legal, the police powers of the state were frequently employed to suppress their activities. Thus, it is not surprising that a significant minority within the labor movement wanted to use political power to rectify the situation. Between the

NB

1880's and the 1930's, the economic unions faced serious competition first from the Socialist Labor Party and then from the Industrial Workers of the World (an anarchist organization).

The years from the turn of the century until the end of World War I were the heyday of the craft-dominated federation. The union membership steadily increased, the federation successfully beat off the attacks of the politically oriented left (both the Socialist Labor Party and the Industrial Workers of the World) and remained staunchly committed to "bread-and-butter" unionism, and, under the aegis of a friendly government between 1916 and 1918, it successfully organized several new industries (shipbuilding, meat packing, and so on). Moreover, although unions were prosecuted under the Sherman Antitrust Act during a part of the period,

TABLE 6–2

Union Membership in the United States

		AFL		CIO	
Year	*Total Membership*	*Membership*	*Number of Unions*	*Membership*	*Number of Unions*
1886	1,000,000				
1887	440,000	265,000	58		
1900	791,000	548,000	82		
1910	2,116,000	1,562,000	120		
1920	5,034,000	4,079,000	110		
1930	3,632,000	2,961,000	104		
1940	8,944,000	4,247,000	105	3,625,000	42
1950	15,000,000*	7,143,000	107	5,500,000*	30
1956	18,477,000	16,904,000†	137†		
1960	18,117,000	15,072,000			

* Estimate
† AFL–CIO
Source: *Historical Statistics; Statistical Abstract,* 1963.

the Clayton Act (1914) supposedly removed this threat to union action. As Table 6–2 indicates, union membership grew from three quarters of a million to over five million. In 1900, unionized workers represented less than 3 per cent of the labor force; however, in 1920 they accounted for over 12 per cent. Although the AFL effectively organized the skilled trades, it failed to solve the problems of the growing group of unskilled and semiskilled workers. The AFL leadership was not unaware of this problem, but because of their commitment to craft-based organization, they were unable to do much about it. This problem, then, was to plague the labor movement through the first third of the twentieth century. Even when the federation appeared willing to organize the new mass-producing industries, its constituent unions were almost sure to become embroiled in jurisdictional disputes (each union claiming the still-unorganized workers as their own). Although the federation attempted to solve this problem through the amalgamation of related crafts and through its industrial departments (organized to coordinate the activities of the competing crafts without asking them to surrender their autonomy), these attempts were never successful. After the failure to organize United States Steel in the immediate postwar period (the twenty-seven competing unions devoted more resources to their jurisdictional disputes than to the organizational drive), the federation largely left the mass-producing industries alone until the emergence of the Congress of Industrial Organization in the 1930's.

The period of 1920's was marked by a steady decline in union membership and a concomitant reduction in union powers under steady pressure from management, the courts, and the public. In that decade, the labor force increased by over seven million, but union membership declined by almost a million and a half. The gains of the war period were wiped out, and even the old-line unions (for example, the miners) lost membership. The 1920's were marked by a series of court decisions that once again brought unions under the antitrust laws. Moreover, they saw an unsympathetic judiciary make sweeping use of the injunction against union activities; they saw the public (worried about the "Red menace") take a strong antiunion attitude; and they saw management once again take the offensive in the labor-management struggle. During the decade, management attacked directly with force and propaganda and indirectly by offering its workers the benefits of unionism through welfare capitalism, scientific management, and company unions. In addition, the industrial structure of the economy continued to shift against the unions. The crafts came to represent an ever-decreasing portion of the total labor force; no progress was made in organizing the mass-producing industries; and the importance of the service industries (even more poorly organized than the industrial sector) continued to increase.

The depression, however, wrought significant changes in the position of trade unions in this country. By 1932 there were 13 million persons unemployed and probably another 7 million working at less than full capacity. The public became disenchanted with the pro-business environment that had typified the previous decade and elected a reform administration to national office. Thus, with the aid of a sympathetic public, a legislative and executive branch of government committed to a program of social welfare, and even a judiciary gradually adopting the new social philosophy, the union movement finally emerged in the United States. In 1931, Congress passed the Norris-LaGuardia Act, largely prohibiting the use of injunctions in labor disputes. In 1933, the most significant single piece of labor legislation was passed as section 7a of the National Industrial Recovery Act (later repassed as the National Labor Relations Act of 1935). These laws made union membership a right, and made it illegal for any employer to interfere with workers in the exercise of this right. Moreover, they required employers to bargain collectively. Since the Hunt decision in 1842, unions had been neither legal nor illegal. In the case of the *Jones and Laughlin Steel Company* v. *The National Labor Relations Board*, the Supreme Court upheld the constitutionality of the National Labor Relations Act. Thus, the Court held that unions are legal entities, and entitled to the protection of the law. In 130 years, the legal position of unions had shifted 180 degrees, from illegality in 1806 to legality in 1937.

Even before the court handed down its decision, union activity had increased. The AFL, still unwilling to make a major effort to organize the mass-producing industries, watched most of its industrial unions secede and organize the rival Congress of Industrial Organization (CIO). The CIO launched a blitzkrieg organizational drive that by 1940 had made great gains in every mass-producing industry except petroleum. In fact, as Table 6–2 indicates, total union membership during the 1930's rose from slightly more than 3½ million to almost 9 million. Of these, over 40 per cent were in the new CIO.

Since 1940, however, the path of further union organization has been more difficult. The return of prosperity, coupled with the capricious actions of some union leaders during the war, has tended to again alter the average American's view of labor unions. In response to this change in attitude, the government has acted less generously toward the unions during the postwar decade. The Taft–Hartley Act (the Labor Management Relations Act of 1947), although largely ineffective, has restricted certain union powers, and it has catapulted the government more than ever into union-management relations. Furthermore, it certainly indicated a change in the temper of the American public. Equally important in limiting union gains in the postwar decade has been the continual shift in the structure of industry. Most of the crafts were organized in the first decade of the century, and the northern mass-producing industries brought into the fold in the third; however, little progress has been made in organizing labor employed in the other sectors of the economy. Organized labor's failures have been particularly marked in the South and in the service industries.

Organized labor has, however, made one important step since the war. In 1955, the memberships of the AFL and the CIO agreed to merge their unions. Despite reintegration, the problems that tore American unionism apart in the 1930's had not all been solved. Major unions still remain outside (the teamsters and mine workers, to name two); and in addition—thus far at least—the joint union has shown little ability to increase union membership in the still-unorganized areas.

Suggested Readings

Hutchinson, E. P. *Immigrants and Their Children, 1850–1950.* New York: John Wiley & Sons, Inc., 1956.

Long, C. D. *The Labor Force Under Changing Income and Employment.* Princeton, N.J.: Princeton University Press (NBER), 1958.

Millis, H. A. and Montgomery, R. E. *The Economics of Labor,* Vol. III. New York: McGraw-Hill Book Co., Inc., 1945.

Rostas, L. *Comparative Productivity in British and American Industry.* Cambridge: Cambridge University Press, 1948.

Chapter 7 THE ENTREPRENEURIAL FACTOR

7–1. *Introduction*

Any developing economy requires that the factors of production be mobilized, organized, and regrouped constantly according to changes in demand, changes in technology, the discovery of new resources, the opening of trading opportunity, and so forth. These things don't "just happen"; some agency, be it organizational, or individual men acting under their own motives, must manipulate the requisite power to change the flow of resources. Decisions must be made and acted upon.

In a planned economy such decisions might be made by "authority." But in an economy such as ours, where until quite recently virtually all decisions about the *direction* of economic growth rested upon individual desires and motivations "cleared" through the marketplace, the quality as well as the quantity of economic leadership has been of crucial importance. Indeed, the American economy in its present state is largely the consequence of the sum of individual actions—an artifact—and can scarcely be comprehended at all unless the vital role played by the economic leadership of the mass of our entrepreneurial[1] talent is understood.

It is easy to lose sight of individuals when one considers the past as collections of historical statistics, forces, movements, and so forth. Such views are convenient and are of course great temptations to historians seeking general explanations of history. Indeed, to view history at all we usually must abstract so much from detail that, except for a handful of outstanding heroes, individuals tend to be

[1] We follow the usage of the word "entrepreneur," or enterpriser, developed by Professor Joseph Schumpeter, referring to those individuals who introduce a change in the direction of flow of resources in economic life. "The carrying out of new combinations we call 'enterprise'; the individuals whose function it is to carry them out we call 'entrepreneurs.'" (*The Theory of Economic Development,* [Oxford Press, Galaxy edition, New York, 1961], p. 75.)

lost. But one should not lose sight of the essential artificiality of such procedures. After all, there is really no gross national product as such, there is only an accounting estimate of a rate of flow of output in a given period, produced by millions of separate individuals. The GNP is an accounting fiction, largely used up while it is being estimated by the millions of people who created it. The amount of output created depends upon how efficiently the people used their skills and resources, and this depends to a large extent upon leadership, especially where it is necessary to organize large agglomerations of productive factors.

The United States has benefited exceptionally in the past from the contributions of thousands of really extraordinary leaders in economic life, entrepreneurs who seized a new idea or a new technique and raised productivity by a skillful introduction of economic change, an "innovation" into the stream of economic life. Such men are not usually, or even often, inventors of anything but are men of vision, energy, skill, luck, nerve, or a combination of all these things, who by their own action change the course of development. Not all business leaders are, or have been, men of this kind—in fact, relatively few have been important innovators. Consider a single illustration: there were many producers of automobiles in this country before Henry Ford entered the field with Ford Motors in 1903. But when Ford seized upon the idea of changing the auto from a rich man's toy to a cheap mode of basic transportation —"I will build a motor car for the great multitude"—a new industrial revolution was born, and the age of the automobile was really begun as the "age of Ford."

Every industry boasts such men now and in the past. Indeed, it is in the creation of these kinds of economic revolutionaries (Ford was, more than anyone else, responsible for destroying a whole American society; he possibly changed life for the average American more than Lenin changed life for the average Russian) that the United States stands in a really unique position among nations. The classic American "tycoonery" is a roll call of veritable economic Caesars: from old Commodore Vanderbilt (1794–1877) down to Henry Ford (1863–1947) the nation's growth was molded by such men. Call them "robber barons," "bloated capitalists," or what have you, the fact is that the American economy, especially the industrial sectors, was shaped to its present form to a large extent by the Vanderbilts, Hills, Carnegies, Rockefellers, Fricks, Harrimans, Morgans, and thousands of lesser industrial and financial leaders who, like the great tycoons, organized the economy to exploit its resources, its land, its technical genius, its growing markets, and the power of its labor.

An earlier generation of historians had fun pillorying these men for their foibles, but the passage of the decades has given us a new appreciation of them, both of their achievements and their failings. We have come now to see that innovating entrepreneurship on every scale, great like that of Ford and small like the thousands of men of only local fame, has been one of our great resources, and, incidentally, the lack of such men a hindrance to economic development under free-market economies in most of the economically underdeveloped parts of the world.

7–2. *Some Functional Categories*

The contributions made by entrepreneurial action can be viewed in various ways. One could simply note the major agricultural, industrial, financial, governmental, and other sectors, look into their histories, and identify the characteristics of leadership industry by industry. One might gain some impressions of entrepreneurial contributions by simply looking at the "scoreboard," the names and histories of the major families of great wealth, since American capitalism has tended to reward its successful leaders most generously. Both of these approaches are useful but have the limitation that they are collections of specific cases, and it is difficult to generalize from them. Such difficulties do not arise if we consider the entrepreneurial contributions on a *functional* basis. What sorts of entrepreneurial activities were generally needed throughout the nation's economic life? To leave this question unanswered in the history of a capitalist nation like ours would be like studying the human body without inquiring into the characteristics and actions of the cells and organs that make the body work the way it does.

We suggest that, on the most general level, as few as five kinds of activities can be used to represent entrepreneurial action in the American economy: (1) abstract thought, (2) invention, (3) innovation, (4) intersectoral organization, and (5) management. All changes in economic activity, petty or dramatic, begin with the conception in the abstract. The power of idealization of abstract thought in American development can scarcely be overemphasized; from the Pilgrims in Massachusetts to the Mormons at the end of the physical frontier, Americans have changed their surroundings because of motivations of the most abstract and even nonsensical kind.

The power of the idea does not depend upon the correctness of that idea, at least in the short run. Adherence to abstract notions about religion, optimal automobile prices, balanced diets, or what have you, have other than rational roots in human behavior. For any idea to be pushed in the face of opposition a trace of fanaticism may be necessary.

The remote intellectual sources of creativity are not known. Any nation may well contain as high a proportion of creative persons as any other nation. The Western nations certainly have had their fair share of creative persons, and seem, in the world of inventions based upon Newtonian science, to have had perhaps more than their share. Clearly this is due in the Western nations to the existence of institutions which systematically propagate all forms of scientific knowledge to a wide segment of the population. In addition, Western society rewards inventiveness because demand for the products of scientific invention exists and, based upon income, is ever growing. If productivity is to grow continuously, there needs to be more efficient capital equipment as well as a better-educated and motivated labor force. Invention is thus a necessity in an independently viable economy. The United States has had, along with the Germans, the English, and others, a particularly rich heritage of invention.

However, the success of invention itself does not assure that productivity will be increased. Invention, be it mechanical, organizational, or entirely intangible (e.g., the drive for improvement of the nation's mental health), must be introduced into the economy—as Joseph Schumpeter put it, to change the direction of flow of the stream of economic life. It is the job of the "innovators" to do this. Innovators are men who may not have any inventive talents at all but who see the chance to introduce successfully new ideas, products, techniques, tastes, and what have you. The American people, with their restless longing for novelty and a richer material life, have been particularly generous to innovators and receptive to innovations. As a consequence, we have had an abundance of men who have changed the material and intellectual structure of the nation through innovation.

A particularly effective form of organizational activity in the United States has been that concerned with linking up different sectors of the economy which benefited each other by the fusion of needs. The most dramatic intersectoral organizing has doubtless been that linking up transportation and manufacturing industry with the wealth and savings of the consuming public. The men who learned to do this through the capital market institutions in New

York, Boston, Philadelphia, and other money centers, mostly in the last third of the nineteenth century, created American investment banking. This singular and powerfully effective system of financial communication enabled every sector, from coal mines and railroads to retail trade and publishing, to find financial resources for investment that probably could only have come much later if investment sources had been limited to accumulated current profits of the business firms concerned. As American firms grew up with the economy, in many important instances the skill of the organizer, blending the financial needs of industry with the safety and earning desires of the savers, provided for "breakthroughs" in scale of plant and operations that permanently changed the structure of the American economy and the lives of its citizens.

Finally, soundly established industries, and declining ones, may continue for considerable periods without growth, needing only competent management to continue operations profitably. Similarly, management of operating government bureaus requires only men of modal energy and resourcefulness, with sufficient education to comprehend the paper work and forms of office manners and protocol. The "manager" fills a useful role, somewhat like that of a shepherd, in maintaining productive routine in the flow of resources. The manager does not perform the same dynamic role in shaping the growth of the economy as do the men of thought, invention, innovation, and organization. Management makes a *given* pattern of flow move efficiently. Management, in this view, allocates resources among given uses, husbands and reaps what has been started by men who mobilized resources, and in so doing *changes* the structure of the economy and the direction of its growth. Managers manage what has been built—and is being built—by the "entrepreneurs," the men of originality who guarantee that our children's America will scarcely resemble our own.

Relying upon this simple frame of reference, let us consider briefly the basic contributions of four men who can be taken as representatives of all entrepreneurs and whose lives span the nation's development up to 1914. William Penn, Eli Whitney, Andrew Carnegie, and John Pierpont Morgan can be considered as surrogates for thousands like them, in the past, around us now, and, hopefully, in the future.[2]

[2] For a more thorough treatment of this theme, see Jonathan Hughes, *The Vital Few* (Boston: Houghton Mifflin Company, 1965).

7–3. Four Entrepreneurial Contributions

1. One lucky fact in American history is that the basic institutions of our government and economic order, which were transplanted from seventeenth-century England, represented the *best* of the English experience, and not that which was either typical or successful in England at the time. William Penn (1644–1718), whose colony, Pennsylvania (named after his father, the Admiral Sir William Penn of Samuel Pepys's *Diary*) proved to be a major fountain of American tradition, was a man mixing religion with business, hoping to make a profit. As Penn put it, "I have led the greatest colony into America that ever any man did upon a private credit. . . ."

As is well known, Penn received his extensive grant of land from Charles II in payment for, or recognition of, certain obligations owed by the Crown to Admiral Sir William Penn. Young William Penn had been a thorn in the side of his father's associates. From an early date he had been a follower of the (then heretical) doctrines of the Society of Friends, or "Quakers," and had become a leader of that much-persecuted sect. Quakers were already in the New World in some force by 1680 and there was great hope of establishing a society there which could adhere to Quaker principles. It was this chance that Penn seized when he agreed to accept the grant of land on a feudal basis (an annual "quit rent" of two beaver skins ". . . to bee delivered at Our said Castle of Windsor on the First Day of January in every year. . . .") from King Charles.

What were the principles Penn transplanted from England to America? Seventeenth-century England was a maelstrom. In the great political, economic, social, and intellectual revolutions of the age the germ of egalitarian democracy began to spread. It appeared dramatically in the demands of the "Leveller" soldiers, the "Agreement of the People" of 1647. The Leveller ideas, based upon "abstract principles new to English politics . . . ," were revolutionary, and Cromwell had several of the Leveller leaders executed. One Leveller leader, John Lilburne, became a Quaker, and the Friends came to profess Leveller doctrines.

What were the Levellers' revolutionary demands? That power should be transferred to the House of Commons, that there should be complete and free manhood suffrage, without property qualifications, that Parliament should be regularly reelected, that there should be more power in local government, that all men should be treated equally before the law, that monopolies should be broken, that small landowners should be given freedom of tenure, and that, throughout England, there should be complete religious freedom. These principles are old friends to the modern American but were strangers to England, even until this century.

Penn, as the feudal lord of Pennsylvania, could have given it any government he pleased. In the *Concessions* of 1681, and in the *Charter of Liberties* and *Frame of Government* of 1682, when England was being ruled despotically without even a Parliament and had just undergone a great and bloody purge (the "Popish Plot"), a remarkably liberal and democratic government, which realized many of the old Leveller demands, was organized for Pennsylvania. For a nominal quitrent (Penn's main hope for profit) smallholders were given security of tenure, and land was set aside to increase the number of smallholders as indentures were worked off. All free men (not slaves or indentured servants) had the vote, all could serve in the assembly or in the governing council where membership was staggered. The assembly had the power of impeachment, taxes could only be imposed by due legal processes, all men were to be treated equally before the law (justice was to be ". . . neither sold, denied, or delayed"), and there was to be trial by jury (twelve peers). The government could not confiscate property, and all persons ". . . who confess and acknowledge the one Almighty and eternal God . . ." were granted complete religious freedom. The Pennsylvania government was not perfect, but its ideas were to permeate the American mind so completely that William Penn has become every American's intellectual ancestor, and, as the American historian Edward Channing put it back in 1906, William Penn, more than any other man, ought to be considered the "founder" of the United States.

Penn's tremendous service to his American posterity was part of a business venture, and a relatively unsuccessful one at that (he estimated his net loss in the colony at £30,000), yet our country has scarcely known a more profound entrepreneurial contribution. Penn, in a violent and cynical age, was committed to the ideals of a struggling religious sect, to abstract ideas in which few others believed; his great contribution was made within that intellectual framework and because of it. Penn wanted to start a government that would attract good men to Pennsylvania, believing that good men would triumph:

"Any government is free to the people under [it] . . . where the laws rule, and the people are a party to those laws . . . Governments, like clocks, go from the motion men give them; and as governments are made and moved by men, so are they ruined too. Wherefore governments rather depend upon men, than men upon governments."

These beliefs were incorporated in the basic documents of the United States when, in 1789, our government, like a clock, was "given motion" by "We the people."

2. Eli Whitney was an inventor and entrepreneur whose life spanned the years 1765–1825, a period which saw this country grow from rebellious British colonies into a robust adolescence as an independent state. Whitney, and people like him, built the first foundations for the viable inventive culture which underlay so much of subsequent technological and economic progress. Whitney himself was a man who dealt in both the public and private sectors, and his work was crucially important to the development of both southern agriculture and northern industry.

Whitney's background, like that of so many early American inventors, was the Yankee farm and forge. After graduating from Yale in 1792, Whitney went as a tutor to his first job in the South. Noting the need for a machine to clean cotton, in 1793 Whitney made the first model of his cotton gin. A partnership was formed and was financed by the widow of General Nathaniel Greene. Her funds came from the proceeds of the General's estate, which formerly belonged to the British governor of South Carolina. Hence the great inventor was launched on his career by that oldest friend of the manufacturer, government money. The results of the introduction of the cotton gin were immediate. Cotton exports had been 487,000 pounds in 1793; in 1794 the figure rose to 1,601,000 pounds, a year later to 6,276,000 pounds, and by 1800 was nearly 18,000,000. The great bottleneck in the growth of the southern economy had been broken.

Whitney's factory in New Haven burned down, and his gins were widely pirated in the South—the new patent laws not yet having been tested for infringement. Despairing of revenues from the cotton gin, Whitney turned to the federal government and won, in 1798, a contract to manufacture 10,000 "stands of arms" (musket, bayonet, and cleaning and loading equipment)—a prodigious number for a single manufacturer to undertake to deliver in those days. He erected works near New Haven and began the long process of designing and making machines and machine tools to manufacture the arms with interchangeable parts. In 1801 the interchangeability of the locks of the muskets was demonstrated to President Jefferson (who noted that he had seen a similar demonstration in France).

Whitney continued as an arms maker and as a maker of machine tools the rest of his life. He is commonly, although perhaps excessively, credited with being the father of the "American System" of manufacturing in the nineteenth century, with its emphasis on standardization and interchangeability of parts, and where machinery was used as a substitute for skilled labor. Whitney was explicit about this, saying that he had to make "not only the arms, but the armourers" and, like Henry Ford a century later, preferring *completely* unskilled labor with no formed working habits to overcome to tend the machines. From Whitney and the handful of Yankee inventor entrepreneurs like him, the new nation was launched on its career as one of the nations of the world with a viable and developable fund of technological information rooted in the populace, which could be transmitted through time as the growing nation provided opportunity for technological advance. This form of entrepreneurship was a vital force; already in the 1830's standardization of models and parts was becoming a leading characteristic of American manufacturing. In decades to come the habits thus formed were destined to pay enormous dividends to the growing economy.

3. Andrew Carnegie (1835–1919), who invented nothing but put together new combinations of men and capital, was almost the classic Schumpeterian entrepreneur. His life was also the embodiment of two powerful forces in the American past, the great Atlantic migration of the nineteenth century and the industrial transformation of 1870–1914. Carnegie was a child of the industrial age. His father, a Scottish hand-loom weaver, was displaced by the power loom and emigrated in 1848. Carnegie began working in textile mills in the Pittsburgh area as a youth. He learned telegraphy, found employment with the Pennsylvania Railroad, and by 1859, at age twenty-three, was division superintendent. He served in the telegrapher's corps in 1861 and saw the first Battle of Bull Run. During and immediately after the Civil War Carnegie invested in bridge and iron foundry works. He also spent some years at that time transporting securities to London for sale to English investors.

But the financial life did not occupy Carnegie for long. He was a man of enthusiasms, and his entry into the business of making steel was an enthusiastic response to an experience, characteristic of the man. In 1872 Sir Henry Bessemer demonstrated his converter to Carnegie, who was then in England. Although Carnegie had earlier vetoed a proposal by his partners to make steel, he now came back to Pittsburgh and pushed "Bessemer's volcano" vigorously. A new plant, the Edgar Thomson works at Braddock Field near Pittsburgh, opened a new era in American heavy industry in 1873. Carnegie Steel was destined to revolutionize the industry, capture a quarter of the ingot market, and eventually become the nucleus of the United States Steel Corporation.

Carnegie's innovations were many. Although he participated at times in the cartel arrangements of the industry, basically he operated to meet the conditions of a perfectly competitive market (Chapter 1), telling his salesmen to meet the market price and to let his production managers worry about the costs of operating. He argued that a profit must come from operations themselves, not from price-rigging with the other members of the industry. Here Carnegie was a forerunner of Henry Ford, the revolutionary of automobiles. Carnegie also preceded Ford in the neglect of the capital and money markets, relying solely upon internal profits to finance expansion. Carnegie pushed technological change to its ultimate logic, introducing new methods wherever their advantages could be proved. In the 1890's, for example, he demolished most of his great Bessemer installations in order to adopt the more efficient open-hearth furnaces. Carnegie was a pioneer in scientific and incentive management. He introduced cost accounting in his mills, and hired chemists to learn to control the quality of the blast-furnace charges. "Rule of thumb" was eliminated. Carnegie was also an early (if at times reluctant) practitioner of vertical integration, beginning when he added Henry Frick's coke properties (by amalgamation). In the end Carnegie Steel had its own ores, barges, railroads, and Carnegie was about to enter the field of steel fabrication, making wire, rods, nails, tubes, and so forth when he sold out in 1900 to Pierpont Morgan's new steel combine, United States Steel.

In the realm of management Carnegie was a major innovator. His investment policies were "inspired." He understood enough of the workings of the business cycle to anticipate its periodic movements, building up reserves during booms and making his major investment expansions and buying out competitors during the depressions of the 1870's, 1880's, and 1890's. As a result, his capital costs were minimized and those cost advantages were pressed vigorously during boom periods when his new plant and equipment, purchased at rock-bottom prices, gave him great competitive powers. As a result, Carnegie Steel led in the giant secular fall in steel prices (rails fell from over $120 per ton in 1874 to less than $18 per ton in 1898) which made steel the basic metal of America's industrial transformation.

The method of selecting managerial talent at Carnegie Steel was also revolutionary. Carnegie had no respect for "tradition" in industry (here again he was Henry Ford's spiritual predecessor) and advanced men of talent as fast and as far as they could go, buying partnerships in his company for men like Charles Schwab (first president of U.S. Steel) who started as unskilled labor in the Carnegie mills—Schwab was president of Carnegie Steel at 30 years of age. Carnegie's great steelmaster, "Captain" William Jones, who refused a partnership, but who asked for "a hell of a salary" instead, was paid annually the salary of the President of the United States. Carnegie, once upbraided for his extravagance in his salaries, replied that his men were the best in the world and that paying them enough to keep them happy at Carnegie Steel was the cheapest thing he could do, so great were their contributions to his profits. Contemporaries considered Carnegie's management team one of the wonders of the industrial world. A whole generation of great managers in American industry came up from the ranks of Carnegie's Pittsburgh mills.

Carnegie's greatest failure was, paradoxically enough, in labor relations. Like so many industrialists of his time (and our own, for that matter) Carnegie found the aims of organized labor completely incomprehensible, with the result that the Homestead Strike, one of the bloodiest and most infamous in American industrial history, was against Carnegie Steel, and Andrew Carnegie's name was forever tarnished as a result.

Believing that "he who dies rich dies disgraced," Carnegie devoted the last decades of his life to *giving away* his great fortune—he lived to give away some $350,000,000 and left a host of illustrious institutions, philanthropies, and the great foundation that bears his name today. He hoped that the development of the art of "giving" by those who had benefited most from American economic growth would be his greatest innovation. With the help of income tax laws which nurture and succor the tax-free foundation, Carnegie's dream may well be realized. But historians would be remiss in their duties if they ignored the contributions which made the fortune of Andrew Carnegie and the other great innovators like him. As Carnegie said himself, there was no philanthropy in his business operations, business was "war." It is indeed paradoxical that the "Little Boss" of Pittsburgh is now mainly remembered as a benign figure, a diminutive Scottish Santa Claus, who gave away library buildings and hero medals.

4. High finance, as few people need to be told, plays an essentially conservative role in economic growth, even when it contributes directly to inflation. The source of the conservatism is both functional and traditional. Functionally, the financial institutions must be rationers, as well as mobilizers, of savings and wealth. The rationing typically considers both risk and earnings, so that the "safety" of investments and loans must be balanced with revenues —a defaulted loan is bad for profits even though the prospective earnings might have been high. Tradition enters in through the formal apparatus of borrowing, lending, and investing. Finance is one of our oldest arts; for example, the Code of Hammurabi (21st century B.C.) contains penalties for defaults on bills of exchange. Schedules of repayment, criteria for security, and so forth tend to impose certain forms upon the modes of behavior of the financial community. Indeed, J. P. Morgan, one of the founders of modern investment banking, and our final representative entrepreneur, placed himself and his partners in the management of their clientele in order to insure the financial impeccability of the motives behind management decisions.

John Pierpont Morgan (1837–1913) was the scion of an old Yankee banking family. His father, Junius Morgan, became a partner in 1854 of George Peabody, a Yankee merchant banker resident in London. Morgan's grandfather, Joseph Morgan, was a Hartford hotel owner who did banking business and was a founder of the Aetna Fire Insurance Company. Pierpont Morgan was the greatest financial organizer in American history. Indeed, he ranks in that arcane field of enterprise with Nathan Rothschild, Jakob Fugger, and Cosimo di Medici. When Morgan died in 1913 he had been the major innovator in American investment banking, with its intimate connections between corporate finance, commercial banking, and the investing public. In a perverse way, he could even be named a father of the Federal Reserve System, since it was Morgan's actions in the financial crisis of 1907 which showed that, in New York City at least, the financial system was capable of stabilizing itself through concerted action when struck by panic. Unfortunately, in 1929 the lesson had not yet been digested, but the Federal Reserve System, then in operation, was an outcome of the National Monetary Commission, an investigating body organized after the events of 1907.

J. P. Morgan was one of the few "intellectuals" among the tycoons of his age. He had been well educated in Hartford and Europe, studying mathematics at Göttingen before entering merchant banking in 1857. During the Civil War, as was customary among the wealthy, Morgan hired a "substitute" to serve in his place in the Union Army. Although Morgan was implicated in a scandal concerning resale of rifles to the Union Army, subsequent investigation cleared him of any complicity. Morgan continued in the merchant banking business and only in 1869 did the first hint of the future appear. In that year the 32-year-old Morgan entered the comical "Susquehanna War" against Jay Gould and Jim Fisk, the notorious Barons of the Erie Railroad, and beat them. He was obviously a man marked for a high destiny, and he did not disappoint his admirers—and his enemies.

What Morgan did essentially was to turn the vital position occupied by the merchant bank, a clearinghouse for information as well as for foreign exchange, into a communications and control center for public utilities, banking, and industry. The basic mechanism for this was Morgan's firm (first Dabney, Morgan and Co., later Drexel, Morgan and Co., and finally just Morgan and Co.) and his foreign associates. By 1873 this hegemony was established. Morgan had his father's business in London (the old Peabody firm), a Paris associate (Drexel, Harjes), and powerful French connections to use as allies.

In 1870 the London firm, Junius Morgan & Co., had astounded the financial world by marketing, privately, through the well-used merchant banking channels, \$50 million of French government bonds when French fortunes in the war against the Prussians were at their nadir. The same methods were used in 1873 when Morgan displaced the great Civil War financier Jay Cooke. In 1871 Cooke had failed to market satisfactorily a huge refunding issue of the Civil War debt. In 1873 another refunding was undertaken, and this time Morgan succeeded in placing some \$200 million abroad and at home. The London firm had allied itself with the Barings (a great Anglo-American merchant bank) and with the Rothschilds, in addition to the usual Morgan connections. Cooke's reputation was eclipsed by the Morgan coup, and, in fact, in 1873 Cooke's firm failed in a great financial crisis, leaving Morgan alone atop the New York financial structure.

In 1877 Morgan again utilized his international power dramatically in the New York Central Railroad reorganization. Old Commodore Vanderbilt had left his unhappy son, William, 87 per cent of the NYC common stock. William Vanderbilt became the continuous target of public opprobrium and rising taxation imposed by a New York legislature that levied with impunity against the unpopular millionaire. Vanderbilt sought an audience with Morgan to solicit help. Morgan agreed to take on the job of relieving Vanderbilt of 250,000 shares of NYC stock valued at $25 million. Through discreet private placement abroad, the job was done in near secrecy without disturbing the American market. Drexel, Morgan & Co. held the proxies of the English investors, and Pierpont Morgan was a power in American railroading.

Relying upon both his foreign and domestic connections, Morgan repeated the basic pattern again and again as, one by one, the major railroads succumbed to a Morgan reorganization, or "Morganization" as it was called. Morgan was the greatest of several financial organizers (E. H. Harriman was another) who used the power of the financial sector to take American railroads from the control of the plungers who built them, squeeze out the fat in the capital structures, and try to make them pay. The unique abilities of the financiers to handle the problem of "money" successfully created a new kind of financial power, the investment bank, as an outgrowth of the old merchant banking system. The Morgan system, the placement of investment bankers on the management of firms using investment banking services, is followed to this day.

Morgan's financial organizations are probably better known today in industry than in railroads. In 1892 Morgan organized General Electric out of a group of companies which included Thomas Edison's own Edison Electric, and in 1900 came the great U.S. Steel combine with a capital of $1.5 billion, by far the largest ever seen. Even Andrew Carnegie didn't believe that U.S. Steel would succeed—but it did.

The list of Morgan organizations was a virtual roll call of the major industrial and transportation companies of his day. He was attacked in his lifetime as the embodiment of the great financial monopolist; and, with his portly figure, blazing eyes, bulbous nose, fancy waistcoat, inevitable cigar, his yachts, his dogs (purebred collies), Morgan was the delight of cartoonists and is the prototype of the bloated capitalist in political cartoons even today. Such interpretations of Morgan's actions are amusing, but are largely beside the point. In the period roughly 1870–1914 the great industrial transformation occurred in this country. The huge scale of the developing economy, and the possibilities of achieving economies of large-scale production through heavy capital investment and industrial reorganization, called for entrepreneurial talents of the kind supplied by men like Carnegie in manufacturing and Pierpont Morgan in finance. Their contributions were direct and easily identifiable. Until the establishment of the Interstate Commerce Act in 1887 and the passage of the Sherman Act in 1890, the rules of governing this vast economic revolution were few, and men, as well as governments, played the game largely "by ear." In fact, the interested student may follow the affairs of the Antitrust Division of the Justice Department today to see the extent to which the rules of the game are still being worked out. How big is "big" in an industry like steel or railroads? What is "monopoly" power in pricing policies, in labor negotiations, in "fair trade" legislation? Morgan was a pioneer in the development of finance-linked giant industry, and, since he didn't know the answers to those questions any more than people do today, his good name suffered accordingly whenever the courts ruled against him. But the companies and procedures he started surround us today.

J. P. Morgan's business career was of vast dimensions, and we have only scratched the surface in these paragraphs. He was also a man of public affairs, raising money in 1877 to pay the U.S. Army when Congress failed to pass an appropriations bill before adjournment, using his international connections to stem the tide of gold losses in 1895 in response to an appeal by President Cleveland, and, in the crisis of 1907, organizing, as a one-man central bank, the New York financial community to avoid massive bank suspensions in that city. He also endowed the Metropolitan Museum of Art with a large part of his $60 million collection of European and Egyptian treasures. John D. Rockefeller once commented that Pierpont Morgan's role in American life was astonishing in view of the fact that Morgan wasn't even a wealthy man. Of course by Rockefeller's standards Morgan was virtually "working class." Morgan's great power was not due to his personal wealth, but to his *authority* as a virtuoso financial organizer. When he died the London *Economist* noted of him: "All his competitors regarded him as their superior. He was the Napoleon of Wall Street. . . ." We have not seen his like since, and probably won't again. Morgan answered the needs of his era; our modern financiers are not required, fortunately, to undertake such powers.

7–4. *Conclusion*

The decisions for mobilizing and organizing resources for economic change must be made in any economy. In American economic development, with the majority of the expenditures made by individuals within the framework of a free-market capitalist economy, the role played by the entrepreneur has been of central and vital importance. Indeed, to understand the present structure, as well as the past development, of the American economy the contributions of individuals must be understood. Because of the sheer magnitude of the problem, we have used an arbitrary system of functional categories to analyze the contributions of individuals. The four men whose careers were briefly surveyed, Penn, Whitney, Carnegie, and Morgan, may be considered "representative" entrepreneurs, surrogates of the vanished army of men in our past who contributed similarly to our country's development. Today the same kinds of contributions must be made daily, on every scale, great and small, and it need not be emphasized that our modern capitalism should make room for such contributions now and in the future if the great advances of the past are to be continued.

III
The Public Economy

Chapter 8 THE EMERGENCE OF THE PUBLIC SECTOR

"In every human soul there is a Socialist and an individualist, an authoritarian and a fanatic for liberty. . . ."
R. H. TAWNEY[1]

8–1. *The Conflict of Private and Public Interest*

Any thorough study of the utilization of the power of the state to mobilize and develop resources must necessarily confront a basic dilemma: many times the interests of individuals are in apparent opposition to those of government. Looking about us in our own times we see manifestations of this dilemma on all sides. Conflict between individuals and the collective power of government is apparent in nearly all fields of economic activity: in the granting of tariff protection to certain favored interests, in the regulation of interstate commerce, in the licensing of radio and television stations, in the conservation of natural resources, in the regulation of the preparation of food and drugs, in the licensing and regulation of private enterprises all the way from medicine to the sale of alcoholic beverages, in the denial of certain kinds of printed matter the use of the federal mails, in the regulation of agriculture, and in a host of other areas. This extension of the power of government into the private economic affairs of individuals is not new; it has been a part of our national experience since the Jamestown Settlement. Before that, the dilemma has a long history in our common European heritage, stretching back as far as one cares to pursue the subject.

The economic conflict between the individual and the society as a whole—government—is not only ubiquitous and endowed with an ancient history; it is probably a natural part of our form of government and our organization of economic life. It has always been with us, but the form in which the conflict manifests itself

[1] *Religion and the Rise of Capitalism* (London: Pelican edition, 1948), p. 211.

changes with technological progress and other innovations in our social environment.

This fundamental conflict between the American citizen's private desires and those of his chosen government was neatly put by Thomas Jefferson in his dictum, "That government is best which governs least." Does this mean that the ideal would be no government at all? Obviously not. What Jefferson was expressing was both an admission of the necessity of some government functions and his abhorrence of them. In our basic documents, the Declaration of Independence and the federal Constitution, the conflict is apparent for all to see. In the constitution this is especially clear in the appendage of the "bill of rights" to the instrument of government. After setting up the framework of government, the founding fathers saw fit to expressly prohibit to that government certain actions deemed destructive of individual liberty, one of the basic premises of generally accepted American philosophy.

8–2. *Individual Liberty in Economic Life*

Virtually since the rise of the national state from the chaos of the feudal system, the state power has mixed extensively in economic life to tax, regulate, extinguish, or promote industry and trade, according to the needs of the state. Such a system of state economic control necessarily meant a large degree of political control as well. To a large extent, the English revolutions of 1640–1688 represented revolts against this odious mixture; and, of course, the American Revolution was, in large part, a product of protest against economic regulation that was combined with political repression. The system of state control as it appeared by the end of the eighteenth century came to be known as "mercantilism," the name which it has carried ever since.

At the end of the eighteenth century the British world, of which the American colonies then formed a part, together with portions of Western Europe, experienced the development of a strong and vocal sympathy for individual freedom as opposed to state action in economic affairs. This development came to be known as laissez faire, or "hands off"; a phrase taken over from the French physiocrats, it was later to become, according to its enemies, a "secular religion." Although the policy says "hands off," as it has developed it is clear that most of its advocates have not opposed government aid to business, only government hindrance.

After the great revolutions and wars of 1776–1815, the reaction against state intervention achieved great ideological powers. Even though the government began to take action against business late in the nineteenth century, by the early twentieth century, so complete had the power of laissez faire become over the minds of men, the prospect of an extension of government economic activity in the Great Depression was widely viewed as being by itself a dangerous innovation (as if it had not existed before), subversive and destructive of the valuable national virtues of individualism. Since the 1930's, there has been a very considerable expansion of government activity into the private economy, not only in areas like social security and conservation, but in other areas as well; and this expansion has not ceased to be viewed by some with alarm and apprehension. There are no signs of return to the older system and practices of mercantilism, but the "welfare state" and "creeping socialism" are widely viewed as threats to individual liberty and to the efficient functioning of the capitalist economy.

8–3. *Laissez Faire—Philosophers and Economists*

It is useful to note that, even though we have always had a "public sector" (government sector) in our economy playing widely differing roles in our history, the belief has persisted that this sector was to some extent a tyranny, and was, in addition, by its very nature inefficient. This idea comes to us to a large extent from British empiricism, one of the major origins of American political and economic philosophy. It was the great British empiricist, John Locke (1632–1704), writing after the English Revolution, who found "life, liberty, and property" to be inalienable rights founded upon natural law (Jefferson later found their inalienability to be "self-evident"). Locke argued that man "mixed" his labor with nature to create property, which was his to dispose of essentially as he pleased. State intervention was destructive of this right. Moreover, Locke argued that only individuals acting in their own best interests could create the "common good," that, in fact, the protection of private rights was *ipso facto* the protection of the common good, or the general welfare. Private rights were known clearly to each individual, but what government could possibly know what the sum total of all those individual rights, the common good, might be?

In his intellectual demolition of mercantilism, *An Inquiry Into the Nature and Causes of the Wealth of Nations* (1776), Adam Smith (1723–1790), the "father of economics," put Locke's doctrines to work on practical problems and came up with the same conclusions, but applied to business. He argued that without government regulation the system of free prices and free competition would, by directing the allocation of resources according to individual preferences, assure the most efficient production according to what the society desired by way of goods and services. An "invisible hand" would effect this optimal allocation—the economic equivalent of Locke's common good.

> As every individual . . . endeavours as much as he can both to employ his capital in the support of domestic industry, and so to direct that industry that its produce may be of the greatest value; every individual necessarily labours to render the annual revenue of the society as great as he can. He generally, indeed, neither intends to promote the public interest, nor knows how much he is promoting it. By preferring the support of domestic to that of foreign industry he intends only his own security; and by directing that industry in such a manner as its produce may be of the greatest value, he intends only his own gain, and he is in this, as in many other cases, led by an invisible hand to promote an end which was not part of his intention. Nor is it always the worse for the society that it was no part of it. By pursuing his own interest he frequently promotes that of the society more effectually than when he really intends to promote it. I have never known much good done by those who affected to trade for the public good. It is an affectation, indeed, not very common among merchants, and very few words need be employed in dissuading them from it.
>
> What is the species of domestic industry which his capital can employ, and of which the produce is likely to be of the greatest value, every individual, it is evident, can, in his local situation, judge much better than any statesman or lawgiver can do for him. That statesman, who should attempt to direct private people in what manner they ought to employ their capitals, would not only load himself with a most unnecessary attention, but assume an authority which could safely be trusted, not only to no single person, but to no council or senate whatever, and which would nowhere be so dangerous as in the hands of a man who had folly and presumption enough to fancy himself fit to exercise it.[2]

In the sweep of nineteenth-century economic history, with the rise of free trade abroad (not noticeably in American foreign policy, however) and a pervasive industrial and commercial society at home, there developed an atmosphere of economic freedom which was so free from extensive government control that its like is unknown elsewhere in the recorded history of the great commercial nations. There was no time when business enterprise was completely free of government regulations, but by 1875 such regulations were

[2] Adam Smith, *The Wealth of Nations* (New York: Modern Library ed., Random House, 1937), Book IV, ch. ii, p. 423.

minimal, finding expression mainly in foreign commerce, Indian affairs, regulations controlling the public domain, appropriations for rivers and harbors and in similar specific areas. Although he was relatively free of control, the American entrepreneur did frequently benefit from government aid. In this country, reaction to that degree of economic freedom was already gaining ground by the last quarter of the nineteenth century, but laissez faire was by then as generally accepted by economists, statesmen, and businessmen as the old mercantilist system had been centuries before. Indeed, the doctrine of "the invisible hand" became hallowed, and even today an assertion that the "welfare" of the country calls for public action at the expense of private profits is quickly and easily condemned as subversive. Is the pendulum swinging back in the other direction?

8–4. *What Should the Government's Role Be?*

The government's power continued, however, to be used in economic life by the courts, by Congress, and by the executive, and was capable at any time of being expanded. In the early 1930's, when the private enterprise system seemed to fail, we turned once again to expanded government economic action for a remedy; and the government sector was again thrown back into public debate after a long slumber.

Are there any workable criteria for the "proper" role of government anywhere, either in our experience or in our heritage of economic ideas? If it is the case that government action is both dangerous and inefficient in economic affairs, why have we not set definite limits to its sphere? We have not done so simply because we are not agreed on those limits. Here is the basic dilemma in economics as well as in politics—we want government action, yet we abhor it. We want a free economy, yet we want certain regulations on it (recall the television scandals of 1959 and the public outcry for controls over advertising and broadcasting).

In point of fact, we have not set the limits of government action in economic affairs except in a myriad of specific cases that have scarcely any general principle whatever uniting them. Can we do better than this? If so, we probably need to look beyond laissez faire economics for an answer. In 1932, at the Democratic convention, Jim Reed, an old-time political leader, was opposed to the nomination of Franklin Roosevelt; Reed was appalled by the prospect of tampering with the economic system through government action. In a fiery call for a return to fundamentals he said: "There has been no improvement on the philosophy—the economic philosophy—of John Stuart Mill, and there never will be an improvement." What was that? John Stuart Mill (1806–1873), a many-sided genius, had in his *Principles of Political Economy* (first edition, 1848) summed up the liberal and British empiricist viewpoint on economic theory and policy. But what did he say of the proper role of government?

> . . . enough has been said to show that the admitted functions of government embrace a much wider field than can easily be included within the ring fence of any restrictive definition, and that it is hardly possible to find any ground for justification common to them all, except the comprehensive one of general expediency; nor to limit the interference of government by any universal rule, save the simple and vague one that it should never be admitted when the case of expediency is strong.[3]

"Expediency" is not exactly a mark that could be set up for immediate legislative action! But it is a practical mark, since—as will be seen shortly—we have certainly made good use of expediency in our history in defining the government's role and the prerogatives of private property whenever they have been in conflict or, in the not unusual cases, when the interests of government and of individuals seemed to be the same. We have been expedient, but we have not gotten out of the basic dilemma. What is the proper role of government in a capitalist economy? Perhaps we can learn something from our own history in dealing with this issue. Government in the history of the United States has been involved in economic activity through the constitution. The judiciary has involved itself through its role as ultimate interpreter of the constitution. The Congressional and the executive branches have concerned themselves through their legislative, enforcement, and control functions. We shall consider first the development of judicial involvement, reserving until later discussions of the Congressional and executive roles.

8–5. *The Federal Judiciary and American Business*

One of the fundamental bases of free commercial activity is the reign of calculable law, the existence of generally understood and relatively unchanging rules upon which the contractual obligations of a complex economic life can find a sure foundation. This economic function of legality made the adoption of a general body of law of fundamental importance to the new American nation after

[3] John Stuart Mill, *Principles of Political Economy* (New York: The Colonial Press, 1899), Vol. II, Bk. V, p. 305.

the Revolution had removed us from the jurisdiction of British courts, and after the Articles of Confederation had failed to provide the nation with a workable basic legal instrument.

The United States of America came into existence in the spring of 1788 when New Hampshire and Virginia became the ninth and tenth states to ratify the Constitution. However, the Constitution adopted at that time was a relatively simple document whose authors had made no attempt to anticipate every possible eventuality. Thus, the Constitution became a living document, and the way it has been interpreted has done much to affect American economic life. Much has been written about the power of judicial review, and no controversial court decision has yet been made without someone beginning to agitate for a limitation of the authority of the courts to review the enactments of our legislative bodies. However, at the time that Justice Marshall wrote "a legislative act contrary to the Constitution is not law . . . It is emphatically the province and duty of the judicial department to say what the law is"[4] no one took particular exception to this extension of judicial powers. In fact, most statesmen at the time thought it was a necessary step for any government based on a written constitution, and many state courts had already accepted this responsibility vis-à-vis the state constitutions. Under any conditions, this decision placing the ultimate power in the hands of the courts once and for all was destined to have powerful and long-lasting effects upon the course of the American economy's development.

The laws of the United States are derived from both enacted and common law. Hence, in addition to the powers gained by judicial review, the courts also exercised considerable influence on economic affairs through their continual reinterpretation and further applications of common law. In fact, it was through interpretation of the common law that the U.S. Supreme Court had its greatest effects on economic development during the first ninety years of the nation's existence (a period that saw only two federal laws declared unconstitutional).

In American history, the decisions of no single justice have had such far-reaching influence as have the decisions of John Marshall, chief justice (and almost sole spokesman) of the U.S. Supreme Court from 1801 until 1835. During this period, Marshall was responsible for a series of decisions which contributed fundamentally to fixing the relationship of government to the business community.

[4] 1 *Cranch,* 137, 1803.

Although many scholars have viewed Marshall as a spokesman for the centralization of authority, Professor Carl Swisher has cogently argued that the justice was really attempting to free the business community from government control, and in Marshall's time such freedom usually meant removing business from the restrictions of state and local governments (and thus increasing the sphere of the federal government). In fact, however, the motives behind Marshall's decisions are irrelevant. What is important is that his decisions, together with those made by his followers, set the stage for two important trends in American development: (1) free-wheeling capitalism and (2) judicial supremacy. Let us then examine some of these decisions that were to do so much to shape the direction of economic development.

First, in the matter of contract, the court interpreted the law in such a way that business practices were greatly strengthened. In the case of *Fletcher* v. *Peck* (1810), the court ruled that the legislature could not rescind a sales contract even in the case of fraud, because an innocent third party might be injured. Nine years later, in *Dartmouth College* v. *Woodward,* the court held that the charter of a private corporation is a contract that may not be impaired by state law. In that same year, in the case of *Sturgis* v. *Crowninshield,* the court held that states could not pass bankruptcy laws that would make already existing contracts unenforceable (eight years later, however, with Marshall dissenting, it held that state bankruptcy laws could apply to new contracts).

In cases concerning corporations, the court extended the protection of business from local regulation. In *Bank of Augusta* v. *Earle* (1839), the court ruled that states could not exclude foreign (i.e., out-of-state) corporations, and while affirming the states' rights to regulate foreign industries the court limited this power. Two subsequent cases also strengthened the foreign corporation; in *Louisville, Cincinnati, and Charlestown Railroad* v. *Letson* (1844), the court held that a corporation was a citizen and was therefore entitled to access to the federal courts if sued or being sued by a foreign person. In *Terral* v. *Burke Construction Co.* (1922), the court limited even further the rights of a state to regulate a foreign corporation. On a slightly different issue, in the case of *Warren River Bridge* v. *the Charles River Bridge* (1837), after Marshall's death, the court held in favor of free enterprise and against monopoly (without ever saying this) when it ruled that a corporate charter should be narrowly interpreted and that the granting of one charter does not prohibit a state from granting competitive charters.

A series of post-bellum decisions in a similar vein did much to free business from an increasingly vocal populace that had become progressively disenchanted with some of the excesses of the "free-wheeling" capitalism of the period. In fact, in the earliest years of this criticism the court appeared to favor some state regulation, for in *Paul* v. *Virginia* (1869), the court held that insurance companies were subject to regulation; and in *Munn* v. *Illinois,* two years later, the court upheld the states' rights to regulate prices in Chicago grain elevators because "when private property was affected with the public interest it ceases to be *juris private* only, and becomes clothed in the public interest." However, during the next fifty years the courts engaged in steady retreat from this revolutionary doctrine. For a few years after the Munn decision the court upheld state regulation of intrastate railways; but in a series of decisions they continually narrowed their definition of the public interest, charging the courts rather than the legislature with the determination of the definition of "fair" (see for example, *Georgia Railroad and Banking Company* v. *Smith* [1888], and *Chicago, Minneapolis and St. Paul Railroad* v. *Minnesota* [1890]). In 1886, in the famous Wabash case, the courts ruled that the states could not regulate the rates charged on intrastate portions of interstate lines. This decision delayed much-needed railroad regulation for twenty years and, while it helped the railroads at the time, it probably intensified their long-run problems.

Only during the 1920's did the courts begin to take a less defensive position toward business and to consider whether completely unbridled business is necessarily the most healthy condition for the entire economy. In 1921, in upholding a Washington, D.C., wartime rent-control act (*Block* v. *Husch*), the court held that "circumstances might change in time or space as to clothe with the public interest what at other times and in other places would be matters of purely private concern." Finally, in 1923 the court attempted to spell out once and for all the areas of business covered by the phrase "in the public interest." At that time (*Wolff Packing Company* v. *Court of Industrial Relations*) the court included as subject to some government regulation (1) those businesses which operate under the authority of a public grant of privileges either expressly or implicitly imposing the obligation to render services demanded by any member of the public (this would include railroads, common carriers, and public utilities); (2) exceptional occupations regarded as having public interest attaching to them and recognized from the earliest times (this would include inns, cabs, and so on); and (3) businesses that had not been "public" at their inception but that had risen as such. This latter area obviously has no clear boundaries and in 1934 this ruling was actually used as the basis for a court ruling upholding a states' right to regulate milk prices.

Thus it has only been in the more recent years (and particularly since the 1930's) that the courts have adopted anything but an attitude favorable to business in cases where the public interests and those of private business seemed to conflict. Although through their decisions the judiciary has undoubtedly contributed to some of the excesses that have many times been associated with business in the nineteenth century, there can be no doubt that these same decisions did much to lay the framework for a free-enterprise system, and contributed to the rapid growth of the American economy in the past 150 years. However, although the courts have recently examined business with a much more jaundiced eye, most of the ultimate safeguards have been part of the common law too long for the courts to change. Hence, if, as many think today, business has reached a state of development where perhaps it too needs a little more control than was thought necessary in the past, such control will probably need to come from Congress. But each new legislative enactment will further involve the courts. Their role in economic affairs has long been an accepted part of the American economic system. They have indeed become something of a "watchdog" on business practices. Some recent (and hotly protested) decisions, for example, have contributed to the maintenance of economic growth. In the Schechter Case (1935) the court indicated that it would not tolerate even government-sponsored interindustry cartelization and price fixing; Supreme Court decisions in *Carmichael* v. *Southern Coal Company* (1937), which upheld state unemployment compensation laws, and in *Helvering* v. *Davis* (1937), which affirmed the Social Security Act, doubtlessly helped to promote economic stability and therefore have had favorable effects upon growth.

The court's more recent treatment of businesses prosecuted under antitrust has doubtless resulted in a freer and more efficient economy than would otherwise have evolved. In passing, however, it is interesting to note that the same groups who, in John

Marshall's time, sought federal protection from state regulation now want to return to the jurisdictions of the state and local units.

Suggested Readings

GALBRAITH, J. K. *The Affluent Society*. Boston: Houghton Mifflin Co., 1958.

LERNER, ABBA. *The Economics of Control*. New York: Macmillan Co., 1944.

MILL, JOHN STUART. *Principals of Political Economy*. New York: The Colonial Press, 1899, Book V.

SCHUMPETER, J. A. *History of Economic Analysis*. New York: Oxford University Press, 1955, chap. 5, sec. 4.

SWISHER, C. B. *American Constitutional Development*. Boston: Houghton-Mifflin Co., 1943.

Chapter 9 THE ROLE OF THE PUBLIC SECTOR

9–1. *Introduction*

In any democratic free-enterprise system, the public —speaking directly as savers, consumers, and workers, and indirectly through their government—has a powerful voice in determining the shape and direction of economic development. The direct effects are discussed elsewhere; this chapter deals with the attitudes of the American people toward the business system and the government policies that were the expression of these attitudes. In addition, this chapter will attempt to provide a set of economic criteria for government intervention in the free-enterprise system and explore the history of government spending in the American economy.

9–2. *Business, Public Attitude, and the Growth of Public Policy*

In the early nineteenth century, the lack of transportation and communication facilities segmented the country into a number of small and largely independent economic units. It is not, therefore, surprising that the authors of the Articles of Confederation thought that a weak central government could best serve the needs of the nation's four million people. In fact, despite the adoption of the Constitution in 1787, state and local units continued to dominate government business relationships until after the Civil War (the important exception was, of course, tariff policy). Moreover, since most economic activity was confined to a relatively small geographic area, the reliance on state and local authority made good sense.

As the economy grew and improvements in transport and communications made it possible to organize a single national market, state and local regulations were no longer adequate. Thus, beginning about mid-century, the federal government gradually began to displace state and local units in government–business relations.

The forty years following the Civil War were marked by a close working relationship between business and government. The Civil War had for a time destroyed the political effectiveness of the Democratic party with its southern and agrarian ties, and had brought to office the new Republican party, dedicated to the encouragement of business. Within a short period, the new office-holders had effected legislation that encouraged immigration, made sizable grants of western land to support the construction of an integrated railway network, strengthened the nation's banking system, and established higher protective tariffs.

While most of these measures did encourage rapid economic growth, they were not without costs. The new immigration, for example, quite likely kept wages below the levels they otherwise would have attained; and the land grants resulted in a transfer of resources from the public to the builders of the railroads. Still, they may be viewed as necessary adjuncts to long-term growth. As time passed, however, the government's pro-business bias led to policies that not only engendered high social costs but also had adverse effects on economic growth. This later period was characterized by a movement toward business monopoly and cartelization. Although monopolies of one sort or another had existed since classical times, in the United States important noncompeting market organizations were first introduced in the railroads during the 1870's and thereafter quickly extended to most other major industrial groups (see Chapter 20). Although they resulted in much higher profits, these monopolistic practices were severe hinderances to economic progress. Of course, the reader must remember that, since the period was also characterized by rapid technological progress and the exploitation of the geographic and industrial frontiers, in many areas economic growth was very rapid; and even the monopolized areas frequently experienced growth, although at a slower rate than might otherwise have been the case. Since the mergers and cartels were market-oriented, they seldom altered the structure of production; and, thus, they failed to attain any new economies of scale (even if such economies did exist). In fact, the only direct results appear to have been a misallocation of resources in the short run and a tendency to resist innovation and, thus, to slow economic growth in the long run (without competition there was no pressure to risk the innovation of techniques). For example, the steel industry—which in the 1880's had been the most progressive in the world—in 1920 was characterized by a reluctance to make *any* innovations until these had proved absolutely successful. In addition, certain indirect effects also tended to restrict growth. It appears likely that these business practices engendered an even greater degree of income inequality; and this tendency may have worked (through poor diet, bad living conditions, and adverse moral effects) to reduce the efficiency of the labor force without, because of the conspicuous consumption of the Gilded Age, resulting in any large increase in the rate of savings.

For some reason, perhaps because they were unwilling to destroy what had been accomplished in twenty years of rewarding cooperation, or perhaps because business had used its economic power to entrench itself politically, the government was slow to take any action against the business community. For whatever reasons, the period from 1880 to 1914 was marked by an increasing public hostility toward business and ever more vocal demands for effective government action against "monopolistic" business practice. Public pressure resulted in the passage of antitrust legislation, in growth of effective railroad regulation, and culminated in 1912 in the legislative implementation of Woodrow Wilson's "new freedom." Thus, by the 1920's immigration had been reduced, labor had gained more rights, tariffs had been lowered, the first steps toward monetary reform had been taken, and new teeth had been put in antitrust regulation. Although not all of these measures could be said to have been in the best interests of economic growth (particularly the new immigration laws), all did act to redistribute income from the business sector to the rest of the economy. They can, therefore, be viewed as yet another proof that in a democracy "the people will be served" (although sometimes it may take quite a while).

Conservative critics have often viewed the changes in government–business relations during the first decades of the twentieth century as marking the abandonment of the free-enterprise system and the first steps down the road to socialism. An alternative interpretation, however, appears to better fit all the facts. More reasonably, it appears that throughout our entire history public policy has been directed neither toward aiding nor toward hindering business but rather toward the achievement of a satisfactory rate of economic growth. In this view, the twentieth century brought no change in fundamental public policy. Instead, it may be argued, the people speaking through their elected representatives were willing to make considerable sacrifices for business, if business, thus encouraged, had continued to grow. However, when business practices began to impede growth, these same citizens were equally willing to use the power of government to control business.

Whatever the explanation, by the 1920's business' new look appears to have allayed almost all fears; and where twenty years before it had been hard to find a single business apologist in public or academic circles, it was now equally hard to discover a critic of the business system. John Raskob, financier and chairman of the board of General Motors, was Democratic national chairman; and almost no one was surprised when Our Savior was pictured in the image of the businessman. Unfortunately (for the people in the short run and business itself in the long run), business began once again to pursue the profitable monopolistic practices of the late nineteenth and early twentieth centuries. Moreover, although national income was rising the upper-income groups received a greater share of the gain; tariffs were increased, antitrust enforcement was blunted, and many of labor's gains were lost.

The stock-market collapse in 1929 and the ensuing depression did more to alter the public's (and ultimately, therefore, the government's) attitude toward business than any other series of events in the nation's history. It became apparent that, unaided, private enterprise could not solve the unemployment problem; and a series of business scandals shattered whatever was left of the public's belief in the unmitigated wisdom of the business community. For example, during the first month of the market collapse, a top-ranking officer of the Chase National Bank sold short over 42 thousand shares of Chase stock. To cover this sale the officer borrowed more than $6.5 million from the bank itself; and his profits from this transaction were in excess of $4 million. When he was questioned about these activities, he defended officers' loans for stock speculation on the grounds that such loans permitted the officers to develop an interest in their institutions.

In fact, given the state of public opinion, the New Deal was surprisingly easy on the business community. Certainly the employers lost something in the legalization of unions under the Wagner Act and in the passage of minimum-wage and hour legislation. However, although many of the other New Deal policies did not make much economic sense, they should not have made the business community particularly unhappy. For example, the National Industrial Recovery Act would have effectively cartelized industry and protected the existing firms from the rigors of free competition; and the Miller-Tydings and Guffey Coal Acts went a long way towards prohibiting "illegitimate competition"—that is, price cutting.

Thus, although business did not suffer excessively under the New Deal, the growth potential of the economy may have suffered considerably. Some progress was made toward an acceptance of the government's role in economic stabilization; but even here the policies actually adopted tended to be "too little and too late." On the other side, the period was characterized by an increasing willingness on the part of the public, business, and government to abandon free enterprise in favor of government regulatory agencies and subsidy payments. While these expedients may have temporarily alleviated the short-run problems, they have since hampered (and probably will continue to hamper) the growth of the economy. In the first instance, the dependence on quasi-government–quasi-business regulatory authority (the NIRA, for example) represents the worst of all possible worlds. Such a system loses both the dynamic elements of the free-enterprise system and the growth orientation of other forms of central direction. In their place, they produce something akin to the nonprogressive chartered-town economies of the Middle Ages. In the case of subsidies, government payments have, for example, saddled the economy with an agricultural policy that not only prevents the transfer of resources from agriculture to other more productive fields but even fails to utilize all the output of the factors so tied to agricultural production. Furthermore, since the 1930's the public has appeared increasingly willing to subsidize other producing groups (transport and small business, to cite two), and each additional subsidy further distorts the allocation of resources on the basis of nothing more than political power or simple pork-barrel favoritism.

Although quasi-judicial regulatory agencies had been a force in the American economy since the establishment of the Interstate Commerce Commission, during the 1930's new regulatory bodies were organized and greatly extended powers were granted to bodies already in existence. The regulation of the trucking industry was added to the ICC's duties; the powers of the Federal Power Commission were greatly extended; and the Securities and Exchange Commission, the Federal Communications Commission, the Civil Aeronautics Board, and the U.S. Maritime Commission were all established. Although regulation of industries not subject to free competition makes economic sense, these quasi-judicial agencies have tended to make economic decisions on noneconomic grounds and have continually attempted to extend their authority into areas where competitive market forces can act. The result has been an almost certain misallocation of resources and a probable retardation in the economy's rate of growth.

Despite the importance of the depression years in shaping public policy, at no time has the federal government exercised greater effect on economic life than during the years of World War II. In an attempt to quickly mobilize the economy for war, the government in part abandoned the free-enterprise system. Instead of permitting the price system to allocate resources, the government performed this function directly through a system of rationing, priorities, and price controls. It is generally agreed that the war emergency made it necessary to temporarily abandon parts of the free-enterprise system if the military were to get the equipment it required, while the civilian population received at least minimum amounts of the necessities of life (in fact, because of the low level of income during the depression, civilian real income rose during the war). On the other hand, the existence of black markets and their sudden growth during the period of postwar controls proves how much the effectiveness of rationing depended upon the patriotism of the average American and how, in any but the most extreme emergencies, the price system better solves (in terms of meeting consumer desires) the allocation problem. Moreover, the fact that the United States, depending only in part upon central direction, was able to mobilize its resources more effectively than Germany suggests that there is nothing inherent in central direction that guarantees rapid and efficient allocation.

In the postwar decades, although politicians of both parties have talked loudly about the need for economic growth, the record of achievement has been spotty, at best. The Employment Act of 1946 clearly stated that the government would no longer tolerate mass unemployment and would use its fiscal powers to prevent future depressions. In fact, however, despite a continued high level of government expenditures, unemployment has persisted. Moreover, the government has appeared curiously reticent to take effective action against the quite serious depressions of 1949 and 1958. In addition, the continuation of high tax rates no longer accompanied by rapid write-off provisions may have adversely affected the rate of savings; and, almost certainly, continued excise taxes and regulation on transportation and communication have had an adverse effect on growth. Furthermore, in those areas the free market cannot reach effectively, the postwar record has not been good. Although the economy already possesses transport, communications, and power networks, basic research represents an equally important investment that the private sectors cannot profitably make. In this instance, the government, though apparently willing to spend millions on applied research, has not done its job. In addition, our investment in education has probably been less than optimum at the state and local level; and, almost certainly, much of what has been supposedly invested in future training has been spent on items better classified as consumption (driver training and social adjustment, to name only two).

In summary, if the public wants the government to play an effective role in economic growth, it should insist that the government remove itself from those areas where the free-enterprise system can operate and extend its activities in those areas where the system breaks down. In the next section we will examine the area where government investment is economically warranted, and in the final section we will examine the case for direct government regulation of business.

9–3. *The Government as a Source of Investment: Theoretical Considerations*

As we have seen (Chapter 1), in a centrally directed economy allocation decisions are made by a central authority; however, in a free-enterprise economy the desire of entrepreneurs to make profits, the existence of a market mechanism, and certain demand-and-supply considerations combine to direct resources into the employment yielding the highest returns. Since the free-enterprise system operates without central direction, it is frequently argued that any government interference (aside from the passive role of providing a healthy business environment) distorts the allocation of resources. This argument, while not entirely fallacious, is certainly misleading. In many instances government expenditure will distort the allocation of resources; but in certain circumstances it is only through government action that an optimal allocation can be achieved. First, an economy requires investment in certain kinds of social-overhead capital before its development can begin; however, these investments cannot be profitable until the process of development has proceeded some distance. Second, in certain areas there are divergencies between private and social costs and revenues; and in these instances some government expenditure may be required to attain an optimal allocation of resources. Finally, the government in its attempts to maintain a healthy economic environment may, from time to time, be required to make certain investment expenditures.

a) ***Social-Overhead Capital.*** Many underdeveloped economies require a certain level of investment in social-overhead capital before they can fully realize their growth potential. For example, the United States needed an extensive transport and communications network before its internal market was large enough to support a modern industrial economy. Again, in the modern world some economically feasible power source is required before development can begin; however, because of technological indivisibilities, minimum plant size is frequently so large that the underdeveloped economy cannot profitably utilize its output in the foreseeable future. Finally, if an economy is to develop industrially, a certain amount of technological education is required for a portion of its labor force. In all these cases, it would likely be unprofitable for a private entrepreneur to make the investments, since the extended cost-recovery period would delay profits far beyond his planning horizon. On the other hand, unless the investments are made the market for their services will never be developed.

In the case of the United States, transport into the trans-Appalachian area was a necessary condition for the settlement and economic development of this vast region. Because, however, the demand for transport waited on development and settlement, it is doubtful if unsupported free enterprise could have lured resources into intercontinental transportation. During the first half of the nineteenth century most government transport support came from state and local units. In part, this local bias was the result of constitutional objections to federal interference; but, more important in the early period, problems were usually local rather than national in scope. The best estimates indicate that in the ante-bellum period, government units together financed about 70 per cent of canal construction and between 25 and 30 per cent of railroad construction. Of this total, the federal government's contribution was largely limited to a few million dollars of direct financial support and, more important, permission of the transport companies to draw on the corps of engineers for technical advice. In addition, some small assistance was also received in the form of occasional survey grants and refunds on duties paid on railroad iron.

After 1850, however, the federal government came to play the dominant role in providing overhead transport capital. In total, the government contribution in this later period was higher than in the earlier era, but as the market developed, government's relative share of investment declined. However, government support was largely responsible for pushing the first railroads across the prairies and for providing the first internal east-west links. After 1850, aid most frequently took the form of grants of public lands. These grants were usually in excess of right-of-way requirements, and their sale could provide an extra revenue source to the railroads. The first federal grants were made in 1850; they included some 2½ million acres to support the Illinois Central and some additional land for the Mobile and Ohio. The decade 1862–1872 saw a rapid increase in the number and size of grants; and before the practice was halted grants ultimately exercised included over 131 million acres of federal and an additional 49 million acres of state land. These grants ranged from 10 square miles of land per mile of road constructed in the states and 20 square miles per mile in the territories (the Union Pacific–Central Pacific grant, for example), to 20 and 40 per mile (as typified by the Northern, Southern, and Atlantic Pacific Lines). Land in almost every state west of the Mississippi (Texas, Oklahoma, and South Dakota were the only exceptions) and in Illinois, Michigan, Wisconsin, Florida, Alabama, and Mississippi was included. In North Dakota and Washington, the grants represented over one fifth of the states' total land area, and in Minnesota, Kansas, and Montana, between 15 and 20 per cent.

These land grants have been the objects of much criticism. Public indignation arising from the exposure of the Union Pacific's profits halted further grants in 1872 and resulted in forfeiture of about 35 million acres of unexercised grants between then and 1890. Taking the long view, it appears that much of this criticism has been undeserved. Although better administration could probably have furnished more transport and less speculative profits, still, such a contention is not a criticism of the principle of government investment in social-overhead capital. Moreover, the rapid development and integration of the trans-Appalachian and trans-Mississippi areas into the economy appears to be a strong argument in its favor.

The nation's power network also provides an example of successful investment in social-overhead capital. Although the technology of electric power was well known in the last quarter of the nineteenth century, private investment was, as late as 1930, limited to the already developed areas. Thus, the potential of the Tennessee and the Columbia Valleys was left largely unutilized. In these latter areas industrial development waited on an adequate power source and the power source waited upon development. During the 1930's, the federal government began to make large investments in electric power. The Tennessee Valley Authority was empowered to develop the resources of the Tennessee Valley, and other organizations were established to develop the potential of the western rivers. The extent of government activity can be seen in the growth of public power in the past two decades. In 1930, the federal government produced less than ½ billion kilowatt hours out of a national total of 91 billion. In 1961, while total production had risen to 879 billion, federal power had increased to 112 billion. Although more recently the growth of some federally supported utilities has brought them into competition with private companies, there can be little doubt that, in its early period at least, federal investment facilitated greatly the economic development of the South and West.

Yet another example of investment in social-overhead capital can be found in the development of free education in the United States. Economic development requires investment in human resources, but this investment is characterized by the same vicious circle that marked the physical investment in railroads and electric power. As early as 1642, the Massachusetts Bay Colony adopted a public-school law, and since that time every state has come to recognize the need for educational investment. Although much of the investment has come from state and local governments, during the nineteenth century the federal government gave the states up to four sections of public land per township for the support of public schools; more recently, it has made contributions to school transportation, lunchroom programs, and classroom construction. Examples too can be found in more specialized education. If an economy is to develop, certain highly special technical skills are required; but until some progress is made there is little demand for these skills. In the case of the United States, for example, trained engineers were needed if the railroads were to be built, but no engineers were needed until construction began. In this instance, the government made the necessary investment by training army engineers; and, until development had proceeded quite far, West Point was the most important engineering school in the country. Again, an industrial nation requires technical education; and both state and federal governments have provided substantial sums for vocational training.

The government contribution to social-overhead investment appears to have greatly aided American economic development;

however, the techniques of administrative control have frequently had undesirable side effects. In the case of the railroads, the payment of direct subsidies without proper administrative controls resulted in some waste in the form of speculative profits and unreasonable construction expenses. In the case of electric power, government ownership has at times resulted in direct competition between the government and private industry. In this latter case, the administrative organ, originally established to prevent the misuse of government funds, has attempted to increase the scope of its activities outside the area of social-overhead investment. In the future, perhaps, some third method of capital transfer may evolve that will avoid the evils of both unrestricted subsidies and government–private competition. The fair success of government investment in atomic energy, administered through a form of public-private partnership, may indicate the direction such a solution should take.

b) *The Divergence between Public and Private Costs and Revenues.* An optimum allocation of resources is usually attained when each individual and firm in the economy equates its marginal costs and revenues. In certain special cases, however, these optimization decisions, while maximizing each individual's profits, do not lead to a social optimum. Such a divergence occurs each time the individual (or firm) does not bear the entire cost or reap the total benefits of its decision. In the former case, although a change may improve an individual position (his revenues exceed his costs) society will be worse off because the social costs are higher than the social revenues. In the latter, the individual may fail to initiate a change because its potential benefits to him do not cover its costs, but society would have been better off had he done so. In either case, government action based on a consideration of all costs and all revenues could improve the allocation of resources. Pittsburgh, for example, was for years covered by a dense industrial smog that made the city an unattractive place to live and work. The total profits of smog control in terms of labor-force recruitment were quite large; however, since only a fraction of these revenues would accrue to any single firm, it paid no one to undertake the necessary expense. Government action to control smog has, thus, improved the allocation of resources.

The history of the United States provides numerous examples of public–private cost-revenue divergences. For example, it pays no single individual or firm to carry on the broad range of activities in pest control, sewage treatment, and hygiene education that are required to reduce sickness and death rates. On the other hand, the social benefits of these reductions are apt to be large. During the first three quarters of the nineteenth century, malaria epidemics frequently raged across the South and were not infrequent visitors to the eastern port cities. Although the social costs of these epidemics were high, no single firm could profit from their control. On the other hand, benefits to the economy from investments in improved sewage treatment, filtered-water supplies, and mosquito control far exceeded their costs.

Another, although less obvious, case may be found in the areas of urban redevelopment, slum clearance, and public housing. There appear to be some external economies available to firms in large cities; however, these cities also tend to spawn slums. The existence of slums and crowded living conditions make it very difficult to recruit certain kinds of labor. Moreover, it appears likely that living conditions, at least in part, determine the economic usefulness of the work force raised there (many persons raised in the slums tend to be lost to jails and to jobs far below their capacity). Thus, although no one firm could profit, the economy could gain from urban redevelopment that makes cities more attractive places to live. Furthermore, although dwellers in subsidized housing may never be able to pay rent sufficient to cover costs, the economy may well reap a net gain because of the increased efficiency of future generations.

Since Sputnik we have become more aware of yet another area where social and private costs diverge—basic research. Basic research is, by its very nature, far removed from profits. Ultimately, however, all technical innovations depend upon it. Business has long known that applied research (related to current or potential productive processes) is profitable; and, in fact, over the past two decades business has financed about 40 per cent of such research. Most firms have, however, been equally quick to realize that basic research is unprofitable. In the latter case, the benefits accrue not to any one firm but to society; and, in addition, revenues are likely to be temporally far removed from expenditures. As a result, basic research has been ignored by any but the largest business firms (DuPont and Bell labs are almost the only exceptions). If fundamental research is not continued, our rate of technological improvement will ultimately decline as the present state of technology exhausts itself in a sea of gimmicks. In 1953, for example, of the almost 4 billion dollars spent on total research, less than 4 per cent went to basic inquiry. The obvious answer to this dilemma is government subsidization of basic research, while applied research is left to private business. In fact, this is largely what has been done. Before World War II the state governments, through subsidization of research in the state universities, were the leaders in the field, but since that time the federal government, through a myriad of research grants, has come to share a substantial portion of the burden. Unfortunately, in the most recent past the government has begun to apply the profitability criterion to fundamental research. If this trend continues, we could easily lose the military and economic races to the centrally directed powers.

Education too is an area that offers an example of the benefits of government investment when private and social costs diverge. In this instance, however, the example is not so clear-cut as in those cases we considered previously. We have already seen that some proportion of educational expenditure can be classified as investment in necessary social capital. Again there are portions of the educational process where there is no need for government support. A part of total education should be viewed as a consumption good (a service consumed to make life more pleasant). In this case, it appears far more rational to let the consumer choose between this form of consumption and some alternative, in the same way that he allocates funds between a new television set and a season ticket to the Metropolitan Opera. Further, no economic argument can be made for government investment in those forms of education whose private and social costs do not diverge. On these grounds, for example, it would appear more economic to withdraw government support from driver training and social adjustment in the high school, from business administration on the college level, and from the study of medicine and law on the graduate level (although, of course, it might be well to establish government-supported loan funds to help bear the cost of education, such loans to be paid back when the student graduates and earns an income).

There are, however, areas in the field of education that do require government expenditures if private and social costs are to be equated. The rewards that will accrue to a society with a relatively literate population may be greater (in terms of good and stable government and responsible interpersonal relations) than the costs of the education, but the costs to any particular individual may be higher than the rewards that come directly to him. Cuba and the Congo provide recent examples of the high economic costs associated with democratic government and a low level of literacy. A similar divergence probably occurs in the education of specialists in the sciences and the humanities. The rewards to the individual for his contribution in these areas are unlikely to cover the costs of his training (take Einstein, for example), but the rewards to society may be much greater. In both instances, a program of government investment seems warranted.

c) ***Expenditure Made in the Process of Government.*** Thus far we have confined our discussion to expenditures necessary to achieve an optimum resource allocation and a sustained rate of economic growth. It is obvious that from time to time the government must also undertake certain investments that are related to some of its more generally understood functions.

During every war, the federal government has embarked upon a greatly increased program of expenditures; and, while a large portion of this has gone into strictly military production, some also has flowed into productive investment. It is apparent that bases and airports built during both world wars are new investment. Moreover, during both wars the government made extensive investments in capital goods not specifically tied to the war effort. In 1918, and again in 1945, the government held stocks of machine tools, trucks, ships, and factories that were then available for peacetime production. More recently, the cold war has forced the government to invest in science, education, and the nation's transport network. The recent expenditures on a system of national defense highways are only the most recent of a long history of expenditures rationalized, at least in part, on the grounds of military necessity.

Since the '30's, the government has been more or less committed to a full-employment policy; and such a program involves expenditures in periods of declining income. In the 1930's, this antidepression policy led to a much increased level of government expenditure; and a myriad of federally supported agencies (including, among others, the PWA, the WPA, and the CCC) directed federal investment into highways, dams, public buildings, and recreation areas. More recently, although unemployment has not reached the level of the '30's, the recessions of 1949, 1954, and 1958 have engendered increased expenditures. In such cases, it should be obvious that we are not concerned with possible resource misallocation, since any use is better than no use at all.

Finally, a certain amount of government investment is justified in terms of noneconomic goals. Since such expenditure rests on the nation's value judgments, it is impossible to say that they are not economic. Thus, government expenditures on public housing and health may be defended on no other grounds than our dislike of the worst manifestations of poverty.

d) *Conclusions.* Nothing in this section should, however, be taken as a blanket endorsement of government expenditure. In fact, many government programs appear unjustified on any of the grounds discussed. The current farm program and the Small Business Administration are two cases in point. In both instances, the government has effected a net transfer of resources from consumers and business to special-interest groups; and, in both cases, the rationale has been the supposed economic effects of the program. If the government had chosen to base its rationalization on some social or political grounds (e.g., the farmers have lots of votes, or the need of American society for the small-business man), the economist could say little about the desirability of the programs. Since their defense has been cast in economic terms, it is legitimate to argue that expenditures on agricultural storage facilities, investments in agricultural inventories, and capital transfers to small-business men at subsidized rates fly in the face of all rational economic policy. On the other hand, were the justification made in terms of social or political stability, the voter at least would be able to weigh intelligently the costs with the supposed gains.

This section is designed to indicate the areas in which careful government investment can aid the free-enterprise system in attaining an optimum allocation of resources, full utilization of facilities, and a rapid rate of economic growth. Each request for additional government investment should, however, be evaluated on its own merits.

9–4. The Government Control of Business

Not only has the government acted as a source of investment, but also from time to time it has attempted to directly control the activities of business. While not all government regulation is a good thing, there are at least three areas where careful control can improve the allocation of resources. First, where monopolies and other noncompetitive market structures exist, the government can attempt to destroy them. Second, where these monopolies are "natural" and can be destroyed only at great economic loss, the government can regulate them. And finally, where noncompetitive firms are neither regulated nor destroyed, the government can move to equate bargaining power between them and the more competitive sectors.

Chronologically, it was the state and local governments that first moved into the area of business regulation, but in the past three quarters of the century it is the federal government that has played the most important role. The rights of local units to license certain occupations and regulate quality and weights extend far back into ancient times; and, in the United States, such regulations were common over a century before the Revolution. Moreover, as the extent of the business system became more pervasive, the state and local governments attempted to increase the scope of their regulations. Before the Civil War, most of the eastern states had passed laws regulating railroads, canals, banks, mutual savings banks, and insurance companies; in the latter part of the nineteenth century, the list was increased to include the new public utilities. Moreover, wage and hour legislation (particularly for women) was enacted in some states in the middle of the nineteenth century, and almost every state had some such regulations on its books by the end of World War I.

However, as the market area widened and business expanded across state lines, state and local regulation could no longer be effective. Although some federal regulation has always been present, it is in the more recent period that national regulation has surpassed state control in importance. In fact, most of the federal regulatory laws can be traced to the two periods (1890–1914 and 1930–1940) when public criticism of the business system reached its peak.

Federal (like state) regulation has been designed to prevent monopolies, regulate those that are natural monopolies, and equalize bargaining power between competitive and noncompetitive groups. In the first area, federal policies were an outgrowth of the postbellum merger and trust movement. Before the 1880's, reliance had been placed on the antimonopolistic threads of common law, but common law was too weak to resist the steady pressure toward merger and trustification that marked the period. Public resistance to monopolies increased; as a result, antitrust legislation was passed by eighteen states; and, in 1890, the Sherman Antitrust Act was signed into law. This statute, although several times modified, still sets the direction for antitrust policy. In part, it says:

> 1. Every contract, combination in the form of a trust or otherwise, or conspiracy, in restraint of trade or commerce among the several states, or with foreign nations is hereby declared illegal. Every person who shall make any such contract or engage in any combination or conspiracy, shall be deemed guilty of a misdemeanor. . . .

2. Every person who shall monopolize or combine or conspire with any other person or persons to monopolize any part of the trade or commerce of the several states or with foreign nations, shall be deemed guilty of a misdemeanor. . . ."

Twenty-four years later, further progress was made with the passage of the Clayton Act, designed to strengthen antitrust regulation. The Clayton Act specifically outlawed certain business practices (discrimination in prices, exclusive and tying contracts, intercorporate stockholdings, and interlocking directorates), and established the Federal Trade Commission to enforce the antitrust laws. Since then, three more statutes have been enacted (Robinson-Patman, 1936; Wheeler-Lea, 1938; and Celler Antimerger, 1950), but these do little more than close loopholes in the earlier legislation.

Despite the enactment of this series of laws, concentrations of economic power have not been broken up as effectively as most economists would have liked. Although part of the failure can be attributed to spasmodic Justice Department prosecution, much more can be traced to the decisions of the Supreme Court. In one of the earliest cases (*U. S.* v. *E. C. Knight and Co,* 1895), the court actually ruled that manufacturing enterprises were not within the definition of commerce. Although this interpretation was overturned in a few years, it was not until the Standard Oil and the American Tobacco cases (1911) that the first real victories were won. Even these were, however, not without cost. In the former case, the court ruled that the law did not prohibit all restraint, but only "unreasonable" restraint. Thus, the court gave to itself the power to decide what constituted a violation of the antitrust laws. Furthermore, in the U.S. Steel Case (1920) the court held that mere size and the existence of unused monopoly power did not in itself constitute a violation of the law. Thus, by 1925, antitrust laws did little more than prohibit outright collusion among competitors.

After 1929, however, public feeling once again demanded more stringent controls, and the court belatedly responded. In the Alcoa case (1945) the court held that there was no such thing as a good trust, and, therefore, the mere existence of a single producer could be taken as evidence of a monopoly. Although the court has not reversed itself, it has recently gone a long way toward tempering its decision. In the Cellophane case (1953), the court held that the proper market for consideration was not cellophane but all packaging materials. Again, in the United Shoe Machine case (1953), the court held that since the monopoly had not been attained through illegal means, the firm would not be dissolved, although it would be expected to conform to stricter standards than those prevalent in competitive industries.

In practice, the antitrust acts have not resulted in the destruction of the large corporations; instead, they have established a set of ground rules by which these companies must play. The laws have not reestablished a perfectly competitive economy, but they have prohibited many of the worst features of oligopoly (for example, collusive price agreements, market divisions, and monopolies from merger). In some areas, strangely enough, they may have been too effective. For example, it appears quite possible that fear of antitrust action has made the auto industry less willing to engage in competitive price cutting than they might otherwise have been. If one admits that a return to a perfectly competitive world is impossible (and this seems likely) how best can we achieve the benefits of competition? Effective antitrust policy is one attempt to achieve a workable compromise.

In certain areas, however, natural monopolies exist, and here any attempt to dissolve them would result in considerable economic loss. Such natural monopolies are the result of indivisibilities in use; that is, the duplication of facilities necessary to insure competition could be attained only at such high cost that the enterprise would become economically unfeasible. Examples are readily found in the public utility and transport industries. One set of telephone or electric lines is obviously sufficient to serve a large area, and duplication would greatly increase costs without resulting savings. Similarly, a single railroad line may carry traffic sufficient for a town, and line duplication would bring no advantages. In these instances, we can hardly expect the free-enterprise system to assure competition. Typically, the solution has been public ownership or public regulation.

Historically, the state has been the first to institute regulation of natural monopolies. State railroad regulatory bodies were common in the 1880's; and the growth of electrical power resulted in utility regulation in most states. Such regulatory bodies were established in New York and Wisconsin in 1907; and, since then, have spread to almost every state. Moreover, their functions have frequently expanded to include gas, telephones, and other natural monopolies. Ideally, these bodies attempt to set utility prices at a level comparable to those that would rule if the industry were competitive. In some states (New York, Wisconsin, Illinois, and California), the commissions have achieved a reputation for aggressive and sound regulation. In others, the results of regulation have been less good; and, at times, the commissions have even been accused of acting as agents for the utilities.

An alternative approach is, of course, the socialization of the utilities. In the field of electric power, for example, we have historically had a number of local and, more recently, federally owned monopolies; and the federally supported rural cooperatives are only half a step removed from government ownership. In 1958, for example, publicly owned facilities accounted for about one fourth of total output.

More recently, in response to the ineffectiveness of state regulation, the federal government has also become active in public-utility regulation. In 1910, the Mann-Elkins Act gave the federal government the power to regulate interstate transportation and communications rates. The Public Utility Act of 1935 gave the Federal Power Commission the power to regulate interstate electric rates; and the Natural Gas Act of 1938 gave that Commission power over gas-pipeline rates. In general, it is agreed that, until recently, the federal regulatory bodies have pursued an aggressive policy in the public interest. Recent developments have, however, caused some concern that the bodies may become subject to utility pressure.

Finally, the government has, from time to time, passed laws to equate the bargaining power of workers and consumers in an economy dominated by noncompetitive businesses. In 1933, for example, the federal government entered the field of labor–management relations. Section 7a of the National Industrial Recovery Act required employers to bargain in good faith with workers who were exercising their union rights. When the NIRA was declared unconstitutional, these provisions were legislated again as the Labor Relations Act of 1935. In 1947, the government became even more directly involved in the labor contract. The Taft-Hartley Act explicitly excluded certain issues (e.g., the closed shop) from the bargaining table. Although there had been state laws limiting the hours of work, it was not until the NIRA that the federal government took action in this area. In 1936, the Walsh-Healy Act established the forty-hour week in government contracts; and this limit was extended to all interstate commerce by the Fair Labor Standards Act (1938). A similar story unfolds in the history of minimum-wage legislation. The Davis-Bacon Act (1931) required that certain minimum wages be paid in government construction; the NIRA insisted on wages of

30 to 40 cents an hour in covered industries; the Walsh-Healy Act required payment of prevailing union rates on government contracts; and the Fair Labor Standards Act set minimum wages in all interstate commerce.

Good economic arguments can be made for government regulations in the three areas we have discussed. That such a case can be made does not, however, insure that the policies pursued were necessarily the best. In all of the areas, the lack of a standard against which to test policy leaves the economist unsure as to whether there has been too little, too much, or just enough direct regulation. In a competitive world, competition provided the standard; in a world of monopolies, there is no standard.

Suggested Readings

GALBRAITH, JOHN K. *The Great Crash, 1929.* Boston: Houghton-Mifflin Co., 1948.

GOODRICH, CARTER. *Government Promotion of American Canals and Railroads.* New York: Columbia University Press, 1960.

HANDLIN, OSCAR AND MARY. *Commonwealth: A Study of the Role of Government in the American Economy.* New York: New York University Press, 1947.

HARTZ, LOUIS. *Economic Policy and Democratic Thought: Pennsylvania, 1776–1860.* Cambridge, Mass.: Harvard University Press, 1948.

WILCOX, CLAIR. *Public Policies Toward Business.* Rev. ed. Homewood, Ill.: Richard D. Irwin, Inc., 1960.

IV
The Accumulation of Capital and the Mobilization of Resources

Chapter 10 SAVINGS AND INVESTMENT

The classical economists, writing at the end of the eighteenth and the beginning of the nineteenth century, were concerned with problems of economic growth; and, therefore, they devoted considerable attention to the process of capital accumulation. Today, an understanding of the savings and investment mechanism has again become important as interest has recentered on questions of economic growth and development. Within the past quarter century, economists have both damned the act of savings as a cause of economic instability and applauded it as a necessary precondition for economic growth. This chapter will explore the effects of savings and investment on the economic growth of the United States, and the next four chapters will examine the growth of those financial institutions that encouraged savings and facilitated the transfer of these savings to productive investment.

Unless an economy is characterized by a high and continued rate of technological progress, it is almost impossible to achieve sustained economic growth with no net savings.[1] In fact, most economists agree that sustained economic growth requires annual net savings of at least 12 per cent of gross national product (gross savings of about 20 per cent). The typical underdeveloped country saves net only 2 or 3 per cent of its gross national product, and this amount is insufficient to support sustained growth. In this case, savings, instead of leading to permanently increasing incomes, have forced these economies into a vicious circle from which they show little ability or willingness to escape. The small increments in investment lead to slightly higher standards of living. Higher living standards lead, in turn, to lower mortality rates (as food supplies increase

[1] Net savings are defined as income–(consumption + depreciation), and gross savings as income–consumption. In the case cited above, a sustained rate of technological innovation could result in rising per-capita incomes, as capital freed by depreciation is reinvested in new capital of greater productivity.

and investment in public-health facilities are made) that cause the population to increase. As the population increases, per-capita income begins to fall, and soon the country is back where it started. A much higher rate of investment would be required to lift incomes to the point where family planning could cause a decline in birth rates to offset the fall in mortality. (See Chapter 5.)

It is obvious that the underdeveloped countries must increase their rate of savings if they are to develop; however, we have little evidence of any countries making the transition from 3 to 12 per cent savers. Although evidence for the earlier periods is sketchy, it suggests that the developed countries have been high savers from an early period. For example, Goldsmith's estimates of the growth of physical capital (a magnitude related to savings) indicate that, in the United States at least, the rate of wealth accumulation has been relatively constant since the beginning of the nineteenth century. Apparently Japan is the only case of an economy actually moving from a 3 to a 12 per cent saver. Whether we in the United States have, in fact, increased our rate of savings is really unimportant; what is important is the way we were able to maintain a rate of savings sufficient to underwrite rapid economic growth.

Professor Goldsmith has recently published his pathbreaking work, *A Study of Savings in the United States*;[2] and his research provides us with reasonably accurate measures of savings and its components as far back as 1897. Before that date, however, we must rely on very fragmentary data. Investment data appear slightly better. Estimates of capital have been extended back to 1805, and the figures become reasonably reliable soon after the Civil War.

Let us first analyze the trends in savings that Professor Goldsmith has uncovered. Over the entire period (1897–1950) savings rates have been fairly constant, although they have shown considerable short-term variability. The absolute volume of real savings per capita has increased at something less than 2 per cent per year; and, although this rate appears to have declined slightly over the period, the decline is relatively small. The trend in the savings/income ratio (a rough aggregate consumption function) also displays these same characteristics. It averages about one eighth of net national product, and declines gradually over time. In general then, it appears that, though there may have been a peak in savings sometime in the post–Civil War decades, the peak was small; and, secularly, consumption

[2] Raymond W. Goldsmith, *A Study of Savings in the United States* (Princeton: Princeton University Press, 1955).

has been a relatively stable share of income. At any point in time, however, there has been a close correlation between the incomes of spending units and their savings. Thus, in any year higher-income groups tend to save a higher percentage of their incomes than do lower-income groups.

Moreover, in the short run, too, savings appear closely correlated with income. In the 1930's, for example, savings (both absolute and as a percentage of income) fell drastically; and, throughout the entire period they have tended to move with the level of national income. If one assumes (as Goldsmith does) that the American consumer does not consciously bring total savings into his spending equation, but instead considers at least a portion of it as a residual, then an explanation for the short-run variability can be found. It can be argued that the saver first makes his consumption decisions and then saves what is left of his income. It follows that as income rises, consumption, geared to a lower level of income, declines as a percentage of total income, and savings rise. Conversely, as income falls, consumption bulks larger in the total, and savings decline both relatively and absolutely.

There are three major savings groups in the American economy: households, business, and the government; and although all save, their motives differ markedly. We have already seen that individuals appear to treat savings as a residual. However, the fluctuation of the level of savings around a positive figure seems to indicate that these individuals are consciously attempting to save something, at least in the long run. Studies of savings motivation suggest that householders save for a variety of reasons. Most important among these are a desire to acquire durable tangible assets for use in the household, a wish to provide for future expenditures (including retirement, estate provisions, future expenses, and emergencies), and, at times, a need to provide funds to enter business. In the case of corporations, savings are usually motivated by a desire to increase profits. At times, however, business savings may be motivated solely by management's attempts to increase its own power. This latter motive frequently provides an explanation for corporate savings in the form of liquid assets, or in plowbacks when the firm's profits are substantially less than those earned elsewhere. Governments save to acquire assets needed in their day-to-day activities, and at times are forced to dissave as current consumption expenditures exceed current income. Expenditures on military equipment, for example, caused the federal government to dissave heavily during both world wars. Intended government savings most frequently take the form of military and civilian tangible assets (the latter including buildings, equipment, and land) and increases in the stock of monetary metals. Since the 1930's, the adoption of farm price supports has contributed to federal government savings in the form of inventories. More recently, mortgage-guarantee programs and contributions to international lending agencies have increased investments in paper securities. (It should be noted, however, that almost half of all government savings is unintended and represents nothing but tax accruals that will be spent as soon as they are received.)

During peacetime (and excluding the 1930's), personal savings have represented about 70 per cent of total savings, corporation savings about 20 per cent, and governmental savings, the remainder.[3] The trends in personal savings have been almost identical with those in total savings. The rate of increase of personal savings has been relatively constant over the entire period, and the savings/income ratio has averaged about one tenth in normal periods. Moreover, like total savings, personal savings have shown extreme short-term variability and, if consumer durables are excluded, a slight tendency to decline over time. Although there exists no incontrovertible proof as to the causes for this decline, indirect evidence suggests some possible causes. First, higher incomes have engendered increasing pressures for higher standards of living. The sociologists agree that, as a society, we are ever becoming more "other directed"; and, if this is true, pressure to "keep up with the Joneses" is likely stronger today than it was in the 1920's, and stronger in the twentieth century than it was in the nineteenth. Second, the entire period has been characterized by migration from country to city; and we have good reason to believe that farmers have always displayed a much stronger propensity to save than have their counterparts in the cities. Third, the period has been marked by a steady shift of workers from employer to employee status (and with this shift, a relative increase in the factor share of income accruing to employees); and, again, the entrepreneurial class has historically shown a greater willingness to save than its employees. Finally, the decline in income inequality may have also tended to reduce the savings/income ratio.

[3] This breakdown includes additions to social security reserves and government pension funds in personal savings. If they are instead attributed to the government, the share of government savings rises and that of personal savings falls. Also, it excludes consumer durables. If these are included, personal savings amount to about 5 per cent more, and the other categories are reduced a like amount.

Corporate savings amounted to about 30 per cent of net corporate income from 1897 to 1930, were negative during the depression (dividends were larger than profits), and averaged about 40 per cent during the 1940's. While no trends are apparent in the savings/income ratio, there do appear to be important interindustry differences in savings habits. In particular, railroads and public utilities (industries with low profits), and finance (low capital requirements) have tended to save relatively small proportions of their incomes; and manufacturing, mining, and trade have traditionally been high savers. If it is true that corporate (like personal) savings are a residual, then corporate savings may have distorted capital allocation less than some critics have indicated. The evidence shows that the low-earning industries and those with relatively small capital requirements have tended to retain less, and the profitable industries have tended to retain more, than their proportionate share of income. This distribution of capital is not unlike the one that a free market could be expected to produce.

If the huge government deficits of the depression and World War II are included, the federal government has been a net dissaver over the entire period. In normal periods it saved about 8 per cent of its income from 1897 to 1916, and slightly less from 1945 to 1950. During the 1920's, however, the savings/income ratio rose to 25 per cent. State and local units together saved about 10 per cent of their income during the first two decades after 1897, 20 per cent during the 'twenties,' and 5 per cent since World War II. In both cases, although the ratios have fluctuated, no discernible trends are present.

It appears, then, that the major elements of savings have displayed little change over the past half century, although the slight decline that appears in the savings/income ratio might cause some difficulties if it continues into the future. A more immediate cause for concern, however, can be found in an examination of the trends in the forms savings have taken over time. Since 1897, there has been a steadily and fairly rapid increase in savings implemented through the purchase of life insurance and through investment in pension and retirement funds. At the same time, the relative importance of savings channeled through purchases of stocks, bonds, and real estate has declined. Thus, the proportion of funds made available directly to the capital markets has been reduced; and the share indirectly transferred, through financial intermediaries, has increased. If these financial intermediaries were permitted to invest in assets yielding the highest returns, there would be no cause for concern in this shift in the nation's mode of savings. If, however, legal and cultural restrictions artificially limit the intermediaries' investment horizon, it is quite possible that certain demands for funds will not be met; and this failure could have severe repercussions on the economy's rate of growth. In fact, financial intermediaries are frequently unable or unwilling to make any but the most conservative investments. For example, the law requires that government pension and social security funds be invested in government bonds. Again, it is common to place stringent restrictions on the proportion of life-insurance accumulations invested in stocks. As long as a substantial proportion of total savings is free of such restrictions, misallocation will be minor; but, as an ever-increasing share of savings becomes subject to these limitations, both the allocation of resources and the economy's growth potential may suffer.

We know, of course, that actual savings always equal actual investment. Therefore, since we know that savings have averaged (net) about 12 per cent of gross national product, it follows that net capital formation has also amounted to about 12 per cent of gross national product. Still, an economy's ability to grow depends not only on the amount of the net investment figure, but also on the quality of that investment. To understand the role of capital accumulation in the American economy, therefore, it is necessary to examine the trends in the composition of net capital formation as well as those in the ratio of net capital formation to net national product.

As in the case of savings, there appears to have been some slight downward trend in the ratio of net capital formation to net national product. Although a part of this trend can be accounted for by the greater productivity of new capital (that is, because of technological improvements the same amount of investment now yields higher output), nevertheless, some portion still represents an actual decline in the ratio of capital formation to national product. The portion that does reflect an absolute fall could represent a threat to the economy's rate of growth. How serious, then, is this decline?

There can be little doubt that, if the decline should begin to accelerate in the future, it could lead to serious repercussions. At present, however, several factors appear to be mitigating its effects. First, most of the decline has been manifested in the reduction of inventories and a fall in residential and public-utility investment.

The decline in utility construction almost certainly reflects the completion of much of the nation's social overhead investment—the dams and railroads that required heavy construction investment. Once these internal investments have been made, further investments are frequently less capital intensive (have a lower capital/output ratio) and require, therefore, less investment. In the case of the United States, the capital/output ratio rose from 1880 until World War I, but has fallen steadily since that time. The decline in inventory investments, too, presents no serious problems to economic growth. In large measure, the inventory decline reflects the improvements in transport and communications, which have permitted a greater degree of inventory centralization and, thus, reduced the total demand for inventories. Finally, it has been argued that there are quality differences between types of capital and that investment in housing is not as "good" (in growth terms) as investment in other types of construction or machinery and equipment. If this argument is true, the secular decline in residential construction would have less severe repercussions on growth than would a decline in investment concentrated in other sectors. The effects of the present decline in savings may well, then, not be too serious at the moment. Whether a continuation of this decline, with its effects spreading to other sectors, would also have only limited repercussions on growth, is another matter. We will examine this question in more detail in a moment.

First, however, the trends in one other component of net capital formation appear worthy of comment. The investment in producers' durables, while remaining relatively constant, has shown some tendency to increase in the past two decades. More important, within that group individual industries have altered their investment habits markedly. New growing industries have increased their share of capital formation, and the older industries have tended to reduce their share. Thus, between 1880 and 1940 the proportion of producers' durable investment flowing into the electric, automobile, aircraft, and scientific-instrument industries rose from 2 to 28 per cent, while the proportion going to the farm and railroad equipment and the carpenters' and machinists' tool industries has declined from 41 to 18 per cent. These changes in capital formation provide further proof of the thesis that a retardation in its rate of growth appears to characterize almost every industry at some point in its development. (See Chapter 20.)

What is the optimum level of savings, and does the decline in the savings/income ratio represent a long-term threat to the economy? Economists have, during the past two decades, been very concerned with this question; but there has been considerable lack of agreement on whether the level is too high or too low, or whether the decline is apt to stimulate or retard the economy's growth. On the one hand, some economists have argued that the level of private savings is too high to maintain full employment without considerable negative government savings. Thus, they conclude, although a fall in the propensity to save may imply a lower maximum rate of growth, it also implies a higher actual rate. These economists argue that the twentieth century has been marked by a decline in investment demand (the result of a declining rate of population growth, the completion of investment in social overhead capital, and a less capital-intensive technology); thus, they continue, if full employment is to be maintained the decline must be offset with a reduction in the supply of savings. These economists tend to view the gradual decline in the savings/income ratio as one manifestation of the fall in investment demand and argue that a further decline would benefit the economy.

On the other hand, some economists have concluded that the decline in savings is not a result of a change in demand (a movement along a supply curve) but of a change in savings motives (a shift in the curve). This shift they attribute to two characteristics of American growth. First, as income has risen, present economic emergencies have become less worrisome. Thus, the need for retirement income has become the most important motive for savings, and the average American has a relatively low estimate of the level of annual savings needed for retirement. Second, for the remainder of its personal savings, the economy must depend upon the upper-income groups. In a less dynamic economy, the upper groups are traditionally drawn from the same families, generation after generation. In this case, expenditures aimed at attaining social position need only be made once, and thereafter these families are able to increase the portion of income flowing into savings. In the United States, however, the composition of the upper-income groups is continually changing; and in each generation a new set of families is required to spend to achieve social acceptability. These expenditures, of course, reduce their potential contribution to the savings stream.

For purposes of policy, it makes a considerable difference which argument is correct. If the decline in the savings/income ratio is due to a fall in investment demand, far from being a matter of concern, the decline in savings should be encouraged. If, however, the push is really from the other side, efforts should be made to encourage additional savings. Although no one can yet say that either group is correct, with the postwar experience behind us most economists have concluded that, with proper government action, the economy is able to maintain full employment (at least, most of the time). Thus, for a few years at least, saving has again become both a public and a private virtue.

However, one should not forget that, at times at least, high rates of savings may be associated with high social costs. For example, there appears to have been an increase in the savings/income ratio during the 1870's and 1880's, but a study of the period indicates that this increase was a sign of economic weakness rather than of strength. A part of the increase, of course, can be attributed to the rapid rise in incomes and the relatively slow adjustment of consumption to the new income levels.[4] At the same time, however, the higher rates of unemployment and the monopoly profits and capital gains (the result of the growth of large corporations and the emergence of the trusts) that characterized the period led to increasing income inequality. In part, the rise of the savings/income ratio can be attributed to this redistribution. In this case, higher savings rates may have increased the maximum rate of growth, but they almost certainly reduced the actual rate.

Despite occasional short-term setbacks (as in the 1930's), the American people have continued to save enough to underwrite rapid industrialization. Furthermore, the growth of financial institutions has made it possible to mobilize these savings for productive investment. The evolution of a market mechanism capable of encouraging savings and making them available to the new industrial entrepreneurs is the subject of the next four chapters.

Suggested Readings

GOLDSMITH, RAYMOND. *Financial Intermediaries in the American Economy Since 1900.* Princeton, N.J.: Princeton University Press (NBER), 1958.

GOLDSMITH, RAYMOND. *A Study of Savings in the United States.* Princeton, N.J.: Princeton University Press, 1955.

KUZNETS, SIMON (ED.). *Income and Wealth: Series II.* Balitmore: The Johns Hopkins Press, 1952.

KUZNETS, SIMON. *Six Lectures on Economic Growth.* Glencoe, Ill.: The Free Press, 1959.

[4] Since some portion of savings is apparently a residual, this part tends to be more closely correlated with the rate of change than with the level of income.

Chapter 11 INVOLUNTARY SAVINGS: THE EVOLUTION OF THE COMMERCIAL BANKING SYSTEM

11–1. *Credit Creation and the Process of Economic Development*

We have learned in Chapter 2 that banks can create money. They issue claims on assets (demand deposits) to borrowers in exchange for IOU's. Since checks written against these newly created accounts can be spent (people are willing to accept these claims in payment for assets and services), the money supply has been increased. In effect, capital claims against resources have been made available to the borrowers through *involuntary savings* by the nonborrowing public. When a loan is made, the money supply is increased; and, by definition, money represents claims on assets. The total amount of goods and services available on the market has not changed, but the number of claims on these assets has increased. The market adjusts to the increase in demand (supply remains unchanged) through an increase in prices. As a result, the nonborrowers find that their money entitles them to a smaller share of the total (they have the same amount of money, but at higher prices it buys less). On the other hand, borrowers have money—they had none before—and are capable of claiming a share of the total. Thus, through the process of credit inflation, resources have been transferred from nonborrowers to borrowers; and the nonborrowers have been forced to save (i.e., they have reduced their consumption), although this decision was not a voluntary one. In periods of less than full employment, of course, bank credit creation can put unused resources to work, resulting in more goods and services for both borrowers and nonborrowers.

Because of their power to transfer resources, the commercial banks can make an important contribution to the process of economic development. Their ability to force savings from an unwilling economy and transfer these savings to producing groups allows them to effect an increase in the rate of savings and to assure the employment of these savings in areas yielding the highest returns. On the other hand, the commercial banks' power over the money supply is not an unmixed economic blessing. If it is to be effective in periods of full employment, bank credit creation must be inflationary and result in a redistribution of asset claims. The nonborrowers, however, can claim fewer assets; and, if the rate of bank-induced inflation is too high, they may object. Moreover, credit creation can aid economic growth only as long as the public accepts the asset claims issued by the banks. Although it is hard to conceive of such an eventuality in the United States today, in a less-sophisticated world excessive lending can destroy confidence in the banking system, start a flight from money, and seriously disrupt the economic system. In the United States we have seen serious and widespread bank runs (although engendered by different causes) as recently as 1933.

America's history has been marked by a continual struggle between people interested in rapid economic development (who, therefore, argue for unrestricted bank lending to assure an adequate supply of involuntary savings) and people who fear the effects of unrestrained credit creation on the stability of the economic system and the distribution of income. Thus, development has brought with it an increase both in the influence of the commercial-banking system and in public pressure for its regulation. This chapter will explore the evolution of the commercial-banking system; and the following chapter will examine the nature of the institutions that have evolved to regulate it.

11–2. *Commercial Banking, 1800–1860*

Because of the undeveloped state of the colonial economy and the legal restrictions imposed by the British, commercial banking developed late on the American continent. Except for a few abortive land banks, no banks operated in the colonies before the Revolution. During the war, the Bank of Pennsylvania was chartered to help organize the colonies' financial resources. That bank passed out of existence when the war was over, but it did serve as a model for later peacetime banks.

Despite early success, commercial banking was slow to develop in most of the new nation; by 1810, only eighty-eight banks had been chartered. Thereafter, growth was more rapid and in 1820, the number exceeded 300; by 1860, 1500; and by 1920, 30,000. Over the first half of the nineteenth century, the number of banks increased about four times as fast as the population; and in the postbellum period the relative increase was even greater. Between the Civil War and the outbreak of World War I, the number of banks increased about sixteen times, while the population increased only three times. More recently, the number of banks has declined but their assets have continued to grow very rapidly. For example, between 1915 and 1940, the number of banks declined by almost 13,000, but bank assets tripled while population increased about a third. In fact, if assets are used to measure the pervasiveness of the banking system, the comparisons with population growth are even more spectacular. Between 1860 and 1914, for example, while population increased three times and the number of banks sixteen times, bank assets increased twenty-seven times. There can be little doubt that American economic development has been temporally associated with the rapid expansion of the commercial-banking system.

The banking system that emerged in the nineteenth century was much simpler than its present descendent; however, in many respects banks then performed the same basic functions in much the same manner as they do today. There was, however, one important difference, and unless the student is aware of it much of the monetary controversy of the period makes little sense. Today, as we have seen, a bank creates money by granting borrowers the right to draw checks against demand deposits. In the earlier period, checking accounts were rare. It was not until the 1830's that they became common in the large cities, and not until after the Civil War that they became a generally accepted means of payment. Instead, bank credit creation was a much more direct process; the banks printed their own money and issued it to their borrowers. These private bank notes resembled the paper money we know today and, since the Federal government was not permitted to issue paper currency, they served as the usual medium of exchange. There is no functional difference between the issue of bank notes and the creation of demand deposits. In the case of checks, however, it is a matter of course to return them immediately to the bank of issue. With bank notes such was not the case. Instead, once issued, they stayed in circulation, just as paper money does today, unless they were returned to the issuing bank for payment in specie. As a result, by the middle of the nineteenth century the notes of several thousand banks were in circulation (including the issues of some banks long defunct). Since the value of any note depended upon the willingness of someone to accept it, and since this willingness varied with people's estimates of the possibility of converting the note into a generally accepted medium (gold or silver), note issue represented an obvious source of economic instability.

Economic problems also stemmed from the looseness of banking practices in the early period. First, actual fraud appears to have been considerably more prevalent then than now. Second, and more important, banking theory was little understood; as a result there was a general failure to recognize the need for cash reserves. Although most bankers realized the need for *some* limit on bank credit expansion, they thought in terms of a limit based on some multiple of the bank's capital stock. If banks had received cash payment for their shares and had held these funds in liquid form, credit limits in terms of stock issue would not have led to serious trouble. However, it was customary for bank promoters to pay for their shares with IOU's; and at no time did the size of the capital-stock account bear any fixed relation to the bank's liquid reserves. In the 1820's the banking community became aware of the need for liquid reserves, but it was not until the 1840's that talk of *legal* reserves became general.

Furthermore, although most banks claimed that they stood ready to redeem their notes in specie (gold and silver), this statement was far from the truth. In periods of economic stress, all banks tended to suspend specie payments; and almost every bank in the nation suspended payments in 1819, 1837, 1857, and again in 1860. At other times, local conditions caused local suspensions. For example, although the New York banks maintained payments through the depression of 1840–1842, the banks in Philadelphia and the Southeast suspended. Thus, while no individual bank could suspend and hope to avoid bankruptcy, general suspensions were taken as a matter of course. The failure of the banks to centralize their reserves kept reserves (for a bank that wanted to remain liquid) higher than they would otherwise have been. However, the willingness of the public to accept specie suspensions permitted the banks to maintain lower reserves than they would have needed had they been required to meet all demands.

Another source of instability can be found in the hesitancy of some banks to pay out specie at any time. Although many banks (particularly those in the northeastern cities) *almost* always stood ready to redeem their notes, others went to extreme lengths to avoid disbursing their carefully hoarded specie reserves. While these activities helped the banks conserve their reserves (and thus permitted them to extend credit further than they otherwise would have been able), they also increased the uncertainty attached to accepting bank notes.

Banks that tended to overexpend credit and dodge specie payments were dubbed "wildcats" by their contemporaries, and this title has frequently been used by historians to characterize all country banking in the ante-bellum period. There can be little doubt that the "wildcat" banks added a colorful chapter to American economic history, but the extent of their contribution to the economy's development is still in doubt. The name "wildcat" refers to the tendency of frontier bankers to locate in places where redemption was difficult—that is, "where there were more wildcats than people." Legend has it that loans were frequently made on the condition that the recipient would not spend his borrowed funds in areas close to the bank. The truth of this story is of little importance; the fact that it was generally accepted strongly implies that country bankers were concerned with redemptions that threatened bank reserves. Certainly, the frontier banks tended to lend more freely than their counterparts in the cities. It is, however, more difficult to determine whether these practices contributed to or hindered economic development. Industrial development was concentrated in the eastern cities, where there were few "wildcat" banks. On the other hand, although the term "wildcat" has become synonomous with unsound banking practices, it is difficult to determine whether, in fact, the banks were unsound or merely given to making longer-term loans than eastern bankers thought prudent. In fact, given the agricultural orientation of the frontier areas, long-term loans may have been necessary if the banks were to serve their customers. Even in the East, as industry grew and demanded longer terms than were common in commercial transactions, the banks gradually began to lengthen their terms.

As the economy grew, the continued demand for credit put pressure on the banking system and gradually the system began to change. Originally, corporate bank charters (and the benefits of note issue and limited liability) were special privileges only sparingly granted by state legislatures. Special charters provided some safeguards against the worst effects of unrestricted banking, but they also resulted in monopoly profits, legislative corruption, and perhaps a limit on the level of involuntary savings. As the needs for finance increased, even the business community began to agitate for "free banking" (the right of anyone to organize a bank). Free-banking laws were first passed in Michigan and New York (1838) and, within a few years, most other states had followed suit. The rapid increase in the volume of lending under the aegis of free-banking legislation greatly increased the amount of capital available to business; however, in some states unrestricted banking also brought with it poor financial practices that, ultimately, tended to disrupt the economy.

Forces were also at work to change the nature of the banking function. The first banks had specialized almost completely in short-term mercantile credit. However, under pressure from a growing business sector for long-term (at times, almost permanent) credit, this specialization gradually broke down. The first banks had been organized by merchants to provide them with temporary loans to finance their trade balances. Although refusals to lengthen maturities elicited complaints from farmers and manufacturers, the banks, at first, did nothing. During the second decade of the nineteenth century, however, banks began making longer-term loans to governments, and, on occasion, to large business enterprises. Even then, however, they continued to refuse mortgage loans to agriculture, and long-term manufacturing loans were a rarity.

In fact, because of the unfulfilled demand for long-term capital, corporations were, at times, granted banking powers in their charters. (Such powers were, at one time or another, granted to gas-light, canal, fishing, and railway companies). The failures following each financial panic proved that such industrial banks were financially unsound. A large proportion of their liabilities were bank notes subject to payment in specie on demand, while most of their assets were fixed; and, as a result, they were unable to meet the sudden cash demands precipitated by a panic. The industrial banks were never numerically important, nor was their influence long lasting. However, their growth did underscore the need for long-term capital in an economy shifting from trade to manufacture and from hand to mechanized agriculture.

The demise of the industrial banks further intensified the demands for long-term capital. The manufacturing and agricultural sectors represented the largest portion of this demand, but even the mercantile sector began to insist on longer terms to support their greatly increased volume of business. Finally, even the most conservative banks began to bow to their customers' demands. For example, the Banks of Massachusetts and New York, among the most conservative in the country, had never made any but short-term loans and had always refused renewal requests. Under customer pressure, however, both began to lengthen maturities and grant almost automatic renewals.

Although these changes in banking policy had temporarily stilled the demands for longer-term credit, the banks' failure to re-adjust to the new loans greatly intensified the effects of financial panics and forced many banks to permanently close their doors. Unaccustomed to long-term loans, the bankers failed to recognize the need for spaced portfolios and greater reserves. As long as only short-term loans were made, loan repayments provided a continued source of liquidity. Unspaced long-term loans do not, however, possess this characteristic. Because they attempted to provide both long- and short-term credit in unlimited quantities, the banks found themselves unable to supply either.

The bank failures resulted in substantial losses to note holders and engendered public demand for severe limitations on the banking system's ability to issue current liabilities (bank notes) supported only by fixed assets (long-term loans). Had the banks adopted more sophisticated portfolio and reserve policies, they could have extended a certain amount of long-term credit without jeopardizing their financial position. However, given the nature of their liability structure, they could never have supplied all the long-term capital required by an expanding economy. Thus, new financial intermediaries were needed to supply the bulk of the economy's long-term capital. The rise of these nonbank intermediaries (savings banks, life insurance companies, and so on) and the evolution of the direct-investment markets is considered in Chapter 13. Henceforth, although the commercial banking system would one day make some long-term loans, it never again could attempt to supply the entire demand for long-term capital; and it would be many years before the system was willing to make any significant volume of long-term loans.

Before the Civil War, almost all commercial banks were state-chartered enterprises. The exceptions were the First and Second National banks; and, although they exerted considerable influence, they operated for only about a third of the century's first sixty years and could exercise no direct control over state bank operations. As a result, banking practice varied considerably over the country. Despite these considerable differences, by 1860 financial development (in the economic centers, at least) had proceeded quite far. Free commercial banking had become established in most states, and sufficient financial capital was made available to meet the needs of development. Moreover, in many areas the growth of regulation had abolished the worst features of unrestricted banking. More important, the dozens of separate short-term capital markets had been linked together in something very close to a single national market. Very early, movements of short-term funds between eastern cities had aided the development of an eastern capital market; and, by the outbreak of the war, western and southern banks, too, had begun to move funds to eastern banks when such transfers appeared profitable. Although these short-term capital movements were to have serious repercussions, they did succeed in tying the eastern capital markets to those in the less-developed areas.

Moreover, during the period the bankers themselves had gained considerable sophistication. By 1860 there were few bankers who failed to realize the necessity of reserves or to understand that these reserves should be tied to short-term liabilities. Further, they had come to talk of balanced portfolios; and most would admit that it was impossible to commit all a bank's funds to long-term loans and hope to maintain solvency. As a result, although their contribution to long-term finance was limited (limited, perhaps, more than was really necessary), what there was rested on a firmer footing than it had in the earlier decades. Furthermore, because of their greater stability, the banks were able to supply the economy with an ever-increasing volume of short-term commercial credit and to provide agriculture and industry with their working capital requirements.

Although evidence seems to indicate that the banks were responsible for making a large volume of involuntary savings available to the economy, there appears to have been less inflation than one might have expected. (Between 1820 and 1860 the price level was relatively stable.) It appears that something akin to full employment existed at least during the early thirties, the late forties, and the early fifties. Thus, it is unreasonable to assume that bank expansion did nothing but put unemployed resources to work. The period was, however, characterized by continued technological advances that should have led, other things remaining equal, to price declines. Since these declines did not occur, it may be reasonable to assume that the inflationary tendencies engendered by bank credit expansions offset the deflationary tendencies stemming from the technological advances. Involuntary savings, therefore, were effected not through price increases, but through foregone price declines.

11–3. *Commercial Banking Developments, 1860–1950*

Commercial banking developments in the decades after the Civil War largely represent a continuation of trends rooted in the ante-bellum period. Although the number and size of banks increased and checking transfers became more common, the basic banking function did not change. Most important of the events of the period was the passage of the National Banking Act in 1863. The act permitted banks to take out federal (as opposed to state) charters and established a uniform set of rules for all chartered banks. As a result, for the first time the economy could boast of a national currency (the national bank notes redeemable at par by *any* national bank) instead of the thousands of different notes previously circulated. More important, the act established a national banking system with all member banks required to maintain minimum standards.

Subsequent amendments to the act in 1866 placed a 10 per cent tax on notes issued by state banks, forcing most state banks to take federal charters. By 1870, almost 90 per cent of the nation's banks had joined the national system. Thereafter, the widespread innovation of checking transactions, combined with the greater freedom and lower reserve requirements permitted under most state regulations, touched off a resurgence of state banking (see Table 11–1). Although the number of state banks soon exceeded the number of national banks, the latter continued to exert a strong influence on banking developments. For example, by 1910, national banks represented just over a third of the number of banks in the United States; but they accounted for more than two thirds of total bank assets. The new state banks tended to be smaller than the national banks (in 1910 average assets of state banks were $338,000 against a national bank average of $1,385,000), and located in the country away from the greatest centers of economic development. Most of the large banks were federally chartered, and these more strictly regulated institutions dominated the credit market in the eastern and upper midwestern cities. Thus, because their number included the largest and most influential banks, the national banks tended to set standards; and, because of their ability to present checks for immediate payment, they were also able to limit the credit expansion of state banks. By 1875, therefore, a uniform set of federal tandards had been imposed on much of the banking community. Moreover, even in areas with few national banks, the growth of tate regulation had, by 1880, spelled the end of "wildcat" banking.

As we have seen, as early as the 1830's the country banks had egun to place surplus funds in the hands of the city correspondnts. This trend, important in the 1840's and 1850's, was greatly ccelerated after the Civil War. The National Banking Act, as well s most state laws, permitted banks to maintain a fraction of their eserves on deposit in other banks. Since reserve deposits must be ubject to instant recall, country banks tended to send their reserves o New York, where rates on demand deposits were highest. The New York banks, in turn, loaned the funds on call to stock and

TABLE 11–1

OMMERCIAL BANKS: GROWTH OF STATE- AND FEDERAL-REGULATED BANKS, 1870–1961

ear	*Number of Commercial State Banks*	*Number of* Federal Chartered and Regulated Banks*	*Assets of State Banks (Millions)*	*Assets of* Federal Chartered and Regulated Banks (Millions)*
870	174†	1,612	$ 149†	$ 1,566
880	650	2,076	882	2,035
890	2,250	3,484	1,743	3,062
900	4,659	3,732	2,625	4,944
910	13,257	7,145	4,482	9,897
920	20,690	9,399	23,836	33,618
930	15,860	8,315	34,494	47,349
940	9,239	6,398	31,194	57,846
950	9,081	6,873	72,216	144,660
961	8,444	6,113	128,280	235,112

* Includes national commercial banks, 1870–1910, and all members of the Federal Reserve ystem, 1920–1957.
† Estimates.
Source: *Historical Statistics; Statistical Abstract,* 1963.

ond brokers. The need for short-term balances to finance stock ransactions permitted both the city banks and their correspondents o profit. This tendency for reserve centralization was certainly rofitable; however, it contributed to the economic instability of the eriod. When funds were withdrawn by the country banks (as, for xample, they were each spring and fall), the price of call money ose precipitously. Moreover, when seasonal drains coincided with ny unusual demands, credit stringency in the stock market could, nd frequently did, reach disaster proportions. Throughout the atter nineteenth century, stock market panics were concentrated in the fall, when heavy seasonal withdrawals coincided with some other demand for funds.

In addition, a further element of instability was added by the character of the deposits themselves. Since the deposits were the reserves of the country banks, they tended to withdraw them at the first whisper of danger. Such action further intensified credit conditions in New York, and made the New York banks even less able to meet their liabilities. After the panics of 1873, 1884, 1893, 1903, and 1907, New York bankers came to understand that the possession of short-term assets does not necessarily assure the ability to meet depositors' demands; and the country bankers learned that deposits in New York banks were not always perfectly liquid and perfectly safe. Bankers throughout the country finally realized that it is necessary to hold reserves in a form safe from loss due to economic fluctuation and in a place where their withdrawal does not add additional stresses to an already trembling economic system. These lessons were learned, however, only at considerable cost. What was needed, of course, was a central bank that could *create* reserves in times of pressure.

The banks' ante-bellum experience with long-term loans convinced many bankers that such lengthy commitments should be avoided at all costs. During the last half of the century, even loans that could safely have been made (loans based on proper maturity spacing and portfolio balance) were frequently denied. This bias toward short-term paper may have been commendable from a safety standpoint, but it is thought by some that it tended to restrict the rate of economic development. Moreover, the resurgence of the "real-bills" doctrine (loans based solely on self-extinguishing commercial paper) had adverse short-run effects. In periods of prosperity, banks tended to immediately expend credit contributing to inflationary pressures. In periods of commercial decline, they reduced loans equally fast and contributed to further decline. The money supply, thus, became largely tied to the state of mercantile prosperity. As a matter of fact, it has only been within the past two decades that banks have again begun to make significant quantities of long-term finance available to business and industry.

Although developments in banking during the late nineteenth and early twentieth centuries had resulted in better practice than the "wildcat" operations of the earlier era, there was still room for improvement. Bank failures were high in every decade but reached a spectacular figure during the 1920's and 1930's. Over 15,000 banks failed in that twenty-year span (see Table 11–2). Many of these banks were small country banks, but, especially in the 1930's, a not insignificant number were large city banks. The causes of failure were numerous. In many states, regulation was lax and banking practice not tightly supervised. During the 1920's the agricultural depression had pushed many country institutions into bankruptcy; and, during the 1930's, overly close connections between banks (particularly in New York) and the securities markets forced many city banks to close their doors as security prices collapsed. Moreover, the decline in asset values caused by the depression forced many banks, both in the cities and country, into the hands of the receivers. Such frequent bankruptcies could not but interfere with the economic process; and, in an attempt to strengthen the banking system, a host of legislation was enacted during the 1930's. (The regulative aspects of this legislation will be discussed in the following chapter.) Out of the depression and failures came satisfactory deposit insurance, and this insurance has done much to protect the banks from

TABLE 11–2

BANK SUSPENSIONS BY DECADE, 1871–1962

Decade	*Number of Suspensions*
1871–1880	365
1881–1890	286
1891–1900	1,234
1901–1910	808
1911–1920	944
1921–1930	7,066
1931–1940	8,067*
1941–1950	28
1951–1958	31
1959–1962	16

* Most of these suspensions came before 1934.

Source: *Historical Statistics; Statistical Abstract,* 1963.

panic withdrawals. Deposit insurance had been tried at the state level in the first decade of the twentieth century; but inadequate premiums, the refusal of large banks to participate, and the agricultural bias of the banks that did join, led to its failure. Beginning with temporary insurance in 1933, the federal government had, by 1935, made insurance with the Federal Deposit Insurance Company compulsory for all members of the Federal Reserve System and large state banks, and had offered it to the remainder of the banking community. Today, about 95 per cent of the nation's banks (plus many other financial institutions) are insured, and these insured banks account for all but about 2 per cent of the nation's deposits. With adequate insurance, it is difficult to conceive of banks forced to close their doors because of the sudden cash demands of panicky depositors. As a result, the commercial bank's position in the economic process has been greatly strengthened.

11–4. *Present Banking Problems*

In terms of industrial organization, the banking community is unique. Not only has it been subject to regulation, but, from an early period, state laws have prohibited certain kinds of banking growth. For example, almost nowhere is it possible to engage in interstate banking; as a result, banks are not faced with out-of-state competition. In some states, laws are even more stringent, frequently prohibiting intercounty branch banking and, at times, limiting competition to even smaller areas. As a result, local bank monopolies have been common; and, in many areas, growth has been limited by the unprogressive character of the local banking monopolies. (If local banks refuse loans to business and industry, it is very difficult to attract finance from distant banks.) On the other hand, in California, where the laws permit statewide branches, the Bank of America has been an important force in the state's development. Recently, agitation for at least cross-county banking has been increasing in many states. It could well be argued that, from the point of view of rational development, growth could be more rapid and the allocation of resources improved if all laws prohibiting branch banking were repealed.

England and Canada have few individual banks (there are eleven clearing banks in England and ten in Canada), but these have thousands of branches and banking services are more readily available than they are in parts of the United States. Ten or eleven banks might be too few to assure competition, but there is little reason to believe that branch banking could result in a greater degree of monopoly. In the past half century, concentration in banking has increased, but, as yet, this trend does not appear too dangerous. Mergers and increased branch banking resulted in an increase in the share of the 100 largest banks in the nation's banking assets from 30 per cent in 1923 to almost 60 per cent in 1940; but this fraction has since declined to less than 50 per cent. Even 100 banks are probably enough to assure something close to competition and, under any conditions, it is difficult to see how any further misallocation can result from large banks replacing local monopolies. It is not, after all,

he size of a firm that distorts resource allocation but the size in re-
ation to the market served.

In addition, the trend toward larger units has had some un-
loubtedly beneficial effects. Large banks have frequently intro-
luced more sophisticated banking techniques, they have often
hown a greater willingness to pursue an aggressive loan policy, and
hey have made larger blocks of capital available in small cities and
owns.

The commercial bank also differs from firms in other industries
n yet another important respect. Unlike prices of other commodities,
egal limits have often been placed on the rate of interest (the price
f money). Usury laws have, of course, long historical precedence.
uch laws were common in the Middle Ages and were in effect in
lmost every American colony long before the Revolution. Usury
aws were usually rooted in the belief that earning interest was evil.
'heir authors failed to realize that the interest rate is a price like any
ther, and that it should be allowed to allocate resources if we want
he free-enterprise system to produce an optimum allocation. In fact,
he usury laws have resulted in a denial of credit to the riskiest
orrowers who, though willing, are not allowed to pay a rate high
nough to compensate for their risk. Instead, these people are forced
o borrow illegally or go without funds. It would be better, from an
conomic viewpoint, to abolish all usury laws. As long as free en-
erprise is maintained, competitive pressures would force banks to
end money at the lowest possible rates; and banks could lend to
isky borrowers at rates high enough to compensate for the risk.

During the later nineteenth and early twentieth centuries, the
merican banker had become an ever more conservative figure in
he American economy. The day of the entrepreneurial "wildcat"
anker had passed; banker domination of industrial firms had led
oward noncompetitive market forms and a lack of innovation; and,
nally, in the 1930's bankers were even accused of abnegating their
oan function. In 1934, bank investments in paper securities ex-
eeded their loans, and among the securities the largest portion was
nvested in government bonds. By 1945, after the massive govern-
ent bond issues of the war period, government bonds accounted
or almost three quarters of total bank assets.

Recently, however, some changes have occurred. The semi-
onopolistic position of the banker has been broken in many areas
y the development of branch banks and by the growth of the sav-

ings and loan associations competing for the deposits and investments that traditionally had belonged to the commercial bank. These competitive pressures have tended to make the banker much less conservative, and, in some areas, he has become a veritable merchant of money. The progressive banker of the 1960's has shown a greater willingness to innovate and to make loans that before would have been considered unthinkable. His sole criterion is profitability. The past ten years have seen commercial banks vigorously competing for consumer credit, automobile loans, loans to risky business at high interest rates, and long-term industrial loans. Only a few years ago, any of these loans would have been considered taboo for a "respectable" bank. The effects of this resurgence of entrepreneurship are visible in commercial-bank portfolios. By 1963, loans again accounted for more than half of the bank assets and investments in formal securities have fallen to less than 40 per cent. The banker, then, once again appears capable of making great contributions to the American economy during the forthcoming decades.

Suggested Readings

DEWEY, DAVIS R. *Financial History of the United States.* New York: Longmans, Green & Co., Inc., 1934.

HAMMOND, BRAY. *Banks and Politics in the United States from the Revolution to the Civil War.* Princeton, N.J.: Princeton University Press, 1957.

MINTS, LLOYD W. *A History of Banking Theory.* Chicago: University of Chicago Press, 1945.

Chapter 12 INVOLUNTARY SAVINGS: THE GROWTH OF REGULATION

12–1. *The Need for Regulation: Theory*

We have seen that commercial banks can make important contributions to the process of development; in fact, few economies have ever realized their full growth potential without the aid of some credit-creating financial intermediary. The benefits derived from a commercial banking system, however, are not costless.

First, aside from the government, banks are the only institutions in our society empowered to issue money claims. The public, of course, must be willing to accept these claims if the banks are to operate effectively. Thus, fraud and excessive credit expansion, culminating in frequent failures, can seriously affect the banks' position in the economy and can force the public to bear the cost of illegal or unwise decisions. Although such practices may profit particular bankers at some point in time, in the long run any decline in the public's willingness to hold bank claims results both in lower profits for the banking sector and in a slower rate of economic growth.

Second, at times of full employment bank credit creation is inflationary and, although a transfer of resources from consumers to business can speed the process of economic growth, it does result in a redistribution of income away from the consumers. As long as the growth process permits the consumers to ultimately recapture their income, few problems are presented. If, however, bank inflation results only in higher prices, income redistribution may have both political and economic repercussions.

Third, the process of bank credit creation can amplify fluctuations in the level of income. Bankers, interested in profits and the safety of their loans, have tended to increase the number of loans (and thereby the money supply) in times of prosperity and to reduce their lending activities in periods of depression. Thus the actions of the banks have contributed to further increases in prices when prices were rising, and to further reductions in incomes when incomes were falling.

As theory suggests, the growth of the banking system in the United States has been associated with periodic flights from bank notes and panic bank "runs," with periods of marked income redistribution and with increasing monetary instability. As a result, there has been a continued and growing pressure throughout American history for banking regulation. The pressure came at first from the public, but their pleas have been echoed by the more farsighted of the banking institutions themselves.

What was needed, of course, was a central bank capable of supervising and regulating the activities of the commercial banks. Such an institution can stand ready to lend to commercial banks (i.e., create reserves) when public panic threatens the liquidity of the system. Moreover, the central bank, by discouraging lending in periods of inflation and encouraging the banks to lend in times of depression, can help stabilize the level of income and prevent continual bank-induced inflations. The bank, too, can establish minimum banking standards and protect the public from poor banking practices. Historically, the central bank has also served as the fiscal agent for the central government and thus helped that unit mobilize its resources. The history of bank regulation in America can, then, be viewed as the gradual evolution of a central bank capable of supervising and regulating the commercial banks.

12–2. *Private Regulation*

a) ***The Suffolk System.*** Through the years, banking regulation has been privately, often state, and occasionally federally initiated. Chronologically, the first deliberate regulatory attempt was privately sponsored. The Suffolk System was introduced by the Suffolk Bank in 1819 to curb the lending policies of the country banks located near Boston. In 1824, six other Boston banks joined the Suffolk, and together they were able to force the country banks to redeem their notes in specie. Thus the system gave the city a more uniform currency. The seven cooperating institutions demanded that the country banks deposit reserve balances with them sufficient to cover any note that might be received. If the country banks failed to heed the demand, the members of the Suffolk System threatened to accumulate notes and present them for redemption in embarrassing quantities. If the country banks acceded, the seven agreed to accept their notes and to present them gradually.

The rural areas usually were faced with a trade deficit with the cities (they bought more than they sold) and the city banks were almost always net creditors with their country counterparts. Thus, the extension of the system to the seven largest city banks forced the country banks to reduce their circulation. By 1825, almost all New England bank notes were exchanged at par (i.e., notes from any bank could be converted at face value into the notes of any other bank or into specie.) From 1825 to 1860, New England had an almost uniform currency, a phenomenal achievement in the America of the early nineteenth century.

The Suffolk System continued to serve the area until the late 1850's, when it was replaced by another private organization and the Boston Clearinghouse. During its period of effective regulation, the Suffolk System rewarded the seven cooperating banks with the deposits of the country banks, as well as the higher interest rates on the extra loan business that must have accrued to them as the country banks were forced to contract their issues. The country banks gained little, and protested vigorously against the demands of the city banks. The people of the Boston area received the benefits of a stable currency; but, on the other hand, the amount of loan capital available to them was probably less than it otherwise would have been. The system's requirement that reserves be deposited in a central depository set the pattern for future American central-bank development. In general, the Suffolk experiment underscores again the conflict between the need for additional involuntary savings in a growing economy and the public's demands for a reasonably stable money supply.

b) ***Private Clearinghouses and Financial Crises.*** Local bank clearinghouses, although originally established solely to overcome the mechanical difficulties of interbank settlement, at times also acted as private regulatory agencies. The first clearinghouse was established by the New York banks in 1853; the idea was copied in Boston two years later; and within a very short time clearinghouses were in operation in most of the nation's largest cities. Because they speeded the process of collection and payment, the clearinghouses could maintain a tight rein on the credit-creating ability of individual banks. Moreover, the innovation of the clearinghouse certificate added another dimension to the central-banking powers of the clearinghouses. The certificates that were issued against bank assets during periods of general specie suspensions were used to settle interbank balances in lieu of specie transfers; and at times they even circulated as currency. Although the certificates were only a substitute for reserves, they did permit the banks to survive in periods when a shortage of legal reserves would otherwise have spelled disaster.

Although the certificates were not legalized until the Aldrich-Vreeland Act of 1908, they served to ease almost every financial crisis of the post-bellum period. In 1873, the New York clearinghouse issued $10 million worth of certificates; in 1884, $25 million; in 1893, $38 million; in 1907, $88 million; and in 1914, $109 million (however, only $58 million actually circulated). Moreover, clearinghouses in other cities issued $25 million worth of certificates in 1893 and $150 million in 1907. Today, because we have a central bank capable of creating reserves in time of crises, it is no longer necessary for the clearinghouses to issue certificates. In the earlier period, however, although clearinghouse action was incapable of preventing financial panics, it did, by ameliorating the worst effects of fixed-reserve requirements, lessen their severity.

12–3. *State Regulation*

Except for the Suffolk system and occasional clearinghouse action, private regulation was atypical in the United States. During the first half of the nineteenth century, the most important regulatory bodies were the state legislatures. In the earliest years, banking privileges had been granted by charter and the number of banks was not large. Thus, it is not surprising that regulation was limited to spasmodic attempts to control certain banking practices without providing any long-term regulatory policies. For example, as early as 1792, the Massachusetts legislature restricted the Massachusetts Bank's obligations to double its capital held in specie. In 1814 and 1824, the Pennsylvania legislature enacted laws revoking the charters of banks suspending specie payment (although this law was seldom enforced). No state bank commissions with power to require reports and conduct bank examinations were established before 1829, and even by the time of the Civil War most states were still without effective commissions.

a) ***The Safety-Fund System.*** The first important step toward banking regulation was taken by the New York legislature in 1829. Before then, as we have seen, banks frequently failed with large note issues outstanding, and the holders of the notes bore the cost of failure. Public pressure for legal protection for noteholders grew, and in 1829 the legislature began to require all new banks (and banks whose charters were renewed) to join the Safety-Fund System. The safety fund was a reserve established to insure the note issues of the banks. Each member bank was required to pay ½ per cent of its capital into the fund each year, until its total contribution had reached 3 per cent. The fund so constituted was to be used to honor the notes of defaulting banks.

On the surface, the Safety-Fund System had much appeal. In fact, it attempted to accomplish the same ends as the Federal Deposit Insurance Corporation, established over 100 years later. There was, however, one significant difference. Contributions to the safety fund were not based on the volume of notes and deposits that were insured; instead, they were based on the bank's capital. Such a scheme tended to penalize the banks with the highest ratio of capital to liabilities (the most conservative banks) and reward those that had the greatest percentage of loans outstanding. It is not, therefore, surprising that the banks in New York City (whose loans-to-capital ratio was less than half that of their country competitors) protested against the subsidy they were forced to pay the "reckless" country banks. Had it not been for the upstate bias of the New York legislature, it is quite possible a more satisfactory scheme would have been adopted. If, for example, contributions were based on the volume of short-term liabilities insured, the scheme might have effected permanent changes in the banking system.

Despite its defects, the system did work fairly well for eight years. Bank defaults during the panic of 1837 and the subsequent depression, however, exhausted the fund and the state was forced to make up a deficit in excess of a million dollars. Because of this failure, the legislature granted no more safety-fund charters after 1839, and the charter of the last safety-fund bank expired in 1866. Although the act was short lived, it was the precursor of future banking legislation. Not only was it the forerunner of the FDIC, but also its insistence on periodic state bank examinations foretold future developments.

b) ***Free Banking.*** New York took the lead in initiating the second step in state banking regulation. The "Free-Banking Act" of 1838 was primarily designed to encourage the growth of a competitive banking system. (It granted banking privileges to any group that complied with a simple set of regulations laid down by the

Secretary of State.) The law did contain some regulatory provisions. Most important, the act, as originally passed, required the banks to hold liquid reserves behind their liabilities. Although this restriction was dropped in subsequent amendments, it was the first attempt to require legal bank reserves based on the volume of short-term liabilities (deposits and notes). The insistence upon cash reserves, coupled with the Suffolk system's demand for a central reserve depository, set the pattern for most subsequent banking regulation and distinguished the American banking system from its European counterpart. The act also required that bank notes be backed 100 per cent by state obligations. Again, like the Suffolk and safety-fund systems, this requirement represented an attempt to restrict the issue and increase the safety of bank notes. Neither of the reserve requirements remained long in the law; nor, for that matter, were they ever closely observed. They did, however, indicate a desire on the part of the legislature to regulate the banking system, and they did set the pattern for future regulation.

c) ***The Forestall System.*** By far the most important set of state regulations in ante-bellum America were those embodied in the Forestall System. During the depression of 1842 all Louisiana banks had suspended. As a result, the state legislature, in an attempt to prevent future suspensions, established a set of detailed regulations to govern the future operation of the state's nine commercial banks. The law required that all loans of deposited funds (as opposed to loans of capital) be limited to ninety days. Renewals were prohibited, and the banks were required to publish the names of borrowers requesting them. Moreover, the law required that all short-term liabilities be backed one third by specie reserves and two thirds by short-term commercial paper.

Operating under the new regulations, the Louisiana banks proved themselves resistant to economic fluctuations. When, in 1857, they were among the few banks that continued specie payment, legislatures elsewhere began to insist on cash reserves. In fact, it may have been the success of the Forestall System that accounts for the American predilection for cash reserves. Certainly, the success of regulation in Louisiana affected the structure of post-bellum regulation throughout the country. So conservative were the Louisiana banks that, well after the outbreak of the Civil War, they continued to remit balances to their New York correspondents.

d) ***Miscellaneous Changes.*** Changes in the pattern of state regulation were not, of course, limited to these three laws. Other regulations too had a lasting effect. For example, states began to require banks to publish financial statements very early, and by the Civil War these statements actually began to provide adequate and reliable information. Again, in 1827 New York imposed double liability on bank stockholders; and this requirement became common throughout the country in the 1850's.

After the war, state regulation became even more common. Although federal regulations ultimately supplanted much of the states' efforts, the period saw the growth in the regulatory power of state bank commissions and the general innovation of legal reserves.

12–4. *Federal Regulation*

a) ***The First Bank of the United States.*** In 1791, the Congress of the United States granted a charter to the First Bank of the United States. Originally, the bank was intended to act as a fiscal agent for the government. While it served the Treasury well during its twenty years of life, it also performed many of the other functions today associated with a central bank. Because it pursued a conservative loan policy, the bank remained a net creditor with the state banks. Therefore, it was able, through its eight branches scattered over the country, to present state bank notes for payment and thus to limit the credit creation of the commercial banks. Moreover, because it could create credit it was able to act as lender of last resort. Finally, because of its ability to issue notes through its branches, it provided something akin to a national currency.

Unlike central banks abroad, the First Bank of the United States was organized as a private-government partnership. The original capitalization was $10,000,000; the federal government owned one fifth and private persons the remainder. While central banks in other countries have tended to be either government or private owned, all three of the institutions that have served the United States as central banks have been, to some extent, private-public partnerships either in terms of ownership or control.

During its life, the bank loaned the Treasury over $13 million dollars, acted as a depository for government funds, and, through its branches, facilitated the movement of government funds over the country. Despite its success, its policies of credit restraint and its ability to make private loans engendered the animosity of certain interests. What is more important is that, as a creature of a Federalist administration, it earned the resentment of most of the members of the party of Jefferson. As a result, when its charter expired in 1811, Congress, by a very close vote (sixty-five to sixty-four in the House and a seventeen-to-seventeen tie broken against the Bank by the Vice-President in the Senate) refused to renew it. The first American experiment in central banking was brought to a close, and the country again returned to complete unit banking.

b) ***The Second Bank of the United States.*** The need for a fiscal agent to handle federal funds became obvious during the War of 1812. The government, pressed by severe military needs, found it difficult to borrow and almost impossible to move funds across the country. As a result of this experience, Congress in 1816 chartered the Second Bank of the United States. The Bank, to act as a fiscal agent for the government, was empowered to open branches in all states and, in addition, was permitted to engage in commercial banking activities. The combination of central and commercial banking functions that characterized both the First and Second Banks represented a development in the European central-bank tradition. It is interesting that this development, almost alone among early American central-bank innovations, did not reappear in the Federal Reserve System. Like the First Bank, the new institution was to be a private-public partnership. The federal government was to subscribe to one fifth of the stock and to appoint one fifth of the Second Bank's directors. The remainder of the capital and management was to be provided by the private sector.

Although the result may have been unintentional, the Second Bank (like its predecessor) was admirably designed to serve as a central bank. Not only could it serve as a government fiscal agent but, because of its branches and lending powers, it could act to restrict credit in periods of inflation and to encourage loans in periods of depression. No feature of the bank's charter caused more criticism than that section that gave it the power to establish and operate branches throughout the country. If the bank had restricted its operations to Washington, it could not have regulated commercial-bank lending. But, with branches in every part of the country, it could present notes for redemption and thus prevent state banks from expanding loans more rapidly than the Second Bank itself.

The process of central banking was, however, even less understood than the process of commercial banking; and from 1816 until 1822 the bank probably made a greater contribution to economic instability than to stability. In that period its managers were first overly expansionist and then, when depression set in, overly conservative in their practices. Moreover, because it did have the power to restrict state-bank loans and because it competed directly with these banks for business, local bankers tended to oppose the bank and its policies.

Under its president, Nicholas Biddle, the bank did, between 1822 and 1834, act as a central bank. Although it remained a private, profit-making institution, the bank did not hesitate to restrict credit when inflation threatened nor to encourage lending in periods of depression or deflation. Moreover, when state banks were threatened by panic withdrawals, the Second Bank frequently acted as lender of last resort.

Although Biddle's action frequently infuriated state bankers and those who desired easy credit (particularly eastern manufacturers and merchants), economic arguments had little to do with the ultimate demise of the bank. Instead, political considerations tended to dominate the recharter controversy; and Jackson's actions (including the withdrawal of federal deposits) appear to have been prompted more by personal animosity toward Biddle and his political maneuverings than by economic considerations. Although the Second Bank was not a perfect central bank, it was probably the most advanced institution of its time. Certainly, it performed most central-bank functions; it did not restrict national economic growth unreasonably; and it does appear to have prevented overly rapid credit creation (the per-capita money supply was almost constant between 1820 and 1830, but doubled during the next decade).

Thus, between 1834 and 1836, America's second experiment in central banking came to an end. Its record had been good, but the pressures against any restrictive force in an expanding economy are tremendous. Although the bank was criticized on many grounds, the only truly economic argument was never directly leveled against it. The bank had been given central-banking powers, but nowhere had it been charged with a responsibility to use them wisely. Its central-banking functions were not mentioned in its charter, nor did subsequent legislation inform the bank's management that its first responsibility was not profitability but the stability of the economy. Biddle himself had been a good central banker, but there was no guarantee that his successors would do as well. Certainly his predecessors had not. Ideally, it would have been better to have revised the bank's charter. In the 1830's, however, the critics wanted nothing less than free and unrestricted banking. It is possible that the absence of a central bank did speed economic growth (although this inference is by no means certain). It *is* certain that the absence of a central bank greatly accentuated short-term monetary adjustments and engendered periodic booms and busts throughout the rest of the century.

c) ***The National Banking System.*** After the failure of the recharter act and the demise of the Second Bank, the federal government largely severed its direct connections with the commercial banking system. After a short and rather unhappy experience with the state banks, the federal government established a complex of sub-treasuries to handle federal funds. These sub-treasuries could, and at times did, act as central banks, but they were not charged with central-banking duties and their first concern was always the day-to-day business of the Treasury. By 1860, however, the existence of over 10,000 types of money and thirty-six sets of banking regulations began to affect the development of a national economy. Even if the nation was still not prepared to accept a central bank, federal action was needed to unify the system. In 1863, therefore, the National Banking Act was passed.

The act gave the country a uniform currency and a system of banks operated under a single and relatively strict set of rules. The member banks were subject to minimum capitalization and legal-reserve requirements, as well as periodic inspections. At the same time, the law did not provide a central bank. In fact, it may actually have intensified short-run instability.

The volume of national currency (national bank notes) depended not on the demand for cash but on the rate of interest and the needs of the Treasury. The notes could only be issued against government bonds, and banks invested in bonds only when bond yields exceeded the earnings on alternative investments. At the same time, the volume of bonds available to the banks depended upon Treasury policy.

The act required member banks to hold reserves, and this requirement undoubtedly contributed to the safety of the system. The law required 25 per cent reserves for banks in central-reserve cities and 15 per cent for other banks. However, the law permitted the banks to deposit a part (three fifths) of their reserves in other banks. This "doubling up" tended to immobilize reserves in periods of crisis, because, as we have seen, reserves tended to move to New York. Moreover, because reserves were not held by a central bank, the law demanded a higher average level of reserve than otherwise would have been required. Thus, the reserve provisions were doubly defective. Country banks' reserves were higher than they need have been; and, therefore, the volume of credit was unnecessarily restricted. At the same time, because of the concentration of reserves in New York, the system encouraged overexpansion of call loans to the stock market.

In addition, the act did not provide an institutional framework for many central-banking functions. It failed, for example, to provide any lender of last resort. There was no way to create reserves in times of financial stress nor to bolster individual banks in the face of runs. As a result, banks that could, if given time, have met their debts were sometimes forced to close their doors because they were unable to meet sudden increases in demand for specie. Moreover, the act provided no authority charged with implementing central-banking functions. The national banks became depositories for some federal funds, and they could be counted on to act as agents for federal fiscal operations. However, even here the Treasury still took primary responsibility. More important, no institution was empowered to assume economic leadership. Actually, leadership was at times assumed by the clearinghouses and the Treasury. But the clearinghouses acted only when total disaster threatened, and the Treasury only when contracyclical programs did not interfere with normal operations.

Although the act failed to provide the full range of control needed in a growing economy, it was not a complete failure. It provided a national system of banks that was fairly reliable, and it laid down minimum capital requirements for these banks. It permitted the banks to issue notes against bonds deposited with the Treasurer of the United States, and thus gave the country a national currency. In addition, the reserve requirement, although leading to short-run problems, probably did contribute to stable banking. Certainly, the failure rate among national banks was below that for state banks. For example, from 1864 to 1914, while 1,975 state banks suspended, only 529 national banks closed their doors. Moreover, the example of the national banks probably also improved state banking practices.

d) *The Federal Reserve System.* The weaknesses in the banking system demonstrated by waves of failure and suspensions during the crises of 1873, 1884, 1893, and 1903 proved to many the need for a central bank; and the collapse of 1907 convinced even the legislators that something needed to be done. Unfortunately for central banking, monetary questions became a party matter. Although both parties agreed that some form of central bank was needed, they disagreed violently over the form that bank should take. Because the Democratic party was in power when legislation was finally passed, the Federal Reserve System reflects the fear of Wall Street that had dominated Democratic party thinking since the Civil War. Instead of a single central bank, the Act of 1914 established twelve central banks. Although general supervisory powers were granted to the Federal Reserve Board, the board actually had little authority. Moreover, although all national banks were required to join the system, state banks were not forced to participate.

In what had become the typical American pattern, the new bank was a private-public partnership, with bankers, the public, and business represented. In contrast to the situation in the past where there had been both government ownership and control, there was now, through the Federal Reserve Board, to be some element of government control without ownership. The law established reserve requirements for all banks in the system. In addition, each district bank was permitted to issue Federal Reserve notes (a new national currency), to buy and sell government bonds on its own account, and to rediscount commercial paper for its member banks. The latter provision was designed to permit the central bank to create reserves in times of crisis and to regulate the lending activities of the member banks. Later, as central-banking techniques became more sophisticated, the open-market powers proved more useful than the rediscount rate. In the early years, however, open-market techniques were not well understood.

The act (slightly amended in 1916) did provide a lender of last resort and did result in reserve centralization (reserves averaged 20 per cent under the National Banking Act, 14 per cent under the Federal Reserve Act). It did not, however, establish a true central bank. The central authority initially was too weak to establish and implement any national monetary policy, and no one in the system was given power over reserve requirements. Moreover, in its early years the system was not well accepted. Although the national banks had been forced to become members, by 1916 only thirty-seven state banks had joined. Even the government was slow to use its services. The Treasury did not make any use of the system's facilities until 1916, and the last sub-treasury was not closed until 1921.

Over time, however, the Federal Reserve System has become

an integral part of our financial system. It has handled the government's financial transactions, it has acted as lender of last resort, and it has smoothed the flow of funds between the United States and the rest of the world. It has not, however, proved itself capable of maintaining economic stability. A portion of this failure can, of course, be traced to the general inefficacy of monetary controls. However, a part can be laid directly at the door of the Federal Reserve Act and the system as it developed. First, the original act did not grant the system a full set of economic controls. No one had the power to alter reserve requirements and no single authority could set rediscount rates in all twelve districts. Second, neither the framers of the act nor the men who came to operate it were skilled central bankers. Thus, the system frequently failed even to utilize the tools it did have. It was only gradually, for example, that the system's accounts and open-market transactions were welded into a single unit of control. Third, there was no central authority charged with the duties of regulation and given the power to effect this regulation. Finally, in several periods of crisis, the bank found it impossible to fulfill both its mission to maintain stability and its duty to act as fiscal agent for the government. Such conflicts of interest occurred during both world wars and during the years 1946–1951.

Let us examine the effects of each of these weaknesses on the system's attempts to stabilize the economy during the past forty-five years. The system had hardly been launched when the United States was propelled into war. Thus, almost immediately the system was required to help the government raise the funds needed to prosecute the war. During hostilities, the economic effects of Treasury-Federal Reserve cooperation were not bad. At the war's end, however, the system was forced to underwrite the Treasury's victory loans, and the method of loan finance chosen by the Treasury almost certainly encouraged inflation. The Treasury stressed the advantages of borrowing to buy bonds and demanded that the system maintain low enough interest rates that such loans would look attractive. The result was a rapid increase in both the money supply and the velocity of circulation, and a concomitant increase in prices.

Moreover, when the system was finally freed from its Treasury commitments, inflation had already become depression. However, because of a lack of understanding of the economic system, the banks continued to pursue an anti-inflation policy well into the recession of 1921. Even after the banks finally realized that depression and not inflation was the problem, their actions were ineffective. Manipulation of the discount rate accomplished little and they had no power over reserve requirements. Furthermore, although they had power to institute contracyclical open-market operations, they lacked the requisite skill. The Act of 1914 had empowered the twelve banks to buy and sell government bonds on their own account. Such action, if pursued intelligently, can create and destroy bank reserves (and thus affect credit creation). In the early years, however, the banks usually bought and sold government bonds only to adjust their portfolios. Even had the system known what to do, it was almost impossible for the twelve banks operating independently to effect any common policy. It was not until the 1920's that, under the leadership of Benjamin Strong of the New York Bank, the Open-Market Committee was established, without legal authority, to coordinate the activities of the district banks. By the mid-twenties, however, the Open-Market Committee was functioning effectively, and the system had another weapon in its fight for economic stability.

The need for central authority was well demonstrated by the vacillations in central-bank policy during the critical stock-market inflation of the late 1920's. The Federal Reserve Board was generally regarded as a political creature and was largely distrusted by the member banks. The Federal Reserve Banks, at times, appeared willing to accept the leadership of the New York Bank, but this institution was, in turn, distrusted by the political authorities. Throughout the period, the New York Bank wanted to introduce quantitative general credit restrictions to halt the speculative stock market fever (i.e., they argued for a general restriction of credit). The Federal Reserve Board, on the other hand, disliked general restrictions and insisted on taking qualitative actions against stock-market loans. As a result, although quantitative restrictions were tried briefly during 1928, little was done to stop the stock-market inflation. Even today it is difficult to ascertain who was "right." Either quantitative or qualitative controls might have reduced the speculative fever if they had been applied soon enough. However, with authority divided between New York and Washington, the system was completely immobilized. For example, on the day in 1929 when the board appealed for a reduction in stock-market loans, Charles Mitchell, a director of the New York Federal Reserve Bank, announced that his bank (the National City) was willing to place an additional $25,000,000 on the call market. The result of hesitancy and divided authority was, not too surprisingly, the collapse of 1929.

The depression too brought with it proof of the inability of the system to cope with severe economic crises. In 1929, the system attempted to ease the monetary situation; however, all they could do was to make it easier for banks to lend. In this instance, the permissive controls failed. Moreover, throughout the depression, because of conflicts over motives and goals, the board frequently failed even to utilize the tools they did possess. Between October 1931 and February 1932, for example, the bank actually raised the rediscount rate to halt the flow of gold out of the United States. Moreover, throughout much of the period the Board feared an inflation (though how any informed person could have feared inflation with 13,000,000 unemployed is hard to understand). As a result, the rediscount rate was increased several times, and in 1936 reserve requirements were actually increased to mop up excess reserves and reduce inflationary pressures.

Despite the policy of the period, the banking acts of 1933 and 1935 did much to strengthen the commercial banks, and gave the United States its first true central bank. The Act of 1933 increased the required capitalization for national banks and increased the scope of the Federal Reserve System by permitting savings and Morris-Plan banks to join. Moreover, it attempted to sever the close connections between the commercial banks and the stock market by forcing banks to divest themselves of their security affiliates (see Chapter 13) and by giving the board the power to refuse a member bank credit if that bank made an undue number of speculative loans. Finally, it legalized the Open-Market Committee and formalized its composition. The Act of 1935 went even further toward reconstructing the entire system of central-bank controls. The scope of the Federal Reserve System was further broadened by requiring membership of all state banks with deposits of more than $1 million. The Federal Reserve Board was reconstituted as the Board of Governors. The new board was less subject to political pressure than the old, and it was granted authority to direct the open-market and rediscount activities of the district banks. Moreover, the board was permitted to set reserve requirements.

For the first time, central control replaced the separate powers of the twelve district banks. The law had been changed to grant full central-banking powers to the Federal Reserve System, but the system's performance since 1935 has indicated that American central-bank problems have not been completely solved.

During World War II, the bank acted efficiently as a financial agent for the government; and the system of wartime controls largely eliminated the need for economic stabilization. In 1946, however, the economy was faced with an incipient inflation engendered by the wartime heritage of liquid assets and pent-up consumer demand. Although the newly reworked system should have been ideally designed to cope with the problem, the system was faced with the same conflict of interest that had limited its effectiveness in 1919. Although sound economic policy would have dictated tighter money and higher interest rates, the Treasury demanded low rates to reduce the interest charges on the federal debt. Because of its commitments to the Treasury, the system's hands were tied from 1946 to 1951. At that time the two institutions reached something of an accord, and since then the system has had more flexibility in the use of its powers.

Overall, the record of the Federal Reserve System since its inception has not been as good as one might wish. Many of the defects in the original law have been changed, but even today the system has not been completely freed of its commitments to the government. More importantly, the political pressure against any bank action for higher interest rates and tight money has been sufficient to limit the system's effectiveness during periods of inflation. Because of these defects, and those inherent in monetary policy, while the system will probably continue to do yeoman service in other central-banking functions, it will likely be incapable by itself of maintaining economic stability.

12–5. *Appendix: The Monetary Standard*

In our discussion of the monetary system we have studiously avoided the subject of the monetary standard—that is, the way "precious metals," gold and silver, have been priced in American currency. We have done this because of our concentration upon economic rather than social and political aspects of the nation's growth and development. We do not intend to rehash all the fantastic, amusing, muddleheaded, and largely ill-conceived policies related to the problem of the monetary standard. Nor do we intend to resurrect the heroes and villains of these long-dead controversies. But we do wish briefly to examine the bare facts of this aspect of our monetary history. For the "romance of silver," or of gold, or both, the reader is urged to consult a general American history book.

From the beginning of its history as a nation, America, like France and some other European nations, had a bimetallic standard; that is, the legal tender (generally, money which the government would accept in payment of taxes) was defined in both silver and gold. The inspiration for American bimetallism is usually credited to Robert Morris and Thomas Jefferson. Under the terms of the Coinage Act of 1792, the Congress instructed the United States Mint to buy each ounce of standard gold offered at a price equal to fifteen ounces of standard silver. Since other countries had legal prices for precious metals at their own mints (or treasuries), the United States dollar could be valued in foreign currency by its gold (or silver) content.

This bimetallic system lasted in law until 1900. During the long period of 1792–1900, the standard for the currency had a bizarre life. The original valuation of an ounce of gold as 15 ounces of silver, or 15 to 1, was too low relative to the world-market price of gold. Gold was "undervalued" and, according to the workings of Gresham's Law (light coins will tend to drive heavier coins of the same denominations out of circulation), the gold coinage did not circulate. In fact, in some states certain foreign coins were actually made legal tender. In 1834 Congress attempted to rectify the undervaluation of gold and set a new mint price at 16.002 to 1 (in 1837 a further adjustment set the mint price at 15.988 ounces of silver to one ounce of gold). Following the California gold discoveries (and those of Australia in the 1850's), this price proved to be too high; and silver, being undervalued in terms of gold, became extremely scarce in circulation.

It was during the period of silver undervaluation that all metallic standards were abandoned temporarily by the rival governments of the Civil War period. Specie payments were finally resumed in 1879 on all currency, including the unretired greenbacks,[1] according to the terms of the Gold Resumption Act of 1874. The mint ceased coining silver dollars in 1873 (the Crime of '73) but, as a sop to the silver-mining interests and to the inflationists,[2] acts passed in 1878 (the Bland-Allison Act, amended in 1886) and in 1890 (the

[1] The currency of the Union government, a purely paper issue which reached a maximum circulation of $415 million in 1864.

[2] These forces in American history, from the Greenback Party and the Populists through William Jennings Bryan down to the Silver Purchase Act of 1934, have provided not only a tradition rich in eccentricity and oddball economics, but they are the direct forerunners of the modern bias toward "cheap money."

Sherman Silver Purchase Act) provided for the purchase of some $500 million of silver at above-market prices by the Treasury from 1878 to 1893.

In 1900, the Gold Standard Act ended the long and checkered life of American bimetallism (although we had been on a *de facto* gold standard since the resumption in 1879) and placed the United States currency on a single-metal standard. Gold was then valued at the mint at $20.67 per standard ounce. This price lasted until the United States suspended gold payments in 1933. In that year the price of gold was raised to nearly $35 an ounce (hence, at that price, compared to the previous price, the dollar had been "devalued" in terms of gold by 40.94 per cent). This price was reached by stages in 1933 through gold-market operations conducted by the Reconstruction Finance Corporation under the terms of the Thomas Amendment to the Agricultural Adjustment Act of 1933. The Gold Reserve Act of 1934 *required* the President to reduce the gold content of the dollar to not less than 50 per cent and not more than 60 per cent of the old price. That price had already been reached by the earlier gold-market operations, so that price was then fixed in law. The power of the President to change the price of gold was renewed by Congress in 1937, 1939, and 1941. It was not used. Since that time the price of gold has remained fixed and the standard dollar has been equal to 1/35 of an ounce of standard gold. To change that price would require an act of Congress.

In 1933 we abandoned the gold standard in fact, but a fiction of "gold backing" was maintained by requiring the Federal Reserve System to own gold certificates[3] equal to 35 per cent of its demand deposits and 40 per cent of its issues of Federal Reserve notes, even though under the law the Federal Reserve banks cannot own monetary gold themselves. In 1945 Congress reduced this requirement to a "gold backing" equal to 25 per cent of all Federal Reserve demand liabilities. That is the present (1964) state of the standard. It might be called a "managed-paper currency" standard, or a "partially gold-backed paper currency" standard, or some other appropriate name. It is neither a silver standard, a gold standard, nor a bimetallic standard. As the reader can readily see, the present United States currency standard reflects a historical experience with money standards that is indeed rich and varied.

[3] Essentially receipts given by the Treasury for gold, just as the common silver certificate is such a receipt for silver (read the face of the $1 bill in your wallet.)

Suggested Readings

BACH, GEORGE L. *Federal Reserve Policy Making.* New York: Alfred A. Knopf, 1950.

CHANDLER, LESTER V. *Benjamin Strong: Central Banker.* Washington D.C.: Brookings Institution, 1958.

SMITH, WALTER B. *Economic Aspects of the Second Bank of the United States.* Cambridge, Mass: Harvard University Press, 1953.

STUDENSKI, PAUL, and KROOS, HERMAN E. *Financial History of the United States.* New York: McGraw-Hill Book Co., Inc., 1952.

Chapter 13 VOLUNTARY SAVINGS: THE DEVELOPMENT OF NON-BANK INTERMEDIARIES AND THE CAPITAL MARKET

13–1. *Introduction*

In the previous chapters it was shown that the commercial banks, because of their power to create money, could speed the process of capital accumulation by forcing savings from the incomes of unwilling consumers. However, all savings are not involuntary; instead, an important segment of total savings flows voluntarily from those income recipients who choose to save rather than spend some portion of their income. In a Robinson Crusoe economy, the same individual would perform the acts of savings and investment. In such an economy, the level of desired savings would always be equal to the level of desired investment and the capital would always flow into the most desired use. As an economy develops and specialization increases, the savings and investment decisions become separated; and, unless some market institutions evolve, the risk of an imperfect utilization of savings becomes very real. This chapter is devoted to a discussion of the evolution and the role of such financial market institutions in the American economy.

In the absence of perfectly competitive product and factor markets and an omniscient central-banking system, the evolution of nonbank financial institutions can increase the rate of savings and, even more important, can alter the uses to which these savings are to be put. In the absence of institutions specializing in the transfer of capital from the saver to the investor, the investment alternatives open to any saver are limited to those within his own range of experience. Thus, societies without financial intermediaries have been marked by higher relative investment in land, housing, and other land-associated industries than relative profitability would have dictated. English history provides an excellent example of the effects on the allocation of capital of such an economic system. Although as early as the fifteenth century there were in

England several individual fortunes each large enough to have financed the entire industrial revolution several times over, as late as the early nineteenth century these new industries, despite their high profitability, continued to suffer from capital starvation. At the same time, industries closely associated with the land (agriculture, brewing, milling, and mining) were receiving the bulk of new investment, although net returns there were close to zero.

In short, given the risks that people attach to the unknown, it is only the very sophisticated saver who would be willing to place his funds in investments far removed in distance or experience from his own environment. Nonbank financial intermediaries can, by placing themselves between the saver and the investor, substitute known alternatives for investments outside the saver's immediate knowledge.[1] In addition, the evolution of a formal capital market can promote direct investment by increasing the saver's knowledge of his investment alternatives and making these alternatives more liquid (and thus, in some sense, "safer") than they would have been in the absence of a formal market.

In addition to altering the form of savings, the evolution of certain financial institutions can also increase an economy's propensity to save. It is obvious that, to the extent that savings are interest-elastic (though recent studies indicating that savings are a residual would tend to deny this premise), the rate of savings will be lower if the market is so sectored that investments offering the greatest returns are unable to make effective bids for new savings. More important, if one assumes (as appears highly likely) that there is an increasing risk to the saver associated with the growth of cash hoards, then an increase in hoards (even though offset by loans by a commercial banking system) would lead to a shift from savings to consumption, a shift that would not occur if the savers had a safe depository for their funds.

One word of caution. Despite the evolution of an imposing list of intermediaries, perfect capital mobility has not been attained. Because of custom and legal restriction, intermediaries are frequently either unable or unwilling to invest in the most profitable alterna-

[1] Throughout the remainder of this book the term "nonbank intermediary" will be used to describe those financial institutions that collect savings from individuals and in turn invest these savings in some investment portfolio, but that do not possess the power to create money. This list would include, for example, savings banks, insurance companies, pension funds, and so forth. Logically, the savings departments of commercial banks should also be included, but they have been omitted in order to avoid confusion.

tives. Despite a segment of the market that is profit-oriented, this sectoring frequently prohibits the attainment of an optimal distribution of capital.

13–2. *The Nonbank Intermediaries*

Although we do not have adequate aggregate data on the importance of nonbank intermediaries during the nineteenth century, contemporary chronicles make it apparent that these institutions played an important role in the process of capital accumulation. Table 13–1, taken from Professor Goldsmith's excellent study of financial intermediaries, indicates that by the end of the nineteenth century the nonbank intermediaries were providing about four fifths of the finance flowing into the nation's nonfarm mortgages, about

TABLE 13–1

RELATIVE SHARES OF HOLDING OF PRIVATE NONBANK FINANCIAL INTERMEDIARIES IN TOTAL VOLUME OF SELECTED INVESTMENT OUTSTANDING*

Investment	*1900*	*1952*
1. Nonfarm household mortgages	60.4%	57.2%
2. Nonfarm non-real estate debt (excluding tax accruals)	8.2	28.6
3. Farm mortgages	25.6	26.3
4. Corporate bonds (domestic)	24.7	86.1
5. Corporate stock (domestic)	6.8	20.3
6. Government issues		
(1) State and local	49.1	18.7
(2) Federal	11.9	18.7

* Includes: mutual savings banks, private life insurance companies, fraternal insurance organizations, private noninsured pension funds, fire and marine insurance companies, casualty and miscellaneous insurance companies, savings banks' life insurance departments, investment companies, personal-trust department.

Source: Raymond W. Goldsmith, *Financial Intermediaries in the American Economy Since 1900* (Princeton, N.J.: Princeton University Press, for the National Bureau of Economic Research, 1958), pp. 195, 201, 210, 224, 225, 262, 269.

two fifths of that into state and local issues, and over one quarter of the total into farm mortgages and corporate bonds. This distribution becomes particularly significant if one remembers that during the nineteenth century much of the nation's capital was pouring into construction and state and local governments were bearing the significant proportion of the expenditures on social-overhead capital.

The nonbank intermediaries certainly played an important role in our early development, but their importance has increased every decade since 1900. Thus, by 1952 these institutions were making available sufficient claims on resources to finance almost 90 per cent of the outstanding domestic corporation bonds, a quarter of the nonfarm-nonmortgage credit, and a fourth of the stock issued of domestic corporations while, at the same time, retaining their former position in the mortgage market.

a) ***The Mutual Savings Banks.***[2] From the point of chronology, the first nonbank intermediary to play a significant role in the process of capital accumulation in America was the mutual savings bank. The rise of mutual savings banks owes much to the character of the New England upper classes in the early years of the nineteenth century. These groups had long been concerned with the condition of the lower classes, but their desire to aid those less fortunate than themselves was tempered by a fear that outright charity would make the poor even less willing to help themselves. Attempts to implement this dual philosophy led to a whole series of self-help experiments, of which the savings banks were probably the most successful.[3]

These early savings banks (the first was established in Philadelphia in 1816) were organized on the mutual principle. In theory ownership lay in the hands of the depositors, although in fact control resided with the "men of substance" who served the institutions as officers and directors. In their formative years the banks were literally nonprofit institutions operated solely for the benefit of the poor. They had no paid officers and the business affairs were conducted by the directors who received no remuneration above, perhaps, a feeling of satisfaction. Later, however, as their size and importance increased, management was assumed by professional bankers and paid staffs were employed.

The early banks were well managed and successful. Although legal restraints and a certain provincialism in their investment criteria tended to hinder the geographic movement of capital, they did (because of their fine safety and earnings record) encourage the poor to save and save in a form that could be transformed into productive investment. The safety (and safety is always a prime motive for the small saver) of the mutuals during an era of numerous commercial bank failures is nothing short of phenomenal. In the case of the Savings Bank of Baltimore, for example, between its organization in 1818 and 1854 its losses totaled $1.54. When the bank was threatened by a run, disaster was averted because the city's business-

[2] A savings bank, unlike a commercial bank, can accept only time deposits. Thus it cannot make loans by creating money and can act only as an intermediary between saver and investor and not as a creator of savings.

[3] Savings banks had already proved very successful in England and Scotland

men were willing to pledge their personal funds in support of the bank.

Some quantitative impression of the size of the savings bank movement can be seen in the fact that by 1860 there were 278 such banks with assets of almost $150,000,000 (see Table 13–2). Indeed, some of the banks were even more important than these figures suggest. Those located in the larger cities were giants among contemporary enterprises. In 1860 nine of the ten largest business organizations in the nation were savings banks (in that year the banks in Boston, Baltimore, New York, and Philadelphia all reported deposits in excess of $6,000,000 each).

Because of their ability to provide their depositors with both safety and sizable returns, the savings banks became an important instrument of capital mobilization. Two factors did, however, work to limit the geographical scope of their capital-mobilization efforts.

TABLE 13–2

THE GROWTH OF SAVINGS BANKS IN THE UNITED STATES

Year	*No. of Banks*	*No. of Depositors*	*Deposits*
1800	0	0	0
1820	10	8,635	$ 1,138,576
1830	36	38,035	6,973,304
1840	61	78,701	14,051,520
1850	108	251,354	43,431,130
1860	278	693,870	149,277,504

Source: *Annual Report of the Controller of the Currency,* December 4, 1916 (Washington, D.C.: GPO, 1917), Vol. I, pp. 85–86.

First, for some reason—perhaps related to the culture or the class structure of the period—the savings bank movement was geographically localized. There were no mutuals south of Maryland nor were there many west of Pennsylvania. Second, both cultural and legal restrictions tended to limit the banks' investment horizon to their home states; and, as a result, they contributed little to the interstate mobility of capital. Thus, although the banks effectively mobilized small savings in the Northeast, those of the remainder of the country were largely untouched. Because of such investment policies, not even the savings of the Northeast were made available to the rest of the economy.

Although the mutuals continued to grow after the Civil War,

they dwindled in importance relative to other nonbank intermediaries, and today they are less important than either the life insurance companies or the savings and loan associations (see Table 13–3). The relative decline of the savings banks can probably be traced in part to a decline in the need for self-help societies as per-capita income rose, the increased role of government in social welfare, and the decrease in income inequality—all of which have characterized America since the Civil War. In addition, the banks have lost their competitive position because of the restrictions placed by law and custom on their investment portfolios and because of the competition of the life insurance companies. The portfolio restrictions weaken the mutual position vis-à-vis the savings and loan associations; and the insurance companies feature contract savings and a

TABLE 13–3
TOTAL ASSETS OF SELECTED NONBANK INTERMEDIARIES
1900–1958
(In Millions)

Year	*Life Ins. Companies*	*Savings and Loan Associations*	*Savings Banks*	*Postal Savings*
1900	$ 1,742	$ 571	$ 2,624	$ —
1910	3,876	932	4,481	
1920	7,320	2,520	5,619	.1 (1911)
1930	18,880	8,829	10,295	157
1940	30,802	5,733	11,952	175
1950	64,020	16,846	22,385	1,293
1958	107,580	55,115	37,779	3,035
1962	133,291	93,816	46,086	1,212
				583

Sources: Institute of Life Insurance, *Life Insurance Fact Book 1959*, p. 65. United States Savings and Loan League, *Savings and Loan Fact Book 1960*, p. 70. *Historical Statistics of the United States, 1789–1945* (Washington D.C.: GPO, 1949), pp. 226, 272. *Statistical Abstract.*

thorough confusion (at least in the saver's mind) between savings and insurance.

b) ***Life Insurance Companies.*** Life insurance companies can play a key role in the process of capital mobilization because they usually sell their products (life insurance and savings) today for delivery ten, twenty, or thirty years in the future. Unlike other types of insurance companies whose premiums just cover their costs in any year, life insurance companies (even on straight-life policies) charge more than cost in the early years of the policy and, as a result, have long-term funds available for investment. In addition, the life insurance companies have at times combined insurance with savings programs. In these cases they have available for investment the savings portion of the premium for the length of the contract.

Although the idea of life insurance is not new, it became important in the United States only at a relatively late date. The Presbyterian Ministers Fund of Philadelphia was writing life insurance during the 1750's; however, it was not until the middle of the nineteenth century that life insurance companies became an important force in the processes of capital accumulation and mobilization. In part, growth awaited the accumulation of vital statistics and reliable death tables; more important, however, were rising income levels (permitting people time to think about the future) and the innovation of new insurance techniques. Most important among these innovations was the application of the mutual principle to insurance. By the 1840's, the success of the savings banks had convinced the public of the desirability of mutual financial institutions. In fact, so firm was the faith in mutual management that, during the second half of the century, the insurance companies were granted a much freer hand by policyholders and government than common sense would have dictated. Although the companies did, in fact, frequently abuse this trust, the growth of life insurance sales did facilitate the accumulation of capital in the hands of an entrepreneurial group willing to make it available to business and industry.

In addition to the organization of mutual companies, other innovations also speeded the growth of the life insurance industry during the last three decades of the nineteenth century (a period that saw life insurance in force increase from a few million dollars in 1860 to over $7½ billion in 1900). Until the year 1860, the typical mutual company collected premiums based on actuarial estimates of the death rates. If in any year these premiums exceeded the amount necessary to pay the firm's expenses and maintain the company's reserves, the excess was returned to the policyholders in dividends. Following the Civil War, however, a new type of insurance, "tontine," was introduced; and the subsequent growth of the industry was closely correlated with the sales of tontine insurance. The new policy did not pay the holder a dividend amounting to the extra earnings on his policy; in fact, it frequently paid no dividends at all until the term of the policy (usually five or fifteen years) had elapsed. At the end of the period, persons with effective policies divided the accumulated dividends, heirs of the dead received only the face of the policy, and those whose policies had lapsed received little or nothing. While tontine insurance possesses many merits in theory, it fell into disrepute in the latter decades of the nineteenth century. In the post-bellum decades salesmen were frequently overly optimistic in their estimates of the potential end-of-policy dividends and the companies tended to fritter away earnings in unwise investments and lavish expenses. Thus, the policyholders oftentimes were paid much less than they had been promised. But the quantity of capital available for investment increased both because of the increase of sales associated with tontine and because the companies retained the earnings for a longer period of time.

A third innovation of the century was industrial insurance. These were small-value policies with premiums payable weekly or monthly, designed to provide life insurance for the increasingly important groups of unskilled and semiskilled workers. These policies were marked by an extremely high lapse rate; and, later, considerable public resentment was evidenced against the treatment of defaulting policyholders. Despite this shortcoming, industrial insurance did permit the mobilization of the funds of small savers that would in all probability otherwise have been lost to the market.

By the turn of the twentieth century the insurance companies were faced by steadily mounting public pressure for reform. Most states, at an early date, had established regulatory bodies to protect the policyholders; and if they had done their job it seems probable that capital could have been accumulated without the social costs actually incurred. Unfortunately, during much of the period the insurance companies were able to bring sufficient political pressure to bear to prevent the regulatory commissions from acting effectively. In one instance, a disgruntled policyholder, after being denied any help from the local insurance commission, was informed that he could not quote from the proceedings of the commission because the entire minutes had been copyrighted by the insurance company in question. Again, evidence indicates that in a single decade a New York company paid one lobbyist $1,312,197 to prevent any tightening of the insurance regulations (it is interesting to note that the money was charged off as an operating expense by the company.)

By the turn of the century, the life insurance companies had assets of $1¾ billion and had made a large portion of their accumulation available to business and industry. However, the public clamor against the policies of the companies threatened the future of the industry. Public resentment finally culminated in the Armstrong Committee investigations in New York in 1905. These investigations uncovered those business practices previously alluded to and other equally unethical practices. As a result of this careful investigation, the insurance laws of the state of New York were extensively rewritten to provide full protection for the policyholder. These New York laws subsequently became the model for regulation in many other states. The new laws prohibited tontine insurance, they required at least a partial refund to be made to the holders of lapsed policies, they prohibited the expenditure of company funds on lobbying activity, and they greatly strengthened the powers of the state regulatory commission. Although the insurance companies bitterly resented the new laws, these statutes did much to reestablish the faith of the American saver in life insurance and to provide the basis for the rapid growth of the industry in the twentieth century.

Table 13–3 provides some evidence on the growth of insurance companies since 1900. An examination of the table indicates that in the past half century insurance companies have become the dominant nonbank intermediary and, since the 1930's, have had assets greater than the next two largest intermediaries combined. Moreover, because of the nature of the insurance contract, the life insurance companies are not faced with the liquidity considerations that dominate the portfolio policies of the commercial and savings banks. They are, therefore, able to make funds available for a much longer period than these other institutions. As a result, they have become the most important source of "brick-and-mortar" money for industry as well as an important source of other types of long-term capital. In the late nineteenth and early twentieth centuries the life insurance companies were an important source of capital for the railroad industry then completing the transport network. More recently, as the capital requirements of the railroads have declined the insurance companies have moved increasingly into the public-utilities and industrials markets and have become a major capital source for these two growing sectors. Moreover, throughout the whole period the insurance companies made important contributions to the financing of commercial and residential construction.

The growth of the life-insurance companies in the twentieth century, while making a vast pool of finance available to industry, has caused certain distortions in the allocation of these funds. Since the turn of the century the companies have been marked by a growing conservatism in their investment policies. This trend may be traced to a multitude of factors (restrictive investment regulation, lack of competition in the industry, an ever-increasing belief among investment officers in the trust nature of the insurance contract, and so on), but whatever the cause it has resulted in an inability or an unwillingness to make certain types of investments. For example, the insurance companies have made very little contribution to the growth of new industry or to the development of foreign operations, and they have appeared much more willing to absorb debt than equity issues. Since the life insurance companies exercise a position of considerable importance in the long-term market, their investment policies tend to distort the allocation of funds between firms and, at the same time, to distort the capital structure of particular firms.

During the past few years certain new trends are noticeable and, if these continue, there appears to be hope that the worst effects of the allocation problem will ultimately be alleviated. In the first place, because of the fine record of the industry over the past half century, state governments have appeared more willing to broaden the legal investment alternatives (in 1951, for example, the New York state law was changed to permit at least some investment in common stocks). In the second place, the recent growth of stock life insurance companies has brought a resurgence of entrepreneurship to the industry, and the new competition has forced even the old-line companies to become alert to new investment opportunities. Finally, the long period of inflation has increased public interest in some form of inflationary hedge, and such an interest could either cause a relative decline in the importance of the insurance companies or cause the companies to experiment more fully with some form of variable-annuity policy.[4] Either result would induce more savings to flow into equity investments.

c) ***The Savings and Loan Associations.*** Although the savings and loan associations trace their origins back to the cooperative movement of the 1840's (see Chapter 16), they have exercised a significant influence in the capital markets only during the past quarter century. Today, however, they stand second in importance among the nonbank intermediaries. Their tremendous growth in this recent period can probably be traced to four factors: the attitude of the commercial bankers, the activities of the federal government,

[4] A variable-annuity policy instead of yielding a fixed number of dollars per year would represent only a claim on some fraction of an equity portfolio whose value (and yield) would fluctuate with the state of the stock market and the economy.

the booming post–World War II real estate market, and dynamic entrepreneurial leadership. Since the Civil War, commercial bankers have frequently pursued an extremely conservative investment policy. This fact, coupled with a lack of competition that has been a frequent result of state banking regulations, has given the savings and loan associations a profitable area in which to operate. For example, in those areas where competition among the commercial banks has been insufficient to force them into mortgage loans, the savings and loans have provided this needed competition, and they have at times acquired a lion's share of the business. The federal government has contributed to the growth of the savings and loan associations both directly and indirectly. During the 1930's public confidence in the associations was badly shaken when the association suffered more than any other form of intermediary (in that decade some 1,706 savings and loan associations failed, with losses to stockholders in excess of $200 million). Since then, the government, through the Federal Savings and Loan Insurance Company, has provided deposit insurance somewhat similar to that given the commercial banks by the Federal Deposit Insurance Corporation; and, as a result, savers have largely regained their confidence in the savings and loan associations. In addition, limits placed by the Federal Reserve System on the interest rates commercial banks could pay on savings deposits (limits established during the low-interest period of the 1930's and not increased until the mid-1950's) have played into the hands of the less-regulated savings and loan associations. The postwar real estate boom too has proved helpful to the savings and loan associations since most of their investments are, by definition, directed into mortgage credit. Finally, these institutions have demonstrated a considerably greater degree of entrepreneurial ability than have their more well-established competitors.

Despite their growth during the past fifteen years, it is doubtful if the savings and loans will be able to continue to grow as rapidly as they have in the past. The recent increase in the maximum interest payments permitted the commercial banks, coupled with a resurgence of entrepreneurship there and in the life insurance companies, should tend to make these latter institutions relatively more attractive to savers.

d) ***Miscellaneous Institutions.*** The United States in the twentieth century has seen a proliferation of financial intermediaries. In general they serve an economic function similar to the institutions already discussed and no attempt will be made to consider each type. Several have, however, left their mark on American development and three of these will be touched on here.

The Postal Savings System was organized by act of Congress in 1910. At that time politicians in both parties thought that such a system would, by providing the small saver with a safe place for his accumulations, play an important role in encouraging thrift and savings. The system has, however, never played the role envisioned for it by its founders. Its growth coincided with the development of other financial intermediaries, and these other forms appear to have been more attractive to the savers of the nation. Certainly, the system designed almost solely for the small saver could have served as a useful tool in capital mobilization. Its required reserves were small (5 per cent) and, although the law required 30 per cent of assets to be invested in government bonds, the rest could be deposited in national and state banks where it would swell the loan potential of these institutions. Since the system failed to attract a significant volume of savings, its primary importance today is the example it provides of a governmental attempt to establish a system of public intermediaries.

During the 1920's the investment trust played an important role in the process of capital accumulation, and in the future it again may be significant. In principle the investment trust is not new, and such an institution certainly provides many benefits for the small saver. In its simplest form, the investment trust pools the funds of a number of individuals and with this pool buys a diverse list of securities (usually equities). The pool members hold shares in the investment trust, and these shares represent some fractional claim on the total investments of the trust. Thus, the small saver is able to place his funds in the equity market but, at the same time, retain the benefits of portfolio diversification.

In the United States the investment company did not become a significant factor in the capital markets until the 1920's. By 1927, some 160 such trusts were operating, and between 1927 and 1929 an additional 591 were organized. In that latter year alone, the trusts issued over $3 billion in securities to savers. By the time of the stock market crash of 1929, their assets were in excess of $8 billion (making them, then, as large as the savings and loan associations and almost as large as the savings banks). Unfortunately, many of the trusts were characterized by weak management that caught the speculative fever of the period. As a result, the companies were capitalized in a manner designed to attain maximum "leverage" and pursued investment policies designed to yield the highest capital gains possible.[5] Frequently their investments were in shares in other investment trusts (for it was their prices that were rising most rapidly) whose value rested more on expectations than on their ability to earn profits. Moreover, although the leverage provided by the capital structure tended to increase profits in times of rising security prices, it could serve equally well to increase losses in periods of falling prices—and stock prices fell drastically between 1929 and 1932. The effect of these investment and capitalization policies can be seen in the history of the price of Goldman Sachs stocks. The shares issued in 1929 for 104 were selling in 1932 for 1.75.

The performance of the investment trusts during the stock market crash so shook savers' confidence that by 1940 total assets of the trusts had fallen to less than $2 billion. Since that time, however, closer government regulation, better management, and a rising stock market have contributed to a new surge of growth. By the mid-1950's, the trusts had almost regained their 1929 size.

The most important recent development in the capital markets has probably been the growth of private pension funds. Currently, savings through pension funds (including both insured and uninsured plans) amount to somewhere between $2 and $3 billion per year, and the total accumulation of such funds amounts to over $20 billion. This growth has been largely the result of business' increasing awareness of the typical American's desire for security and a continued pressure by the labor unions. Pension funds, almost nonexistent before World War II, have since that time represented an ever-increasing share of the total wage package. Since payments into the funds are made during the working life of an employee and are not withdrawn until his retirement, there is a considerable pool of funds available for investment (this is particularly true in an expanding industry where payments are continually in excess of withdrawals). Unfortunately, because of the fiduciary character of these pension funds, the tendency has been to invest only in the safest alternatives (most frequently in government bonds). These accumulations, therefore, have been only indirectly (through releasing other funds from the government-securities market) available to finance business and industry. Here too, the future may hold con-

[5] Leverage refers to a capital structure containing both debt and equity finance. The interest charges on debt instruments are fixed, and when earnings exceed these charges all extra profits accrue to the equity holders. Thus, in periods of high profits the greater the ratio of debt to equity the greater are the profits (as a per cent) of equity.

siderable hope for improvement, since the threat of inflation has caused an increased interest in variable annuities and this would, by definition, mean investment in business equities.

e) ***Summary.*** There can be little doubt that the growth of nonbank intermediaries in the United States has greatly increased the ability of the economy to mobilize capital. However, some of the benefits of capital mobility may well have been lessened because of the investment policies of the intermediaries. Regulation (either by law or custom) has tended to force intermediaries to make only the most conservative investments. Because the credit market is not perfect (instead it appears to be fairly highly sectored), such a bias in investment policies acts against an optimum allocation of funds (that is, a movement of funds toward their highest returns). Recently the intermediaries, under a gradual loosening of government regulation and the threat of inflation, have appeared more willing to make "risk investment." If this trend continues, the economy may in the future be spared the worst costs of misallocation.

13–3. *The Securities Markets*

Financial intermediaries are not the only institutions that aid the flow of capital from savers to investors. As an economy develops the importance of direct transfers increases; but if direct transfers are to be efficient, it is usually necessary to have yet another institution, a formal securities market. There persons and firms with symbolic capital to sell (investing units) can meet persons and firms with excess funds (savings units) who are willing to buy these instruments—at a price.[6] The market facilitates the flow of information; and, while the market cannot affect the safety of funds invested in symbolic instruments, it can greatly increase their liquidity. The liquidity benefit is easily illustrated by the experience of investors on Black Thursday in 1929. On that day, while the market collapsed, some 13 million shares were sold by investors who wanted out and, by definition, 13 million shares were purchased by someone else. One need only compare the financial experience of an unlisted firm with that of a firm that has acquired access to the formal markets to realize how important the securities markets are to the capital transfer process.

Although formal securities markets originated long before 1860, they did not play a major role in capital mobilization, except

[6] Symbolic capital refers to all paper claims on assets. These would include both stocks (equities) and bonds (debt instruments).

for governments and the transportation industry, until after the Civil War. In their embryonic stage, because of difficulties of transportation and communication, markets began to grow in each of the major cities. As early as 1797 the New York brokers formally agreed on commission charges and, thus, began to move along the path that was ultimately to lead to the world's largest securities market. Twenty years later they took another giant step by organizing the New York Stock Exchange Board, a self-governing body empowered to establish rules for securities trading among its members. By 1830 well-organized (but largely locally oriented) markets were also functioning in Boston, Philadelphia, and New Orleans, and a few years later in St. Louis and Chicago as well.

In their formative years these capital markets largely handled government, utility, and transport bonds. Although Boston was generally regarded as the leading industrial capital market of the period, industrials were only infrequently traded even there. Even the semiofficial market publication warned its readers not to rely too heavily on its industrial quotations because they were so seldom traded; and the situation in New York was even less favorable to the mobilization of industrial capital. As late as 1835 no industrials were listed on the "big board," and in 1856 less than twenty appear. Moreover, although much of the economy's post-bellum industrial growth was financed through issues floated on the New York exchange, it was not until World War I that bankers specializing in stock market loans accepted industrial stocks as collateral on the same basis as other issues.

Today we are accustomed to buying symbolic capital in a myriad of forms, ranging from common stock through various types of preferred equities to junior subordinated debentures to senior mortgage bonds. The nineteenth century saw the evolution of most of these forms. Common stock issues were widely used as soon as the corporate form became generally adopted (the New England textile industry was, for example, financed through the sales of common stock), but preferred shares did not appear until the 1830's.[7] At that time, railroads and canal companies in financial difficulties began to market these instruments for the first time, but it was not until the 1870's that preferred stock was widely innovated in industrial finance. Bonds, too, only slowly became used as instruments of industrial capital mobilization. Although state governments had issued

[7] Although common stock issues were widely used, such sales were very frequently direct transfer processes between the issuing firm and ultimate buyer, thus bypassing the formal market. Almost all of the textile issues were of this sort.

bonds since the revolution, and such instruments were frequently used in the finance of railroads, roads, and canals during the first half of the nineteenth century, they were not used in industrial finance until the time of the Civil War. The slow evolution of industrial financial techniques probably reflects not a lack of knowledge but a lack of need, for in the period there were few investors willing to hold symbolic industrial capital.

The most important step in the development of our all-pervasive capital market was the evolution of a single market to replace the complex of small, loosely connected markets that was characteristic of this country until the 1840's. A study of the capital markets in 1835 indicates that both State Street (Boston) and Chestnut Street (Philadelphia) were at least as important as Wall Street. Twenty-five years later, however, even the most biased observer would have to admit that, though local markets continued to exist, Wall Street was *the* American capital market. Although improvements in communications and transportation were necessary conditions for this concentration, they were not sufficient by themselves to bring it about.

Foremost among the factors working to strengthen the New York market vis-à-vis those in the other cities was the development of a money market in New York. If a capital market is to function smoothly, there must be funds available to finance the market transactions; and these funds can best be provided if the capital market coexists with a short-term money market. In the case of New York, an active short-term money market was one of the by-products of the city's role in international and interregional trade. With the opening of the Erie Canal, New York became the major entrepôt between the Midwest and the rest of the world. Because of the volume of trade, New York merchants were in almost constant need of funds to cover their purchases; as a result, their commercial paper became an attractive investment to the New York banks and, through these banks, to commercial banks across the country. With large country-bank balances in their vaults, it was easy for the New York banks to begin to make call loans, and such demand loans were admirably well designed to serve a capital market whose traders were in continual need of very short-term funds to facilitate the purchase and sale of securities.[8] It is interesting to note that, aside from New York, London is the only other city with a continuously operating

[8] A call loan is a loan granted on hypothecation of formal securities without fixed maturity. Instead of a fixed term, either lender or borrower can terminate the loan agreement at their discretion.

money market capable of serving the needs of the capital markets and, equally interesting, that London and New York have been the world's dominant capital markets for the past century.

The New York call-loan market, although it began to function in the 1830's, did not reach maturity until after the Civil War. In that later period the market drew primarily on three sources of funds. First, and most important, were the funds of the New York banks themselves; second were the reserves of the country banks (the National Banking Act had permitted the country banks to keep part of their reserves with the New York banks—see Chapters 11 and 12); and third were the funds placed on loan by the city banks for their country correspondents. The call loans made for security brokers on stock-exchange collateral continued to grow and by 1912 totaled more than $750,000,000. These loans provided the finance without which the market could not have operated efficiently. However, because of the extreme seasonal and cyclical variability of the country-bank contributions, they tended to destabilize the market (and through the market, the economy).

A second factor necessary to assure New York dominance among the American capital markets was the failure of the Second Bank of the United States. As long as the United States bank was located in Philadelphia, that institution's prestige made Chestnut Street a worthy competitor of Wall Street; but with its collapse in 1842, no other banking system could match New York in size or stability (Boston was perhaps the one exception, but that city possessed none of New York's other advantages). Thus, even before the Civil War, country-bank reserves poured into New York banks, and these funds were an ideal base for stock market credit.

Although the American capital markets had made great strides before Lincoln's election, it was the Civil War that placed these markets in the center of the mobilization process. During the war the federal government borrowed very heavily (by nineteenth-century standards) to finance its defense efforts. For example, between 1860 and 1865 government debt rose from $64,844,000 to $2,677,929,000. The public absorbed these bonds and in so doing became far more accustomed to holding symbolic capital than they ever had been before. The war-formed investment habits carried over into the postwar years, with the result that sales of private issues were much easier. Moreover, the techniques developed to market the huge volume of government securities were also to serve the process of capital mobilization in the later period.

The first wartime attempts by the government to sell bonds clearly indicated that what had been the normal marketing channels would never be adequate to handle the new demands. Therefore, in October of 1862 the government contracted with Jay Cooke, a private banker, to act as general agent for the sale of Treasury bonds. Through the use of subagents, investor education, high-pressure sales techniques, advertising, and a willingness to deal with anyone who had $50 to invest, Cooke and his workers were able to sell $157,000,000 worth of government bonds in nine months, and $362,000,000 in fourteen. After the war, Cooke and others were quick to see the possibilities in his system, and they began to use these "time-tested" techniques in private promotions. With his wartime experience behind him, Cooke and Company became the first large investment house capable of underwriting and marketing the issues of the emerging industrial giants. During the first six years of peace, Cooke's firm had taken the lead in the underwriting and sale of the issues of the Northern Pacific; the Chesapeake and Ohio; the New York, Ontario and Western, as well as several smaller roads. With the collapse of Cooke and Company (along with their Northern Pacific bonds) in 1873, leadership passed into the hands of J. P. Morgan. It was the house of Morgan that undertook the sale of the first issue of United States Steel stock ($1,400,000,000); and, of course, his firm played a leading role in the finance of many other ventures of the period. It was also Morgan who forged the first direct link between the financiers and the management of producing companies by insisting that the underwriters be given seats on the board of directors and an active voice in management. As time passed, these investment houses, desiring additional securities to sell, began to take an active part in the organization of new industrial complexes. Morgan, for example, was largely responsible not only for the security sales but also for the organization of U.S. Steel.

At the end of the war, the volume of securities traded on the nation's capital markets was still relatively small. As late as 1879, 700,000 shares were a record day's sale of stock on the New York exchange; and the 1 million mark was not reached until 1886. Thereafter, however, growth was rapid, and in 1901 a new high (to last as a record until 1916) of 3,281,226 was reached. The impressive gains chalked up by the markets in the thirty-five years after Appomattox were the result, in large measure, of increasing investor sophistication, the innovation of the new marketing techniques proved during the Civil War, the continued development of the call-loan markets, and the rise of the investment banking house. On the other hand, one cannot deny that without the demand for finance engendered by the rapid economic growth of the period, there is little even the most sophisticated market institutions could have done (this is, of course, just one more example of the chicken and the egg problem).

The post-bellum growth of security sales and the resulting increase in capital mobility was not obtained without cost. The cost in terms of increasing economic instability has already been noted. In addition, there were also social costs associated with the issues sold the public through the exchanges and the operations of the exchanges themselves. The New York stock exchange was a voluntary association of securities dealers, and the brokers themselves established membership requirements and operating rules. As a voluntary organization, the governing board did little in the exchange's formative years to discourage the practices that throughout the 19th century made the typical American wary of the "wolves of Wall Street." By 1868, however, the much-publicized activities of Daniel Drew, treasurer of the Erie Railroad (particularly the fraudulent stock issues made during an ownership contest with Commodore Vanderbilt), and others, raised such serious questions in the minds of the American investors that the exchange was forced to attempt more stringent regulations if it were to survive. Beginning with the demand that stock registry be a condition of listing on the board, other regulations followed. Within forty years the exchange had come to require public financial reports from listed companies and had outlawed many of the more flagrant technical abuses of the market itself (including artificial sales entered into to maintain activity—wash sales—and obvious market jiggling).

By the end of World War I the stock exchange had apparently cleaned house to the satisfaction of the American public. During the war the government leaned heavily on bond financing and, because of the Liberty Bond sales, even the smallest investor became aware of symbolic capital. Moreover, the government's "borrow-and-buy" campaign had shown the saver that great gains could be realized from buying securities on margin (the leverage principle again).[9] The stage was set for the speculative boom of the 1920's.

Although the capital markets did suffer from the depression of

[9] A purchase or margin involves making only a small down payment and then pledging the security for a loan to cover the remainder of the purchase price.

1920–21, in the 1920's America became the land of symbolic capital. Table 13–4 shows the increases in corporate issues during the period (over 40 billion as compared with about half that amount in the preceding and following decade), and Table 13–5 shows the even greater increases in capital-market activity. In 1921, for example, 173,000,000 shares were traded, but by 1929 this figure had reached 1,125,000,000. At the same time, the character of the market was undergoing a significant change. Before 1920, government bonds had represented a large proportion of total placements, but during the 1920's such issues represented a steadily declining proportion of the total. For example, although total bond transactions declined from $3,324,000,000 in 1921 to $2,982,000,000 in 1929, corporate bond transactions rose from $1,043,000,000 in the former year to

TABLE 13–4

CORPORATE ISSUES OF SYMBOLIC CAPITAL
1910–1962
(Dollar Amounts in Millions)

Years	(1) *Total*	(2) *Stocks*	(3) (2)/(1)	(4) *Bonds and Short-Term Notes*
1910–1914	$ 8,594	$ 2,375	27.6%	$ 6,219
1915–1919	9,236	3,424	37.1	5,812
1920–1924	15,502	3,577	23.1	12,925
1925–1929	35,201	14,951	42.5	20,250
1930–1934	9,529	2,723	28.6	6,806
1935–1939	13,670	1,811	13.2	11,859
1940–1944	10,686	1,442	13.5	9,244
1945–1949	31,378	6,884	21.9	24,494
1950–1954	38,141	8,331	21.8	29,810
1954–1957	30,372	7,633	25.1	22,739
1958–1962	70,935	28,267	39.8	42,678

Source: *Historical Statistics,* p. 282. *Statistical Abstract.*

$2,182,000,000 in the latter. At the same time, equity issues increased in importance among total corporate issues of symbolic capital (see Table 13–4).

A comparison between Tables 13–4 and 13–5 indicates that while funds were made available to industry during the 1920's, not all the increase in stock market volume can be traced to a growth in business' demand for capital. Instead, the American investor, entranced with the lure of windfall profits, supported a level of security demand that led to continually rising security prices during the twenties, and much of the increase in market volume reflects nothing but the greatly increased volume of transactions that characterize any period of rapid price inflation. For example, between 1921 and 1929 the wholesale price index (1926 = 100) was practically constant (from 97.6 to 95.3), while the index of common stock prices (same base) rose from 52.2 to 190.3.

The rapid security price inflation was underscored by a number of developments that contributed to further increases during periods of rising prices, but that were to combine to make the ensuing crash the worst in America's history. First, the rapid increases in stock prices were unmatched by any concomitant increase in corporate earnings. Thus, very early in the inflation, stock prices were related only to expected windfall gains rather than to any potential business profits. Any change that affected expectations

TABLE 13–5

VOLUME OF SALES, NEW YORK STOCK EXCHANGE
1900–1958

Years	*Stocks (Millions of Shares)*	*Bonds*		
		Total	*Corporate* (*Millions of Dollars*)	*Noncorporate*
1900–04	937	n.d.*	n.d.	n.d.
1905–09	1145	n.d.	n.d.	n.d.
1910–14	553	$ 3,164	$ 2,933	$ 231
1915–19	1053	9,040	3,201	5,839
1920–24	1177	18,265	7,688	10,577
1925–29	3527	15,525	10,617	4,908
1930–34	2791	15,877	9,753	6,124
1935–39	1846	13,164	10,247	2,917
1940–44	1047	12,042	11,239	803
1945–49	1562	6,534	6,033	501
1950–54	2235	4,465	3,970	495
1955–58	2513	4,579	4,320	259

Sources: *Historical Statistics,* p. 282. *Statistical Abstract,* 1959, p. 463.
* No data.

even slightly could, then, touch off a long cumulative fall in the demand for securities. Second, the growth of investment trusts relying heavily on leverage in their capital structures and holding large blocks of symbolic capital tended to buoy up demand in the period of rising prices. However, because of their capital structure, these same institutions were extremely susceptible to price declines and were ready to unload large blocks of securities on the market at the first sign of trouble. Third, the experience of the American saver with "borrow and buy" had shown him the advantage of leverage, so that throughout the period an increasing volume of shares were bought on margin. Margin purchases can serve to increase profits in periods of rising prices, but they can also cause an investor to be wiped out by even a moderate decline in security prices. During the last years of the boom, margins had fallen to 8 to 10 per cent and, because of the leverage effects, the psychological effects on expectations of a price decline were greatly magnified. Fourth, the 1920's had seen an increased volume of American savings flowing overseas. In that decade, foreign investment rose to almost 10 per cent of total savings (the highest in history) and a significant portion of this increase was effected by the public's purchases of foreign securities. Behind this flood of securities lay many projects reminiscent of the American canal boom of the 1830's; and, although no one should have been surprised, the collapse of many of these foreign ventures had an adverse effect upon domestic expectations. Fifth, an increasing volume of funds was placed in the call-loan market by persons and institutions who were ready to recall them at the first sign of danger. These funds supplied the speculation before 1929, but their withdrawal at the first break in the market brought on a severe credit shortage that greatly intensified the market's problems. Finally, the growth of a new link between the commercial banks and the capital markets, the wholly owned investment banking corporation, was to increase even further the areas affected by a stock market collapse. The first investment banking subsidiary was not organized until 1908, but by 1930 they were handling one half of the new issues floated on "the street." A well-run investment bank can be a useful tool in the process of capital mobilization. In times of stress, however, the commercial banks were frequently tempted to use their resources to save their investment affiliates. Thus, within a year of the crash several large commercial banks had gone under and broadened the area of crisis from the securities markets to the financial community.

When the break came, it was the most serious in the history of the American capital markets. So great were the declines in stock prices (from an index of 190 in 1929, to 63 four years later) and so far reaching were the effects on confidence and business psychology of the multiple bankruptcies that followed in the wake of the crash, that the American saver largely lost faith in symbolic capital. Nearly two decades were to pass before the average saver appeared once again willing to make use of the stock exchanges and to absorb symbolic capital.

Although the crash greatly impeded the process of growth, it did produce new legislation designed to correct the defects that had become apparent in the market. The Federal Reserve Board was given power to regulate the margin requirement (the size of the down payment), and over the past twenty-five years margin levels that largely eliminate the possibility of leverage have been maintained. Further, banking regulation forced the commercial banks to divest themselves of their investment banking subsidiaries. In addition, the two securities acts (Securities Act of 1933 and Securities and Exchange Commission Act of 1934) forced firms issuing symbolic capital to publicize their capital structures and obtain SEC approval for new issues.

In the past decade, the stock exchange has once again resumed its place as one of the most important institutions in the process of capital mobilization. Table 13–4 indicates that the secular movement in total volume is once again upward. It is doubtful, however, whether the stock market will ever again capture the imagination of the American people as it did in the 1920's. Moreover, recent increases in self-finance (out of retained earnings) and direct sales of securities by borrowing corporations to financial institutions have tended to reduce the area served by the formal market. Despite these trends, however, the market has continued to grow. In 1961, for example, 1,021 million shares were traded. Although this volume was below the 1929 peak, it represents a vast increase over 1946.

Suggested Readings

BULEY, R. CARLYLE. *The Equitable.* New York: Appleton-Century Crofts, 1959.

MYERS, MARGARET G. *The New York Money Market.* New York: Columbia University Press, 1931.

NORTH, DOUGLASS C. "Capital Accumulation in Life Insurance Between the Civil War and the Investigation of 1905–6," in W. MILLER (ED.), *Men in Business.* Cambridge, Mass.: Harvard University Press, 1952.

WILLIAMSON, HAROLD F., AND SMALLEY, ORANGE A. *Northwestern Mutual Life: A Century of Trusteeship.* Evanston, Ill.: Northwestern University Press, 1957.

Chapter 14 THE ROLE OF FOREIGN SAVINGS IN NATIONAL DEVELOPMENT

14–1. *The Purpose of International Capital Movements*

Our purpose in this chapter is to explore briefly the role of foreign investment and lending in the economic development of the United States. This method of mobilizing the capital needed for American economic development has received relatively little attention from historians. Yet we know that in major periods of rapid growth—for example, the 1830's, the 1850's, and the late 1860's and early 1870's—foreign capital flowed into the United States in considerable quantities, providing crucial margins of purchasing power that were not forthcoming from domestic savings for developmental investment. Part of these foreign funds were more or less "automatically" made available in ordinary trade with foreign countries. In part, these funds came in through sales of United States securities (stocks and bonds) to foreigners, plus direct foreign ownership and development of some American industry. Finally, some part of these funds were a direct consequence of the massive nineteenth-century immigration into the United States from Europe (that is, the new immigrants brought with them the capital they had saved prior to immigration). Eventually, as American industry expanded into foreign markets, opened branches abroad, and increased their imports of raw materials, America became a major source of international funds for the development of foreign countries. These in turn have become important sales outlets for American industries whose continued growth depends in part upon an expanding export market.

Before we treat these topics in detail, let us consider briefly the general characteristics and functions of international capital movements. Although immigrant transfers and direct investments were not insignificant, most foreign capital flowed into the United States as a result of international borrowing. Such debt can arise in the simplest fashion, as in the case of an American order of French perfume not paid for until six months after shipment; or the debt can result from sales of private or government bonds to foreign individuals or governments. If stocks are sold internationally, or foreigners otherwise buy directly into a domestic business, there has been an exchange of money for equity. This is not debt in the sense that it must be repaid at some finite future date, but it is debt in the sense that part of one country's assets are now owned in another country and cannot be "repatriated" except by repurchase (or, of course, by expropriation as was done recently in Cuba). All of these forms of capital movements serve a fundamental purpose in international economic development: they are methods of transferring the "surplus" of one nation to another for immediate use. As we have noted already in Chapter 3, growth is primarily a problem of mobilization of resources. Just as the American financial system mobilizes savings from those who earn a surplus over their normal expenditures, so the flows of international capital—whether for periods of thirty days or thirty years—transfer "surplus" purchasing power from savers to those who use it for current expenditures. International capital flows can augment a nation's supply of savings (and, hence, its command of additional investment) and at the same time provide employment for surpluses raised in other countries.

In the economic development of the United States, extensive international capital flows were utilized; first as a borrower, and later as a lender, the United States has been an important part of the world of international capital movements. There is very little agreement among scholars regarding the importance of foreign funds relative to investment funds derived from internal sources in the period before 1875 when the United States was mainly a borrower on current account importing more than she exported, and was a net seller of long-term issues. Indeed, there can be no solid agreement on this issue until research into this matter has gone *far* beyond that which has already been done. It is argued by some that foreign investment in the United States simply freed American funds for purposes other than capital formation, and that without such foreign funds we could have done it ourselves. This is a bit like arguing that the public school system simply made easy the accumulation of knowledge which students might otherwise have achieved in the Lincolnian way. On an a priori basis, the present authors think that the role of foreign capital in American economic development was of great importance, especially up to the 1870's, not primarily because of the absolute amounts involved (although they were very large) but because they were "at the margin." Whether in commercial credit or in long-term bonds of states or basic public utilities, foreign capital gave us an extra margin in crucial periods beyond the quantities provided by domestic savings. Foreign funds gave us an extra "push" without which our economic development would doubtlessly have been considerably slower than it was.

In the discussion that follows we shall confine ourselves mainly to private capital movements. Transfers by governments, except in the case of the Export-Import Bank, are treated in the discussion dealing with the balance of payments in a later chapter.

14–2. *Short-Term Capital Movements*

There are essentially three types of private short-term capital flows: those primarily related to international differentials in interest and exchange rates; those related to political disruptions (refugee funds, or "flight capital"); and those arising from trade in commodities. Those of the first kind, "arbitrage" funds that move from market to market and serve the function of reducing the differentials, are of very short term, often twenty-four hours. Insofar as stability of exchange and interest rates are, and have been, helpful in accelerating economic growth, arbitrage funds are of interest. Similarly, flight capital can have important effects, but this is not a systematic force in economic development and hence is not of interest as an economic phenomenon. Our attention is focused here upon those short-term funds that arise from trade and take primarily the form of commercial credit.

At least from the time of the Massachusetts Bay Colony, commodities have been imported into this country on credit. The amount of this credit depends upon, and fluctuates with, the difference between American earnings from sales of goods in international trade and the dollar volume of foreign imports which must be paid for. In other words, the amount of this credit is currently determined by the balance of payments. A detailed account of the relationship of the American balance of payments in the larger sense and economic growth is given elsewhere. Here we will concentrate on the record and role of capital flows, a critical part of the total balancing mechanism.[1]

[1] Our account up to 1860 relies upon the work done recently by Professor Douglass North and his assistants. They have gathered together the important estimates of United States foreign indebtedness from 1790 to 1860. We are grateful for permission to utilize these figures in advance of their publication.

In the United States, the short- and long-term international credit institutions grew out of our country's participation in the international market for money. An understanding of these institutions thus involves, initially, an understanding of the nineteenth-century system of international commercial payments.

At that time, commercial credit was usually either granted as straight ledger credit (like a charge account in a modern department store) or embodied in a negotiable legal document (an order to pay) called a bill of exchange. In the case of a bill, payment was usually not due for sixty or ninety days, or longer. (A modern bank check is an order to pay on demand and is a descendant of the older trade bill of exchange). If a London merchant bought Georgia cotton, the seller of the cotton would, at the time of shipment, "draw a bill" (write out a dated order to pay) on the London merchant. Once that merchant had, either personally or through an agent, "accepted" the responsibility to pay, the bill could be turned into immediate cash at a slight discount. The bill, payable in London, could then either be held to maturity and sent to England for payment, or purchased by an American with a debt to pay in Britain and used for payment there. When the bill matured, it was presented by whoever then held it to the London merchant for payment. In this way, American exports gave rise to a supply of pounds sterling to be used by American importers. Reverse the process and you can see how British exports to the United States made a supply of dollars available in Britain to use in the American dealings of British merchants.

Since there was an element of interest charges involved, the bill of exchange became a favorite form of short-term investment for bankers, and a brisk business developed very early in the purchase and sale of bills emanating from the Anglo-American trade. As long as payments were forthcoming and the bills could be negotiated for cash, trade gave rise to short-term credit creation. In both Britain and the United States, bill-discounting houses frequently later evolved into investment banks; J. P. Morgan's firm, for example, was originally engaged in bill discounting. British manufacturers early established agents in this country to receive and market their goods, and these agents took American bills, or bills payable in London, in payment. Before 1830, so efficient were the British at this kind of short-term finance that very few American houses were able to compete in this trade. Later Americans, either independently or in partnership with British merchant bankers, entered the bill trade, and the system enabled the trade of both countries to mutually prosper when the economic development of both countries proceeded apace. The net short-term credits arising from this system were part of the "financing" of trade deficits. A market for this kind of credit grew up in several major American cities and was later centralized in New York. In Britain, the London money market handled most of the American paper. Bills arising from American trade with other British cities (e.g., Liverpool) could be discounted in London. Even the Bank of England would ordinarily discount American paper if it had been endorsed (responsibility for payment "accepted") by London firms. For this reason, specialist "acceptance houses" charging a small fee for underwriting foreign bills thrived in London. This system still exists in international trade, but it has been modified greatly to make use of cash transfers by international cable and of checks and demand deposits.

The international market for American long-term debt grew up on quite a different basis, but through essentially the same channels. Here, since no shipments of goods "guaranteed" the payment of debts, the calculation of risk and profit involved greater judgments about the eventual ability of borrowers to pay. Markets for long-term paper thus tended to be dependent upon the spread of detailed information about regions and industries and were not closely connected to trade itself. But financial firms engaged in the marketing of American trade paper in Europe were particularly well placed, with connections on both sides of the Atlantic, to judge the quality of American long-term issues (or at least better placed in this regard than was the ordinary private investor); and to find buyers for such issues in Britain. Hence, the London money market, and not the stock market, became the vehicle for the placement with private individuals, as well as with financial institutions, of American bonds, and later stocks. The British purchaser relied upon his trust in his own merchant banker to select American issues for his investment funds. Famous international financial houses, such as Baring, Rothschild and later Morgan, Brown Shipley, and others, dominated this market. Considering the rough course of the Anglo-American long-term investment connection, it is one of the wonders of American economic development that this connection did not succumb early in its life. Instead, the arrangements continued throughout the nineteenth century and into the twentieth. The British investor was able, again and again, to renew his appetite for American securities in spite of the periodic and widespread default, repudiations, and suspensions of payments that reflected the stormy history of American internal development in the nineteenth century.

Until the early 1870's, during periods of rapid internal expansion the United States developed large current-account deficits in her balance of international payments, while in periods of relative stagnation the deficits were small, or even became surpluses. The deficits measured in part the extent to which rapid American expansion was financed from abroad. Hence both the short- and long-term indebtedness of the United States could be expected to expand considerably in periods of rapid growth. We can measure these flows of (both short- and long-term) foreign capital at various points of time by treating estimates of American and foreign holdings of foreign and American short- and long-term debt as the physical evidence of such capital flows. The data are admittedly only rough, and to a large extent uncorroborated, estimates. All we need for our purposes, however, is that their general order of magnitude be roughly correct. The data we use will support this much weight with some confidence.

Except for a short-lived burst of economic development in 1815–19, it is generally agreed that the first major period of American expansion came in the 1830's. During that decade settlers poured into the midwestern states that lie between the Alleghenies and the Mississippi; and the country was alive with schemes for banks, canals, roads, and land improvement. In 1829, estimates of the total volume of American securities held by foreigners ranged from $30 to $38 million; by 1839, however, that figure had reached $285 million. Of the latter figure, short-term indebtedness alone accounts for $85 million. British and European merchants had greatly expanded their credits to American merchants to finance part of the boom of the 1830's. After the defaults on public and private debts in the early 1840's, that figure by 1843 had fallen to about $28 million. The next wave of expansion (in the 1850's) was again underwritten in part by foreign commercial credit and, by 1857, American short-term debt reached $150–$155 million. Accelerated expansion came again after the Civil War. We have no reliable figures on short-term debt for the great expansion of the early 1870's, but the enormous increase in our *trade* deficit from an annual average of $87.2 million in 1866–1870 to $180 million in 1872 (the largest single-year trade deficit in our history) indicates that, in all probability, there was also a very considerable rise in short-term credit. By 1897, when the United States had swung over to the position of exporting more than she imported, the level of short-term credit extended to us had reached some $300 million.

Available data indicate that U.S. short-term debt has risen in the twentieth century proportionally less than increases in our foreign trade. As our industrial, commercial, and banking systems developed, our short-term credits to others expanded. But, curiously enough, we have remained a net borrower on private short-term account. Until World War II (1939), the largest figure for *net* short-term U.S. indebtedness had been $1.6 billion in 1927. In 1940, the figure was $4.4 billion; it was $7.2 billion in 1945, and has been in excess of $5 billion in every year since that time.

There are several possible explanations of this curiosity. Until the late 1930's, it may just have reflected a continuation of the tradition of the earlier years. Beginning in the late 1930's, foreign funds came here on short-term as "flight capital" from areas affected by the rise of totalitarianism and, later, by World War II. During that war and even since then we have made vast quantities of dollars available free to foreign countries as economic and military aid. This has eliminated a large part of the traditional area of short-term credit in our export trade while, at the same time, we have continued to receive credit from foreigners for imports on a greatly expanded scale. Hence the record of U.S. short-term indebtedness since the late 1930's is misleading. We have not required these large-scale net short-term credits for our own development, but have had them as a residual because we have been giving dollars to foreign countries rather than lending them through the ordinary mechanism of international commercial credit. The extent to which we still would be a debtor on short term in "normal" trade is purely an academic question now. But if we were to fill the role for underdeveloped countries that Britain and other countries did for us in short-term transaction in the nineteenth century, we would certainly become a net creditor on short term if foreign aid were to be discontinued.

The story of our position in the international flow of long-term capital is similar to that of short-term flows until the late nineteenth century, but then it becomes radically different as the American economy matured and the effects of World War I were felt throughout the international economic community.

14–3. *Long-Term Capital Movements*

The main kinds of private, international long-term capital movements are, of course, those that arise from sales of securities, stocks, and bonds of various kinds. These funds move in a more deliberate way than do short-term funds; that is, they represent the intention on the one hand to borrow (or sell equity for) stated amounts of funds for long periods of time, and on the other hand to lend on such terms. On both sides of long-term transactions an element of planning appears that is quite different from the sorts of short-term commercial decisions made in the movement of short-term funds. There are, in addition, net funds brought in by immigrants. Whether these have been of much significance in American economic development is not clear at this time.

Private long-term funds arising from sales of securities have played a critical role in American history. Estimates of the amount of total American debt held abroad in the 1820's range from $30 million to $38 million, and contemporary accounts suggest that over half of this was long term. In the great boom of the 1830's—fostered by state governments, builders of roads and canals, and by private land speculators—long-term funds flowed in, as did the short-term funds we noted earlier. To raise the funds for these schemes, state governments as well as private companies issued or sanctioned the issuance of millions of dollars worth of bonds that were sold to British and other investors. By the end of the 1830's American long-term debt held abroad reached an estimated $200 million, of which some $125 million were issues of public authorities. During the 1840's many of the banking, canal, and land-development schemes failed to produce anticipated earnings, and many of the states that had borrowed to finance improvements repudiated their debts, leaving foreign investors "holding the bag."

These securities were marketed in Europe (mainly Britain) primarily through the merchant banking network discussed above. The successful issuance of such a volume of American securities, including those of state governments, was due partly to the great success of the Erie Canal (which opened in 1825). That enterprise was initially financed by the issuance of bonds ($7 million) by the state of New York. Interest on these bonds was paid in the first year from revenues, and within ten years the canal was able to redeem its bonded indebtedness at a premium. Many Erie bonds were held by British investors, and such a successful venture was not kept secret. During the 1830's many of the American states embarked upon schemes of internal improvement, issuing their own bonds for financing. These bonds passed into the hands of agents of British exporting and merchant banking firms in exchange for goods exported to the United States. These firms then placed the issues privately in Britain. As a result, before 1873 American securities were scarcely ever traded publicly or listed in the London stock exchange. The network of commercial finance had proved itself capable of absorbing long-term funds as well as short term.

At the same time that the initial internal-improvement financing had been carried off so successfully, the conflict over the organization of American banking came to a head in the notorious battle between the Jacksonians and the Second Bank of the United States. Jackson vetoed the bank's recharter in 1832 and, with the subsequent withdrawal of Federal funds, the banking system was cut loose from central control. The chaos in the financial system that followed the crises of 1837 and 1839 was matched by disruption of commercial activities and by the failure of many of the ambitious internal development schemes to meet their financial obligations. By 1840, a deep depression spread through the American business community and widespread defaults followed in private business as well as among the state governments. In 1841–42, nine states, Arkansas, Florida, Illinois, Indiana, Louisiana, Maryland, Michigan, Mississippi, and Pennsylvania, suspended payments on their debts. It is estimated that British investors were left with $100 million of defaulted American securities. In addition there were, of course, losses on mercantile debt and other forms of investment, as depression and business failure gripped the economy. Although American credit was momentarily damaged by this massive defaulting (for some years the United States was virtually without credit abroad), in later decades the British and Europeans showed no hesitancy about returning to the American investment market. Some scholars believe that, relative to national income, foreign-capital imports were of greater importance to American economic development in the 1830's than they ever were again. In absolute terms, of course, we imported much more capital in later periods than we did in the 1830's.

In the 1850's, America experienced her first great railway boom. Once again we relied heavily upon foreigners to supply us with long-term funds, and, curiously enough considering the scandalous repudiations of the 1840's, once again the Europeans (again mainly British) investors accommodated us. By 1857, estimates of United States long-term indebtedness ran as high as $500 million. The governor of the Bank of England in that year told a Parliamentary Committee that there were an estimated $390 million of U.S. railway securities held in Britain alone. By the end of the 1860's, American long-term indebtedness was more than $1 billion. There were large-scale long-term capital imports in the 1870's, 1880's, and early 1890's, and by the end of the nineteenth century the total value of American long-term securities held by foreigners was $2.5 billion. By 1914, our *net* long-term indebtedness was in excess of $3 billion. During the period from 1820 to 1914 we had successfully mobilized vast sums from abroad to supplement our own savings in the financing of our economic development. These sums were mainly embodied in bonds and preferred stocks in the transportation system. Curiously enough, in the long period to the close of the nineteenth century, American common stocks had not proved to be much of an attraction to European investors.

By 1914 we were the world's major industrial power; our exports had exceeded our imports in every year since 1895; and we were already becoming a major *supplier* of long-term funds to other countries. From 1897 to 1914, private American long-term investment abroad rose from $690 million to $3.5 billion. But the United States was still a very attractive investment to Europeans, and foreign long-term investment in the United States rose from $3.15 billion to $6.7 billion in the same period. We were, therefore, still a major net debtor on long-term account.

World War I greatly affected world holding of long-term securities, and the United States emerged in 1919 as a net creditor of $4 billion of private long-term funds. The pattern established in 1914–18 has persisted, and even today we remain the world's largest creditor in terms of private long-term funds. In the 1914–18 war, the European belligerents were forced to liquidate their dollar and other foreign holdings to finance the war. The extent of American "repatriation" of its overseas debt was enormous. From 1914 to 1919, foreign holdings of long-term American securities fell from $6.7 billion to $2.5 billion. At the same time, Americans greatly expanded their foreign holdings, increasing the supply of long-term dollar credit to the world from $3.5 billion to $6.5 billion.

The process begun in war continued in the 1920's as Americans went on a binge of foreign investment, and by 1930 the private long-term foreign holdings of American investors reached $15.2 billion (compared to foreign holdings of our private securities of only $5.7 billion). This made us a net creditor of some $9.5 billion on long-term account. During the 1930's there was considerable debt repudiation by foreigners; American investors became disenchanted with foreign securities; and a substantial volume of foreign funds poured into the United States. As a result of all this, by 1940 we held only $11.3 billion of foreign long-term securities and foreigners held \$8.1 billion of American securities. Our net long-term creditor position had declined by nearly two thirds from the high level of the 1920's.

In World War II there was no dramatic reversal of the flow of private long-term capital as there had been in 1914–18. Instead, the process started in 1914–18 and continued in the 1920's was resumed. By 1945 we were, on private account, a net creditor of \$5.7 billion (just over half of the 1930 figure). This sum represented a fairly stable level of foreign investment in American securities and an increase of just over \$2 billion in American private long-term investment abroad.

Since World War II, the movement of long-term debt contrasts sharply with the direction of movement of short-term debt. It appears that, despite its effects upon short-term movements, foreign aid has not interfered significantly with long-term flows. In point of fact, insofar as American aid facilitated industrial recovery abroad, it doubtless induced American capital exports. American capitalists, in need of overseas supplies and plants, and responding to the opportunities of economic development in foreign countries, vastly expanded the supply of dollars to the world. Most of the private investment was direct (stocks) rather than in debt instruments. From a figure of \$13.7 billion in 1945, U.S. holdings of foreign long-term securities reached the unprecedented total of \$77.3 billion by 1961. At the same time, foreign long-term investment in the United States (largely restricted by foreign-exchange controls during the period of the "dollar shortage," i.e., roughly the first postwar decade) rose from only \$8.0 billion to \$21.5 billion. Thus, private United States investors were left *net* creditors of nearly \$55.8 billion in long-term capital. Since then, American long-term funds have continued to pour into developing foreign countries. These funds have by no means been evenly distributed; about one third of all American private direct foreign investment is in Canada alone, and investments in other parts of the world have been heavily concentrated in oil production. Yet there has been, since 1945, a growing volume of U.S. investment in other areas and industries. Depending upon the course of world affairs, of course, the future of foreign investment would seem to be encouraging.

No account of American capital movements would be complete without mention of the role of the federal government. We treat foreign aid at some length later, in connection with American trade and the balance of payments. Here we will note briefly the role of an extraordinary institution that is now, as it has been for some time, a source of American government export of dollars. Since 1934, the United States government has involved itself in the supplying of dollars on credit to foreigners. The Export-Import Bank, organized in 1934 (and reorganized in 1936) was originally meant to be a device to prop up American export credit during the Great Depression. Originally its resources were relatively modest. With a capital of $175 million (subscribed by the all-purpose Reconstruction Finance Corporation), it was to make short- and medium-term commercial credit available to foreigners. Its current commitments were originally limited to a total of $700 million. In subsequent years of war and and crisis, the Export-Import Bank has proved to be an enormously flexible and useful institution; and it has become an important agent of the government's foreign policy. Its loans (now including long-term loans) have gone to a broad range of industries, including transportation, manufacturing, and agriculture. These loans have been good business for American manufacturers. The loans usually have included tying clauses obliging the borrower to buy goods (except those made in the borrowing country) from American manufacturers and to transport such goods in American ships. The bank has become a major source of discretionary foreign aid; and, since new appropriations are not directly involved, it has been at the disposal of the executive branch of the Federal government. From July 1, 1945, to December 31, 1962, of net United States aid and credits to foreigners of some $92 billion, $8.2 billion were made available through the auspices of the Export-Import Bank. However, most of the $92 billion (about $72 billion) was composed of outright gifts; and of the net credits (transfers subject to repayment) made available in this period, nearly half were supplied by the Export-Import Bank alone. This remarkable government institution remains the largest official source of dollar credit, both on long and short term, available to foreigners. It supplies a powerful supplement to capital exports from the private sector of the economy.

Thus, we see that in the mobilization of international long-term funds the United States has benefited both as a debtor nation and later as a creditor nation. In a flourishing world of peacetime international trade and economic development, the United States helps itself as it helps others by moving its surplus funds to areas where yields are high. Foreign investment adds as much to our economy today as British and European investment a century ago added to their economies through their willingness to export capital to the

United States. In both cases, of course, the borrowing countries participated in the gains from capital exports.

Suggested Readings

BLOOMFIELD, ARTHUR. *Capital Imports and the American Balance of Payments.* Chicago: University of Chicago Press, 1950.

HIDY, RALPH. *The House of Baring in American Trade and Finance.* Cambridge: Harvard University Press, 1949.

JENKS, LELAND H. *The Migration of British Capital to 1875.* New York: Alfred A. Knopf, Inc., 1927.

KINDLEBERGER, C. P. *International Short-Term Capital Movements.* New York: Columbia University Press, 1937.

KNAPP, JOHN. "Capital Exports and Growth," *Economic Journal,* September, 1957.

LARY, HAL B. AND ASSOCIATES. *The United States in the World Economy.* Washington, D.C.: U.S. Government Printing Office, 1943.

NORTH, DOUGLASS C. *The Economic Growth of the United States, 1790–1860.* Englewood Cliffs: Prentice-Hall, Inc., 1961.

PAUL, GATES. *The Illinois Central Railroad and Its Colonization Work.* Cambridge: Harvard University Press, 1934.

V

The Expanding Dimensions of the American Economy

Chapter 15 ASPECTS OF SIZE IN THE NATIONAL ECONOMY

15–1. *The Advantages of Size*

There are distinct advantages in large-scale economic units under certain conditions, primarily where population is numerous enough and productivity high enough to provide markets for the products of modern technology. In such conditions, all the economies of specialization and mass production can be achieved. In our world, with rigid barriers to trade and political instability, the advantage of large-scale economic units may be restricted to those countries large enough to afford such conditions internally. Where productivity is high, a large and rapidly growing population means powerful and rapidly expanding markets. Such markets warrant the massive use of capital instruments in specialized production. These instruments, moreover, can be readily improved upon by advancing science and technology. The highly productive population provides a growing tax base which will support heavy public expenditures upon skilled personnel, laboratories, libraries, buildings, and the other accoutrements of the institutions of learning which make the massive improvement of human capital possible. Where such improvement has taken place successfully there is likely to be a high degree of mobility of resources (including mobility of labor) between kinds of occupations, as well as over widely spaced specialized areas differently endowed by nature with mineral, agricultural, and other resources, enabling the economy to adjust "at the margin" to changes in technology.

Moreover, a high degree of occupational mobility usually means a high degree of social mobility, thus avoiding the excessive waste of human resources which characterizes highly structured and rigid caste or class systems. With high social mobility a country is well placed to get maximum returns from its own technological progress; the corps of leaders in science, industry, and related fields is constantly being refreshed and replenished by the successful recruitment and training of men and women of the highest ability from families in all levels of the income strata. The whole population is the source of new leadership, instead of just certain privileged classes and castes as in some unfortunate countries.

Even such a sketchy introductory statement of the advantages of scale in economic development suggests a view of America's industrial history, for the United States is one of those countries abundantly blessed with such advantages. Economically we are a giant among nations, and our imposing wealth has been largely based upon the abundance of natural endowments within our own borders that Americans have always been challenged to develop. Our social structure has been so ordered as to enable us to create a system of industrial, social, and educational institutions to successfully develop our natural endowment. We may have squandered some of our heritage to be sure, we have doubtlessly failed to utilize all of our advantages (as our history of racial discrimination, monopolistic market constraints, depressions, shortages of schools, parks, roads, and so forth abundantly indicates), but it would have been, after all, fairly difficult to starve in the Garden of Eden; and it would have been an inefficient people indeed which could not have flourished to some extent on the territory of the United States. In point of fact we have done well for ourselves. We have reaped advantages from our huge country, just as the Soviet Union is now doing in that vast area, and as the Common Market[1] countries of Western Europe are now doing.

It is important to note that thus far we have concentrated our attentions only upon the possibilities of achieving the advantages of scale within the bounds of a large national market. In a world more perfect than ours, i.e., one with complete free trade, such advantages would be just as easily available to smaller countries as well. With free trade, other things being equal, the whole wide world would be their market and their source of freely available raw materials. Needless to say, some countries have prospered on this basis even with less than perfectly free trade between themselves and the rest of the world. Countries like Great Britain, Sweden, Denmark, New Zealand, Canada, and others, by a rela-

[1] Under the terms of the Treaty of Rome of 1957, France, Italy, the Netherlands, Belgium, Luxembourg, and West Germany are proceeding rapidly toward the creation of a single market in Western Europe, serving some 180 million Western Europeans. Political union of this new "country" seems possible within the near future, and a new economic giant will have been born.

tively efficient husbanding of their resources, human and natural, have through a favored position in trade with the world enjoyed higher living standards than could be supported by their own narrow bases of resources and their small populations.

On the other hand, some countries, and these include most of humanity (about two thirds of it) have not been able to achieve the advantages of scale either through international trade or, thus far, by developing potent internal markets which can support large-scale capital accumulation, mass production, and the accoutrements of modern industrial society. Some, like India and Indonesia, are heavily overpopulated relative to output and developed natural resources; and the tragic failure to develop this human capital has resulted in low productivity, weak markets, low rates of savings, and other intractable obstacles to industrial development. Whereas success breeds more success in the utilization of the advantages of large-scale units, the failure to achieve this utilization only breeds more failure. Compared to the United States, the Soviet Union, Great Britain, or any of the other industrial nations of the world, the underdeveloped two thirds of mankind seem to illustrate the cruel message of the *Parable of the Talents.*

> For unto everyone that hath shall be given, and he shall have abundance: but from him that hath not shall be taken away even that which he hath.
>
> And cast ye the unprofitable servant into outer darkness: there shall be weeping and gnashing of teeth. (*Matthew 25:29–30.*)

15–2. *Some Comparisons*

As we noted earlier, only Canada has achieved a per-capita income anywhere near that enjoyed by the United States, and Canada exhibits many of the characteristics of the U.S. economy and is heavily influenced by it. The United States and Canada have per-capita incomes more than double those of the wealthier European countries, and of course the rest of the world does not compare at all by this measure. For example, in 1961, when the income per capita of the United States was $2,311, that of the United Kingdom was $1,144; Brazil, $268; Mexico, $297; and India, only $69. Chinese annual per-capita income in that year was estimated at $83. Here we see one measure of the extraordinary American economy: its abundance. What about its size?

Before the entry of Alaska and Hawaii into the Union, the area of the United States was 3,022,000 square miles. Of the other nations of the world only Brazil (3,287,000 sq. mi.), Canada (3,846,000 sq. mi.), China (3,897,000 sq. mi.), and the U.S.S.R. (8,603,000 sq. mi.) were larger. With Alaska and Hawaii, our area jumped to 3,600,000 square miles, surpassing Brazil. These five are all physical giants compared to other countries. All of Europe (1,902,000 sq. mi.), excluding the U.S.S.R., for example, would almost fit twice into the area of the United States, and would fit twice inside Canada. The United Kingdom (England, Wales, Scotland, and Northern Ireland) has only 94,000 square miles and could be virtually lost in the U.S. or in any other of the giant countries. The same can be said of any other single European nation.

In all the giant countries, a great part of the land is desert, forest, natural pasture, jungle, or wasteland of one sort or another. Only about 28 per cent of the United States land surface is under cultivation (roughly 478 million acres). But only the Soviet Union (with about 556 million acres) exceeds the United States in this respect, and only India (with about 325 million acres) and China (with 223 million acres) are roughly of the same order of magnitude as the U.S. and the U.S.S.R. in this regard. The other physical giants are not so well off. Brazil, with less than 47 million acres of arable land, actually has less than little Spain; and Canada, with about 97 million acres arable, leads the remaining nations (except, curiously enough, the Congo, which has some 121 million arable acres).

How do these countries compare in population and in arable acres per capita? The United States again ranks with the larger nations in population. We now have more than 183 million people (which gives us a labor force of some 77 million). Let us, for comparative purposes look back to 1958, the last year for which complete world estimates are presently available. In that year we had about 174 million people, China had 647 million, India had 413 million, and the U.S.S.R. had about 210 million. The nations of the new Common Market should also be reckoned with. In that year, the combined populations of France, West Germany, Italy, Belgium, Luxembourg, and the Netherlands came to some 168 million. After these, the most populous countries were Japan with 92 million, Indonesia with 90 million, and Pakistan with about 89 million. Except for the U.S.S.R., Japan, and the United States (and the Common Market countries), the other countries with huge populations were desperately poor nations.

In terms of arable land per head of population, in 1950 (the latest year for which we have complete international data), the United States had about 3.2 acres of arable land per capita and the Soviet Union had 2.8. The Common Market countries had 0.6 acres, China had only 0.5, India 0.9, Japan 0.2, Pakistan 0.8, and Indonesia 0.4. In fact, among the world's major countries, only Canada (7.1 acres per capita), Argentina (4.3 acres), and Australia (5.6 acres) exceeded the United States in acres of arable land per capita. And none of these, of course, were populous nations. With the great productivity of American agriculture, we alone among the nations with huge populations possess an abundance of food to provide for present needs and for expansion in the future. This is a critical point in American history. The U.S. alone among the nations of giant size and population has not experienced famine or severe food shortages in modern times.

Thus we see in the physical magnitudes of land and people that the United States is a giant among nations. As we noted earlier, in terms of national income, absolute or per capita, we stand alone (except for Canada on a per-capita basis), and we are the world's largest single seller and buyer in international trade. In terms of production, the U.S. surpasses all other countries (although in some areas, in steel for example, the U.S.S.R. and the Common Market countries are rapidly gaining on us).

There are, of course, many ways to measure the scale of American achievement—in production, motor cars, bathtubs, and so forth; but many of our products are peculiar to the American culture and are not meaningful items to compare with output in other countries. We will confine ourselves to a few resources basic to all industry to compare the scale of our economic performance with others.

The production and consumption of mechanical energy is a good measure of relative economic activity in a world where the use of human and animal power in production are measures of technological backwardness. In 1961, the United States produced 879 billion kilowatt hours of electrical energy. Our nearest rival, the U.S.S.R. produced 328 billion KWH. The United Kingdom produced 146 billion KWH. By comparison, production in some other large countries was miniscule. India, for example, produced just under 23 billion KWH, and Brazil about 24 billion KWH. The industrial countries, of course, fall mainly between these extremes: West Germany produced about 125 billion KWH; France, 76 billion KWH; and Italy, 61 billion KWH. Here again, the combined output of the countries which now form the new Common Market makes an impressive figure: 297 billion KWH, less than the U.S. by a large margin, but no longer higher than the U.S.S.R., as was the case three years ago.

Another measure of energy consumption is the combination of all forms of mechanical energy into units equal to that produced by the consumption of coal in metric tons. By this measure, in 1956 the U.S. consumed about 1,600 million metric-ton units; the U.S.S.R., 540 million units; the U.K., 284 million units; Canada, 146 million units; and the Common Market countries combined, about 472 million units. India consumed only about 53 million units and Brazil only about 26 million units.

We have already noted how the uses of all these productive factors in combination produced a per-capita income in the United States (and Canada to nearly the same extent) out of all proportion compared to anyone else. In terms of certain basic industrial items, crude petroleum, coal, steel, and cement, the point is further underscored. Again our figures are for 1961. In that year American crude petroleum output was 2,600 million barrels; the U.S.S.R. produced 1,243 million barrels. Production among other industrial countries was negligible, because, except for the U.S. and the U.S.S.R., the wells are located in nonindustrial countries. Of these, Iraq produced 367 million barrels; Iran 438 million barrels; Saudi Arabia, 512 million barrels; and Venezuela, 1,065 million barrels.

Our coal output in 1961 was 417 million short tons; the U.S.S.R. produced 416 million tons; the U.K., 213 million tons; Poland (a major producer), 117 million tons; Japan, 61 million tons; and the Common Market countries together, 254 million tons (of which West Germany alone produced 158 million tons). Coal is, however, a declining industry. In steel, the U.S. also leads even though we scarcely used 70 per cent of our capacity. In 1961 we produced 98 million short tons, compared to 78 million in the U.S.S.R., 25 million in the U.K., and 14 million in Japan. The Common Market countries produced in that year about 76 million tons. In 1961 we produced 63 million metric tons of cement, compared to 56 million in the U.S.S.R., 16 million in the U.K., 32 million in Japan, and 75 million (more than U.S. production) in the Common Market countries.

When we study the development of the United States, then, we are studying an economy built upon a giant scale in nearly every physical measurement. One can expect the advantages of large-scale economic units to be achieved in such an economy, and that is important to remember in any study of the development of American industry—especially because much of the "traditional" emphasis in this area is upon the personal vices of early industrial leaders (e.g., "the robber barons"). Because of, or despite, the influence of these early industrial entrepreneurs, we did not develop our industrial output on the basis of small producing units. Neither is the U.S.S.R. so doing today. One further word here. An economic history book is not the best place to forecast the future. But the student might bear in mind how comparatively recent is America's leadership in industry in the world, how much it depended upon aggressive and inventive leadership in its development, and how any other country similarly endowed with human and material resources might be expected to do likewise. We used comparative data for 1961, a year when American industry was running at 70 per cent of productive capacity. If we had comparable international data it would be preferable to use more than one year, perhaps decennial averages. The 1961 figures, then, should be considered mainly as guideposts to what more complete data could be expected to show. Our output is not so gigantic that we can afford to use less than full capacity and expect to stay ahead of others. The race belongs to the swiftest; and in the race for industrial power, where there are at present comparatively few contestants, the balance could easily shift significantly. In recent years both the U.S.S.R. and the Common Market countries have been growing faster than has the United States.

When did the United States emerge as an economic giant? Historical comparisons of output are difficult to come by. Not all countries have adequate data going back into the nineteenth century. But we can produce some data covering the materials we have already discussed to illustrate the way the United States has grown, compared to other industrial countries.

In terms of population, the United States has long been a giant. In 1880 the main European populations were: The United Kingdom, 30.7 million; France, 37.4 million; Germany, 45.1 million; Italy, 28.2 million; and Belgium-Luxembourg, 5.7 million. In that year the United States population was 50.3 million. Except for Russia, the United States already was the most populous Western country. However, in that age of iron and steam, and fifteen years after the end of the American Civil War, we were still behind the United Kingdom, and far behind the main Western European countries combined, in crucial areas of production. In 1880 Great Britain produced 149.3 million tons (short tons, 2,000 pounds per ton) of coal; Germany, 47.0 million; France, 19.4 million; Belgium, 16.9 million; for a combined total of 232.6 million tons, while United States' output was only 64.8 million tons. British output of pig iron and ferroalloys in 1880 stood at 7.9 million metric tons; Germany produced 1.8 million; France, 2.0 million; and Belgium-Luxembourg, 1.0 million tons; or a total for the four European producers of 12.7 million tons, compared to American output of only 3.9 million tons. In output of crude steel the United States had already equaled U.K. production of 1.3 million tons. Germany had 600 thousand tons; France, 400 thousand tons; and Belgium, about 100 thousand tons (a total of 2.4 million tons). Except for steel output, the United States in 1880, in spite of its resources and population, still lagged behind Great Britain.

In the thirty-three years between 1880 and 1914 the transformation of the United States into the kind of industrial state we have known ever since was completed. A new technology based upon steel, electricity, petroleum, and chemistry, plus the opening of vast new reserves of raw materials and the completion of the system of railway transportation, combined with an enormous growth in population, catapulted us to the front rank among the industrial powers. Let us consider the same units of comparison on the eve of the 1914–1918 war.

In 1913 the U.K.'s population was 42.5 million, Germany had grown to about 67 million, France had 39.8 million, and Belgium-Luxembourg about 7.8 million. American population in that year had increased to 97 million. Our increase of just less than 100 per cent since 1880 outstripped even that of Germany, the most rapidly growing of the major West European countries. In 1913 British coal production was 292.0 million short tons; Germany, 118.7 million; France, 43.8 million; and Belgium-Luxembourg, 22.8 million; for a total of 477.3 million tons. American coal production in 1913 was 517.1 million tons, greater than all of the major Western European producers combined. British output of pig iron and ferroalloys in 1913 was 10.4 million tons; Germany produced 10.7 million tons; France, 8.9 million tons; and Belgium-Luxembourg, 5 million tons; for a total of 35 million tons. American output in that year was 31.9 million tons. Crude steel production in Great Britain was 7.8 million tons; in Germany, 11.0 million tons; in France, 3.4 million tons; and in Belgium-Luxembourg, 3.9 million tons; for a total of 26.1 million tons. American crude steel output was 31.8 million tons—as in the case of coal, more than all the major West European producers combined.

We see in these data evidence of the rise of the United States from a major industrial nation second to Great Britain to an economic giant which dwarfed all others. This period of our history is one of the least understood and one of the most critically important. For our great industrial transformation was precisely the period in which the giant business units made their decisive entry into American economic history. Obscured by the cloud of semi-Populist literature regarding the rise of "monopoly," "the trust busters," "the decline of laissez faire," and other similar slogans which have so long bemused American historians lies the fundamental change in industrial organization which created modern America. Unfortunately, we are still ignorant of most of the concrete facts regarding this great transformation. All we know, and this only in a very general way, is that the scale of American industrial organization expanded to match the great transformation in the scale of the American industrial economy. The two were obviously causally related. Let us consider this transformation to the twentieth-century American economy in more detail.

15–3. The Existence and Growth of Large-Scale Business Units

Before we discuss the origins and growth of large-sized business units in American economic development, let us consider for the moment some aspects of the size structure of modern American industrial organization. In 1958, in all of manufacturing industry a significant part of the value added was produced by the largest four firms alone, and of some 299,000 manufacturing establishments, the largest fifty produced 23 per cent of the total value added. In some industries the concentration of manufacturing in the hands of a few firms was greater than in others (we will treat this in more detail shortly). This tendency for giant firms to develop has been characteristic of American industry almost since the period of accelerated growth began in the late 1860's. It is still one of the most prominent characteristics of American economic growth. The same fact emerges from employment data. In 1958 (the latest year for which we have complete data of this kind) 0.2 per cent of the manufacturing firms employed 17 per cent of the total workers, and less than 1 (0.8) per cent of the total firms employed more than 30 per cent of the total workers.

Such data for the entire manufacturing sector indicates the existence of giant firms (incidentally, data for retail and wholesale

TABLE 15–1

SIXTEEN LARGEST INDUSTRIES BY VALUE OF SHIPMENTS, NUMBER OF COMPANIES, PER CENT OF SHIPMENTS OF LARGEST COMPANIES IN EACH INDUSTRY IN 1958

Industry (1)	*Number of Companies* (2)	*Value of Shipments ($ Billions)* (3)	*Per Cent of Shipments Accounted for by* *4 Largest Companies* (4)	*8 Largest Companies* (5)	*20 Largest Companies* (6)
1. Petroleum refining	285	14.1	32	55	82
2. Motor vehicles and parts	989	6.4	75	81	89
3. Sawmills and planing mills	15,731	6.2	8	12	18
4. Blast furnaces and steel mills	148	6.0	53	70	84
5. Fluid milk and products	5,008	5.8	23	29	37
6. Paper and paperboard mills	375	4.9	21	34	52
7. Bread and related products	5,305	3.7	22	33	42
8. Newspapers	7,947	3.6	17	24	35
9. Aircraft	113	3.4	59	83	99
10. Aircraft engines	186	3.4	56	77	92
11. Organic chemicals	250	3.1	55	70	85
12. Prepared animal feeds	2,016	2.9	22	30	43
13. Canned fruits and vegetables	1,347	2.9	29	39	55
14. Cotton broad-woven fabrics	321	2.7	25	40	59
15. Paperboard boxes	1,447	2.7	17	27	45
16. Commercial printing	13,023	2.6	10	16	25

Source: U.S. Bureau of the Census, *Statistical Abstract of the United States, 1963* (Washington, D.C.: U.S. Government Printing Office, 1963), pp. 788–89.

distribution show roughly the same proportions). These firms are distributed among the whole range of American industry, from grocery stores to blast furnaces. In some industries more than in others, however, the technology of the big firm (mostly with several separate plants) has come to predominate. The extent of the dominance, measured as proportions of output, employment, capital assets, and so forth, held by a few large firms is sometimes called "the degree of concentration." The notion of concentration is useful in several respects. For some it is synonymous with "degree of monopoly" and has become a kind of hatchet to be used in pressing antimonopoly policies. It is also useful, however, as a crude measure of industries in which large plants or large multiplant single firms have proved to be profitable methods of organizing production.

Tables 15–1 and 15–2 provide some evidence on the extent of "concentration" in the fifteen largest American manufacturing industries. In this case, the proportions of total products shipped by the four, eight, and twenty largest single firms in the industry have

TABLE 15–2

SIXTEEN LARGEST INDUSTRIES RANKED BY CONCENTRATION OF PRODUCTION IN THE FOUR LARGEST FIRMS IN 1958

Industry	*Rank by Value of Shipments*	*Per Cent In* 4 *Largest*	*8 Largest*	*20 Largest*
1. Motor vehicles and parts......	(2)	75	81	89
2. Aircraft..................	(9)	59	83	99
3. Aircraft engines..............	(10)	56	77	92
4. Organic chemicals............	(11)	55	70	85
5. Blast furnaces and steel mills...	(4)	53	70	84
6. Petroleum refining...........	(1)	32	55	82
7. Canned fruits and vegetables...	(13)	29	39	55
8. Cotton broad-woven fabrics....	(14)	25	40	59
9. Fluid milk and products.......	(5)	23	29	37
10. Bread and related products....	(7)	22	33	42
11. Prepared animal feeds........	(12)	22	30	43
12. Paper and paperboard mills....	(6)	21	34	52
13. Newspapers..................	(8)	17	24	35
14. Paperboard boxes............	(15)	17	27	45
15. Commercial printing..........	(16)	10	16	25
16. Sawmills and planing mills.....	(3)	8	12	18

Source: Table 15–1.

been used as an index of concentration. This is a crude measure, but it will suffice for our purely illustrative purposes. Table 15–2 indicates that, except for sawmills, newspapers, cotton textile, and paper products, the four largest manufacturing firms typically ship more than 20 per cent of the industry's output; in the cases of aircraft engines (56 per cent), aircraft (49 per cent), blast furnaces and steel mills (53 per cent), and motor vehicles (75 per cent), the concentration among the four largest firms is very heavy indeed. Among relatively smaller industries not shown in Table 15–2, concentration by this rough measure is also marked. Thus, in 1958 the four largest producers of tires and inner tubes (in an industry with thirty-eight producers) shipped 74 per cent of the total. Again, in 1958 the four largest firms in the cigarette industry (with 12 manufacturers) shipped 79 per cent of the total. There were, in 1958, 2,646 meat-packing firms in the United States, but the largest four firms accounted for 34 per cent of total shipments; with 84 producers of tin cans and tinware, the four largest firms accounted for some 84 per cent of total shipments. As the number of firms is expanded to include the largest eight and then twenty firms, the proportions of total shipments increase, but only relatively slowly—indicating that production is widely spread among many firms in each industry once the giants in that industry are accounted for.

We do not argue either that this kind of concentration is undesirable or that there is any magic element in big industry which brings automatically greater concentration as industry grows. Indeed, as Table 15–2 shows, among the sixteen largest industries there is only a very rough relationship between the degree of concentration in the four largest firms and the size of the industry. The point we wish to make is simply that in American industry large firms hold a dominant place. In most industrially developed countries this is true. Indeed, there is a great deal of emphasis in the new literature on economic development on the *necessity* for creating economies with wide enough markets to support large units which can achieve economies of scale. Moreover, let it be noted that the trend toward bigness does not typically develop into the single-firm monopoly. It might be argued that this is due to the efficiency of our antitrust legislation even though in some isolated industries, like shoe machinery, monopolistic elements appear to be quite strong. But there is also evidence that in every industry there is an optimal-sized firm, beyond which bigness brings inefficiency in management.[2] In any case (see Table 15–1) although some firms have attained a very large size there are—with a few important exceptions—many producers in the largest industries. Of course, the conditions of perfect competition (a large number of small producers, each unable to influence the market) are not met. Actually, this "textbook case" rarely seems to exist in American manufacturing industry. On the other hand, it would appear that with a few large firms dominating so many industries, "collusion" between producers on prices, output, market sharing, and so forth would be

[2] Joe S. Bain, "Economies of Scale Concentration, and the Condition of Entry in Twenty Manufacturing Industries," *The American Economic Review,* Vol. XLIV (1954), pp. 15–39.

a constant danger in our economy. As our history of antimonopoly legislation shows, Americans have long been aware of the dangers as well as of the advantages of bigness in industry.

Study of the growth of large-scale economic units in the United States has been obscured by the related issues of "monopoly" and "concentration of economic power." From the end of the Civil War to the Northern Securities Case in 1904, many of our greatest companies came into existence (partly by merger with other similar companies) and grew to enormous size; Standard Oil, United States Steel Corporation, the great railroads—all of these and others existed at the beginning of the twentieth century. It was during the same period, as we noted earlier, that this country was transformed into an "industrial state." Whether or not the two sets of phenomena might have developed separately is an academic point. The fact is that the greatly accelerated industrial development of the late nineteenth and early twentieth centuries and the rise of giant business and industrial units came together and may have been causally related.

Publicists and historians have generally concentrated their attentions upon the spectacular personal eccentricities and chicaneries of the tycoons, the appalling corruption of both business and government, and the ruthless market practices of many of the emerging industrial giants. While there was some truth in these charges, as "history" they have been grossly overdone. As a result, we know a great deal about such trivial phenomena as John D. Rockefeller's activities in forming Standard Oil, the "midnight rates," the "watered stock" of the Erie Railroad, the machinations of the early trusts, the extent of the "good will" in U.S. Steel's first balance sheet, and so forth. But we know very little indeed about the structure of markets and the changing character of the economy of the late nineteenth century which, in a very short space of time, bred a number of giant business units where many small firms had previously existed and set the tone of the U.S. manufacturing industry in the twentieth century. What were the *economic* conditions which favored the development of "big business?"

Undoubtedly the answer lies in changing technology and institutions. We cannot hope to provide the complete answer to this question in this book. We can offer some suggestions for the reader to consider. First, of course, was the development of a huge national market which came with the completion of the national railway system. Small administrative and production units of the pre-Civil

War kind were inappropriate in many industries where a system of central administration over a multiplicity of production units meant that the fruits of research and the financial power of a national organization could bring the most efficient methods to production units scattered over enormous areas.

The institutional foundation of the giant business unit is the corporate form of organization. The limited liability attached to ownership and the permanent life of the corporation enable it to issue long-term debt, sell shares of itself, and hence to mobilize the savings of the entire economy. Some students of the American economy think that the ease of incorporation, which began when New Jersey started to compete with other states for corporate charters in the 1880's, greatly assisted the growth of large units. Certainly the old alliance of banking and industry (J. P. Morgan organized U.S. Steel through a syndicate of bankers and industrialists) owes its origin to the protective cover of limited liability. Not only did the corporate form enable industry to be financed through the capital markets, but by making the growth of giants possible it limited entry of new firms, at times, to organizations of similar gigantic size that could compete efficiently with the existing giants. Hence, the paradox that a "perfect" capital market may have contributed to industrial concentration.

It is sometimes said that "every businessman wants a monopoly." The extent of the truth in that statement might also measure the extent to which giant organizations were put together originally in order to control the market. It is argued by some that until 1904 (the Northern Securities Case) the main motive of the merger movement was to gain monopoly power. Actually, although there were plenty of monopoly actions among the new giants like Standard Oil and U.S. Steel, this is not *ipso facto* proof that monopoly was the guiding motive of the mergers, any more than that the desire for monopoly was more prevalent among large than among small business. After all, when Adam Smith wrote in 1776 that ". . . people of the same trade seldom meet together, even for merriment and diversion, but the conversation ends in a conspiracy against the public, or in some contrivance to raise prices," he did not specifically allude to large businesses. The aversion of the public to bigness in this country which was embodied in the antitrust laws probably indicated an awareness that, however the desire for monopoly power may be distributed among the business community, such power is more likely to be achieved by large than by small units. The fact that the mergers of 1870–1904 did tend to reduce the *number* of competitors in each industry also contributed to fears of incipient monopoly. In fact, the reduction in the number of individual firms in American manufacturing industry until the 1930's while manufacturing output expanded was thought to be solid evidence of a decline in competition, and bigness was thought necessarily a promoter of monopoly practices. The extent to which monopoly power has been the goal of large business units is not certain. It is certain that the courts have not been impressed with the motion that mere size is a measure of monopoly.

Finally, it is felt by some that our laws regarding patents have encouraged bigness because large firms who employ the main body of industrial researchers are able to maintain monopolies on new processes that they develop under the patent laws (for example, in 1955, out of about 56,000 scientists and engineers employed in 2,443 research laboratories in American industry, the largest twenty companies employed one third of the total). One of the conditions of a competitive market, freedom of entry, is thus violated, and the rewards, in terms of more efficient production and new markets that may well contain the germ of growth, remain reserved to firms that are already well established. The economic growth force derived from technological change serves as a support for large-scale enterprises.

The heat of argument generated by those who think the question of monopoly is indissolubly linked with large units is not unreasonable, nor is it irrelevant. Whereas bigness may be of great advantage to economic growth, monopoly is not. If the large units do in fact automatically tend toward certain constraining monopoly practices—restriction of output and higher prices, for example—then the large-scale companies deservedly need to be watched, perhaps controlled, or even nationalized, if they threaten to cripple our economy. But large firms can compete as vigorously as small firms (in fact it is usually the large firms which have been charged with "ruthless" competition) and, as we have seen, large firms in any industry do not necessarily impede the entry of smaller firms into the industry. Moreover, as we have noted, the degree of monopoly or even of the degree of "concentration" is not necessarily a function of size. Curiously enough, even if this were not the case it would appear that in most of this century there has not been even a movement toward greater concentration in spite of the mergers and the success of the industrial giants.

According to recent studies, from 1910 to 1947 there was most probably a decline in the degree of concentration in American manufacturing industry. In 1901, just under one third of value added by manufacturing was contributed by industries where the degree of concentration was high (i.e., industries whose four largest firms contributed more than 50 per cent of the value added). By 1947, only about one fourth of value added came from such industries. This does not mean that the heavily concentrated industries became less so; nor does it mean that a reduction of concentration implies a reduction of monopoly practices. It simply indicates that in the period under discussion the relatively less concentrated segments of American industry grew more rapidly than did the relatively concentrated sectors. A recent student of the subject put it thus: "The odds are better than even that there has actually been *some* decline in concentration. It is a good bet that there has been no actual increase; and the odds do seem high against any substantial increase."[3]

Any decline in concentration has ordinarily been due to the growth of new firms in the same industry, and not due to large firms breaking up. United States Steel is a good case in point. In 1901, when it was organized by Charles Schwab, J. P. Morgan, and James B. Dill, the steel industry had recently passed through a technological revolution. In the previous five years organizations like Federal Steel, National Tube, American Bridge, and others through innovation of the new open-hearth technology had more than doubled steel output. The giant, newly merged corporation controlled firms producing 8.8 million tons, or about 65 per cent of the 1901 output (13.5 million tons). By the end of the 1940's, when steel output in this country was just less than 100 million tons, U.S. Steel's share was only about one third of the total. In large part this decline was due to rising demand for fabricated steels which could not easily be produced by U.S. Steel's plants and equipment. Moreover, the number of individual firms in the American economy has been increasing since World War II, thus reversing a trend half a century long. In manufacturing, for example, from 1899 to 1914 the number of firms whose production exceeded $500 per annum declined from 512,191 to 268,450; and, although the evidence is less conclusive, the decline probably continued through 1933. In 1919 there were 210,268 manufacturing firms producing output annually valued at more than $5,000; by 1929 the number was

[3] M. A. Adelman, "The Measurement of Industrial Concentration," *Readings in Industrial Organization and Public Policy* (Homewood, Ill.: Richard D. Irwin, Inc., 1958), p. 40.

206,663. Then, after a sharp decline to 139,325 in 1933, the number recovered to 184,230 by 1939. By 1947 the number was 240,807; and by 1958 it had reached the neighborhood of 299,000 firms. In spite of heavy concentration, the expanding economy has apparently made room for more entrants into the industrial race.

15–4. *Final Comments*

Several points may be made to conclude this discussion. First, in spite of existing industrial concentration, the expanding American economy makes room for new entrants. Second, it certainly does not seem to be the case, as many have feared, that the tendency for American industries to develop large-scale units with resulting intraindustry concentration produces ever more concentration (and possibly monopoly) in the economy. The economy grows and absorbs more units. Since there seems to have been no further growth of concentration in this century in the economy at large, the possibility arises that the great mergers of the late nineteenth and early twentieth century—mergers that were, in fact, massive industrial reorganizations—represented a once-over necessity required to produce a national economy. Finally, it appears that the resultant economy owes much of its extraordinary success to the achievement of the economies of scale that came with the growth of the giant corporations. Even if it is conceivable that U.S. Steel's output could be as economically achieved by 10,000 charcoal furnaces in 10,000 backyards, the fact is that it isn't. Our economy is one of huge size, based largely upon giant economic units. This fact has been a fundamental reality in modern American life and economic development since the end of the Civil War.

Suggested Readings

ADAMS, WALTER. *The Structure of American Industry.* New York: Macmillan Co., 1951.

BURNS, A. R. *The Decline of Competition.* New York: McGraw-Hill Book Co., Inc., 1936.

HEFLEBOWER, RICHARD B., AND STOCKING, GEORGE W. *Readings in Industrial Organization and Public Policy.* Homewood, Ill.: Richard D. Irwin, Inc., 1958, chaps. 1–3.

KUZNETS, SIMON. *Economic Change.* London: William Heineman, 1954, chaps. 6–8, 10.

MYRDAL, GUNNAR. *Rich Lands and Poor.* New York: Harper & Brothers, 1957.

WOYTINSKY, E. S., AND WOYTINSKY, W. S. *World Population and Production.* New York: Twentieth Century Fund, 1953.

Chapter 16 GEOGRAPHIC EXPANSION AND URBAN GROWTH

16–1. *Introduction*

For the first 300 years of American settlement the frontier was an ever-present reality. Today we are accustomed to speak of the space frontier or the atomic frontier or some other challenge. For the greater part of America's history, first as a colony and then as a nation, the frontier was the West, an unsettled land area into which man could push. While everybody knew where the West was, different people saw various dimensions of it. The farmer, the land speculator, the footloose adventurer, the "Easterner" who never went there, and the settler who made it his home, all saw the frontier from different points of view. In this book we concentrate attention upon only the economic aspects of the frontier: the role played by the existence of, and expansion of settlement into, virgin territory. Important as they are for understanding American history, the sociopolitical ramifications of the frontier cannot be dealt with here.

16–2. *The Geographic Frontier and the Pioneer Economy*

A land frontier is significant only in a pioneer economy. The presently unexploitable hinterlands of Africa and Latin America have no effect upon the coastal economies. Only when pioneers move into the area will a frontier exist; and, as long as there is a frontier, the economy will exhibit aspects of a pioneer economy.

To the early settlers on the eastern seaboard of what is now the United States, the frontier was a forbidding obstacle. For the French in Canada and the Spaniards along the Gulf of Mexico there existed no barrier to the interior comparable to the Appalachian Mountains. It was inevitable that the French, using the St. Lawrence River, the Great Lakes, and the Mississippi Valley, and the Spaniards using the Mississippi and the southwestern plains, should penetrate the interior with trading routes and rudimentary settlements while the English were still tied to the sea. Parenthetically, one might imagine how settlement would have progressed had the Rocky Mountains faced the Atlantic rather than the Pacific Ocean. The English, however, came to dominate the whole North American continent. There were two reasons for this. First, the Royal Navy controlled the Atlantic Ocean and could effectively blockade hostile forces in America. Second, a string of forts along a trade route could not resist the pressure of a moving line of settlement that pushed a solidly based communications and supply system slowly westward. Until the railroad enabled men to bridge great distances swiftly, the movement of settlement would be slow but certain.

The pioneer economies that developed as offshoots of Western Europe—such as the United States, Canada, Australia, New Zealand, and South Africa—developed many common characteristics derived from a shared background and a similar environment. The ratio of natural to human resources was higher than in the economies of Europe. This difference led to high, and in many instances to increasing, output from successive applications of labor and capital along with geographic expansion and technological advances. This increasing output in turn led to higher real wages and interest rates than were common in Europe. There was a constant demand for labor that was filled partially by indentured servants, partly by slaves, and increasingly, particularly in the later periods, by immigration. In Central and South America the indigenous population provided a labor force for the colonizing powers that was not available in North America. A great deal of the explanation for the social and political differences between the two areas has been based on this point. From an economic point of view, some part of the differences in the pattern of economic activity, at least in early periods, can be traced to the existence of an indigenous labor force in Central and South America and the lack of such a labor force in North America. As colonization continued, however, a native North American developed. He was an individual born in the new country who accepted the country as his home with no thought of making his fortune so he could return to Europe. America was not an alien land but an integral part of his thinking, coloring his behavior indelibly and making him easily recognizable when abroad. But his ties with Europe were great for he inherited many of his basic ideas about social order and institutions from European culture. In particular, he had access to the new ideas and new tools for production of a livelihood being developed in Europe, although he changed and modified them to suit the environment with which he was so familiar.

In the early stages of colonization particularly, the colonies of what is now the United States were dependent upon the more mature economy in England not only for reasons of defense but also for the tools necessary for life in their new environment. To be able to import such things the colonists needed to produce something to export. To qualify as an export-staple commodity, a good had to have a production function consistent with the available resource supply, geographic and climatic realities, and a low transportation-cost-to-value ratio. Aztec gold hoards are the best example of a commodity meeting these requirements, but furs, sugar, tobacco, and cotton are also examples. Implicit in this list of characteristics is the condition that the staple commodity have a large and, ideally, an expanding market.

In addition to a high ratio of natural to human resources and a staple commodity, the pioneer economies were characterized by a scarcity of money. The pioneer is of necessity a debtor. In settling new territory capital was required unless one were willing to live in the same manner as the aborigines. North America was not blessed with a supply of gold, and the cash supplied by the staple commodity was used to buy a continuing stream of goods from abroad. Inextricably tied to the frontier was a community either in Europe or, as the frontier moved west, on the East Coast, capable of providing capital for development. The supply of capital on the frontier was never sufficient to meet all needs, and barter was an important part of the frontier life. In the absence of a sufficient supply of capital acceptable as a means of payment on the frontier and with the creditor region, the frontier created its own banks and currency and continually agitated for laws requiring nationwide acceptance of the money they created. By 1870, when a national currency had been established and the confusion resulting from a multitude of currency issues had been cleared up, the frontier was able to see its true predicament. From then on, to use a very descriptive phrase, the frontiersman was "an equity holder in a heavily bonded corporation."[1] Like any such equity holder, the frontiersman was all in favor of inflation or, if not inflation, at least an expanding money

[1] W. A. Mackintosh, "Some Aspects of a Pioneer Economy," *Canadian Journal of Economics and Political Science,* Vol. II (1936), p. 461.

supply based on a paper currency legally acceptable for payment for debts nationwide.

The importance of the Appalachian Mountains as a barrier to westward expansion is clear. Given the technology of the early colonial period, it was economically impossible to transport out of or across the region the commodities that could be grown in or beyond the mountains. Corn and the other cereals formed the basis of early frontier agriculture; but, for export, the corn was fed to cattle that could walk to market or turned into whisky that could absorb the high transportation cost. The Whisky Rebellion of 1794, for example, stemmed from Hamilton's excise tax that reduced the profit margin on the only export available to many settlers on the frontier.

For a long time intensive settlement ended at the fall line, the line marked by river falls that separated the coastal plain from the foothill region of the Appalachian Mountains. This line marked the end of passage up coastal rivers for ships supplying the interior and loading produce, such as tobacco, for shipment abroad. It also provided a source of power—in New England for textile mills, and all along its length for the various milling operations that were an important part of the colonial economy. There was too much wealth in the interior, however, for the American people to remain content on the coastal plain. Out of the need for reduced transportation costs to open the interior areas for settlement grew a governmental interest in internal improvements that has been such an important part of American development. In the pioneering period in particular, the American people looked on the government as a cooperative agency smoothing the way for the untrammelled exploitation of the continent's abundant (but, unfortunately, exhaustible) natural resources. Government support for turnpikes, canals, and later railroads were expressions of this conception of the role of government. The same government involvement is clearly seen in the records of Canadian and Australian development of a later period.

The results of the first large-scale effort to punch through the Appalachian barrier and open up the mountain valleys and the central plains to settlement was the National Pike or Cumberland Road, running from Baltimore through southern Pennsylvania to the Ohio River. By 1820 the road reached Wheeling, West Virginia, and it was later extended through into Illinois. The second major effort produced the Erie Canal (completed in 1825) that ran up the Hudson River and the Mohawk Valley to Buffalo and tied the Great Lakes to the eastern seaboard through the port of New York. Although both routes opened the trans-Appalachian region to settlement by making possible relatively low-cost transportation (in this respect the Erie was more efficient than the Pike), their usefulness for intensive settlement was clearly limited. In addition, the application of such means of transportation was clearly not possible in the vast central plains area. The large-scale settlement of the Great Plains and the economic linking of the East and West coasts waited for the railroad.

16–3. *The Moving Frontier*

The existence of the frontier, the continual movement of settlement westward, was a dynamic force in American development that is difficult to appreciate today. As settlement moved away from the coast, the economic center of gravity shifted westward; and, as a result, the interests of Americans tended to turn away from the markets of Europe to the ever-expanding markets in the interior.

F. J. Turner, in a famous book about America's westward expansion, has given us a memorable view of the way the process of settlement took place. First came the hunters, trappers, and traders, moving out far in advance of settlement, exploring the country, finding the routes through the natural barriers, and bringing back pictures of the fertile land that always lay over the next mountain range or river. These men adapted Indian techniques and knowledge to their own purposes; for without the Indian's knowledge the job could hardly have been done. Second came the first edge of settlement. These people began to clear the land, to set up isolated farms, and to cultivate their holdings on a wasteful one-crop basis. In less-forested regions there would be a pastoral stage as well. Third came the more settled agricultural communities. These people finished the clearing of the land, built substantial houses rather than big cabins, and formed villages where the simple tradesmen supporting the agricultural community settled. Finally, as villages grew into towns and cities, manufacturing and commercial enterprises began; and the final settlement of the land was completed.

This process of settlement did not take place at a steady, even pace. Settlement was held up in areas of Indian resistance or by natural barriers, but it spurted ahead along river valleys. Also, as new areas were opened new methods had to be developed to farm regions where the soil and climate differed markedly from those to which the settlers were accustomed. The soils of the long-grass prairie regions and the dry climate of the middle prairie required modifications in farming tools and methods before settlement could be successful. In some areas, the movement of the frontier took a different form. In New England, in the period of early settlement, an effort was made to establish entire communities at one time in new areas as a defense against Indian attacks. In the coastal plains of the Gulf of Mexico, the southern plantation system moved bodily behind the first edges of settlement.

The fall line marked the earliest frontier; the east slopes of the Appalachians were then settled, with the ridges marking the next barrier. By 1800 the frontier line had moved across into Kentucky and Tennessee and to the north of the Ohio River, but progress to the south was blocked by Indians. By 1830 settlement, although just starting around Lake Michigan, had covered the Ohio Valley, had crossed the Mississippi along the Missouri and Arkansas rivers, and had spread through to the borders of what is now Texas. By 1860, settlement was pushing around the Great Lakes, had pushed up the Missouri and filled in the area between the Missouri and Arkansas rivers, and had been extended halfway into Texas. At the same time, settlement had been begun on the Pacific Coast and a new frontier was being pushed east. The frontier was finally closed during the two decades between 1870 and 1890.

The vast settlement took place with amazing swiftness. The railroad, the invention of barbed wire to enclose the ranges, the quantity production of windmills, and the development of drought-resistant seeds and dry-farming methods all contributed to the speed of settlement. The Homestead Act of 1862 may also have played an important part by providing free land. Finally, large-scale immigration contributed part of the flood of people moving west. In one respect at least, the last movement differed from the patterns that had characterized the preceding periods. After 1870, the search for minerals triggered exploration and settlement in a manner similar to the way the supposed "treasures of the East" had motivated exploration at the very beginning of the discovery of the Americas.

Table 16–1 traces the movement of the center of population of the United States between 1790 and 1950, and the distribution between farm and nonfarm lands between 1850 and 1950. The center of population moved only slowly westward. The proportion of the population actually living on the frontier was always relatively small, and it took a number of decades for settlement to become dense enough to have much effect upon the weight of population on the eastern seaboard. After 1850, land was occupied at a tremendous rate, but notice the quantity of nonfarm land (grazing, forest, other) still remaining. Since 1890, western development has continued, particularly in the development of natural resources other than land (such as oil in the prairie region); but clearly land frontiers still exist. With the development of new farming techniques, particularly in irrigation, a large increase in farm land is possible.

Who were the people who settled the West? The early belief, fostered by the manufacturers of the East Coast, that they were factory laborers dissatisfied with their positions does not seem tenable. Such people probably had neither farming skill nor the capital necessary to finance a new beginning in the West. Immigrants certainly

TABLE 16–1

THE WESTWARD MOVEMENT OF POPULATION AND THE USE OF LAND RESOURCES 1790 TO 1950

	Approximate Center of Population (1)	*Land in Farms (Millions of Acres)* (2)	*Land Not in Farms (Millions of Acres)* (3)
1790	Baltimore, Md.		
1800	Baltimore, Md.		
1810	Leesburg, Va.		
1820	Mooreville, W. Va.		
1830	Mooreville, W. Va.		
1840	Clarksburg, W. Va.		
1850	Parkersburg, W. Va.	294	1,590
1860	Chillicothe, Ohio	407	1,496
1870	Cincinnati, Ohio	408	1,495
1880	Cincinnati, Ohio	536	1,367
1890	Columbus, Ind.	623	1,280
1900	Columbus, Ind.	839	1,064
1910	Bloomington, Ind.	879	1,024
1920	Spencer, Ind.	956	947
1930	Linton, Ind.	987	916
1940	Carlisle, Ind.	1,061	844
1950	Olney, Ill.	1,159	745

Source: Col. (1): U.S. Bureau of the Census, *Statistical Abstract of the United States, 1960* (Washington, D.C.: U.S. Government Printing Office, 1960), Table 5, p. 9. Cols. (2) and (3): U.S. Bureau of the Census, *Historical Statistics of the United States, Colonial Times to 1957* (Washington, D.C.: U.S. Government Printing Office, 1960), Series J 50 and J 60, p. 239.

formed some part of the settlement movement, notably the Germans and the Scots-Irish in the period prior to 1850. Most of the settlers were probably the descendents of earlier pioneering groups, the sons who left the old homestead to try their fortunes farther west. Not all the children moved west, of course; some of them remained to take advantage of the economic opportunities that opened up as the frontier passed by and the new area became more densely populated.

The eastern manufacturers argued that the movement of their workers to the frontier kept a continual upward pressure upon wage rates in the eastern manufacturing region. We have said that this is doubtful, particularly when one considers the large-scale immigration that had such an affect upon the growth in population of the middle and north Atlantic seaboard. In fact, the demands for manufactured goods, originating in part from the frontier itself, easily absorbed all the available labor supply over the long run.

To argue that because one cannot trace a movement to the West from among the laboring classes in the East is, however, no argument against the idea that the existence of the frontier had a "safety-valve" effect. The "safety-valve" theory was essentially that the existence of the frontier provided an outlet for the dissatisfied segments of society so that social conflict was kept to a minimum in nineteenth-century America. While the safety valve did not exist in the sense that there was an actual physical movement of people, it did exist in the sense that the West made possible periods of rapid economic growth in the United States. Social dissatisfaction finds violent expression in communities where opportunities are limited. In a rapidly growing economy, however, new opportunities are continually opening up in all sectors of the economy. In this indirect sense the frontier did provide a safety valve.

16–4. *The Expanding Market and American Growth*

The role of an expanding market as a condition of economic development was set down in the eighteenth century by Adam Smith. In the eighteenth century, economic life in large parts of Europe was carried on in a fashion that appears to us to have been very primitive. Techniques of production had been little changed for centuries, although some new techniques were being introduced in the agricultural sector and in limited areas of manufacturing. Those products that were new and exciting came in almost all cases from newly discovered parts of the world and not from newly found processes of production. By far the largest part of the population was tied to agriculture. While moderate surpluses were created in agriculture, they accrued to the landowning class and to the merchants who acquired their share from trade with the aristocracy. The nonlandowning, laboring classes lived at a low level of income, making the articles they needed to carry on their activities.

Adam Smith contrasted such an economy with one in which the population was expanding fast enough to permit workers to specialize rather than being "jacks-of-all-trades." In his famous example of the manufacture of pins, Smith contrasted the individual workman producing pins by himself for a limited village market, with a pin factory. In a pin factory, the operation was divided into a number of simple operations, "one man draws out the wire, another straightens it, a third cuts it, a fourth points it, a fifth grinds it at the top for receiving the head. . . ."[2] The increased efficiencies resulting from this division of labor led to huge increases in output. In addition, as the operations were subdivided to their simplest parts, it was an easy step to the use of machinery to perform these operations. The modern example would be the assembly line where, for example, the process of producing and assembling an automobile is divided into the simplest constituent operations. Such specialization results in great increases in output per man but, obviously, requires two conditions: first, an agricultural sector with a high enough output per man that a surplus is generated to feed the industrial workers, or—alternatively—access to foreign supplies of food products through trade; second, an expanding market to provide the incentives for the establishment of a dynamic industrial system. In the United States, the abundance of natural resources generated an agricultural surplus; and the frontier provided the expanding market.

An expanding market does not necessarily mean a geographic expansion. An expanding real income for a given population can also be considered an expanding market. In some respects, however, geographic expansion is a simple means of achieving the dynamics of an expanding market. The techniques involved in geographic expansion are likely to be simpler and the demands of consumers less erratic than when expansion takes place in the form of rising real incomes.

The settlement of the American West was accomplished largely through the successive application of the same general level of technology to new geographic areas. This statement does not imply that new ways of doing things were not discovered and applied, but rather that the new ways were essentially modifications of established techniques rather than significant technological breakthroughs. Improvements were made in railroad transportation and in the steamboats that plied the inland waterways. Modifications

[2] Adam Smith, *The Wealth of Nations* (New York: The Modern Library, Random House, 1937), p. 4.

had to be made in farming techniques to meet new conditions, such as those of the semiarid grasslands of the Great Plains. The institutional framework within which people lived and worked had to be adjusted to meet the ever-changing conditions of a country that, in the latter part of the nineteenth century, was sprawling westward over vast areas.

In Europe, by contrast, increases in the stock of resources and in efficiencies of their combination came almost exclusively through the application of new techniques to a relatively slowly growing factor supply. The introduction of new techniques, however, involves a riskier process of investment than the application of proven techniques to new areas. This may explain, for example, the willingness of British investors to invest in railroads in the United States and other new countries rather than in domestic industries, even though the returns at home may in fact have been higher.

The continuing outward shift of the American production function was essentially a result of the discovery of vast new areas of resources that could be worked by the application of existing methods. The expansion of the pool of resources at a rate greater than that at which the supplies of labor and capital were increased led to a continual increase in the productivity of labor, and hence of real income.

This, then, was the expanding market faced by the rest of the economic community. It was also essentially an American market. The contribution of foreign economies became proportionately less important as development continued; and it was not until the first part of the twentieth century that America became involved abroad to any great extent. America's involvement in her own economy was in part a result of a conscious decision to erect tariff barriers around the nation. More importantly, however, American manufacturers held a comparative advantage in the production of those commodities peculiar to the American environment.

Perhaps the best indicator of the growing market is seen in the growth of cities and the increasing specialization of production by regions. The census of 1840 listed 44 cities with a population of 8,000 or more; by 1880, there were 285 such cities; and by 1900, the number had grown to 547. While most of these cities were concentrated in the East, such places as Chicago, Cincinnati, and St. Louis were also listed by 1860. The eastern seaboard from Baltimore north and the eastern part of the Ohio Valley had emerged as the manufacturing heart of America.

16–5. *The Evolution of the Modern City*

Although cities are not new, the metropolitan economy is a product of the past century. As early as the thirteenth century, Paris, Milan, and Venice had populations of over 100,000. None, however, were metropolises in the modern sense of the word; that is, none were dominant economic units.

Early European cities tended to grow up along trade routes. Often the new cities were ports and served as commercial entrepôts, while nonport cities most frequently were located at the junctions of established trade routes or at river crossings. It has been argued that the growth of cities in medieval Europe can be attributed to the need for commercial protection. More recent evidence has indicated that protection was only one among many causes of city growth, but certainly many cities trace their origins to this need. The traveling merchants who conducted intermanorial trade were often robbed by brigands and forced to pay tribute to robber barons; quite naturally, they sought protection in the castles along their routes. Entrepreneurs who wished to service these merchants found it profitable to locate where the merchants concentrated; and from this beginning grew the great commercial cities of the early modern period.

The commercial city did provide a safe market place, and the evolution of the great fairs turned some of these cities into world markets. However, although handicraft manufacture did develop within the cities, it was not until the emergence of the factory system that they became economic units based largely upon resident manufacturing production. Moreover, it was not until the last quarter of the nineteenth century that the city, freed from the factory, became the modern metropolis. In the United States at the time of the Revolution, the largest cities were almost all ports and entrepôts, and this commercial bias continued throughout most of the first half of the century. After the Civil War, however, the pattern changed. Cities tended either to develop an industrial base or to lose their relative preeminence to the new industrial cities of the trans-Appalachian area. (See Table 16–2.)

Not only has the economic base of the city economy undergone drastic change, but also, in the past century, cities have come to dominate American economic life. In 1800, barely 6 per cent of the nation's population resided in urban areas, and by 1870 this figure had reached just 25 per cent. Ninety years later, however, over 60 per cent of the nation's population lived in urban areas. The cities' share of the nation's output has increased even more spectacularly, as secondary and tertiary industry (largely concentrated in urban areas) has increased its share of national product.

Yet another trend in city structure becomes obvious in the present century. Until World War I, cities tended to be well-defined geographic areas, limited by the extent of public transport and central sewage systems. The new metropolitan area is less easy to define. Population, no longer tied to the factory, has spread to the suburbs; and retail trade and light industry have been quick to follow. Today, only half of all urban dwellers live in central cities; and, if present trends continue, this fraction can be expected to fall to two fifths by 1975. The new metropolis, sprawling across old political lines and reaching ever farther into the country, has engendered a multitude of new problems.

TABLE 16–2

SIZE ORDERING OF THE NATION'S TEN LARGEST CITIES
(Selected Data)

1800	1830	1860	1900	1930	1960
1....Philadelphia	New York*	New York*	New York	New York	New York
2....New York	Baltimore	Philadelphia	Chicago	Chicago	Chicago
3....Baltimore	Philadelphia	Baltimore	Philadelphia	Philadelphia	Los Angeles
4....Boston	Boston	Boston	St. Louis	Detroit	Philadelphia
5....Charleston	New Orleans	New Orleans	Boston	Los Angeles	Detroit
6....Salem	Charleston	Cincinnati	Baltimore	Cleveland	Baltimore
7....Providence	Cincinnati	St. Louis	Pittsburgh†	St. Louis	Houston
8....New Haven	Albany	Chicago	Cleveland	Baltimore	Cleveland
9....Richmond	Washington	Buffalo	Buffalo	Boston	Washington, D.C.
10....Portsmouth	Providence	Newark	San Francisco	Pittsburgh	St. Louis

* Includes Brooklyn.
† Includes Allegheny City.
Source: *U.S. Census.*

16–6. *Industrialization and City Growth*

Although the structure of city life has continued to undergo rapid change, the beginnings of the modern city were closely associated with the emergence of the factory system. As long as home industry was dominant, the city could play only a subordinate role in manufacturing activity. When nonhuman power (first water and then steam) was applied to production, it became more efficient to centralize production around the power source; and the factory system began to displace home industry.

Since workers were needed for the new factories, towns began to grow. Factory towns emerged in England during the last quarter of the eighteenth century, but in the United States their growth was delayed some fifty years. In the 1820's, however, the first industrial cities began to emerge. As textile production proved profitable in New England, cities literally grew out of the fields (Lowell and Lawrence, for example). Elsewhere, commercial cities (like New York, Baltimore, and Philadelphia) became industrial centers. Growth in these new cities did not depend entirely on manufacturing development. Specialization in manufactures left room for specialization in the services required to support the new factories and their labor force. Thus, along with the city growth induced by industry came further endogenous growth in city-serving trade and commerce.

Over a certain minimum size there are, apparently, few economies in city operation; and once the half million mark is passed costs rise much more rapidly than population. What, then, accounts for the increasing industrial concentration in the face of rapidly rising city costs? The explanation lies in external economies available to firms locating near other firms and in cities of certain size. First, communication and transportation expenses can be minimized if industries are geographically concentrated. Second, localization can allow small firms to benefit from bulk transport, massed resources, and balanced production—economies that normally could accrue only to large plants. Third, firms of any size can draw on specialized facilities or services available only in large economic complexes. These specialized services include distributors, bankers, lawyers, and a wide range of other services. Finally, localization can produce a force of skilled labor and resources that no one firm could generate, but that all can utilize.

The growth of the machine-tool industry in the textile centers of Massachusetts and New Hampshire provides an early example of city growth induced by external economies. Originally the machine-tool companies depended on the textile mills for orders and a flow of trained personnel, but later they came to serve a much wider market than the textile industry. Again, Pittsburgh grew, both because it became the center of primary steel industry and because firms affiliated with industry (but not primary producers) found it cheaper to operate near the center of production. In the 1920's, Detroit experienced rapid growth as many firms ancillary to the production of automobiles found it beneficial to locate there. Again, in the past decade, the development of the thinking industry (consulting firms) has contributed to Boston's growth. These firms depend upon the complex of great universities located in that city. In each case, external economies added yet another endogenous push to the growth of large cities.

Economies arising from factor indivisibility also have contributed at times to pressures tending to make large cities even larger. For example, the advertising industry appears to require a minimum city size to obtain the services it needs. Since only New York appears capable of supporting the industry, this minimum size may, in some cases at least, be quite high.

Although there has been a close connection between urbanization and industrialization in the United States, these factors have not been perfectly correlated. Woytinsky has shown that close correlation between industrialization and urbanization exists only at the extremes. That is, the most highly urbanized states (Rhode Island, Massachusetts, New York, New Jersey, and Illinois) are the most highly industrialized, and the least heavily urbanized (Mississippi, Arkansas, and the Carolinas) are among the least industrialized. On the other hand, on the basis of industrialization alone it is hard to understand why Utah and Colorado are more highly urbanized than Delaware and Missouri. Most reasonably, it appears that while industrialization has been an important force in urbanization, it has not been the only one. Instead (as Woytinsky concludes), "the pattern of urbanization has been determined by a combination of historical, geographical, and economic conditions."[3]

16–7. *Urbanization Trends in the United States*

As we have seen, in the United States urbanization was temporally associated with economic growth. In 1790, only slightly more than 5 per cent of the population lived in urban areas, and no city could claim more than 50,000 souls. (See Table 16–3.) Thus, it is not surprising that Jefferson envisioned the United States as a land of small agricultural freeholders and looked to that group for the nation's political strength. Even as late as 1870, only a bare one fourth of the nation's population were city dwellers. Since then, however, the nation has become urbanized; and today almost two thirds of the population live in cities, and almost one third live in cities with population of more than 100,000.

Actually, the movement toward population centralization has been even more pronounced than the figures in Table 16–3 indicate.

[3] W. S. Woytinsky and E. S. Woytinsky, *World Population and Production, Trend and Outlook* (New York: The Twentieth Century Fund, 1953), p. 125.

The past decade has been marked by a movement to the suburbs; and, although suburbanites frequently do not live in incorporated areas, in any economic context they are an integral part of the urban complex. In 1950, for example, 58 per cent of the U.S. population lived in metropolitan areas of over 50,000 population. Ten years later, this ratio had passed 60 per cent.

A simple supply-and-demand model appears to provide an explanation for the timing of city growth. On the demand side, growth awaited the rise of industry and the increasing specialization of labor that accompanied industrial development. Moreover, once growth had begun it tended to continue as city-serving functions developed and the benefits of geographic concentration became apparent. On the cost side, large cities were not economic (at least for a state of demand similar to that prevailing in the nineteenth century) until improvements in urban transport and public health reduced the costs of urbanization. More recently, new technological developments have made even larger cities (in a geographic sense) economically feasible. The private auto has made more flexible intracity transport possible and improvements in waste disposal have freed the metropolis, at least temporarily, from its central sewer system.

TABLE 16–3

Growth of Cities in the United States, 1790–1950

	Incorporated Places 2,500 and Over		*Incorporated Places 100,000 and Over*		*Incorporated Places 1,000,000 and Over*	
Year	*Number of Places*	*Per Cent of Total Population*	*Number of Places*	*Per Cent of Total Population*	*Number of Places*	*Per Cent of Total Population*
1790	24	5.1				
1810	46	7.3				
1830	90	8.8	1	1.6		
1850	236	15.3	6	5.0		
1870	663	25.7	14	10.8		
1890	1348	35.1	28	15.4	3	5.8
1910	2262	45.7	50	22.1	3	9.2
1930	3165	56.2	93	29.6	5	12.3
1950	4741	64.0	106	29.9	5	11.5
1960	6041	69.9	132	28.5	5	9.8

Source: Stuart A. Queen and David B. Carpenter, *The American City* (New York: McGraw-Hill Book Co., Inc., 1953), p. 59; *Statistical Abstract.*

The character of the city has also been affected by its population. In the United States the new cities drew on two sources: immigrants and the rural population. Before 1870, new immigrants had tended to move into the agricultural areas of the West. After that date, however, a decline in agricultural opportunities as the nation's arable land was occupied, an increase in urban opportunities as industry grew, and a reduction in personal wealth as the proportions of immigrants from southern and eastern Europe rose (despite the Great American Myth, it cost money to travel west and start a farm) combined to turn the stream to the cities of the Northeast. These new immigrants (a high proportion of working age) provided a large share of the labor required by new American industry and, quite literally, turned the northeastern cities into the melting pot of the world.

The rural-urban migration provided a second major source of city growth in the early period, and has accounted for almost all growth since the passage of the alien exclusion acts. Throughout most of the period, farm incomes have risen less rapidly than urban; and this increasing differential has induced a heavy rural-urban migration. The foreign immigrants tended to bring their entire families to the new cities. However, if the patterns of the 1930's are excluded, relatively few farmers have come to the city. Instead, it has been the grown children of farm families that have migrated most frequently. The size of this stream still continues to increase. Even during the 1930's, it is estimated that some 11 million persons migrated from rural to urban areas; and some 60 per cent of this total finally located in the large cities. More recently, a rise in the proportion of southern Negroes migrating to northern cities has increased the rural-urban flow; and in New York, at least, transoceanic migration has once more become important as Puerto Ricans arrive in large numbers.

Within the cities, certain forces have markedly altered the structures of urban life. Until 1920, the central city typically grew much more rapidly than the surrounding area. Since then, however, this trend has been reversed; and the cities have grown much less rapidly than the nation as a whole, and only about one third as fast as their own suburban areas. Thus, during the 1950's, total population grew by 17 per cent, and the population of suburban areas increased by 47 per cent, but the population of the central cities rose by only 8 per cent. Moreover, several of the largest cities lost population during the past decade. Concomitant with the shift of population to the suburbs, there has been a less spectacular but equally persistent movement of manufacturing jobs out of the central city. In 1929, about two thirds of all production workers in the nation's metropolitan areas worked in the cities, but by 1954 this ratio had declined to 54 per cent. Furthermore, in some central cities the postwar decades have witnessed an absolute decline in manufacturing employment. Between 1947 and 1954, for example, manufacturing jobs in Cleveland, Chicago, St. Louis, and San Francisco declined. In one instance this decline amounted to 8 per cent, and in none of the four cases was it less than 3 per cent.

As an economic unit, the new metropolis does not differ markedly from the older central city, but the movement to the suburbs has intensified transportation problems, made old political units obsolete, and reduced the cities' revenue sources more than their responsibilities.

Again (because of external economies) the growth of cities has been characterized by an increase in industrial specialization. Professor Alexandersson has shown that, while service industries tend to be ubiquitous, manufacturing has developed on a highly specialized basis. Although most cities contain some construction, printing, and food-manufacturing firms, the rest of the manufacturing sector is highly centralized in a relatively few cities.

Although the textile industry was localized in a few New England cities in the early nineteenth century, little specialization was noticeable elsewhere. However, once a national market developed, city specialization became profitable. As we have seen, the gains from city specialization in the modern economy are numerous. In the case of specialized resources, the benefits are obvious. Further, as an industry grows it generates a pool of labor skilled in the occupations of that industry and available to new firms locating nearby. Moreover, if an industry is localized geographically it is easier to develop marketing and financial arrangements tailored to that industry's needs; and it is easier to win for the industry the support of the people and government of the area. Detroit and the automobile industry provide an excellent example of the gains that can be realized from centralization. Although Detroit possesses good port facilities, it is no better located for auto manufacture than any other lake city located near the industrial belt. However, because of its early start, the city was able to develop financial and marketing arrangements particularly suited to the auto industry; and, thus, the city became more attractive to other auto-production firms.

The importance of specialization can be seen in the development of almost every basic industry. One half of the nation's steel is produced in cities located in a band stretching from southwestern Pennsylvania to eastern Michigan, and another 20 per cent comes from the cities on the southern shore of Lake Michigan. The experience of the auto industry has already been mentioned; and, although geographic concentration in other industries is slightly less spectacular, it does exist in aircraft, glass, rubber, machinery, and many others. Alexandersson has shown, for example, that among the twelve metropolitan areas whose populations exceed 1 million, over 7 per cent of New York's labor force is employed in apparel manufacture against a national average of 2 per cent; auto manufacture employs 28 per cent of the Detroit labor force (national average 2 per cent); 18 per cent of Pittsburgh's labor force and 7 per cent of Baltimore's are engaged in making primary metals (national average 3 per cent); and over 5 per cent of the St. Louis labor force is engaged in food production against a national average of less than 3 per cent.

Of course, transportation costs will always limit the extent of concentration, but the advantages of concentration appear to make localization attractive when costs are not prohibitive and to encourage it on a regional basis when wider areas are ruled out on cost grounds. It appears likely, however, that there may be social costs attached to centralization that are not recognized in the individual firm's location decisions. For example, the costs to the nation of loss through bombing attacks would increase with the degree of city specialization; and these social costs should be included in any calculation of optimal industry location. Thus, it is possible that a rational national economic policy would call for extensive industry relocation, even though the firm's search for profits would lead them to greater concentration. Similarly, centralized industry is apt to intensify the local effects of industrial unemployment. Thus, the New England economy has still not recovered from the decline in the textile industry during the 1920's. Since workers are not completely mobile, a weighing of social costs might call for the encouragement of more industrial diversification.

16–8. *The Problems of City Growth*

If people were to live together in dense areas the problem of public health and adequate housing had to be solved. If cities were to be anything more than a few houses huddled around a factory, the urban transport problem had to be solved. Finally, if the modern metropolis is to continue to grow, the problem of administration has to be solved. Satisfactory answers have been found to the first, partial answers to the second, and as yet almost no answers to the third.

Cities have never been healthy places to live, but as long as they were small and relatively unimportant, health conditions did not present a major social problem or an insurmountable barrier to further development. As the industrial revolution transformed the face of the land and the cities became the focal points of economic activity, health conditions seriously menaced further progress. These problems were not, of course, peculiar to the United States. During its period of rapid industrialization, England also experienced the growth of crowded, filthy, disease-ridden cities. By the middle of the nineteenth century, however, that country had taken great strides toward the solution of the worse aspects of its urban problem. In the United States, industrialization came half a century later than in England, and the solution of public health problems was delayed a like time. In 1850, for example, a New York City census report showed that over 8,000 cellars provided the sole living space for one thirtieth of the city's population. In the same year, a Boston census report notes that one twentieth of the city's population resided in "damp, vermin-ridden, underground rooms." Not only were living conditions poor, but competent medical care and adequate sanitary facilities were largely unknown among the poorer classes. Until the middle of the century, most workers had lived in individual shacks scattered around the new factories. In the late 1840's the first tenements appeared; and, while health conditions in the individual dwellings had not been good, the new tenements became the spawning grounds for yellow fever, cholera, typhoid, small pox, and typhus. The effects of the "new urbanization" can be seen in the mortality rates of the period. In New York, for example, infant mortality rose from 146 per 1000 in 1810, to 180 per 1000 in 1850, to 240 per 1000 in 1870.

Even when things appeared worse, however, some progress was made. Although five cities had established boards of public health by 1830, further progress lagged until the publication of *The Report of the Council of Hygiene and Public Health of the Citizens' Association of New York*, in 1864. This report prepared the way for the establishment of the Metropolitan Board of Health in 1866, and from that time there was a steady increase in the numbers and powers of state health boards. These organizations initiated programs of health and sanitation education and spearheaded the drive for better public sanitation facilities. During the period garbage collection became common, and sewers were laid in most cities. The extent of the growth of public sanitation facilities can be seen in the increase in municipal water works from 83 in 1850, to 3,196 in 1896. Concomitantly, great strides were made in the conquest of disease. By the 1880's, most medical authorities recognized the microorganic origins of disease, and these discoveries were transformed into lower mortality rates by the establishment of state public health laboratories (beginning with New York in 1892) and programs of public vaccination. In this latter field, it was 1920 before the first experimental program in public vaccination was attempted (the disease: diphtheria; the state: New York).

Thus, although all health problems had not been solved, by the early twentieth century the critical period had passed. More recently, the spread of cities into the suburb has engendered new health problems. Once central sewer systems had been built, waste disposal offered little further threat to public health. Suburban development has, however, frequently been in advance of sewer systems; and although septic tanks are adequate in sparsely settled areas, in urban communities they pose a serious health hazard.

Although the worst health menaces had been removed by the second decade of the twentieth century, the tenements still remained to spawn disease, high crime rates, and low labor morale. From time to time, both local and private authorities have made attempts to solve the problems of the slums; and in the postwar decades the federal government, through the Housing Acts of 1949 and 1954, has made a further contribution. Although progress has been made in some cities (Baltimore, for example) one need no more than walk through Chicago's South Side or New York's Harlem to realize that much more needs to be done.

The second problem, urban transport, has never been completely solved; and it continues to haunt the twentieth-century metropolis. The first attempt at a solution of the urban transport problem was the horse-drawn street railway. The innovation of electric power in urban transport (beginning in 1890) revolutionized this network; by 1920, some 50,000 miles of electric city railroads were in operation. During the last two decades, however, consumer tastes have shifted away from public transport and toward the private automobile. Needless to say, this shift has intensified metropolitan problems. Before the 1930's, urban transport lines had earned good profits; their shares were considered excellent investments for widows and orphans; and the little government ownership that did exist had been engendered solely by fears of monopoly profits. Recently, however, the situation has changed drastically. (See Table 16–4.) Consumers have expressed a decided preference for auto travel; and urban railroads, unable to raise fares without driving even more customers to their autos, have been forced to reduce service (which induces a further auto substitution) and appeal to state and local governments for help. Some idea of the extent of auto substitution can be gathered from a recent survey that indicates private autos carry 55 per cent of all urban passengers in cities over 250,000; 72 per cent in cities between 100,000 and 250,000; and 83 per cent in cities of less than 50,000 population. Less than forty years ago, autos carried only an infinitesimal fraction of urban passengers in cities of any size.

The choice that faces government on all levels is not a happy one. Apparently they must choose between letting the market decide the fate of urban transport, and granting a transport subsidy. If

TABLE 16–4

TRENDS IN URBAN TRANSPORT, 1940–1955
(1940 = 100)

Year	*Urban Population*	*Transit Riders*	*Auto Registrations*
1940	100.0	100.0	100.0
1945	100.1	177.9	93.9
1950	118.8	131.3	146.7
1955	125.0	87.9	182.7

Source: Wilfred Owen, *The Metropolitan Transportation Problem* (Washington, D.C.: Brookings Institution, 1956), p. 275.

they choose the former, it is quite probable that there will be no public transportation. In the long run, as highway and parking problems increase, the lack of adequate transport may spell the end for the super city. On the other hand, a subsidy may well engender the wrath of the taxpayer, who has indicated he doesn't like the system, won't use it, and may refuse to pay for it. A third, little-discussed alternative would call for no government support, but an absorption of transit deficits by the industries that benefit from the economies of large city size.

The third problem, city administration, has its roots in the present century; and, as yet, little progress has been made toward its solution. As long as urban areas were tied by transport and sewer systems to the central city, there was a single political authority with final responsibility for metropolitan problems. Although corruption frequently prevented the city from exercising wise leadership (and, in large part, accounted for the growth of separate school and sewer authorities), the power was there. In the modern city, sprawling as it does across old political subdivisions, there is no central authority. In 1950, of the 159 metropolitan areas, 23 crossed state lines; and none were restricted to the central city.

Since the problems of the metropolis are area-wide, no one local authority can accomplish much toward a solution of its traffic, education, or urban-renewal problems. Moreover, the suburban movement has imposed an unequal tax burden on the subdivisions of the metropolitan area. The historic source of city finance has been the property tax; and the central cities have found their tax base moving from their control while they are still charged with functions relating to a much larger economic base. Although almost half of the population of the nation's metropolitan areas live outside the central city, the central cities still support the bulk of the business activity for the metropolitan areas. While some manufacturing has joined the movement to the suburbs, the heavy manufacturing and the service industries have tended to remain in the central city. Thus, the cities must provide services for a larger economic base than their populations would warrant. The population of Newark, for example, doubles each morning at nine. Although this condition is atypical, cities must be prepared for daytime population increases of about one third. The only reasonable solution to this problem is a single metropolitan political authority; however, suburban resistance to central control has been so strong that (except in Los Angeles) little has been accomplished in this direction.

Suggested Readings

ALEXANDERSSON, G. *The Industrial Structure of American Cities.* Lincoln: University of Nebraska Press, 1957.

COMMITTEE FOR ECONOMIC DEVELOPMENT. *Guiding Metropolitan Growth.* New York, 1960.

FISHER, R. M. (ED.). *The Metropolis in Modern Life.* New York: Doubleday, 1955.

ROSEN, GEORGE. *A History of Public Health.* New York: MD Publications, 1958.

TURNER, F. J. *The Frontier in American History.* New York: Henry Holt & Co., Inc., 1920.

Chapter 17 TRANSPORTATION AND EXPANDING MARKETS

17–1. *The Nature of the Problem*

While it is misleading to argue that any single factor "causes" economic growth, it is reasonable to conclude that certain developments represent necessary (but not sufficient) conditions for such growth. In the case of the American economy, there can be little doubt that the evolution of a satisfactory transport network was one such necessary condition.

In 1776 Adam Smith wrote that "the division of labor is limited by the extent of the market."[1] In the United States, specialization was forced to await a solution to a transport problem that effectively divided the new country into thirteen (or perhaps more) small, largely independent economies. Moreover, the eastern seaboard is relatively devoid of natural resources, and had development been restricted to that area most of the economy's growth potential would certainly have been lost. Although the effects of lost opportunities can never be precisely measured, an economy limited to the eastern seaboard might well resemble today one of the nations of Eastern Europe. Finally, throughout much of the nineteenth century, the nation relied upon Europe for the manufactured products (particularly steel and machinery) that provided the basis for the industrial economy of the twentieth century. While a small proportion of these imports were paid for with European loans, most were financed through our exports of agricultural products. It is doubtful that in the absence of an adequate internal-transport system the country could have developed an agricultural industry capable of supporting the required flow of imports.

17–2. *The United States in 1800*

The transportation problem that faced the United States in 1800 was a formidable one. America's eastern seaboard (the area of

[1] Adam Smith, *The Wealth of Nations*, Book I, Chap. III.

first settlement) was almost completely cut off from the rest of the continent by the Appalachian Mountains. Furthermore, since its rivers generally flow west to east, they failed to provide an adequate north-south link. Because of these geographic difficulties, east-west transport most frequently depended upon pack animals, and north-south transport on coastwise shipping. Professor George Taylor has adduced some interesting examples of the relative inefficiency of highway transport vis-à-vis coastal shipping in this early period. It was, for example, much cheaper to transport grain from Northampton to Boston by water (a distance of some 300 miles) than by highway (a distance only a third as great). Moreover, a study of the distribution of costs along the water route indicates that it cost twice as much to carry the grain the first 36 miles by road as it did to transport it the remaining 250 miles by water.[2]

That the nation's transport problem was not solved earlier was probably more a reflection of technical difficulties than of any lack of interest. When the British blockade during the War of 1812 forced transport off the ocean, the ensuing cost increases (a doubling in the price of southern cotton delivered in Providence, for example) proved to almost everyone the need for an adequate internal-transport system. Even before the war, many of the nation's leaders (Hamilton and Gallatin, to name two) had been aware of this need. These men realized that it was necessary to build the network ahead of population; and, therefore, that some form of government subsidy was required to finance social-overhead capital. Although the federal government's role in this early stage was limited to the $7,000-000 spent on the construction of the National Pike, state and local governments contributed steadily to roadbuilding activity. So effective was this government aid (charters for private turnpike companies, investment in their securities, and direct support to local road commissions) that by 1820 most of the important cities in the North and East were interconnected by a usable system of surfaced roads.

Despite the nation's need for an adequate transport network and the flurry of roadbuilding activity during the first two decades of the nineteenth century, the turnpikes failed to provide an economically feasible solution to the transport problem. The failure of the highway system can be read in the history of the turnpike companies themselves. Organized with the expectations of large profits,

[2] George Taylor, *The Transportation Revolution, 1815–1860* (New York: Rinehart & Co., Inc., 1951).

only a handful realized any returns. The most successful company averaged dividends of only 5 per cent over its 100-year life. It was much more typical for a company to struggle against rising costs and falling revenues for a few years, then relinquish its roadway to the state (where the roads continued to be maintained at costs that were probably higher than even their social revenues would have warranted). The cause of failure lay not in the competition of a new, superior mode of transport, but in the technology of the period. Given an inland-transport technology based upon horse-drawn carts and wagons, costs (even with good roads) remained too high to compete with ocean transport in the north-south direction and too high to support interregional trade and specialization in the east-west direction.

17–3. *The Canals*

Despite the steady increase in highway mileage during the first two decades of the nineteenth century, the first step toward a solution to the nation's transport problem was not taken until the canal-building era. The history of canals can be traced back into antiquity, and, in the more recent period, private canals had provided the transport network necessary for Great Britain's economic development. As early as 1760 the Worsely Canal had reduced the price of coal in Manchester by 50 per cent. In less than thirty years, navigable waterways had been constructed throughout England.

The success of the English canals did much to encourage their introduction in the United States. The immediate success of the first American canal, the Erie (parts of which were opened in 1817), touched off a great burst of canal building. Unfortunately, important geographic and demographic differences between England and the United States were ignored in the first wave of enthusiasm, and ultimately problems arising from these differences led to the collapse of the American canal movement. In the first place, England is a relatively flat country, cut by numerous rivers. Canals are relatively costly on a per-mile base, but they can be profitable if short stretches of artificial waterway are used to link already existing natural routes. Such linked canals were typical in England. Although 363 miles long, the Erie was successful because it linked together over 2,000 miles of natural routes. In the United States, however, there were only a limited number of locations where the link principle could be applied. Too often the American canal route was a completely artificial waterway, and these were extremely expensive and could be economical only if very high revenues could be generated. In the second place, in England the canals had been built through already developed areas, and they generated revenue as soon as they were opened. In the United States, on the other hand, the western areas (and not even canals could compete with coastal shipping in the north-south trade) were almost completely undeveloped, with no prospect of immediate revenues. Canals through such undeveloped territory provide a perfect example of necessary social-overhead capital (see Chapter 9), requiring government participation. Interestingly enough, aside from the Erie almost the only canals that yielded an immediate profit were the Delaware and Pennsylvania coal canals, which were constructed with little government aid. In these latter cases, the canals (like those in England) were built to connect already developed areas.

Because of the undeveloped state of the areas served, most canals were heavily subsidized. Although the federal government played a minor role in canal finance, by 1860 it had granted over 4 million acres of land and had subscribed to more than $3,000,000 worth of stock of various canal companies. Much more aid did, however, come from the states. State governments on occasion purchased canal-company securities and more frequently provided indirect support through guarantees of indebtedness. Professor Carter Goodrich has estimated that government aid accounted for about 70 per cent of the canal expenditures between 1815 and 1860.[3]

The immediate profits earned by the Erie Canal ignited a wild speculative fever among the American people, who had been waiting for a breakthrough in transportation. The Erie was an immense project for its age involving, as it did, an outlay of over $10,000,000. The canal was 363 miles long, 20 feet wide, and 4 feet deep; it required 84 locks to overcome the rise of 630 feet from the Hudson to the highest point on the route, and the fall of 62 feet from there to Lake Erie. (It is interesting to note, when one considers the magnitude of the transport problem that faced the new nation, that the Erie's route was the most level path through the Appalachian barrier.) The success of the Erie was almost as great as its size. Seven years before it was completed (and only a year after it was begun) revenues from operating sections made substantial contributions to new construction costs. Once completed, the cost of east-west transport was so reduced that the Old Northwest was for the first time

[3] Carter Goodrich, *Government Promotion of American Canals and Railroads, 1800–1890* (New York: Columbia University Press, 1960).

integrated with the East. Although cost estimates for the period are fragmentary, it appears that freight charges between Buffalo and New York were reduced from twenty to two cents a ton-mile by the opening of the canal.

When the success of the Erie was assured, there was hardly a village, town, city, or state whose inhabitants did not think that its economic position could be improved if only a canal could be built nearby—nor did it appear to make much difference where the canal was to lead. In the East the canals were most frequently designed to connect the upland farming areas with the tidelands, and in the West the typical canal connected the inland areas with the Great Lakes (and thus through the Erie to New York) or the Ohio River. These routes were not the only ones selected. The merchants of Philadelphia, for example, in an attempt to recapture some of the trade lost via the Erie to New York, actually completed a canal connecting Philadelphia with Pittsburgh (a canal requiring a portage railway over some of the higher Allegheny peaks). A portion of the canals were rationally planned and almost certainly would have been able to operate profitably had railroad improvements not made them obsolete.

It has been traditional to believe that, despite their early promise, the canals failed to provide an adequate solution to the problems of interregional transport in the United States. As evidence, economic historians have cited the competitive superiority of the railroads (as evidenced by their rapid innovation), and they have buttressed their case by enumerating a sizable list of defects in canal transport. These defects included the relative slowness of canal transport, its inability to operate through the winter, and the high cost of construction in areas not blessed by a plethora of natural waterways. None of the critics have attempted to estimate precisely the aggregate canal-railroad cost differentials nor have they attempted to assess what the course of American development might have been if railroads had not been innovated. Recently Professor Robert Fogel has attempted to answer both of these questions. He has discovered that, although railroads were cheaper than canals, the cost differentials were less than one might have supposed. He has suggested that in the absence of railroads, development probably would have proceeded in much the same fashion as it did. Finally he concluded that it would have been feasible to build additional canals to open the trans-Mississippi west (at least to the 100th meridian), and that the absence of railroads would have reduced gross national product by only a very few per cent.

17–4. *The Railroads*

If Fogel is correct, the railroads were less of a revolutionary innovation than many had thought. Under any condition, however, railroads were a cheaper form of transport than the canals, and with few exceptions, once innovated, they rapidly replaced the canals. It was, therefore, on the basis of the railroad that America's transportation system matured to the point where it could support a continental market and it was the railroad that effected the processes of interregional specialization and trade that were so important for the growth of per-capita income.

Most of the early developmental work on the railroad was carried out in England. In 1825, the Stockton and Darlington became the first regularly scheduled public railroad in the world. The advantages of railway transport did not escape the American entrepreneur, and between 1826 and 1831 several horse-drawn railroads were opened in this country. In 1830 the *Baltimore Sun* announced that the new Baltimore and Ohio Railroad had run a train between Baltimore and Elicott Mills, a distance of thirteen miles, in "the amazing time of one hour and four minutes," and by 1831 three railroads had applied steam power to their trains.

Although the canals were great engineering feats, quite likely their greatest contribution to American development was the impetus they gave the move to adapt the steam engine to inland transport. The merchants of Boston and Baltimore had seen their business decline as the Erie monopolized the western trade. Faced with the same decline in business that had led Philadelphia merchants to build a canal system, they spearheaded attempts to provide their cities with western railroad connections. In Baltimore, the Baltimore and Ohio was launched, and in Boston work commenced on a series of short lines that were to link that city with the Hudson. From this simple start the American railroad network mushroomed, and within twenty years it was the most extensive in the world. (See Table 17–1.)

The term "industrial revolution" frequently is limited to the developments in textiles and iron and steel. While the importance of these developments cannot be minimized, this limited definition tends to cause the student to overlook equally important developments in other industries. In particular, it fails to give sufficient emphasis to the "industrial revolution" in transport. Underlying the new railroad technology were two fundamental developments. First, the evolution of the steam engine, coupled with the concurrent discovery of certain high-test alloys, permitted the development of a high-pressure engine capable of serving as a prime mover. Second, developments in civil engineering made it possible to survey, cut, fill, and grade railway right of ways at reasonable cost. In addition to

TABLE 17–1

RAILROAD MILEAGE BY GEOGRAPHIC SECTOR, 1830–1950

Year	Eastern (1*)	Southern (2†)	Central (3‡)	Prairie and Southwest (4§)	Rocky Mountain and Pacific (5‖)	Total
1830	73	0	0	0	0	73
1840	1,673	1,424	231	0	0	3,328
1850	5,290	2,154	1,435	0	0	8,879
1860	9,627	7,789	12,842	365	23	30,636
1870	14,400	9,712	21,893	4,330	2,550	52,885
1880	20,240	13,192	38,050	15,303	6,886	93,671
1890	25,197	25,346	56,786	38,433	17,819	163,581
1900	28,571	32,980	63,259	45,582	22,929	193,321
1910	30,233	44,740	70,105	62,584	32,752	240,414
1920	30,718	43,407	72,687	65,859	36,029	248,700
1930	30,298	44,812	72,078	68,506	37,142	252,836
1940	27,327	42,726	64,796	64,951	35,282	235,082
1950	25,983	40,555	62,609	62,458	33,544	225,149

Sources: 1830, 1840, 1850, from *Hunts Merchant Magazine,* Volume XXV (September, 1851); 1860, 1870, 1880, from Henry V. Poor, *Manual of the Railroads of the United States, 1870–71, 1880, 1882* (New York: J. W. Greene); 1890 to 1910, from Interstate Commerce Commission, *Statistics of Railways* (Washington, D.C.: GPO, 1890, 1900, 1910); 1920 and 1930, from Slason Thompson, *Railways Statistics of the United States* (Chicago: Bureau of Railway News and Statistics, 1920 and 1930); 1940 and 1950, from Eastern Railroad Presidents' Conference, *A Yearbook of Railroad Information* (New York: 1940, 1950).

* Including Maine, Vermont, New Hampshire, Connecticut, Rhode Island, Massachusetts, New York, Pennsylvania, New Jersey, Delaware.

† Including Maryland, West Virginia, Virginia, District of Columbia, North Carolina, South Carolina, Florida, Georgia, Alabama, Mississippi, Louisiana.

‡ Including Ohio, Indiana, Illinois, Wisconsin, Missouri, Iowa, Michigan, Kentucky, Tennessee.

§ Including North Dakota, South Dakota, Kansas, Nebraska, Minnesota, Oklahoma, Texas, Arizona, New Mexico, Arkansas.

‖ Including Idaho, Colorado, Wyoming, Montana, Utah, Washington, Oregon, California, Nevada.

Improved railroad Technology.

these basic improvements, the nineteenth century also saw many more widely publicized additions to railroad technology. The invention of the T-rail, capable of bearing heavy weights over protracted periods, together with the innovation of steel (rather than cast-iron) rails and an increase in the weight of rails, underlay the steady increase in the weight of rolling stock. The period was further marked by the development of a new road base, the tie-and-graded bed. This relatively simple combination was cheaper, more resilient, and much longer lasting than alternative base forms. It is interesting to note that in England the belief in the need for a very substantial roadbed lasted well into the nineteenth century. As a result, while the capital costs of English railroads were much greater than those in the United States, their operating costs were not noticeably lower. Further, in the 1870's the invention and use of automatic air brakes and couplers increased safety and reduced the costs of freight-car shippings, because there was less freight breakage with controlled stops. Finally, the standardization of the railway gauge (a process not completed until the present century) turned the American railroads into a truly national network. These latter developments were, however, largely frosting on the cake. Although they all tended to make the railroads more economical, it was the developments in

TABLE 17–2

PERCENTAGE DISTRIBUTION OF ADDITIONS TO NET RAILWAY MILEAGE, 1830–1910

Years	*Total Net New Mileage*	*East* (1)	*South* (2)	*Central* (3)	*Prairie and South West* (4)	*Rocky Mountain and Pacific* (5)
1830–1840	3,255	49.2	43.7	7.1	0	0
1840–1850	5,551	65.2	13.1	21.7	0	0
1850–1860	21,757	19.9	25.9	52.4	1.7	.1
1860–1870	22,259	21.4	8.6	40.7	17.9	11.3
1870–1880	40,786	14.3	8.5	39.6	26.9	10.6
1880–1890	69,918	7.1	17.4	26.8	33.1	15.6
1890–1900	29,740	11.3	25.7	21.8	24.0	17.2
1900–1910	47,093	3.5	25.0	14.5	36.1	20.9

Source: See Table 17–1.

engine and engineering technology that made railroad transport possible.

The figures on railroad mileage alone (see Table 17–1) do not totally describe the changes undergone by the nation's transport system between 1830 and World War I. In the earliest years, most of the roads were short lines built to connect local centers in the South and East with the ports of the coast. (See Table 17–2.) During the 1850's, however, the railroads turned west. By 1860, Detroit, Chicago, St. Louis, New Orleans, and Memphis were tied together and with the East Coast (although sometimes this latter tie was rather indirect). The latter ante-bellum years also saw the beginnings of the railroad-merger movement that has continued to the present (at this writing the B & O is considering offers to merge with both the C & O and the New York Central). A few of the early roads had been built as unified interregional systems (the B & O, the Erie, and the Illinois Central, to cite three); but most of the early roads were merely intercity short lines. To these roads the process of merger (although perhaps resulting in a greater degree of monopoly) brought more efficient freight handling and greater pressure for a standard gauge.

Although the United States possessed more railway mileage than any other country in 1850, much more was needed before our national economy could become a reality. In 1870, for example, while the network was adequate east of the Mississippi and north of Washington, D.C., the South was without a northern connection and possessed only a very tenuous one with the West. In the West, the situation, though slightly better, still left room for improvement. By 1870 the railroads had reached Minneapolis to the north and the UP-CP meeting at Promontory Point had linked Chicago with San Francisco; but, while the first railroad bridge had been built across the Mississippi in 1856, it was 1870 before bridging was general.

During the next half century these gaps in the nation's transport system were filled, and total mileage increased to almost a quarter of a million (see Table 17–1). In the East, trunk lines were already built and most of the new mileage was in subsidiary lines and double tracking.

In the South and West, the period saw trunk lines reach almost every large city and subsidiary lines enter practically every local center. In the South, although progress was relatively slow, the C & O completed a trans-Appalachian line in 1873, and there were three more lines operating over the mountains before the panic of 1907. Moreover, the north-south link was completed in 1873 when the Southern arrived in Atlanta. When the Seaboard was completed in 1900, a total of four roads connected New York with the cotton states. Growth in the prairie and southwestern states was even more rapid. In the last quarter of the century, the Sante Fe, Milwaukee, Burlington, the Rock Island, and many smaller lines made major additions to their right of ways. In the far West, the Union Pacific-Central Pacific link between Chicago and San Francisco was followed by the completion of the Southern Pacific and Sante Fe to Los Angeles, and the Northern Pacific, UP, Great Northern, and

Milwaukee to Seattle and Portland, as well as a north-south road connecting Seattle and Los Angeles.

By 1914 the United States possessed a railroad network capable of supporting a large and geographically diverse economic complex. Because of the volumes of literature written on "the railroad problem," it may be useful to comment briefly on the difference between financial and economic capital. The term "financial capital" refers to the paper claims on assets, while the term "economic capital" refers to the physical assets themselves. The issuance of financial capital aided the transfer of resources to railroad construction; but, once the roads were built, the economy continued to benefit from their services even though the operating companies were in continual financial difficulties (financial claims disappear in bankruptcy proceedings, but the real assets continue to function). The railroad system could, therefore, continue to serve the economy even though almost every road built after the Civil War passed through bankruptcy at least once.

There can be little doubt that the story of railroad finance in the post-bellum period provides one of the most colorful chapters in the history of American business. Before the Civil War, most roads had been built through developed areas and usually had been financed by local interests (public and private). In this early period, the investors expected almost immediate returns, both direct (in interest and dividends) and indirect (increased trade and commerce to their cities and states), from their investment. In the post-bellum period, however, conditions were quite different. Construction was frequently ahead of population; and in these instances, returns were, at best, delayed. At the same time, the growth of a national securities market (see Chapter 13) permitted large amounts of financial capital to be raised, through the public sale of securities to individuals far removed from the scene of operations.

The lure of large land grants, and the wave of optimism engendered by the vision of western development, combined to make railroad securities appear very attractive. Securities sales boomed both here and abroad, and promoters realized fantastic profits from railroad organization, reorganization, and merger. As a result, by 1900 over one third of the roads' total equity (1.25 out of a total of 3.1 billion dollars) was pure "water" (that is, investment siphoned off in promoters' profits or unnecessary expenditures, leaving neither assets nor revenues). Nor were the financial scandals limited to the business community. Instead, they grew until they had embroiled much of the political community as well, and, at least once, touched the office of the Vice-President. Because the roads had been built well ahead of demand (like other forms of social-overhead capital, demand depended upon the investment), and because the speculative fever had left the roads with an impossible financial structure (the bonded indebtedness of the Erie, for example, was equal to the company's assets and the stock represented nothing but water), the period was characterized by a steady stream of railroad bankruptcies. In 1872 the Erie, the Northern Pacific, the Kansas Pacific, and several lesser roads went bankrupt; in the 1890's, roads representing 30 per cent of the railroad investment (including, among others, the Burlington, the Norfolk and Western, the Santa Fe, the Frisco, the Union Pacific, the Northern Pacific, and the Georgia Central) passed into receivership; and during the first decade of the present century the Pere Marquette, the Chicago and Eastern Illinois, the Rock Island, the Missouri Pacific, Kansas-Missouri and Texas, and the Frisco all went under.

Despite the high failure rate, the railroads *were* built; and, with but few exceptions, the trade that followed in the wake of the roads generated profits sufficient (at least on the basis of actual assets) to make railroad securities the blue-chip investments of the period between 1910 and 1929. The benefits derived by the economy are easy to measure. Without the roads, the Old Northwest could never have become the nation's industrial heartland, the prairies could never have become the breadbasket of the economy, and the West Coast could never have been more than tenuously tied to the rest of the country.

Although it is almost impossible to obtain any actual figures on railroad freight charges during most of the nineteenth century, it is now widely believed that rates were generally falling in the postbellum period; and as Table 17–3 indicates, this trend continued until the 1920's. The decline in rates can probably be traced to an increase in competition coupled with significant technological improvements (particularly heavier and faster rolling stock). Whatever the cause, there can be little doubt that low-cost interregional transport played an important part in the growth of specialization of industry between the Civil War and World War I.

Despite the contribution made by the railroads to the growth of the economy, during the latter half of the nineteenth century the public became critical of some of the policies pursued by the roads. The railroads' financial activities did much to align public feeling against them; and their cavalier treatment of customers with whom they enjoyed a monopolistic position engendered sufficient complaint that, by 1914, railroads had become the nation's first publicly controlled industry.

By the third quarter of the nineteenth century, although there was considerable railroad competition along major routes, over large areas single railroads exercised an almost complete transport monopoly. In pursuit of short-run profits, management followed practices that, in the long run, led the roads into a nearly hopeless position. Over routes where competition did exist, the railroads tended to collude to maintain prices and divide the market (the famous railroad pools of the 1870's are the results of such policies). Where a single railroad had a monopoly position over a portion of its route and was in competition over the rest, its price structure tended to discriminate against customers on the monopolistic portion and in

TABLE 17–3

INTERCITY RAILROADS' FREIGHT DATA, 1882–1960

Year	*Ton-Miles of Freight Carried (Millions)*	*Revenue per Ton-Mile—Constant Prices (Cents)*
1882	39,302	1.65
1890	76,207	1.65
1900	141,597	1.30
1910	255,017	1.07
1920	413,699	.65
1930	385,815	1.24
1940	375,369	1.21
1950	591,550	.82
1960	594,855	1.40

Sources: *Historical Statistics; Historical Statistics* (revised); *Statistical Abstract,* 1960.

favor of those in the competitive market areas (the long- and short-haul charges so bitterly opposed by midwestern farmers were examples of this practice). Moreover, the railroads were frequently accused (and probably almost as frequently guilty) of providing secret cash rebates to favored customers. Such rebates, of course, gave favored customers an unfair competitive advantage. It is interesting to note that the common thread running through most of the antirailroad charges is one not of monopoly but of inequity. Although the most vocal critics at times claimed the railroads were monopolists, they seldom complained about the effect of the monopolistic prices charged by a railroad possessing a monopoly over its entire route. Instead, most frequently their complaints were cast in terms of the inequity of charging different prices to different people for the same service.

The first serious complaints were voiced by the midwestern farmers who, finding their incomes falling and unable to understand the nature of the world commodity market over which they had no control, chose to blame the railroads for their problems. Although many of their particular complaints were probably unjustified, the transport monopoly undoubtedly did distort the allocation of resources. For a time the railroads were able to ignore the farmers, but when they were joined by members of the business community, it was inevitable that the government would act against the roads. At first the appeals for railroad reform were addressed to state governments, who responded with a series of state regulatory laws. When, however, the Wabash decision (1886) effectively removed the roads from state jurisdiction, the reformers were forced to turn to the federal government.

The Act to Regulate Commerce was passed in 1887 and established the pattern of federal regulation that has existed to the present. The act set up the Interstate Commerce Commission, demanded reasonable rates, and prohibited personal discrimination, long- and short-haul differentials, and freight pooling. Although subsequent court decisions temporarily emasculated the Commission's regulatory powers, the act established the framework for future regulation. By 1910, new legislation (the Hepburn and Mann-Elkins acts) re-established the Commission's powers by, among other things, permitting them to set rates and examine the railroads' books.

Since that time, the railroads have increasingly come to depend on the government for all important decisions, and during World War I they were actually nationalized for a time. More recently, although the area of ICC control has been widened and the process of rate making has become more complicated, the pattern of regulation has not been altered significantly.

It can hardly be denied that where monopolies exist proper regulation can improve the allocation of resources and promote economic growth. On the other hand, in any regulatory mechanism there is a strong tendency to base present practice on past precedent rather than on current need. For American transport, regulation has continually been characterized by attempts to apply nineteenth-century remedies to twentieth-century problems. In the case of the railroads, regulation came half a century too late. From 1850 until 1920, the railroads had an effective monopoly on transport (although there certainly was interroad competition in many areas). But since that time, the roads have been faced with increasing competition from trucks for freight and from autos and planes for passenger traffic. This competition from new transport forms has, in the past two decades, reduced the railroads' share of total intercity freight movements from 62 per cent in 1939 to 44 per cent in 1961.

Although there have been many new technological developments since World War I, there have been few changes in railroad management. Moreover, the changes that have occurred (the growth of the railroad trade associations and a change in management's attitude in favor of regulation) appear to have adversely affected the industry's attitude toward growth. While the ICC has promoted the growth of the trade associations because they make regulations easier, these associations appear far more interested in promoting oligopolistic agreements and in preventing price competition than they do in fostering railroad growth. Management's attitude too, has tended to reflect an increasing reliance on the government. Faced with growing competition from the truck and air lines, management has tended to insist on increases in the scope of federal regulation rather than on greater competitive freedoms for the no longer monopolistic railroads.

At the moment, the problems of the railroads are many and diverse, but it is difficult not to conclude that regulation has contributed immeasurably to (if not actually caused) many of these problems. If regulation had been instituted in 1860, it might have made a significant contribution to economic growth and to an improvement in the allocation of resources. However, at the present it appears to bar the way to further growth and to contribute to greater resource misallocation. Although the authors would be the first to agree that price discrimination (a probable first effect of the removal of regulation) would have an undesirable effect upon the allocation of resources, the adverse effects of continued regulation appear even more serious.

The ICC's unwillingness to permit railroads to drop unprofitable lines has resulted in a continual subsidy from the roads' stockholders and well-located freight shippers to passengers and shippers in uneconomic locations. While there may be nothing wrong with such a subsidy if that is the nation's wish, it appears highly inequitable to saddle a small fraction of the nation with the entire burden. Moreover, the economic results include a misallocation of passenger travel among competing transport forms and of industry between competing geographic locations. In addition, the present rate structure is extremely cumbersome. With some 13,000 individual tariffs to be considered and fifty years of bureaucratic precedence to be overcome, rates do not easily adjust to changes in economic conditions. For example, the rigid rate structure has prevented the railroads recapturing business lost to the trucks—business that, on the basis of cost, should belong to the railroads (e.g., long hauls). The result has been (and still is) a serious misallocation of transport resources.

Regulation has not, of course, been the only problem facing the railroads. They have also been characterized by particularly unimaginative management and plagued by severe labor problems. But in the long run these latter problems are probably peripheral. Their solution would be desirable; but unless something is done about regulation, nationalization or a federal subsidy may be required to keep the railroads operating. Either alternative appears to be a rather high price to pay for the psychological benefits derived from continuing to punish the roads for their century-old crimes.

17–5. *Highway Transport*

Despite the importance of the buckboard and covered wagon in western myth and TV drama, highway transport did not play an important role in the interregional movement of goods and people until after the evolution of the motor vehicle. The effects of the application of the internal-combustion engine to inland transport are readily apparent in the data presented in Table 17–4. The construction of surfaced highways proceeded very slowly from the end of the turnpike era to the close of the 19th century. With the advent of the automobile, the rate of highway construction increased sharply. In the last half of the nineteenth century, total mileage increased only 80 per cent; but that figure was almost matched in the first decade of the twentieth century; and, in the first half of the century, mileage increased by more than 1,200 per cent.

The most immediate effect of the surge of motor vehicles onto the many miles of newly constructed highways was the evolution of a new transport network both complementary to and competitive with the railroads. For passenger movement, it provided a highly flexible commuting instrument that at the same time permitted a greater degree of geographic diversification and wrought immeasurable changes on the structure of urban life (see Chapter 16). More recently, the development of truck transport has added an important new link in the nation's freight network and has made it possible for industry to locate in areas not served by the railroads.

For the government, the advent of the motor vehicle has created new and still unsolved problems. Private enterprise has seldom been successful in road construction. As a result, the local, state, and federal governments have borne almost the entire burden of the million and a half miles of highway built since the turn of the century. While state and local governments have always financed the bulk of highway construction, since 1916 they have come to depend upon federal aid for a significant portion of their highway construction and maintenance costs. The present system of interstate

TABLE 17–4

SURFACED-HIGHWAY MILEAGE AND MOTOR-VEHICLE REGISTRATION, 1800–1962

Year	*Miles of Surfaced Highway (Thousands)*	*Motor-Vehicle Registration (Thousands)* Auto	Trucks and Buses
1800	1		
1850	71		
1900	128	8	0
1910	204	458	10
1920	369	8,131	1,108
1930	694	22,972	3,519
1940	1,367	27,372	4,590
1950	1,679	40,185	8,382
1960	2,179	61,724	12,217
1962	(n.a.)	65,644	12,987

Sources: *Historical Statistics. Statistical Abstract.*

national defense highways is only the most recent of a long list of joint federal-state highway projects.

Although government regulation of the private auto has been limited to certain licensing requirements (all at the state and local level), pressure from the railroads, misguided reformers, and an established bureaucracy has caused the federal government to bring truck lines under ICC regulation. While there may once have been some reason to regulate the railroads, there appears to be no reason to regulate the trucking industry. Highway transport is characterized by extreme ease of entry (anybody who can afford the down payment on a truck can enter); and, since almost all capital costs are borne by the government, the possibilities of monopoly are practically nonexistent. Nor has regulation even effectively protected the railroads. Since regulation applies only to common carriers, shippers have responded by diverting cargoes from common to lease and contract carriers. The only result: a probable misallocation of resources.

The development of the automobile has been felt almost as much outside the field of transportation as within. During their period of growth, the railroads (and to a lesser extent the canals) played an important secondary role in the economy. For almost fifty years they absorbed a sizable portion of the nation's savings and they consumed a significant portion of its intermediate products. What was true for the railroads in the nineteenth century was even more true for the motor-vehicle industry in the present century. Highway construction has continually absorbed a significant share of the nation's total investment (particularly if one includes the gas stations, garages, and public buildings that are tied to highway construction). In addition, not only is the motor-vehicle industry one of the largest employers of labor, but it is also without peer as a consumer of intermediate products. For example, in the past decade and a half it has absorbed about one fifth of the nation's steel production and three fifths of its rubber output. In addition, of course, the 50 million cars and trucks on the highway consume a large portion of the nation's petroleum output.

17–6. *Ocean Transport*

Our ocean-transport system is included in this chapter because, in the early years at least, it provided an important link with our markets overseas and, at the same time, provided us with an important source of foreign exchange. At the beginning of the nineteenth century, American ships not only carried almost all of America's exports but also carried a sizable portion of the rest of the world's trade. American dominance (continuing until the 1830's) was based largely on efficiencies in ship construction. American designs were among the best in the world, and construction costs were only about two thirds those in Europe. However, as time passed, forests receded and costs rose; and in the 1850's the rise of the iron steamship wrote finis to America's competitive advantage.

Even before our cost advantage had disappeared, however, the federal government had begun to aid the merchant marine, and this policy has continued down to the present. In general, the federal government has tailored its programs to fit the shipbuilders' rather than the shippers' or ship operators' wishes. As early as 1818, Congress restricted the coasting trade to American-built ships, and in the 1850's it granted an outright subsidy (the most common form of aid today) to American-built mail steamers in competition with the British packets.

The increasing cost disadvantage, coupled with the government's refusal to let foreign-built ships obtain American registry, resulted in a steady decline of importance of the merchant marine after 1850 (see Table 17–5). In 1840, for example, American ships were carrying four fifths of our exports, but by 1910 they were transporting less than one tenth. The merchant marine revived temporarily in the 1920's when the government sold its war-surplus shipping to American firms at very low prices. Within a few years, however, as these war-surplus ships aged, the merchant marine be-

TABLE 17–5

THE AMERICAN MERCHANT MARINE, 1800–1962

Year	*Gross Tonnage of Fleet (Thousands)*	*Gross Tonnage in Foreign Trade (Thousands)*
1800	972	667
1820	1,280	584
1840	2,181	763
1860	5,354	2,379
1880	4,068	1,314
1900	5,165	817
1920	16,324	9,925
1940	14,018	3,638
1957	29,421	17,265
1960	28,581	14,737
1962	25,456	12,393

Sources: *Statistical Abstract. Historical Statistics.*

gan to slip back to its previous low position. A further recovery was experienced after World War II when again the government sold a part of its fleet (a fleet that then represented about 60 per cent of the world's tonnage), but even this gift is probably insufficient to achieve a permanent reversal in the fleet's decline. In the long run, there appears little hope for this sector of the transport industry. The ships that remain in the fleet will probably do so only because of government subsidy payments. There may be noneconomic arguments (e.g., national defense) for subsidy payments to the fleet; but, like any subsidy, these grants result in a misallocation of resources (goods could be hauled more cheaply in foreign ships); and the costs of misallocation should be carefully weighed against the alleged gains from the subsidy.

17–7. *Miscellaneous Transport Forms*

Although inland-water transport was never as important as one might imagine from reading *Huckleberry Finn,* it nonetheless was fairly important on the western rivers in the ante-bellum period. Because of competition from the railroads, the relative importance of the inland common carriers declined after the Civil War; and since then their significance has been largely limited to the Great Lakes. In the last half of the century there was a gradual merger of these lines with the railroads; and in 1912 intracoastal carriers were brought under ICC regulation. More recently, there has been a steady increase in the importance of single-purpose ships (particularly ore and oil carriers) and these specialists have made important contributions to the integration of two of our greatest industries.

A second development of even more importance is the growth of pipelines in the past seventy years. First laid in the 1870's (to provide the railroads with competition on oil shipments), the pipelines have proved themselves profitable and never in need of government aid (the only transport sector that can make this claim). Designed originally to carry liquid products, more recently pipelines have been adapted to gaseous and solid commodities as well. There were only 10,000 miles of pipeline in 1914, but today (1961 data) there are more than 154,000 miles of pipeline in the economy.

Much more impressive from the typical American's point of view (although probably of less economic significance) has been the growth of scheduled airlines in the past thirty years. In 1961, the airlines handled far more intercity passenger traffic than the railroads, and they flew scheduled flights over almost 107,814 miles of domestic airways. The airlines have not been able to achieve this growth without large public subsidies, although the size of the subsidies has declined in recent years. In fact, since World War II almost all major truck lines have become self-supporting, although as in the case of the trucks the government provides fixed capital. For the industry as a whole, federal mail payments (including subsidies) have declined from about 15 to less than 5 per cent of total operating revenue. The picture is still not perfect, however, since most cost studies have shown that (barring tremendous technological changes or a complete shift in consumer tastes) it will never be economical to carry passengers on trips under 200 miles. If the public continues to demand that the airlines provide such service, it will almost certainly be necessary for the government and the long-flight passengers to continue to subsidize short-flight fares. The noneconomic arguments for airline subsidies seem even less telling than those for other transport forms (e.g., the merchant marine). Much more reasonable from an economic point of view would be an abandonment of all but safety regulations and a return to a free market. Such a policy would, most likely, result in the dropping of service to many small communities and a transfer of resources now committed to feeder operations to the job the airlines can do best—moving passengers rapidly over long distances.

17–8. *Conclusions*

There is no doubt that the development of the transport network has wrought great changes on the economic and demographic face of the nation. In 1820, New York's industry was scattered, more or less randomly, over the counties of the state. Within ten years that pattern had been markedly altered, and industry lay concentrated along the route of the Erie Canal. Every successive link in the nation's transport network had similar, though perhaps less dramatic, effects on the nation's economy. In 1820, there were few economic centers not located on the coast or along navigable waterways, but with the growth of railroad transport industrial complexes developed in such "dry" locations as Dayton, Denver, and Dallas. Moreover, when Washington was elected, both the North and South were agrarian economies; and, if anything, the South may have been the more developed. A century later the North, served by an adequate transport system, had attained a rapid rate of economic growth and was able to match the world's leaders in industrialization, while the South remained an agrarian economy, growing but little more rapidly than it had during the previous century. Southern development awaited transport penetration, and it has been only since the completion of the railroad network in the present century that its economic potential has begun to be realized. Furthermore, the growth of the transport system revolutionized the structure of agriculture during the nineteenth century. The integration of the Old Northwest and the prairie states into the eastern economy caused a radical change in New England agriculture and made the Midwest the breadbasket of the nation. Moreover, adequate transport spelled the end to the economic importance of the subsistence farm and gained for agriculture the benefits (and costs) of specialization more usually reserved for the industrial sectors. Finally, and most obviously, the network supported a westward population shift that in 160 years (1790 to 1950) has moved the center of population from a point twenty-five miles east of Baltimore, Maryland, to a point eight miles north-northeast of Olney in Richmond County, Illinois.

Suggested Readings

DEARING, C. L., AND OWEN, WILFRED. *National Policy on Transportation.* Washington, D.C.: Brookings Institution, 1949.

GOODRICH, CARTER. *Government Promotion of American Canals and Railroads.* New York: Columbia University Press, 1960.

MEYER, J. R., ET AL. *The Economics of Competition in the Transportation Industries.* Cambridge, Mass.: Harvard University Press, 1959.

RIPLEY, W. Z. *Railroads: Rates and Regulations.* New York: Longmans, Green & Co., Inc., 1912.

TAYLOR, GEORGE. *The Transportation Revolution, 1815–1860.* New York: Rinehart & Co., Inc., 1951.

Chapter 18 FOREIGN TRADE

18–1. *Exports and Imports*

The United States is part of a world-wide economy that is composed of nations which buy from each other and sell to each other. In 1962 we exported about $21 billion of our commodities to the world and purchased about $16 billion of imports from the world. These exports and imports made us (as we have long been) the world's largest single international trader. In 1963 we accounted for about 17 per cent of all the free world's exports and about 13 per cent of its imports. The nearest country to us in this regard was the United Kingdom with about 8 per cent of world exports and just over 9 per cent of imports. We use the marketplace of the world in much the same way that members of any economic community use their local market. We sell what we do not use ourselves in order to purchase what we do not produce. Moreover, we are thus able to use goods and services which others make more efficiently than we do, and to concentrate our efforts on the production of goods and services which we are able to produce most efficiently—just as a farmer who *could* make his own clothes and produce his own food knows that he is able to have more and better clothing if he concentrates his efforts on the growing of food, selling it in the market, and using the proceeds to buy clothing that others can make better and more cheaply than he. In this way the farmer specializes in the production of food and the clothing manufacturer specializes in the manufacture of clothing. Both the farmer and the manufacturer acquire more food *and* more clothing by specialization and trade than they would have if they both tried to produce both food and clothing for their own use.

As an economy we import commodities and services that foreigners specialize in making, and they in turn buy our exports—commodities and services that we specialize in making. It is important to note that trade is a two-way street. Just as the manufacturer could not buy the farmer's food if the farmer did not buy clothing, we cannot sell our commodities to foreign countries if we do not buy from them. What we decide to sell and what we decide to buy is determined by a wide variety of factors, including the relative endowment of natural resources, the kinds of crops that can be grown most effectively, the skill of the workers, and the kind and quality of capital equipment available in each country. As we noted in an earlier chapter, the composition of our exports and imports is determined by our *comparative advantage* in the production of goods and services. It is of fundamental importance to realize that any given comparative advantage can be a momentary thing. To be sure, nature's bounty of endowments, distributed unevenly around the world, determines a large part of the specialized production and trade that does exist. But technological change, education, and scientific advances, as well as the opening of new lands, change the balance of specialization continuously. Thus Britain, which formerly was primarily an exporter of woolens, later led the world in output and export of cotton textiles. But Britain is now a major exporter of heavy engineering products and her cotton exports are no longer so important. Similarly, Japan is now a major exporter of cameras and optical instruments whereas before 1939 she specialized in textiles, toys, and other light manufactures.

The United States has a similar history. We began our career in international trade as a country specializing in the production and sale of primary commodities and food that we exchanged for highly manufactured and semimanufactured goods made in Europe (we will discuss this in more detail below). As our industrial sector developed, especially in the late nineteenth and early twentieth centuries, the proportion of manufactured goods in our exports rose while the proportion of primary products and food declined. At the same time, the structure of our imports also changed radically; where we had imported a high proportion of finished manufactured goods we now imported mostly primary products.

These shifts reflect the changes in comparative advantages that occurred as our technology became more advanced and as we changed from an agricultural and rural economy to a manufacturing and urban economy. Part of this transformation was related to improvements in transportation. These alone (the development first of the railways, and later large ocean-going steamers, followed by trucking, and air transport to a lesser degree) were bound to make some local specialties part of our national pattern of specialization. For example, with the advent of railways the great western wheatlands were bound to develop a specialized agriculture that was supplied by trade with manufactured products. Moreover, the wheat and livestock industry of the West naturally enough formed an early base for trade with both European manufacturing countries and with tropical producers of coffee, cane sugar, and other exotic products.

18–2. *Comparative Advantage and Tariffs*

To some extent, of course, our foreign trade was affected by our commercial policies as well as strictly by comparative advantages based upon free markets. A tariff (a tax on imports) that keeps out foreign commodities or reduces their importation may create a market for domestic production that would not exist otherwise. That is to say, whereas we might use men and resources in the production of a given set of commodities where we are efficient, this relative efficiency, measured by the profitability of production, can be altered by tariffs. With protection, resources can be induced to shift into the manufacture of commodities that would otherwise be produced abroad. The structure of our foreign trade is altered accordingly, as regards both imports and exports; and, of course, the result is a misallocation of resources. The reasons for this sort of government interference with free-market specialization are varied. It is sometimes argued that because of certain economies of scale "infant industries" can grow to maturity and efficiency if there is, initially, enough protection to allow the costs of their youthful inefficiency to be absorbed by the consumer. Again, it is sometimes argued that "national defense" requires us to maintain relatively inefficient industries in case war should cut us off from foreign supplies. Other arguments include the curious one—which has wide popular appeal—that men and resources should be used inefficiently by us to make import-competing products in order to protect the economy from the "products of cheap foreign labor."

Tariffs or quotas that place direct controls on physical quantities of commodities that might be imported tend to change comparative advantages. Initially, the balance of domestic industry is changed by making some kinds of production profitable through a limitation of the supply of competing products (restriction of imports). The change in profitability alters the supply of men and resources devoted to the most efficient lines of production in the country and also tends to reduce the supply of dollars available to other nations (by restricting their earnings from sales of their goods and services to us). The structure of international trade is affected accordingly. We cannot say precisely how much the balance of our comparative advantages has been changed by these forces. F. W. Taussig, the foremost student of our early tariff policies, concluded that, with the unimportant exceptions of the American silk industry and the cotton-spinning industry before 1824, our tariffs had had no noticeable effects upon the growth of some of the "infant industries" they were designed to protect. Our protected industries have either always had comparative advantages, or they were never able to achieve comparative advantages even with tariff protection. Moreover, it appears difficult to argue that if the industry has remained "infant" for 150 years there is much probability of its ever attaining adolescence. Thus it would appear that the American tariff has made little contribution to economic growth, but rather that it has been merely a long-term subsidy paid by the consumer to American business.

Although our commercial policies were sensitive to current business conditions, until the Civil War they were not always protective in the extreme. One can argue, in a broad way, that up to 1860 our tariff policy tended toward liberalization (lower tariffs) in times of prosperity, and to restrictionist autarchy (higher tariffs) in times of adversity. The principal ante-bellum restrictionist legislation was passed in 1816, 1824, 1828, and 1842. In each case there had previously been difficulties in the economy that, it was argued, warranted protection of favored industries. In 1832, on the other hand, and again in 1846 and 1857, the protectionist tide was reversed following periods of relative prosperity. The tariff schedules of 1846 were so low that the act of that year was known as the "Free-Trade Tariff" (sic). Up to that point, given a thoroughgoing protectionist bias, our policy was fairly flexible. In Table 18–1, a rough measure of these events is seen. By 1830 the proportions had risen strongly, compared to 1821. By 1840 the proportions were down, reflecting the liberalization of the 1830's. Then, by 1850, the liberal effects of the act of 1846 offset the rigors of the act of 1842. By 1860 the tariff level was the lowest of the whole ante-bellum period.

In 1861 however, with the passage of the high rates of the Morrill Tariff, protectionist interests in this country gained strength that only in recent years has shown any signs of weakening. The Morrill Tariff raised average tariff rates from 20 per cent of value to

47 per cent, or by some 170 per cent above the levels ruling in 1860. It was designed to raise revenues for the hard-pressed Union treasury but, in the longer run, it served to establish protectionism deeply in national economic policies. Protectionism became something of a religion to favored sectors of the economy. Subsequent tariff acts in 1883, 1890, 1894, and 1897 granted even more protection. The protectionist tide suffered a slight setback in the Underwood Tariff of 1913, but went on from there to ultimate triumph, the crippling Smoot-Hawley Tariff of 1930. The Smoot-Hawley Tariff was an act of almost unparalleled protective ferocity, which, together with the retaliatory measures leveled at us by injured foreigners, served to demolish the system of international trade and payments which then existed. In Table 18–1 these developments are seen in the high

TABLE 18–1

TARIFF REVENUES AS PERCENTAGES OF VALUE OF IMPORTS, 1821–1940

	Free and Dutiable Imports	*Dutiable Imports Only*
1821	43.2	45.0
1830	57.3	61.7
1840	17.6	34.4
1850	24.5	27.1
1860	15.7	19.7
1870	44.9	47.1
1880	29.1	43.5
1890	29.6	44.6
1900	27.6	49.5
1910	21.1	41.6
1920	6.4	16.4
1930	14.8	44.7
1940	12.5	35.6

Source: *Historical Statistics.*

proportion of duties up to 1910. By 1920 the proportion was down, but with Smoot-Hawley the proportion rises again and is only slightly ameliorated by the more liberal tariff policies of the New Deal era. Even today we have not been able to undo all the damage that was done to international trade by Smoot-Hawley.

Curiously enough, the United States has long been an advocate of liberal trade policies—for others. But after the Great Depression of the 1930's we began a systematic attempt to promote "multilateralism" (movement toward the elimination of direct and indirect government-imposed controls over international trade and payments).

This attempt was started during Cordell Hull's tenure as Secretary of State in the first Roosevelt administration. Under the Reciprocal Trade Agreements Program (started in 1934), the administrative branch was given powers to negotiate lower tariffs with other countries. These powers were (and still are), however, greatly circumscribed by various escape clauses that can be used by specific industries to maintain protection for themselves. The efficacy of the program, periodically renewed by Congress, has been doubted by many. It is argued that important imports have never been seriously treated to tariff reductions because interested companies have successfully appealed that they are being threatened by foreign competition.

As one student of U.S. foreign-trade policy put it:

> Powerful pressure groups have been successful in obtaining so many exceptions to our trade program, that its effectiveness has been seriously undermined. If left unchecked, this trend may make it very difficult to maintain the political and economic solidarity of the noncommunist world.[1]

Moreover, the imposition of quotas, tied loans from U.S. government agencies, the "Buy-American Act" (passed back in 1933, but still law), and other such quantitative devices have also helped shield favored industries from the full force of competition.

Our tariff policies have had some little-noticed consequences which are worth considering further: (1) their "revenue" function has not been consistent with their "protective" function, and (2) they have long been a systematic transfer from the consumer and farmer to manufacturing industry. It has generally been acknowledged that the earliest American tariffs were imposed merely for revenue purposes with little thought of providing protection. In fact, there is an inherent contradiction between tariff for revenue and one for protection. Revenue can be raised only if goods are brought in, and a protective tariff can be effective only if commodities are kept out. In the tariff of 1816, however, its protective functions were formally acknowledged by its authors, and it is the protective rather than the revenue character of the tariff that has been stressed ever since.

An examination of Table 18–2 shows the extent of tariff favoritism toward manufacturing in the period from 1821 to 1950. As we have seen, the trend in tariffs was upward from 1820 to 1830 and then, because of southern agricultural protest, shifted slightly down-

[1] J. M. Letiche, "United States Foreign Trade Policy," *The American Economic Review,* December, 1958, p. 957.

TABLE 18–2

Percentage Manufactures, Semimanufactures and Agricultural Imports of Total Imports, and Percentage of Dutiable Imports in Each Category of Total Dutiable Imports, 1821–1950

	(1) *Manufactured Imports as Per Cent of Total Imports*	(2) *Duties on Manufactured Imports as Per Cent of Total Import Duties*	(3) *Semi-manufactured Imports as Per Cent of Total Imports*	(4) *Duties on Semi-manufactured Imports as Per Cent of Total Import Duties*	(5) *(1) + (3)*	(6) *(2) + (4)*	(7) *Agricultural Goods Imports as Per Cent of Total Imports*	(8) *Duties on Agricultural Imports as Per Cent of Total Import Duties*
1821	56.9	58.9	7.5	11.6	64.3	70.6	10.7	11.6
1830	57.0	61.4	8.2	11.0	65.2	72.4	11.8	12.7
1840	45.1	54.0	11.6	12.8	56.6	66.8	15.5	0.1
1850	54.9	60.1	15.1	16.3	70.0	77.1	10.4	1.4
1860	48.7	60.3	9.9	10.2	58.6	70.5	12.9	1.3
1870	39.8	40.8	12.8	12.8	52.6	53.6	12.4	13.0
1880	29.4	40.5	16.6	20.8	46.0	61.3	15.0	3.2
1890	29.2	41.8	14.8	18.6	44.0	60.4	16.3	4.2
1900	23.9	38.6	15.8	18.4	39.7	56.9	11.5	6.1
1910	23.6	37.8	18.3	20.2	41.9	58.0	9.3	3.9
1920	16.6	23.0	15.2	11.8	31.8	34.8	10.9	3.0
1930	24.7	39.4	19.9	15.8	44.6	55.2	13.1	6.8
1940	16.1	23.1	22.0	22.3	38.1	45.3	11.2	6.5
1950	17.2	19.0	24.3	39.8	41.5	58.8	20.0	6.5
1821–1910 Average	29.2	39.9	15.6	18.1	44.8	58.0	12.9	6.1
1821–1950 Average	31.5	42.8	15.1	17.3	49.6	60.1	12.9	5.7

Source: *Historical Statistics.*

ward until the time of the Civil War. Here the agricultural sector was to some extent successful in protecting its own interests. In the post-bellum period, however, as the new manufacturing interests became ever more vocal and powerful, we find that tariffs rose steadily (excepting only the downward revisions of the Wilson administration) until the 1930's. As can be seen in Table 18–2, during this period there was a considerable difference in the interindustry impact of these high tariffs. For example, while manufactured products amounted to less than 30 per cent of total imports in the period from 1870 to 1910, duties on these manufactured products amounted to almost 40 per cent of all duties collected. During the same period, agricultural imports amounted to about 13 per cent of all imports, but only about 4 per cent of duties collected. Thus it appears that while almost all business received some subsidy (paid for by the consumers) manufacturing industry received much more than its proportionate share. Up to the 1960's this discrimination in favor of manufacturing industry continued unabated.

An attempt to rebuild the world of relatively free trade and payments became one of the long-run goals of U.S. policy during World War II. Lend-lease aid was made available on the condition that the other United Nations countries pledge themselves to postwar cooperation in the building of multilateralism. In the United Nations and in the great Bretton Woods institutions (the International Monetary Fund and the International Bank for Reconstruction and Development) the goal of multilateralism was made explicit. The American commitment to join the General Agreement on Tariffs and Trade and the British Loan of 1947 were early postwar evidences of our sincerity, at least on the policy-making level. The aid granted in the European Recovery Program, American support of the European Payments Union, our attempts to bolster support of the new international lending institutions, and, more recently, our proposals to organize effective international institutions in the Atlantic economy, all gave evidence of the American desire to build mutual security on a foundation of multilateralism. That our foreign policy should be based on multilateralism at the same time our tariffs remain strongly protective is paradoxical, but perhaps no more so than other aspects of American life where the ideal and the reality conflict.

It should not be assumed, however, that all of our aid programs have contributed to the allocation of resources on the basis of comparative advantage. Just as the export of capital largely determined the flow of British exports before 1914, so recent American capital exports and foreign aid have created markets for our exports in countries that might not otherwise have proved such lucrative customers. It is certainly possible that those domestic industries now buttressed by American aid will never be able to sell competitively in the world market. Here again, government policy has altered the allocation of resources in directions that might not have existed on a free-market, comparative-advantage basis. Nevertheless, our foreign-aid programs, like private capital exports, have built up productivity abroad and doubtless have created viable markets where none existed before. Such a build-up is, of course, a major step forward in the spreading of the advantages of labor specialization and foreign trade.

18–3. The Changing Structure of United States Foreign Trade

As we noted briefly above, our comparative advantages have changed remarkably over time. A student well versed in American economic history could probably guess, in broad outline, the way in which our trade structure has changed.

In 1821 our country was still very much an appendage of the British industrial economy. Our dependence upon Britain was manifested in an exchange of primary products for finished manufactures. This relationship shifted only slowly. It was a fruitful one when our economy was young and not capable of sustaining the growth of basic industry. But as our economy changed, so did the structure of our foreign trade.

To a large extent, the structure of our exports has in fact been reversed since the pre-Civil War era (the notable exception, agricultural commodities, will be discussed shortly). As we have become an increasingly industrial and a proportionately less agricultural and mining economy our exports to the world have reflected this change. In pre-Civil War days, over 65 per cent of our exports consisted of crude materials (mainly cotton) and crude foodstuffs, while the remaining exports (less than 35 per cent) were manufactured food and commodities and semimanufactured goods (see Table 18–3A). In recent years, just over 20 per cent of our exports have been crude materials and foodstuffs and about 80 per cent have been manufactured food and commodities and semimanufactured goods. Our exports of finished manufactured goods have risen from the small proportion we exported early in our history to about 60 per cent of the total. In recent years, our largest single

TABLE 18–3A

STRUCTURE OF U.S. EXPORTS BY CLASS
(In Per Cent of Total)

Annual Averages	*Crude Materials*	*Crude Foodstuffs*	*Manufactured Foodstuffs*	*Semi-manufactures*	*Finished Manufactures*
1821*	60.5	4.8	19.5	9.4	5.7
1851–60	61.7	6.6	15.4	4.0	12.3
1881–90	35.9	18.0	25.3	5.2	15.6
1901–10	31.0	10.6	20.1	12.8	25.6
1921–30	26.0	8.5	11.8	13.3	40.8
1931–40	24.6	3.8	7.2	16.9	47.5
1951–55†	13.0	7.1	5.6	11.6	62.7
1956–60	12.9	7.4	6.0	15.0	58.7
1962	10.5	9.4	6.4	14.3	59.5

* Figures for decade 1821–30 not available.
† 1941–50 omitted as it included war and postwar shipments based to a great extent upon foreign military and aid shipments.
Source: *Historical Statistics; Statistical Abstract.*

group of exports has been composed of machinery and vehicles and they alone have accounted for roughly one third of all of our exports. This remarkable change reflects the successful industrial development of a country that, just over a century ago, was still primarily rural and agricultural.

The history of our imports is similar, but slightly more complex (see Table 18–3B). From the pre-Civil War period until the end of the 1920's, there was a more or less regular increase in the proportion of crude materials and foodstuffs among our imports, accompanied by a relative decline in our imports of manufactured and semi-

TABLE 18–3B

STRUCTURE OF U.S. IMPORTS BY CLASS
(In Per Cent of Total)

Annual Averages	*Crude Materials*	*Crude Foodstuffs*	*Manufactured Foodstuffs*	*Semi-manufactures*	*Finished Manufactures*
1821–*	4.5	11.1	19.7	7.4	56.8
1851–60	9.6	11.7	15.4	12.5	40.5
1881–90	21.3	15.4	17.8	14.8	30.8
1901–10	34.0	11.9	12.1	17.2	24.8
1921–30	37.1	11.8	11.4	18.2	21.4
1931–40	31.0	14.4	14.0	19.8	20.8
1951–55†	26.3	19.5	10.1	27.7	20.4
1956–60	22.4	14.1	10.5	22.1	31.1
1962	20.6	10.9	11.1	20.9	36.6

* Figures for decade 1821–30 not available.
† 1941–50 omitted as it included war and postwar shipments based to a great extent upon foreign military and aid shipments.
Source: *Historical Statistics; Statistical Abstract.*

manufactured commodities. In the pre–Civil War era, crude materials and food imports came to about 20 per cent of the total. The remainder was manufactured commodities in one form or other and about half of these were finished manufactured goods. By the late 1920's, with imports of crude materials and crude foodstuffs accounting for some 45 per cent of the total, our imports of manufactured and semimanufactured commodities and food had fallen accordingly (imports of finished manufactures were down to about 21 per cent of the total). In recent years (since 1950) our imports of finished manufactured goods have been rising rapidly, and they now comprise more than 36 per cent of total imports. The causes of this reversal of a century-old pattern are complex. But as one student of U.S. tariffs has noted, this change may well be partly an "automatic" effect of inflation. First, it is argued by many that American inflation since 1945 has been greater than that experienced in many foreign countries and that, as a result, foreign competition is becoming effective again (a corollary of this argument is the recently heard complaint that the U.S. is "pricing itself out of the international markets"). Possibly of greater significance, however, is the relation between inflation and the mechanics of tariff imposition. Some two thirds of U.S. tariff duties are specific duties—flat rates of so much per item—set years ago. As inflation has affected the American price and income structure, the tariff charge has been "reduced" relatively. Tariffs now are likely a smaller percentage of the total price and they are certainly a less significant barrier against foreign commodities to Americans with an abundance of inflated dollars. It appears that U.S. tariffs have, on the average, been "reduced" in this fashion by about half since 1931–35—an unexpected benefit to international trade from a curious source.

Most of the changes in the structure of our foreign trade have been clearly related to structural changes within the U.S. economy. The structure of trade has not, of course, completely reversed itself. Because of the richness of our natural endowment, we are still a major exporter of crude materials; and they still form a significant part of our exports. We continue to import *different* kinds and qualities of crude materials from countries with natural endowments that differ greatly from ours. For example, we export large quantities of grains and cotton, and import cocoa, coffee, and tea. Similarly, despite our huge domestic market and specialized production, we still depend to a large extent upon foreign manufactured goods; and these items continue to make up a substantial share of our imports.

In this way we take advantage of foreign efficiency as well as of our own.

Whereas there has been virtually uniform transformation of the structure of our foreign trade as regards raw materials and manufactured goods, there has been no such transformation in our foreign trade in food. There are many reasons for this curiousity. American food imports have characteristically consisted largely of coffee, sugar, tea, spices, and exotic fruits, with but slight price and income elasticities. Some domestic substitutes have been developed, but for the most part the tea, coffee, sugar, and assorted spices consumed at the American table are imported from foreign countries. The fluctuations in the relative importance of food among our total exports reflect several episodes of great importance in American economic history. In the last half of the nineteenth century, the great agricultural heartland of the North American continent was opened. In the 1870's, 1880's, and 1890's, our wheat and other cereal products formed a great new source of foreign exchange; and the world wheat economy that then developed was very much a product of the American West. As our manufacturing industries matured, toward the end of the nineteenth and in the first three decades of the twentieth century, world commercial policies reverted to protection—especially protection of domestic agriculture. Thus, new tariffs hampered the further growth of the overseas market. In the 1930's and afterward, U.S. agricultural exports were, to a large extent, noncompetitive because of price supports at home. Only by various forms of "dumping" (including, e.g., farm products as part of foreign aid) could the American farmer continue to enjoy a portion of the great foreign market. In 1957, for example, the Secretary of Agriculture testified that less than 40 per cent of our total exports of agricultural commodities were not underwritten by some form of subsidy or other government assistance. It is clear that a subsidized internal market has largely removed the U.S. farm from the world agricultural market. However, long before there was a Federal program of price maintenance in agriculture, agricultural exports, as a *proportion* of total U.S. exports, were declining.

The decline of American agriculture in world food trade has encompassed almost every type of farm product. In the 1880's (1884–88) our percentage share of the totals of world food exports were as follows: wheat, 35.8; corn, 44.2; beef and veal, 43.0; pork, bacon, and hams, 71.0; cheese, 28.0. By the 1930's (1934–38), following the collapse of farm prices and the rise of world-wide protectionist commercial policies, the U.S. farmer's share of world exports of the same items had declined to 8 per cent of the wheat, corn, and pork, and to less than 1 per cent of the beef and veal, and cheese. After World War II, even with the massive assistance of the U.S. foreign aid programs, none except wheat and corn were brought back to their earlier predominance in international trade. In 1952–56, the percentage figures were as follows: wheat, 33.5; corn, 50.3; beef and veal, 2.1; pork, bacon, and hams, 7.2; cheese, 8.4. Whether American agriculture could be competitive again in free international markets no one really knows; it has now been some thirty years since there was a free market in agricultural products in this country.

18–4. *The Growth and Direction of United States Trade*

Comparative advantage largely determines the composition of a nation's foreign trade. But the volume and direction of trade are determined by the same forces which generate income generally. Thus, over the long run the rate of economic growth both overseas and at home has, in part, determined the volume and direction of our exports and imports. Until the early years of the twentieth century, the growth and direction of U.S. trade can largely be understood in these terms, together with the changing proportions of our trade and their determinants noted earlier.

Thus, from 1821 to 1910 the value of our exports grew at a mean annual rate of 3.6 per cent, and our imports at 3.2 per cent, with the export balance slowly shifting toward manufactures, and imports toward raw materials and food. During this period more than three fourths of our exports went to Europe and more than half of our imports came from there. Our export trade with other areas, especially Asia, was picking up slowly relative to our European trade, and our imports both from Asia and from the southern part of North America were also growing. Despite these trends, as late as 1906–10 the distribution of our exports geographically was not much different from 1860, and of our imports not radically so.

By 1920, however, American foreign trade had changed radically both in magnitude and direction. Four years of world war had wrought vast changes in the balance of world economic power and in the direction of economic development. These changes were, in measure, permanent so far as U.S. trade was concerned. In 1939–45, World War II had similar cataclysmic effects, and the history of our trade since that time is best read either in terms of the disruptions of war or of recovery from war.

That large-scale war should have drastic effects upon trade is. of course, not surprising. First, the two world wars had enormously stimulating effects on the American economy. In both wars we were neutral at the beginning, supplying arms and commodities to the belligerents. Second, once in the wars ourselves we had the good fortune not to be invaded; and our economy continued to expand under the stimulus of unrestrained spending, unhampered by bombardments, bombings, disruptions of communications or transportation, or important losses of life among the civilian population. Since in each case the fighting involved the West Europeans, their markets overseas were left short of supplies. The shortage of European commodities provided our merchants with extraordinary opportunities to sell our manufactures in areas previously dominated by European supplies. Because of the economic chaos of the postwar periods, the United States, here again, was alone capable of supplying much of the world's needs. Second, with Europe either cut off completely or accessible only at great risk and the American economy rapidly expanding, we became a substitute market for the food and raw-material exports of large parts of the world. As a result, after neither war was there a complete reversal back to prewar conditions in the pattern of trade. In large part, the emergency wartime arrangements proved lastingly advantageous (although, of course, the value of trade fluctuated considerably).

After the relatively slow rise in the value of our foreign trade up to 1910 (see Tables 18–5A and 18–5B), there was, from 1910 to 1920, an enormous rise in our exports of from \$1.7 billion to \$8.0 billion (or 4.7 per cent per annum). Our imports rose from about \$1.6 billion to \$5.3 billion, or 3.3 per cent per annum. The greatest single increases came in finished manufactures and in food. But there were extraordinary increases in every category of our exports. The same was true of imports. The pattern of the geographical distribution of our exports also shifted sharply just after the war. There was a sharp drop to about 53 per cent in the European share while the proportions going to Asia and other tropical areas rose. This change, which took place in the early 1920's while chaos reigned in Europe, accompanied a sharp decline in the value of exports. Part of the new-found foreign markets for American goods were maintained, even though the European market contracted; and U.S. exports did not fall back to pre-1914 levels in the immediate postwar era. In our import trade, the impact of the war was immediate. Our imports from Europe fell by more than half while imports from other

TABLE 18–4A

PER CENT DISTRIBUTION OF EXPORTS BY CONTINENT, 1860–1962

Year	Northern North America	Southern North America	South America	Europe	Asia	Oceania	Africa
1860	6.9	8.8	4.7	74.8	2.4	1.5	1.0
1871–75	6.4	7.2	4.0	80.2	1.0	0.8	0.4
1881–85	5.4	5.7	3.6	81.1	2.2	1.6	0.5
1891–95	5.5	6.8	3.7	79.5	2.3	1.6	0.6
1901–5	8.6	6.7	3.2	72.3	5.3	2.0	1.9
1906–10	10.2	8.7	4.6	68.2	5.5	1.8	1.0
1911–15	14.2	7.7	5.2	64.0	5.6	2.2	1.1
1916–20	12.0	7.7	5.5	63.2	8.6	1.7	1.1
1921–25	14.3	10.1	6.8	52.7	11.3	3.2	1.6
1931–35	14.8	8.0	7.0	47.4	17.3	2.4	3.1
1941–45	13.1	5.6	4.9	56.9	7.9	3.5	8.3
1946–50	16.0	11.8	18.0	34.8	15.4	1.6	5.2
1951–55	18.8	10.9	15.1	23.4	13.7	1.5	3.8
1956–60	19.7	10.2	11.4	28.0	15.8	1.8	3.6
1961–62	17.3	7.1	10.0	30.5	19.4	2.1	4.1

Source: *Historical Statistics; Statistical Abstract.*

areas boomed. In the postwar era there was only a small recovery of the European proportion.

In the depressed 1930's, trade was reduced to very low levels; exports, in fact, fell to pre-1914 levels. There was a further reduction in the proportion of our exports going to Europe as protectionism

TABLE 18–4B

PER CENT DISTRIBUTION OF IMPORTS BY CONTINENT, 1860–1962

Year	Northern North America	Southern North America	South America	Europe	Asia	Oceania	Africa
1860	6.7	12.5	9.9	61.3	8.3	0.3	1.0
1871–75	5.9	16.6	11.0	55.6	9.7	0.7	0.6
1881–85	6.3	14.4	11.4	55.1	10.5	1.7	0.6
1891–95	4.6	16.3	14.9	50.6	10.8	2.1	0.6
1901–5	5.4	13.3	12.5	51.3	15.4	0.9	1.1
1906–10	5.9	13.4	11.7	51.3	15.2	1.2	1.2
1911–15	7.7	14.5	12.8	46.6	15.8	1.1	1.4
1916–20	12.7	17.5	17.6	20.3	27.1	2.1	2.7
1921–25	11.5	14.9	12.2	30.4	27.3	1.6	2.1
1931–35	13.8	10.3	14.3	30.1	28.7	0.9	1.9
1941–45	27.4	16.8	22.8	8.1	13.7	5.3	6.2
1946–50	21.5	14.1	22.4	16.8	18.8	2.5	5.6
1951–55	22.5	12.0	21.2	20.2	16.3	2.2	5.5
1956–60	21.2	11.6	18.1	26.6	16.5	1.8	4.2
1961–62	21.8	9.3	15.6	28.4	18.0	2.4	4.3

Source: *Historical Statistics.*

TABLE 18–5A. VALUE OF UNITED STATES EXPORTS, 1821–1962
(Mean Annual Rates in $ Millions)

	Total	Crude Materials	Crude Foodstuffs	Manu-factured Foodstuffs	Semi-manu-factures	Finished Manu-factures
1820*	52	31	2	10	5	3
1830*	59	37	3	10	4	5
1840*	112	76	5	16	5	11
1851–60	232	143	15	36	9	29
1861–70	239	106	33	51	12	38
1871–80	575	216	117	128	26	87
1881–90	750	269	162	190	38	117
1891–1900	1,006	296	183	256	82	190
1901–10	1,589	494	146	317	205	409
1911–20	4,513	971	410	761	696	1,675
1921–30	4,499	1,165	360	528	600	1,916
1931–40	2,578	602	98	175	450	1,252
1941–50	10,797	1,102	569	1,169	1,113	6,845
1951–55	15,196	1,977	1,081	844	1,295	9,527
1956–60	19,029	2,453	1,408	1,145	2,857	11,166
1961	21,359	2,234	2,008	1,366	3,045	12,706

* Selected years.
Source: *Historical Statistics; Statistical Abstract.*

reigned there. To some extent Asia, Canada, Latin America, and Africa made up for the reduction of our European market. The geographic distribution of our import trade did not change significantly.

TABLE 18–5B. VALUE OF UNITED STATES IMPORTS, 1821–1962
(Mean Annual Rates in $ Millions)

	Total	Crude Materials	Crude Foodstuffs	Manu-factured Foodstuffs	Semi-manu-factures	Finished Manu-factures
1821*	55	3	6	11	4	31
1830*	63	5	7	10	5	36
1840*	98	12	15	15	11	44
1851–60	274	27	33	44	36	156
1861–70	332	42	45	63	46	136
1871–80	535	92	85	111	70	177
1881–90	692	148	106	123	102	213
1891–1900	763	202	129	130	106	197
1901–10	1,158	395	137	140	201	287
1911–20	2,612	1,002	321	393	450	443
1921–30	3,742	1,387	445	423	686	801
1931–40	2,074	650	293	291	415	425
1941–50	5,030	1,570	903	553	1,103	901
1951–55	10,784	2,835	2,106	1,089	2,558	2,196
1956–60	13,570	3,033	1,707	1,422	2,993	4,215
1962	16,249	3,342	1,777	1,797	3,393	5,941

* Selected years.
Source: *Historical Statistics; Statistical Abstract.*

The broad results of World War I were (1) a great increase in the volume of our foreign trade during the war and the continuation for some time afterward of trade far above prewar levels, and (2) a significant acceleration of the previously gradual drift of our trade away from Europe.

World War II stepped up this process even more, although, initially, of course, with lend-lease and Allied buying there was a dramatic wartime revival of the European proportion of our exports. In general, our exports tripled during the war period; however, there was no similar wartime increase in imports. Most of the wartime increase in exports was concentrated in manufactured goods; and the European proportion of our exports in 1941–45 rose again to over 50 per cent, recovering, temporarily, the ground lost after 1918. Unlike the post-1918 era, our foreign trade did not decline after 1945. Trade was maintained, due in large part to a reversal of economic policies as compared to 1918, both here and abroad. In the 1945–50 era (from the end of World War II to the outbreak of hostilities in Korea), as our exports increased in value very rapidly and our imports more than doubled their wartime levels, the long-term change in direction of our trade resumed its momentum. Once again the European proportion of our exports fell dramatically, and our European imports failed to regain even the depression levels that prevailed in the 1930's.

Thus, by the early 1960's, with our overseas trade booming, our foreign markets had become increasingly diversified. This diversification, of course, was the end product of an evolution of our position vis-à-vis the world economy which had been developing relentlessly since early in the nineteenth century. By 1946–50, our exports to Europe had fallen to 35 per cent of the total. Subsequently, the European proportion of our exports had fallen below 30 per cent. Partly this has been due to the great industrial expansion of Canada since World War II, to economic development in Latin America, and, finally, to the recovery of Japan as one of our major trading partners. In the case of our imports, the same pattern of diversification now prevails. There has been a recovery in the European proportion since 1950, but generally it is far below the historical levels. We import less from Asia now than we did earlier in this century, but more from Africa and Latin America; and, of course, Canada is now our largest single supplier.

Unlike the post–World War I era, there has not (yet) been any large cutback in the U.S.'s overseas trade. Not only have we maintained the levels reached during World War II, but we have in part, far exceeded those levels. Some of the contributing factors in this change will become apparent in our discussion of our *balance of payments.*

18–5. *The Balance of International Payments of the United States*

Before we examine the historical record of the U.S. balance of payments, let us re-examine some of the more interesting general considerations which arose from our discussion of the balance of payments in Chapter 2. (1) There is no need for exports of commodities to equal imports so long as means exist to finance the difference. In our examples, the rest of the world was not selling us commodities of value equal to those it bought from us, but, because of the volume of other payments in our accounts (sometimes called "invisibles"), there was adequate money available to make up the difference. (2) Part of the balancing mechanism is in a nation's net overseas payments of gold (and supplies on hand of foreign currencies or "foreign exchange"). Since gold and foreign exchange deposits held by nonresidents form part of the total reserves of the banking system, domestic monetary conditions can be influenced by the balance of payments. Moreover, net payments of gold are a consequence of the condition of the overall current account, not of the balance of merchandise trade alone. (3) The balance of our international payments includes both private and government transactions. All three of these facets of the balance of payments are crucially important to an understanding of some parts of American history.

It is useful to subdivide the history of our balance of payments both on the basis of the balance of merchandise trade and on the basis of the state of the current account. With few exceptions, until World War II our current account was closely related to (and heavily influenced by) the trend of exports and imports of merchandise alone. The broad divisions on this basis are: (1) 1820–1875, the developing young industrial economy; (2) 1875–1929, the rise to maturity; (3) 1929–1940, stagnation; (4) 1941–1964, the defense economy. There have been many attempts to link the "typical" structure of a nation's balance of payments with the relative maturity of its industrial development. Our divisions of the American balance of payments do not imply any attempts at systematization. Moreover, our divisions are not meant to be applicable in any way beyond our own discussion. We do not mean here to establish any new system of "stages" of growth. While in the nineteenth century, at least up to 1875, it appears that our balance of payments was a systematic factor in our economic development, in the twentieth century the two world wars and their aftermaths—a period that includes the Great Depression and the "cold war"—render trivial and superfluous any systematic analysis not based upon those harsh realities.

From 1820 until about 1875 there was a consistent pattern in our balance of payments. At first we used our balance of payments as an instrument of growth, quite like any other underdeveloped country. In this period we relied upon current-account deficits to finance periods of rapid expansion (e.g., the 1830's, the 1850's, the late 1860's, and early 1870's) while we built a basic industrial foundation from which a more self-sustaining growth could be supplied. In those periods our merchandise-trade deficits rose strongly, and these deficits largely determined the growth of deficits in the whole current account. By the late 1870's, we began to achieve a more substantial domestic industrial base; and after that time we rarely had deficits again in our merchandise trade. According to some recent estimates,[2] our trade surpluses in the 1880's and early 1890's were offset by increases in American purchases of foreign services and in private transfers. Therefore, according to these estimates, a clear current-account surplus does not appear persistently until 1896, even though surpluses in merchandise trade prevailed after 1875. From 1896 until quite recently we experienced persistent surpluses on current account. Current-account surpluses must be financed, either by gold movements or by extensions of credit, from the surplus country to the deficit countries. Hence, by the early twentieth century we had expanded our surpluses by lending to others; and by the 1920's we became a major capital-exporting country. We had, in the space of a century, reversed our payments position.

In summary, until about 1875 the periodic expansions of our current-account deficits represented net American consumption of goods and services beyond our own production. We "borrowed" from our foreign suppliers to aid our own growth. This process is especially clear in the 1830's, 1850's, late 1860's, and early 1870's, when the current-account deficits took the form of deficits in merchandise trade. In the 1830's, as noted elsewhere, there was a great burst of

[2] U.S. Bureau of the Census, *Historical Statistics of the United States Colonial Times to 1957* (Washington, D.C.: U.S. Government Printing Office, 1960). See the discussion pp. 557–60 and Series U 168–92.

internal expansion, land sales, building of roads and canals, and civic improvements. Our current account developed a strong deficit as we absorbed outside "capital." Again, in the 1850's, concomitant with the immigration wave of 1847–54 and the first great American railway boom, there was, in spite of great exports of the new gold of California, a large net importation of goods and services. In the late 1860's and early 1870's, a period marked by the growth of new basic industries as well as by the extension of the transport systems, we achieved an important marginal "boost" from foreign-credit investment that enabled us again to use more goods and services than we produced. In periods of relative quiescence or stagnation, the pattern was reversed. For example, during the stagnation of the early 1840's we experienced substantial surpluses on current account. These surpluses reflected surpluses in merchandise trade during periods when the economy did not utilize its own production and had no need for "borrowing" resources from other countries. During the Civil War, of course, we borrowed from abroad in every year (the official data are for the Union only), as resources were absorbed both for ordinary uses and by the extraordinary destruction of war. Like so many countries, we have benefited from our trading connections with the outside world through our ability to sustain substantial current indebtedness when our consumption of goods and services outstripped our own production. This does not mean that the United States developed only because of balance-of-payments deficits and foreign borrowing. But it does mean that we probably were able to grow faster and easier than we might have done if we had had to depend entirely upon our own output.

In the twenty-five years following 1875 there were trade deficits (and they were very small) only three times. From 1900 until the present time we have had persistently large trade surpluses. These we have financed by combinations of private and government grants and credits. From 1896 to 1928, as our industrial economy rose to maturity, American businesses and private investors made huge amounts of credit and long-term capital available to foreign countries to finance our surplus of exports over imports. In other words, what foreigners couldn't earn by sales of their goods to us, we made available to them. We granted them credit to buy more than their immediate cash-payment abilities, just as any country-store proprietor might lend to his customers (and just as the countries of Europe had earlier lent to us). During World War I the process was further accelerated when the American government lent foreign governments some $16 billion to buy American commodities. For some years after the war, the pattern was continued by both government and private lenders. From 1919 to 1928, an average annual *net* figure of more than $800 million in long-term credits was made available to foreigners by the private American economy.

American private investment abroad reached its apex in 1928. In the stagnant 1930's, as shown in Table 18–6, we actually had become, again, a net importer of capital on long term. American gross long-term foreign investments were $1.7 billion in 1928; they fell to $67 million in 1933, and were a mere $13 million in 1937. During these years, there was a drastic curtailment of our foreign trade and, at the same time, our trade in merchandise came more nearly in balance. But the enormous inflow of $14 billion of gold from abroad from 1934 to 1940 gave us a strong current-account surplus, with a consequent increase in our monetary gold stock from $4.0 billion at the end of 1933 to about $22 billion by the end of 1940. The export of capital in the 1920's that had helped supply dollars to the world was reversed. We not only greatly cut our imports (from $4.4 billion in 1929 to a low of $1.3 billion in 1932; the 1929 figure was not reached again until 1945), but we absorbed gold at an unprecedented rate. The absorption was partly (about $9 billion) due to the movement of "flight capital" (unilateral transfers of wealth by people for political reasons) from politically unstable Western Europe. A small part of it, around $2.8 billion, also came from our export surplus of goods and services.

During World War II and the succeeding 19 years, our export surplus was again greatly enlarged. As noted earlier, during 1941–45 the average annual exports of merchandise rose to $9.9 billion, compared to imports of only $3.5 billion. But with our foreign-aid program, military expenditure abroad, and private unilateral transfers we gave dollars back to the world in unprecedented amounts and, as a result, we actually had current-account deficits which averaged some $716 million a year in 1949–1953. In addition to ordinary exports and imports we provided a gross amount of $41.6 billion under the wartime Lend-Lease Act. After 1945, American exports continued to climb, reaching a postwar peak of $20.6 billion in 1962 (imports were only $16.4 billion). The difference between imports and exports was covered by credits of all kinds, including more than $2 billion of U.S. government transfers, a considerable reduction from earlier "cold war" years. From July 1,

1945, to December, 1962, total American government foreign grants and credits equaled $91.5 billion, of which $86.3 billion was for "Mutual Security" (only $27.6 billion of this was for strictly military supplies and services); UNRRA and related immediate postwar aid was $3.4 billion; and the Marshall Plan grants totaled about $12 billion. These postwar programs have made a vast total of dollars available that could not have been financed by foreign exports to us, and they partly underpinned the great American postwar export boom. It is essential to realize this fact when one assesses our recent history, and especially when one compares the record of U.S. exports after World War II with those of the post–World War I era. In the earlier period, the job of supplying dollars to the world beyond what we provided by importing was largely left in the hands of the private American investor. Since 1945 we have corrected the "dollar shortage" to a very considerable extent out of taxation. As a result, there has not yet been a collapse of overseas trade similar to that of the 1920's and 1930's.

The question arises of whether the only method of maintaining American exports at or near present levels is a continuation of such foreign assistance. Fortunately, the American investor has largely recovered his poise from the disasters of the 1920's and 1930's and has since 1945 matched the value of the government's foreign investments. As can be seen in Table 18–6, American long-term capital exports began to recover in 1939–43, and, except for 1949–53 (the Korean War), have maintained a brisk pace. Between 1945 and 1961, gross American foreign investments (cumulative) rose from $16.8 billion to some $77.3 billion. American private investment was nearly four fifths of that total, rising from $14.7 billion to $55.5 billion, matching in absolute amount, but not in rate of increase, the rise in the government's total from $2.1 billion to $21.8 billion. In recent years, the yearly gross flow of private capital has come ever closer to the total government foreign expenditure. This increase holds hope for a solid cushion under the U.S. exports of goods and services should the flow of government funds abroad cease or be greatly reduced in the future.

Thus, the surprising reduction of more than $6.5 billion in our gold supply in the last six years can be seen in its true perspective. First, the largest part of that supply (now about $16 billion; it was more than $22.6 billion in 1957, and was at a peak of about $22.7 billion in 1941) came in as flight capital and other extraordinary transfers in the 1930's. Second, the recent reduction of that gold stock represents a tendency by other nations to use a part of the supply

TABLE 18–6

BALANCE OF PAYMENTS OF THE UNITED STATES, 1919–1962
(Five-Year Mean Annual Rates in Millions of Dollars)

Years	Current Account			Capital Account (– Sign Denotes Net Exports)			Net Changes in Gold Stock (– Sign Denotes Increase)	Errors and Omissions
	Net Goods and Services	*Net Unilateral Transfers*	*Balance*	*Net Long-Term Capital*	*Net Short-Term Capital*	*Balance*		
1919–23	2,465.0	–584.5	1,880.6	–1,004.0	–6.6	1,010.6	–216.8	–653.2
1924–28	1,133.3	–364.4	768.9	–740.0	133.8	–606.2	19.4	–183.0
1929–33	681.0	–285.6	395.4	17.6	–397.0	–379.4	–48.4	32.4
1934–38	469.5	–179.0	290.5	406.2	485.0	891.2	–1,504.6	322.8
1939–43	4,527.0	–4,151.2	375.8	–198.8	780.6	581.8	–1,471.2	513.6
1944–48	8,874.8	–6,313.2	2,561.6	–2,938.4	426.8	–2,511.6	–483.4	433.4
1949–53	4,722.4	–5,438.2	–715.8	–923.4	777.8	–145.6	420.0	399.4
1954–58	5,765.8	–4,947.0	818.8	–2,942.8	1,309.6	–1,633.2	302.0	512.4
1959–62	4,780.2	–3,914.7	865.5	–722.4	–2,031.8	–1,888.7	1,141.3	747.4

Sources: *Historical Statistics* and *Statistical Abstract.*

of dollars provided by U.S. foreign-aid programs and private foreign investment to bolster their own gold reserves that were seriously depleted in the 1930's. Finally, the gold loss shows the overwhelming success of our foreign-aid programs in helping war-devastated nations back to economic strength. As we noted in our simple model of the balance of payments, this gold flow is altogether consistent with a surplus in commodity trade. What our commodity trade would be without the foreign-aid programs is probably anybody's guess. But the ability to maintain exports now depends both upon the level of our imports (which supplies dollars abroad) and our exports of "capital"—lending on both short and long term, and direct overseas investment, private and governmental, together with grants, both private and governmental.

The rise of private capital exports augurs well for the future of our exports. An increase in American imports is, however, a necessity if our exports are to be maintained or raised; and this increase can hardly be achieved by any return to protectionism—the classical American reaction to economic difficulties. Given the long-term changes in the structure and direction of our overseas trade, one thing is certain: our policies in the future will need to be intelligent and flexible. Comparative advantages have changed radically in the past and are doubtlessly changing now. As we move away from the "defense economy" of 1940–64, it would be foolish indeed to have a policy based upon the status quo—especially considering the origins and present condition of that status quo!

Suggested Readings

AUBREY, HENRY G. *United States Imports and World Trade.* Oxford: The Clarendon Press, 1957.

BLOOMFIELD, ARTHUR. *Capital Imports and the American Balance of Payments.* Chicago: University of Chicago Press, 1950.

KINDLEBERGER, C. P. *The Dollar Shortage.* New York: Columbia University Press, 1937.

LETICHE, J. M. "United States Foreign Trade Policy," *The American Economic Review,* December, 1958.

NORTH, DOUGLASS C. "The United States Balance of Payments, 1790–1860," *Trends in the American Economy in the Nineteenth Century.* Princeton: Princeton University Press (NBER), 1960.

SIMON, MATTHEW. "The United States Balance of Payments, 1861–1900," *Trends in the American Economy in the Nineteenth Century.* Princeton: Princeton University Press (NBER), 1960.

TAUSSIG, F. W. *The Tariff History of the United States.* New York: Putnam's Sons, 1888.

VI
Structural Change

Chapter 19 TECHNOLOGICAL IMPROVEMENT, INDUSTRIAL LOCATION, AND THE RESOURCE BASE

19–1. *Technology and Productivity*

The total possible output of goods and services with any given aggregate of available natural endowments—the resource base—will vary according to the state of technology and the quantities of labor and capital employed. Similarly, the kinds and amounts of resources that are usable also depend upon the technology employed. Changes in technology, accordingly, will have a profound effect upon the location of industry and upon economic growth. With given combinations of labor, capital, and natural resources, improvement in technical efficiency is usually expressed by economists in terms of rising labor *productivity*, that is, output per man-hour.

In American economic development, a fundamental technical revolution has proceeded almost continuously since the Civil War. It has found expression in man's economic pursuits all the way from basic activities such as fishing, mining, and agriculture to the most sophisticated applications of physical laws in engineering and electronics. More skillful labor, scientific management, more effective fabrication of given raw materials (less waste) and labor-saving machines have all combined to greatly increase the productivity of American industry. This constant revolution is well known, much discussed, and visible all around us in our daily lives. Yet it is well-nigh impossible, with the present state of knowledge, to quantify the individual contributions to the end product—output of goods and services. This problem may be illustrated by a simple example. Suppose a technical change in the money market enables a commercial bank to so adjust its reserves that it may lend money to a resourceful engineer interested in forming a new company. With the loan, the engineer hires skilled workmen to operate a new kind of machine that produces a product so efficient that dollar output per man-hour is double that of a factory making a competing commodity with older methods. Who is responsible, and by how much, for this miracle of production? The money market? The bank? The engineer? The college and school system that trained him? The workmen? The men who trained them? The men who made the new machine? The inventors of the new product? The public that is willing to buy it? It is obvious that the origins of increased productivity are in all of the sources mentioned, and in many more besides. But it is also obvious that it would be a task of virtually insurmountable difficulty to apportion the increase accurately among all the contributors.

If we are to continue to have economic growth our productivity must continue to increase. We know vaguely that to raise productivity we must be "more efficient." But precisely where and how? Efficiency is the product of a whole way of life. It may well be that something as remote as "the competitive spirit," or free public schools, or a combination of these and other equally remote and intangible forces, has mainly accounted for American productivity in economic activities. In a recent study of American economic development, Moses Abramovitz dealt with this perplexing problem effectively.

> . . . between the decade 1869–78 and the decade 1944–53, net national product per capita in constant prices approximately quadrupled, while population more than tripled. The source of the great increase in net product per head was not mainly an increase in labor input per head, not even an increase in capital per head, as these resource elements are conventionally conceived and measured. Its source must be sought principally in the complex of little understood forces which caused productivity . . . to rise.[1]

Typically, economic historians have approached the phenomenon of American productivity by describing the classic innovations that were applied to production. These inventions appear in history books mainly as isolated achievements and their inventors as heroes of industrial history. Increased productivity was, therefore, looked on as a consequence of heroic actions by great men. Until the twentieth century such an approach had the virtue of at least being manageable: Eli Whitney's cotton gin (1793), Cyrus McCormick's reaper successfully developed in the 1830's, the Bessemer converter (1856) and later the open-hearth furnace (1866), the application

[1] Moses Abramovitz, *Resource and Output Trends in the United States Since 1870* (New York: NBER, 1956), Occasional paper 52, p. 6.

of the steam engine in a series of improvements beginning in 1765 in mills and factories, the success of the internal-combustion engine in the development of the automobile, the electric motor, and Henry Ford's successful introduction of the machine-line, mass-production system of output (1913) are frequently mentioned in this regard. But more recently emphasis has shifted away from these early inventions to take into account the rise and impact of American technical education. The fantastic complexity of technological progress in the twentieth century has made it obvious that the role of technical education and basic and applied scientific research in American economic development cannot be overstressed. Also, of course, it was easier to discuss "basic" inventions and to believe that one could observe directly their impact upon productivity when there seemed to be only a few outstanding inventions and when the machinery involved was relatively simple. Hence, one could talk with some confidence about *the* cotton gin, or *the* steam engine, and their roles in the early factory system, and not feel that too much of the story was being left out. Today it is different. What indeed is the "main" machine, process, technique, or what have you at work in any sector of American industry? The proliferation of the output of applied science in the twentieth century makes it apparent that earlier emphasis upon the works of individual "heroes" in industrial history was a very considerable oversimplification. The development of American productivity has been part of the whole complex process of growth. It is useful to bear in mind, however, that the growth of productivity in different industries has proceeded at different rates; and, as a result, some industries have grown more rapidly than others and some have actually declined and died. Let us consider this aspect of growth.

19–2. *Industrial Retardation and Economic Growth*

In the late 1920's and early 1930's two of the most eminent American students of economic growth, Simon Kuznets and Arthur F. Burns, in studies following the earlier work of the German economist Julius Wolf, isolated and measured one of the most fundamental forces in the growth process: the ultimate slowing down of growth rates in specific industries. Kuznets stated the problem as follows.

> As we observe various industries within a given national economy, we see that the lead in development shifts from one branch to another. A rapidly developing industry does not retain its vigorous growth forever

but slackens and is overtaken by others whose period of rapid development is beginning. Within one country we can observe a succession of different branches of activity in the vanguard of the country's economic development, and within each industry we can notice a conspicuous slackening in the rate of increase.[2]

Kuznets measured the rates of growth of output covering thirty-five areas of production over long periods of time in five countries. His findings for the United States are presented in Table 19–1.

We see that in all these major industries there has been retardation. Why should individual industries not continue to grow

TABLE 19–1

AVERAGE RATE OF PERCENTAGE INCREASE DURING FIVE-YEAR PERIODS, SHOWN BY INDICES OF THE VOLUME OF PRODUCTIVE ACTIVITY IN VARIOUS INDUSTRIES IN THE UNITED STATES

		Average Rate of Percentage Increase		
Series	*Period*	*During First Half*	*During Second Half*	*Relative Decrease in Second Half*
1. Wheat crops	1866–1924	20.4	7.3	64.2
2. Corn crops	1866–1924	17.7	6.7	62.1
3. Potato crops	1866–1924	17.6	11.5	34.7
4. Cotton crops	1866–1924	24.2	5.6	76.9
5. Anthracite coal shipments	1825–1924	70.8	16.3	77.0
6. Bituminous coal output	1840–1924	62.9	33.9	46.1
7. Crude petroleum output	1860–1924	70.5	51.4	27.1
8. Pig-iron production	1856–1924	57.7	29.4	37.0
9. Crude steel production	1866–1924	157.7	46.2	70.7
10. Portland cement output	1880–1924	337.4	90.0	26.7
11. Domestic cotton consumption	1871–1924	30.4	19.0	37.5
12. Raw silk imports	1866–1924	66.0	41.8	63.3
13. New York bank clearings	1876–1923	15.2	8.0	47.4
14. Locomotives produced, Baldwin Locomotive Works	1836–1923	47.9	22.3	53.4

Source: Simon Kuznets, *Economic Change* (London: William Heineman Ltd., 1954), p. 256.

rapidly? Kuznets found that in early stages of industrial growth technical progress comes rapidly and the industry, starting from very small beginnings, adopts the new techniques that permit very rapid initial strides. But as an industry grows, the possibility of further technical improvement becomes increasingly difficult (given no fundamental changes in the finished product), and the raw materials and other resources used cannot be expanded at a continu-

[2] *Economic Change* (London: William Heineman Ltd., 1954), p. 254.

ously rising pace. Together, these factors set a brake upon further rapid growth. In addition, if other sectors of the market are more backward in the pace of development, they will not continue to absorb the product of the rapidly expanding industry at the initial pace. The market becomes "saturated" with the new product; and further growth for that industry becomes increasingly limited by the growth of population. Finally, whereas initially a new industry has a virgin market to exploit at home and abroad, foreign competition in that particular line of output will arise and check overseas expansion rates and it may, through imports, even come to compete in the country of original development. Hence, there will not be continuous growth in any single industry at the initial rapid pace.

Interestingly enough, it appears that the decline of the growth of individual industries has been a necessary part of the process of the overall growth of the national economy. Mature and aging industries must make way for the new. Burns, beginning his study in the early 1930's, studied retardation over a very broad segment of the American economy (104 areas of output). He found the presence of retardation very marked. Burns also noted that there appears to have been no resting place. Only continued growth assured further growth: and once any industry reached a plateau and ceased to expand it soon began to decline absolutely. Hence, at any time there were specific "decadent" industries in the economy, following the village smithy to oblivion. By the early 1930's these included whaling—output was 68,000 tons in 1870 and never reached 10,000 tons after 1906; cod and mackerel fishing, with a catch of 109.5 thousand tons in 1873, never reached 50,000 tons again after 1909; non-Portland cement, an industry that grew from 2.0 million barrels in 1880 to a peak of 10.2 billion barrels in 1899—and by 1929 produced only 2.2 billion barrels; and roofing slates, with output falling from a peak of 1.4 million squares in 1903 to less than 500,000 squares after 1918. These four declined because of changes in competitive products, natural supplies, and technology. While whaling declined, petroleum and then electrical output increased. While non-Portland cement declined, output of Portland cement rose by gigantic proportions (42 thousand barrels in 1880 and 176 million barrels by 1928) and became part of America's basic supply of heavy industrial and construction material. One can think of many other industries that have experienced retardation and decline; for example, the construction of sailing ships, equipment manufacturing for draft oxen and horses, and streetcar output—to cite three. The manufacture of railroad passenger equipment presents another example. There were 185 railway passenger cars made in 1871, the number reached 2,195 by 1892, and a peak of 5,353 in 1907. In 1933 only eleven were made. There was, of course, some recovery from that extraordinary figure, but since 1946 there have not been 1,000 passenger cars produced in any year. It is no secret that the railway passenger business had declined drastically in the face of competition from private autos, airlines, and buses.

Each time an industry has entered or left the industrial scene, the economic structure of the country has changed. Since industries are at various stages of growth and stagnation, the economy is almost always in a state of continuous structural adjustment.

The presence of retardation in the national economy in the early 1930's (at the trough of the Great Depression) seemed especially strong; and it was sufficient to suggest to many economists that the national economy must soon begin to stagnate (indeed, that stagnation was inevitable was Wolf's original argument). National retardation must inexorably follow (it was thought by some) the retardation of individual industries, especially since with a deep depression new industries would not be entering the economy at rates rapid enough to offset the general decline. But even at that time Burns was aware that retardation was part of the growth process, and not a precursor of stagnation. Some industries had matured and become old by the 1930's, but would not even newer processes continue to spring up, raising productivity, changing the structure of industry, and promoting further growth? His description of the American data for 1870–1930 suggested a mildly optimistic view on the process of growth, even at the depths of the Great Depression.

> Our evidence is slender, however, and all it permits is this indefinite conclusion: if there has been any decline in the rate of growth in the total physical production of this country, its extent has probably been slight, and it is even mildly probable that the rate of growth may have been increasing somewhat.[3]

Since that time the American economy seems to have resumed a stronger rate of growth. Industries continue to expand very rapidly when they first enter the national economy (the television industry is a recent example); and, as in the past, technological changes combine to raise productivity as new methods, commodities, and industries appear and older industries fail to grow at their earlier rates. Overall, productivity since the Civil War seems to have risen

[3] Arthur F. Burns, *Production Trends in the United States Since 1870* (New York: National Bureau of Economic Research, 1934), p. 279.

fairly constantly in spite of retardation in old industries.[4] Hence it appears that retardation in the older industries has probably not impaired economic growth. If provision is made for short-term cyclical downturns (Chapter 23), and for downturns in the "long cycle" (Chapter 22), Burns's tentative conclusions in the depths of the Great Depression still find considerable support. The statistical problems involved in any attempt to measure overall growth *per capita* over a period as long as that from the Civil War to the present are very great. Writing more than twenty years after Burns, Abramovitz concluded that ". . . any statements about a long tendency in the rate of growth of national product must be treated with the greatest reserve unless the drift is so large and so persistent that no likely combination of biases and errors could account for it. In my judgment the drift of the figures is not so clear."[5] A more recent study, by Edward Ames,[6] indicates that American manufacturing apparently grew at a high rate (average of 4.7 per cent per annum) between 1860–1914 (a rate that gradually declined toward the end of the period), and at a lower rate (average 3.8 per cent per annum) that gradually accelerated from 1915 to 1955.

In any case, the remarkable progress in capitalist society of what the economist Joseph Schumpeter once called "creative destruction" has been characteristic of American economic development, and retardation has been part and parcel of "progress." This pattern also reappears in the history of other industrial countries. Technological change has continually supported rising productivity and the forces of growth have continued to prevail against those of retardation and stagnation in the long run. Even in the older industrial economies such as Britain, growth in the past decade has made a shambles of earlier notions that industrial retardation inexorably led to national economic stagnation. In the case of America, growth has produced a continuously changing economy: one in which the balance of industrial structure and the character of the resource base have been shifting in accord with a rapidly changing technology.

19–3. *Industrial Location and the Resource Base*

The effects of changing productivity, industrial retardation, and growth can be seen in changes in the location of industry and

[4] Abramovitz, *op. cit.*, p. 18.

[5] Abramovitz, *op. cit.*, p. 14.

[6] Edward Ames, "Trends, Cycles, and Stagnation in the U.S. Manufacturing Since 1850," *Oxford Economic Papers*, Vol. XI (October, 1959).

in the exploitation of natural resources. The historical movement of manufacturing industry westward to the industrial Middle West, the far West, and more recently to the South illustrates this point. Let us consider some aspects of this movement briefly. In 1850, nearly 80 per cent of the value of products manufactured in the United States originated in states bordering upon the Atlantic Ocean, and most of this figure in states north of the Potomac River. New York was the leading manufacturing state, followed closely by Massachusetts; overall, New England was the center of American manufacturing industry. Today, over half of the net value of output of manufactured goods in the United States is produced in the East-North Central and Middle Atlantic regions. These two divisions comprise respectively the middle western states of Ohio, Indiana, Illinois, Michigan, and Wisconsin; and New York, New Jersey, and Pennsylvania. In 1954, for example, when the total value added by manufacturing was $116.9 billion, the East-North Central region produced $36.5 billion and the Middle Atlantic region $30.4 billion. In that same year, value added in New England was only $9.1 billion, not as high as that produced by New York ($14.1 billion) or Ohio ($10.1 billion) individually. The rest of American manufacturing was widely distributed throughout the nation. Only the Pacific Coast ($11.2 billion) and the south Atlantic Coast region ($10.2 billion) had appreciable industry, compared to the great concentrations of manufacturing in the Middle Atlantic and East-North Central regions.

The present regional distributions of manufacturing reflect the great changes in the location of American industry that have occurred in the past century and a half; changes that have been largely a response to a changing technology. New England's position as the center of early American manufacturing can be attributed largely to her abundance of water power and capital resources that favored textile development. Except for a primitive charcoal iron industry, some shipbuilding and light consumers' goods industries, the United States was primarily an agricultural country in 1850. Heavy industry, based upon mineral resources (coal and iron), an expanding population, and the development of midwestern agriculture, began to slowly develop. By the 1850's we were still importing most of our iron rails from Britain and our iron industry was characterized by small productive units designed to serve small-scale manufacturing in a disconnected and specialized market operating behind a protective tariff. In the 1850's, the rise of a mass market for agricultural implements and machinery in the Middle West had already begun to provide western Pennsylvania iron manufacturers with an expanding market for their product. The base of the American industrial economy was slowly moving westward. The presence of coking coal in the area also augured well for the future of the Pittsburgh area. Just before the Civil War, the Lake Superior iron ores were first exploited and transported down the lakes to the regions of coal and coke. By the end of the Civil War, these ores were generally smelted at Lake Erie ports, especially around Cleveland and in the Mahoning Valley. At the base of the Great Lakes grew Gary-Chicago-Hammond, Cleveland, Youngstown, and the other steel-producing cities of the Great Lakes region. The machine and machine-tool industries also began the westward migration from New England to the Middle West, where they could benefit from proximity to the steel complexes. Oil, previously of little value, began its career as a new industry with a well in Pennsylvania in 1859. Oil was next found in Ohio and Indiana and later in other states, notably in the Southwest and West.

With these and cognate industries, the foundation was prepared for a gigantic expansion of heavy American industry, but industry located much further west and south than the earlier concentration in New England. Already in 1860, the Middle states of New York, New Jersey, and Pennsylvania had surpassed New England in value added by manufacturing; the figure for the Middle states being $358 million in 1860, compared to $223 million for New England. But the dramatic development of American industry in the post–Civil War period, the union of steel, steam, and petroleum that raised the United States to the front rank among industrial powers and resulted in further concentration of industrial strength in the Middle and East-North Central states, came in the period from 1865 to 1914 and was related to striking technological progress.

As noted above, Lake Superior iron ores began to be used in small quantities about the time of the outbreak of the Civil War. By 1870, steam-driven ore barges appeared in the Great Lakes and their introduction effected a dramatic reduction in transportation charges for the Lake Superior ores. In 1856, less than 11 per cent of American iron was made from Lake Superior ores. Thirteen years later this figure had grown to 24 per cent. With good qualities of coking coal available in Illinois and Ohio and a railway network capable of moving them to the lakes, the stage was set for the rise of the American steel industry along the margins of the Great Lakes.

At first the development was fairly slow, and even the charcoal iron industry still thrived for some time. Of course, Pittsburgh remained a center of iron- and steelmaking, and, in the East, there was a further expansion in the Lehigh Valley of Pennsylvania. But the steam-driven barges, the Lake Superior ores (particularly the crumbly ore from the Mesabi range), and nearby coal reserves now brought a decisive shift. For various reasons, including extensive court actions over patents in the basic open-hearth steel process and technical problems related to the qualities of American ores, American steel was made primarily with the Bessemer process until the middle 1890's. Then, in a matter of only about fifteen years, the open-hearth process was widely introduced and largely supplanted the Bessemer process. Between 1895 and 1910 American steel production rose from 6.1 to 26.1 million tons. At the earlier date, 4.9 million tons had been produced by Bessemer and 1.1 million tons by open hearth. In 1910, the Bessemer process accounted for 9.4 million tons, but the total open-hearth output had risen to 16.5 million tons. The new technology in steel brought great expansion in the East-North Central states. By 1913, about five sixths of all United States iron was smelted from Lake Superior ores. For New York, New Jersey, and Pennsylvania, the new steel technology meant the further expansion of an established industry. But for the middle western states a whole new industry of giant proportions had risen, and steel was soon to be followed by the growth of other related and dependent industries.

Firms tend to consider the sources of their raw materials, the cost of transportation of products to markets, the location and character of those markets, and the location of a labor force when they choose their locations. They attempt to build their plants in the location that gives them the maximum profit. Since the requirements vary in different industries, there is no "rule of thumb" to determine their location. Some locate at their markets, importing raw materials. Others settle at the mines, forest, or wells and ship a manufactured or partly manufactured product. Still others may locate at intermediate points, shipping both raw materials and finished products.

In the case of the new steel technology, the most efficient locations were either near the ore and fuel, or (as in the case of the Great Lakes industry) at the confluence of water and rail transportation routes for the ores and fuels. Basic production was no longer located in or near the point of consumption in the eastern cities. In some cases, for example the U.S. Steel works at Troy, New York, in 1906, the plants were dismantled and shipped west to new locations within easy reach of the Lake Superior ores. Other eastern mills simply were abandoned. In steel, it had become most profitable to ship the finished product from the mills to the points of fabrication.

The increased demand for steel and iron in the new machine technology of the post–Civil War period was matched by increased demand for the other basic ingredients of the new industrialism. Most lubricants had previously been produced from animal fat; and the economy had depended heavily upon whale oil for lighting, machine oil, and grease. By the 1850's the sources of animal oil were already insufficient. The development of the American petroleum industry broke that bottleneck. Growth was spectacular. Crude oil output was 2 thousand barrels in 1859 (generally considered the first year of our oil industry's life); ten years later it was 4 million. Expansion continued; oil output passed the 50 million barrel mark in 1891, and—still accelerating—reached 265 million barrels in 1914. By then the older fields in the East and Middle West were outstripped by the new fields of the Southwest, Gulf Coast, and far West. At the outbreak of World War II (1939), American production of crude oil was 1.3 billion barrels; of the total, the older regions contributed just over 50 million barrels. The mean annual rate of production of the southwest, Gulf, and western fields had risen to more than a billion barrels. In the process of this development, states like Texas, Oklahoma, and California became new centers of the oil industry. In more recent years, with oil imports accounting for an increasing (although still small) percentage of our total supply, a portion of the industry has again migrated to the seaports of the Atlantic and Gulf coasts.

The manufacture of machinery in this country has always tended to locate near the areas of consumption. Hence, the early American machinery industry was located largely in industrial New England. With the rise of the new middle western economy of coal, iron, and steel there was a shift of machine making into the new industrial market. Thus, towns like Cincinnati, Detroit, Cleveland, Toledo, and Chicago rose to prominence as producers of the machines that run the mills, mines, railroads, and docks, and the machine tools that make the machines.

There was a great new market for machinery on the middle western farm. One of the bases of the great expansion of American agriculture after the Civil War (and for the continued rising productivity in agriculture) has been the successful application of machine technology to the farm. In this instance, the industry, agricultural machinery, moved toward its market. As late as 1839, roughly half of America's wheat was grown east of the Allegheny Mountains. Between 1830 and 1860 the thresher, reaper, steel plow, corn cultivator, and a host of other productivity-raising machines were introduced into American agriculture. As the great corn and wheat belt stretching from Ohio to the Rockies came under the plow, the farm machinery industry migrated westward from New York and Pennsylvania. Pittsburgh first became a center of its manufacture. But as agriculture slowly moved west, so did the industry; Columbus and Springfield, Ohio; Chicago, Peoria, Moline, and Rock Island, Illinois; Racine and Milwaukee, Wisconsin; Davenport, Iowa; and Minneapolis—all were at one time or another major agricultural machinery centers. Here a doubly fortunate accident of nature had occurred. The great new agricultural lands were to a great extent contiguous to the Great Lakes and accessible to the railway centers of the Middle West, enabling the industrial thrust of the new manufacturing heartland to support, and at the same time to supply, a growing agriculture.

In the twentieth century, as technology changed and new resources became available for exploitation, the pattern of industrialization began to shift again. The concentration of manufacturing in a wide half-moon from New York to Minneapolis did not remain unchallenged. In the South new strength was developed in textiles and in the manufacture of raw materials absorbed by the new plastics industry. The chemical industry, although mainly located in the north-central half-moon, stretched out in all directions. Development of hydroelectric power shifted some industrial strength to the Northwest and South, and improved ocean and domestic transport enabled industry to develop on the West Coast. In the cases of the South and the West, industrial development is only now beginning, and New England has recently made an industrial comeback in electronics and plastics manufacturing.

This brief survey of the changing location of industry and the exploitation of resources is meant only to illuminate some of the main points of earlier discussion: that changing technology has enabled us to greatly expand the range of resources at our command. But as the process continues, the industrial map of the country has shown steady change and transition. Changes in rates of productivity have attracted capital to some industries and away from others; and new industries have grown up and surpassed older ones. The balance of population and markets has shifted from old to new areas. This kind of economic change is not a rapid process to be sure; but it has been a steady and pervasive one in our history. It would be folly to forecast in any detail the future of this process. New methods, automation in industrial processes, the uses of lighter materials, changes in taste, and movements of population and changes in its rate of growth might easily combine to make the industrial map of this country fifty years hence as radically different from that of our contemporary economy as ours is from the map of the 1850's. Technological change is a truly revolutionary phenomenon, and any enlightened economic policy, whether that of management, labor, or the government, should recognize this fact. Indeed, that is one of the great lessons of the history of American economic development. Moreover, given our system of mass education, free consumer choice, and viable and fluid capital markets, it would seem likely that the process will continue and perhaps even accelerate in the future.

Suggested Readings

ABRAMOVITZ, MOSES. *Resource and Output Trends in the United States Since 1870.* New York: National Bureau of Economic Research, 1956.

BURNS, A. F. *Production Trends in the United States Since 1870.* New York: National Bureau of Economic Research, 1934.

KUZNETS, SIMON. *Economic Change.* London: William Heineman Ltd., 1954, chap. 9.

PERLOFF, H. S.; DUNNING, E. S.; LAMPARD, E. E.; AND MUTH, R. F. *Regions, Resources and Economic Growth.* Baltimore: The Johns Hopkins University Press, 1960.

Chapter 20 THE STRUCTURE OF INDUSTRY

20–1. *Technological Progress and the Industrial Revolution*

Modern economic growth implies large-scale changes in a nation's industrial structure. New products, new occupations, new techniques of production have caused sweeping changes in the way resources are combined to produce goods and services. Prior to the industrial revolution, modern nations devoted the major part of their economic effort to the production of food. With changing knowledge about agricultural techniques it became possible to switch resources to the new areas of manufacturing production and the provision of services. Before we can understand the process of industrial change, it is essential that we have an appreciation of what has been called the industrial revolution.

The phrase "industrial revolution" has been conventionally applied to changes in the techniques of production that occurred in England in the late eighteenth century and early nineteenth century. While the economic change was not as rapid as a political revolution, its effects were thought important enough to justify the use of the term "revolution." The changes involved entirely new methods of combining resources in production, and had wide-ranging effects upon the ability of men to produce new products and provide new services.

The basis of the revolution was the discovery of physical laws that provided men with the knowledge of their physical universe and enabled them to harness new sources of power and apply this power to the extraction of useful products from nature. The rational inquiry into the laws governing the behavior of nature that began with the Renaissance and had such important consequences in all reaches of human endeavor inevitably had economic consequences as well. Any increase in man's knowledge about his physical environment will ultimately have economic effects because economic activity involves the extraction from nature of those things man needs to exist or to improve his existence.

Technological advance is the mainspring of the process of industrial development. We do not know the causes of technological advance but we can by analogy indicate forces that may inhibit the inventive urge. In the chapter on population we described the conditions existing in medieval Europe. At that time, Western civilization was characterized by a very low level of production and also, whether cause or effect, by a prevailing philosophy that stressed stoic acceptance of the conditions of life in a vale of tears leading to a heavenly afterlife. Although these forces may have inhibited technological progress, other societies have not been held down by such forces and yet did not develop the new means of production we associate with the Industrial Revolution. The Greek and Roman empires, while wealthy, not unduly concerned with the afterlife, and well endowed with engineering skill, never developed an industrial revolution. Of nonwestern societies the Chinese certainly reached a level of great achievement from which one might have expected great new developments. In the Western world we have become accustomed to believe that free inquiry is an essential part of the process; and yet the U.S.S.R. has demonstrated an ability to innovate in an atmosphere of nonfreedom. Perhaps all we can say is that the desire to invent new ways of doing things (invention) and then to apply these new ways to production (innovation) is a product of peoples who are inquiring in a rational way and anxious to apply the results of their inquiry to the attainment of some goal. Such a statement does not tell us, however, why invention and innovation appear at some times and not at others and, furthermore, why the accumulation of knowledge proceeds at different rates at different points in time.

The question of fluctuations in the innovation of ideas to the process of production was analyzed by J. A. Schumpeter. He hypothesized that the wavelike movements in aggregate economic activity (changing rates of growth of total output) stemmed from differences in the rate at which ideas were embodied in techniques of production. According to Schumpeter, the existing body of knowledge can be taken as given and growing at some rate. Innovators appear (and there is no explanation of why they do) and, using bank credit, they exploit some part of the existing knowledge in a new form of production. If the project is successful, imitators follow in the breakthrough created; and because of these secondary effects induced by the innovation a general economic expansion follows. As the limits of the innovation are approached and as the supply of bank credit is exhausted, the process comes to an end. The railroads of the mid-nineteenth century, the electrical and chemical industries of the late nineteenth century, and electronics of the 1950's would qualify as examples of initiating innovations explaining swings in the tempo of economic activity.

A somewhat different model of the role of technological progress has been advanced by Professor Simon Kuznets. Professor Kuznets examined the behavior of various sectors of the economy and found that, over time, the output of the sectors exhibited a constantly declining rate of growth. When a new product is introduced the rate of growth of output is high but, right from the beginning, declining. The new product absorbs resources at a rapid rate and reaches a brand-new market. But resources cannot continue to be put in at that rate, and the untapped market gets smaller and smaller. No one industry can grow at a rate greater than that of the economy as a whole for long; although it may spurt ahead when new, its rate of growth inevitably falls back and approaches that of the rest of the economy. Thus the effect of an innovation is inevitably dissipated and, if one assumes only a very limited supply of resources, a wavelike motion is necessary. But if there is a large supply of resources so that innovation can be undertaken easily and exploited rapidly, a wavelike motion is no longer necessary. While the rate of growth of all industries declines, it is still possible for total output to increase if new industries are developed with sufficient rapidity.

While the industrial revolution involved a change in many aspects of production, its initial impact and most impressive offspring was the machine. A machine is a means of transforming a source of power along prescribed channels to perform a particular operation. The power of a machine is determined by its ability to control large sources of energy. The wood-wind-water-animal power technology of the preindustrial revolution period was severely restricted because it lacked either a powerful source of energy or the materials to control it. The history of modern technology can be traced through the development of increasing power sources and more powerful materials. But as machines have increased in size, the initial capital investment has also increased. Thus the history of the industrial revolution can be charted in terms of capital investment, and the increase in capital density explains why capital formation is such an important aspect of the problem of development. Although machines have required heavier and heavier doses of capital, they have also become more and more efficient. As a result, the output per dollar invested has increased over time. In addition, newer and more powerful machines have enabled men to produce entirely new products and services.

The impact of the industrial revolution was originally felt in the iron and steel and cotton-textile industries because it was in these industries that the innovation of the new relatively efficient steam engine first proved economically feasible. The iron industry in England was dependent upon the use of charcoal in smelting, but the forests were being cut back from the production areas. The use of coke in smelting made possible furnaces with a much greater capacity, but required an engine to provide the air pressure necessary for smelting. The cotton-textile industry had a potentially huge market for cloth that was cheap and washable, but output was restricted by the use of hand spinning and weaving machines. The steam engine provided the power for the increasing supplies of iron (and later steel), and the growing knowledge of their structural properties provided the materials for increasing the power of the engine.

As men's efficiencies were enlarged with the extension of the steam engine and the increasing use of iron and steel, their real income began to rise. Undoubtedly all groups did not share equally, but most groups probably benefited to some extent. As incomes rose, so did the market for new products. The increasing market, both in terms of incomes and numbers, provided the incentive for new techniques. Increasing incomes also provided increasing volumes of savings for capital formation. Finally, as tastes and incomes changed the industrial structure, the means of satisfying these tastes changed. It is to this point that we now turn, with reference to the United States.

20–2. Changes in Industrial Structure

Estimates for the long period are not available for a very detailed investigation of the industrial structure of the United States. There is a breakdown of the working force between agriculture and nonagricultural pursuits for census years from 1820 to 1950. In 1820, roughly 72 per cent of the working force were engaged in the agricultural pursuits, and 28 per cent in nonagricultural pursuits. By

1920 these proportions were reversed, and by 1960 the proportions were roughly 6 per cent in agriculture and 94 per cent in nonagriculture. In terms of absolute numbers, there were more people working in agriculture in 1960 than in 1820 (4.3 million v. 2 million), but the growth of the agricultural labor force was obviously very much less rapid than of the nonagricultural working force.

If we begin with 1870, a more detailed breakdown of the industrial structure is possible. Table 20–1 gives the percentage share of the labor force employed in the four industrial sectors of the economy. The first two sectors are the commodity-producing sectors, and the last two are the noncommodity-producing sectors. The most

TABLE 20–1

PERCENTAGE DISTRIBUTION OF THE AMERICAN WORKING FORCE BY INDUSTRIAL SECTOR, 1870–1960

Year	*Agriculture*	*Mining, Manufacturing, Construction*	*Transportation, Trade, Finance*	*Service (Incl. Government)*
		A: Gainful Workers		
1870	50.8	25.1	11.2	12.9
1880	50.6	25.0	11.8	12.5
1890	43.2	28.2	14.7	13.8
1900	40.0	30.5	16.8	14.7
1910	32.1	32.1	19.1	16.8
1920	27.7	34.7	21.5	16.2
1930	22.7	31.9	25.3	20.1
		B: Labor Force		
1930	21.8	31.7	25.8	20.8
1940	18.3	33.1	25.2	23.4
1950	12.1	33.4	29.8	24.8
1960	5.8	27.8	24.8	21.7

Source: J. Frederic Dewhurst and Associates, *America's Needs and Resources: A New Survey* (New York: The Twentieth Century Fund, 1955), Table 313, p. 732; *Statistical Abstract.*

noticeable feature of the table is, again, the decline in the proportion of the labor force engaged in agriculture. Of the other three, the service sector's share almost doubled while that of transportation, trade, and finance more than doubled. Of all the sectors shown, mining, manufacturing, and construction showed the smallest change, increasing its share by only about one third.

The trend away from concentration in the commodity-producing sector is one that can be observed in the records of all developed economies. In 1870, roughly 75 per cent of the American labor force was engaged in commodity production, while in 1960 the proportion was about 34 per cent. Technological developments have made men increasingly productive so that an increasing commodity output can be produced by a decreasing share of labor resources. Moreover, the American consumer has apparently decided to allocate an increasing share of expenditure away from commodities toward noncommodities (i.e., services). Consumers have increased their demands for services more rapidly than they have for goods. In addition, the secular increase in the geographic concentration of production and increasing emphasis on selling has led to substantial increases in the labor-force share of the trade and distribution sector of the economy.

The movement of labor away from agriculture is a necessary adjunct of the process of development. It is obviously impossible to develop a modern industrial nation if all labor resources are engaged in agriculture. But, more importantly, the ability to move resources out of agriculture is a necessary precondition of the process of industrialization itself. That is, if agriculture cannot produce a surplus (output greater than that required to support the farm population), resources can never be maintained in other activities. While the production of an agricultural surplus has never been a problem in the United States, in many countries an agricultural revolution has been an essential part of industrial development. In such countries, increasing agricultural productivity is the only possible way of freeing resources from the production of food so they can be utilized in building and operating an industrial system. Laborers cannot be removed from food production if they would then starve to death.

The increase in the relative weight of the service sector is due to a number of factors. First, the growth of the government. As America has become larger and wealthier, increasingly heavy demands have been made upon all levels of government to control the economic system and ameliorate its social abuses. Moreover, since 1940 there has been the large-scale involvement of government in problems of defense and mutual security. Second, consumers have increasingly demanded services instead of commodities. Some of these services (for example, laundry, haircutting, and entertainment) were in past periods provided from within the household. Others, such as insurance, education, and medical services were only imperfectly provided from within the household. Still others are entirely new in form, if not in concept, and are the products of expanding knowledge and the increasing complexity of modern life. Examples would include the increasing volume of services provided urban and suburban communities by municipalities and private businessmen alike. Third, the great rise in the proportion of labor resources absorbed by the service sector has resulted in part from differences in labor efficiency between this sector and the commodity-producing sector.

A comparison of the shares of the two sectors in national output with their shares of the labor force shows just how unequally productivity increases have been distributed between them. The share in output of the commodity-producing industries (as estimated by Kuznets) has declined from 52.4 per cent in the decade 1869–1878, to 38.9 per cent in the decade 1939–1948. Between 1870 and 1940, the labor-force share of the commodity-producing sector decreased by 25 percentage points from 75.9 per cent to 51.4 per cent. These figures indicate the productivity increases that occurred in this sector of the economy over the period. The noncommodity-producing sector of the economy over the same period increased its labor-force share by 24.5 percentage points but its share of output by only 13.5 percentage points.

The technological revolution has not affected the noncommodity-producing sector of the economy to the same extent as the commodity-producing sector. The provision of services, for example, that call for the rendering of personal judgments are not yet subject to mechanization. There are indications that medical diagnoses may be given by electronic computers, but it is unlikely that the era of personal medical attention is at an end. In fact, one of the factors that has retarded the growth of mechanization in many areas of the service sector has been consumer insistence upon a continued and perhaps increased element of personal service.

20–3. *The Evolution of Business Enterprise*

So far we have concentrated upon the changes in forms of production and industrial structure resulting from the application of the new technology. No less important is the growth of knowledge about means of controlling the new technology. Mechanization, increasing size, and the large volumes of capital required in modern industry posed a problem for businessmen accustomed to managing small-scale family enterprises. Prior to the industrial revolution, the most common form of business organization was the family firm in which the owners risked their capital, directed and controlled the enterprise, and had full rights to the profits (or losses) that accrued. Even in this period there were some large joint-stock companies (primarily engaged in trading enterprises) that through sale of ownership shares were able to accumulate far more capital than the family firm; but they represented only a small part of total activity.

The introduction of the new techniques of production led to a revolution in forms of business enterprise. The amount of capital required to utilize fully the new techniques was so large that few families possessed the resources to finance the new operations. The answer to the problem was the corporate form of organization.

The corporate form has many advantages. First, it is empowered by its charter to issue equity stock. In this way it is able to tap many small pools of savings and direct these accumulations to a single end. Furthermore, the size of a corporation gives it access, through debt instruments, to sources of nonrisk capital. Second, the corporation is a legal entity, and it continues to exist even though those who manage it may die or withdraw. In a sole proprietorship or partnership, the company is dissolved by death of the owner or one of the partners. It would be extremely difficult to run a very large enterprise on such a basis. Finally, the risk of the stockholders in a corporation is limited to the amount of their investment. Under any other business form, the owners are liable for all the debts incurred in the name of the company.

Corporate enterprises in the United States began in transportation and finance. In manufacturing, the corporate form was widely utilized in the textile industry in the 1820's, but it was not an important element in manufacturing as a whole until about 1870. Until after the Civil War most manufacturing was undertaken in small shops by sole proprietors.

Until about 1875 the granting of a corporate charter usually required a special act of a state legislature, and the charters provided strict provisions for guaranteeing the rights of the state, the public, and the shareholders. The charters usually defined carefully the functions of the enterprise and limited the scope of its action. For example, the corporation usually could not begin operations until all capital had been paid up; each share was to be assessed at equal value; and a rigid capital structure that could only be changed by approval of the legislature was established. In addition to these statutory provisions, common law was generally interpreted to mean that all decisions affecting the general interest of the concern had to be approved by all (or, on some issues, a specified majority) of the stockholders, that only old stockholders in the corporation could invest new monies, and that profits could be paid only out of earned surplus. The power of the legislatures to control the number and content of corporate charters frequently led to political corruption and pressure upon the legislatures to weaken the terms of charters. The sharp definitions of scope and function in the early charters gave way to general incorporation acts; proxy voting weakened the responsiveness of the corporation to its stockholders; the majority of stockholders needed to support a vote was reduced (in the case of Delaware charters, for example, to 50 per cent of the common stock plus one share); corporations were authorized to grant shares to individuals contributing property rather than money, a powerful tool in the hands of unscrupulous men when the corporation determined the value of the property; and finally, the rigid capital requirements were waived in many state charters.

20–4. *The Growth of Industrial Concentration*

The large-scale, modern-type corporation began with the incorporation of the New York Central Railroad in 1853. In the case of the railroads, it was perfectly clear that even with lavish government aid a vast accumulation of savings was necessary to effect construction. The railroads led the way in developing methods needed to control large enterprises and, by their very size, created benefits for themselves that were not open to smaller businesses. The economic power of a railroad network permitted it to manipulate rates and service in such a way as to guarantee themselves a large profit as long as there were no competitors in the area. These lessons were duly noted by others, particularly after the depression of 1873 (an event thought by many businessmen of the time to have been caused by "cutthroat" competition). An environment of unrestrained competition is not conducive to stability and high profits for the individual businessman, although it may be a "social good." The record of large sectors of American business since 1873 has been marked by attempts on the part of businessmen to provide a comfortable climate for their operations. At the same time, government has been increasingly concerned to let in enough competitive forces so that business behavior at least approximates the social good. The government has been continually handicapped in this attempt because laws formed on the basis of past experience and court interpretation may be inadequate to control current business practices. It is not entirely wise to condemn businessmen for their behavior. They are charged with the responsibility of making profits, and a monopoly position is the surest way to achieve large profits. It is too much to ask them to have a social conscience when no other group in society is expected to have one; and moreover, the free-enterprise system will operate only if they continue their search for profits. Freedom of individual action and the acquisition of private property are two of the foundations of our economic and political system. Our government is charged, however, with the responsibility for protecting society from the antisocial uses of these rights by any one group.

The depression of 1873 shocked the American business community. They found themselves battered about by a storm of competitive pressures against which they had no defense. Cooperation against the common enemy was a natural solution. At first the business community turned to "pools," agreements among various firms dividing up markets and setting output and price limitations on the member firms. This type of mutual agreement is likely to be very unstable in periods of rapid economic change since any one of the cooperating firms is quite likely to find it to their advantage to break the agreement in the search for profits. Railroad pools that had been attacked most severely by the public were declared illegal by the Interstate Commerce Act of 1887, although the Interstate Commerce Commission has permitted pool agreements among railroads that exist today.

In an attempt to find a more satisfactory mechanism for cooperation, many businessmen turned to trust arrangements. The trust was a much tighter form of business consolidation than the pool. Typically, the stockholders of the firms (or the largest firms only) in an industry deposited their shares with a board of trustees and received certificates in exchange. The trust became, therefore, the legal owners of the firms; and the trustees were empowered to operate them. The concentrations of economic power built up in this way were tremendous. The Standard Oil Company pioneered the movement and its example was quickly followed by other industrial groups including, for example, sugar refiners, whisky distillers, and lead producers. The trusts were effective monopolies and permitted consumer extortion. The trust arrangement gave the trustified firms the power to force favorable rate agreements from the railroads, and it gave them the power to effectively exclude competition from the industry. It is true that during most of the period the prices of the commodities produced by the trusts were frequently falling. However, the explanation of this apparent paradox probably lies in the tremendous technological advances of the period. In this instance, monopolization resulted not in increased price but in smaller price declines than would otherwise have been the case.

The public outcry against the trusts resulted in legislation by the states and, in 1890, the Sherman Antitrust Act. The early prosecutions under the federal act were generally unsuccessful. In fact, it was an Ohio court that ordered the dissolution of the Standard Oil trust (1892) and the New York courts that dissolved the North River Sugar Refining Company (1890). Interestingly enough, the state courts based their decisions upon the grounds that the individual firms that had combined into the trust had violated the conditions of their charters of incorporation, not on the grounds that a monopoly had been formed. Ultimately, however, the Sherman Act spelled the doom of the trusts throughout the country.

After an interlude caused by the unsettled business conditions of the early 1890's, business next turned to the holding company to effect market cooperation. The holding company was made possible by the loose incorporation requirements of certain states, particularly New Jersey. The laws of New Jersey permitted the incorporation of companies whose assets consisted solely of the stock of other companies. A company could, therefore, use the proceeds of its own stock sale to buy a controlling interest in the stock of other corporations. Such firms have been called holding companies. The holding company, although perhaps owning only a relatively small fraction of the voting stock, could by voting as a block appoint the board of directors and determine policy of its subsidiary. These great financial corporations, of which United States Steel is probably the most famous, were intimately tied in with the great banking houses, such as that of J. P. Morgan.

Combinations, mergers, holding companies, and the new forms of consolidation yet to be invented are an inevitable part of the American scene. It must be recognized that these concentrations have in the great majority of cases been organized for quite different purposes than the movements to large scale that occurred as part of the industrial revolution. There is no reason to believe, for example, that the Buick division is more efficient in production because it is a part of General Motors than it would be had it remained a private firm. There may be economies in selling effort and capital mobilization, but such a point is difficult to test. The majority of the great manufacturing combinations had profits as a motive; profits that from an economic point of view were derived from a monopoly position and not from efficiencies in the allocation of resources.

The following section presents a special case study of the growth of a famous monopoly in the American economy.

20–5. *The Standard Oil Company—A Case Study in Monopoly*

The history of the Standard Oil Company is perhaps the classic American example of the growth of a monopolistic organization. Its history spans the period from 1867 through to 1911 and beyond, and the business geniuses who guided the company through its early history developed many of the practices that gave this period of American industrialization its peculiar character.

The modern American oil industry was born in Titusville, Pennsylvania, in 1859, with the first successful oil well. Oil was, of course, known before that date, and its potentialities as a lubricant and source of heat and light were familiar to many. Its derivative, kerosene, was known to be far superior as a source of light to whale oil, the most widely used illuminant. It was not until the discovery of the Pennsylvania oil fields, however, that an economic source of oil was found. The discovery of the "black gold" and the development of new techniques to collect it touched off a speculative boom matching any gold strike. Men poured into the area and set up small independent drilling operations. In spite of the increase in production and refining during the Civil War years, the industry lagged far behind its potential. John D. Rockefeller stepped into this situation in 1865. With money accumulated as a merchant and through profiteering in Civil War contracts, Rockefeller backed Samuel Andrews, who knew how to refine oil, and established the Rockefeller and Andrews oil-refining company of Cleveland, Ohio. During the next five years Rockefeller expanded his firm by uniting with other refineries in the Cleveland area. In 1870 he and four others formed the Standard Oil Company of Ohio with a capital of $1 million. At this point Rockefeller reached a major crossroad in his career. His company had a capacity of about 600 barrels per day when the industry as a whole was refining approximately 15,000 barrels a day. The problem was: how best to extend his power to gain effective control over the industry? One possibility would have been to attempt to gain control of the production of crude oil. To do so would have been possible since all production was concentrated in Pennsylvania, but because of the number of producers involved it would have been very difficult. Rockefeller wisely saw that it would be far better to leave production in the hands of a large number of independent firms because competition among them would keep the cost of crude oil down. Moreover, Rockefeller did not want to be involved in the risks of exploration and drilling when there was always the probability of a "dry hole." By letting independents do the drilling, not all the costs would be reflected in the price of crude oil because of bankruptcies and the pressure of competition. In fact, Rockefeller made it a consistent policy to prevent any attempt by anybody to consolidate the oil-production end of the industry.

Instead, Rockefeller, through the Standard Oil Company, began to take control of the refining of crude oil and, where he could, to control the transportation of the oil and the finished products. As the first step, Rockefeller and the New York Central, Erie, and Pennsylvania railroads gained control of the South Improvement Company, a firm chartered in Pennsylvania with the widest powers imaginable. Rockefeller agreed to ship all his crude oil and finished products with the three railroads and in return received a promise that the railroads would raise freight rates on oil and oil products but give the Standard Oil Company rebates on their freight charges amounting to about 50 per cent on crude oil and 25 per cent on oil derivatives. In addition, the railroads were to furnish to the South Improvement Company (in effect to Rockefeller) complete information on all oil and oil products shipped by them. With this agreement in hand, Rockefeller persuaded twenty-one of the twenty-six refineries in Cleveland either to sell out to, or to merge with, Standard Oil. This operation raised such a storm of protest that the charter of the South Improvement Company was revoked by the Pennsylvania legislature after three months, so the proposed rate increases and rebates never did go into effect. The change of heart of the Pennsylvania legislature did not, however, help the refining companies that had fallen into Rockefeller's hands.

As a result, Standard Oil had a stranglehold on the Cleveland area and controlled 20 per cent of the nation's oil-refining capacity. Cleveland was ideally located to serve as a refining center because of its good rail connections, its proximity to the oil-producing area, and because the Great Lakes and the Erie Canal gave the refiners an alternative route to the east if the railroads used their monopoly power to increase rates. In fact, there was little danger of the railroads combining against Rockefeller even after the South Improvement Company was disbanded. The competition for the oil business was too fierce. In 1872 the New York Central agreed to give rebates on freight charges in exchange for Standard's business. Next,

Rockefeller created the National Refiners' Association, an oil-refinery pool controlling 80 per cent of the refining business of the country. In this same period a group of producers and refiners attempted to get around Rockefeller's control of the railroads by constructing pipelines, particularly to link with the East Coast. Unfortunately they didn't have sufficient capital, and they had to raise the money they needed by selling stock. When they were finished they found that Rockefeller held a controlling interest in the pipeline and was receiving rebates on the shipments he made by pipeline as well as by railroad. By 1879 the refineries on the East Coast had been brought under control, and the Rockefeller group controlled 90 per cent of the refining business of the United States.

How was it possible to gain almost complete control of an entire growth industry in such an incredibly short period of time? The principal reason was undoubtedly the business acumen of Rockefeller and his group of advisors. The organizational ability of these men plus the technical ability of Andrews made them an unbeatable group. It was certainly no easy task to convince the railroads to grant rate concessions when Standard Oil was only another small company. The railroads themselves played a large part in Standard Oil's growth. Once they were convinced that Rockefeller had the ability to control the oil-refining business, the railroads gave him the power to do so. One unregulated monopoly breeds another. From the railroads' point of view, it paid them to cooperate with Rockefeller. The marginal cost of hauling was very slight, and Rockefeller guaranteed them traffic. The railroads could then discriminate against the independents that managed to remain in business.

The process of monopolization was not carried forward completely without opposition. Independent refiners brought lawsuits against Standard Oil on grounds of conspiracy and restraint of trade in the courts of various states. Other suits arose out of the methods used by the company (including arson and sabotage) to gain control of competitors. Standard Oil was big enough that the suits did nothing to halt the progress of the company, but such suits were bothersome and might eventually have led to serious trouble. How could the company maintain its position? To solve the problem, the Standard Oil trust was formed in 1882. By that time the Standard Oil Company controlled thirty-nine separate corporations. The managers of these subsidiaries gave their voting stock to a group of nine trustees and received nonvoting trust certificates in return. The trustees, with Rockefeller at their head, then became the officers of the subsidiaries, but because the trust was not incorporated they were almost immune from prosecution in state courts. It was not until 1890 that a successful action was brought into the courts. An Ohio suit charged that the transfer of a controlling share of Standard Oil of Ohio to the trustees was a violation of the charter of the company. The case was decided by the Supreme Court of Ohio in 1892 when the Court ruled that the voting shares of Standard Oil of Ohio held by the trustees had to be returned to their original owners. The trustees had no intention of complying with the court order, and a series of delaying maneuvers ensued. In 1897 contempt charges were brought, but the company was successful in its attempt to have the charges dropped. As a result, no further attempts to enforce the original order were made.

It is interesting that this action originated in the courts of Ohio and was not instituted in a federal court under the Sherman Act of 1890. The Sherman Act was admirably brief, but the courts did not find its meaning very clear. The act stated that "Every contract, combination in the form of trust or otherwise, or conspiracy, in restraint of trade or commerce among the several states, or with foreign nations, is hereby declared to be illegal." Obviously, the law could be interpreted so broadly as to apply to almost any business agreement, and the courts were left to determine the scope of the act. They tended in their interpretation to be reactionary, to lean over backward in favor of business. In fact, the law was applied in the early period more against labor unions as combinations in restraint of trade than against businesses.

For Rockefeller, the period of the 1890's was marked by continued expansion on the one hand and by legal maneuverings on the other. Finally, in 1899 the Standard Oil Company of New Jersey, a subsidiary, expanded its capital stock from $10 million to $110 million and absorbed the whole Standard Oil group of companies. This move was made possible by a weakening of the New Jersey law on incorporation, and it permitted Rockefeller to gain complete control over the whole operation without laying himself open to prosecution by the various states. A corporation chartered in one state has a legal right to do business in all others. The New Jersey law had been amended to permit corporations chartered in the state to hold stock in other corporations. Standard Oil of New Jersey therefore became a holding company, holding a controlling share of the stock of the corporations in the Standard Oil group. In 1895 the United States Supreme Court had held that buying stock was not an act of interstate commerce and that, even if a holding company held a majority of the stock of corporations in an industry, such control did not represent a restraint of interstate trade. It was, for example, in 1901 that the largest holding company up to that time, the United States Steel Corporation—chartered in New Jersey and capitalized at $1.4 billion—was formed by J. P. Morgan out of a consolidation of steel corporations of which Andrew Carnegie's was the biggest.

From 1882 when the trust was formed until the creation of the holding company in 1899, Rockefeller had been fabulously successful. He held a firm grip on the oil-refining business of the nation, driving out competitors by vicious price wars and other, even less scrupulous, means. His methods aroused the public and led, along with the behavior of other monopolies, to the popularity of "muckraking" literature. Popular resentment, however, had little effect. Rockefeller stayed one step ahead of the government's attempt to control him—either by changing the form of the company or, when that failed, by controlling the government by bribery. Although monopolies were mushrooming in all fields at the turn of the century, they had come to the end of the period of almost complete freedom of action. The public clamor was soon to have some practical effect and "trust-busting" was to become a popular political slogan.

It is easy to overestimate the concrete results of the trust-busting era. While the writings of the "muckrakers" were popular, the large monopolies were well entrenched and possessed political power far in excess of their numerical strength. Presidents Theodore Roosevelt and William Howard Taft had some success in dealing with transportation and industrial monopolies, particularly in the matter of rebates and rate adjustments by railroads. In the period, the two most significant decisions of the Supreme Court were on the Northern Securities case (1904) and the Standard Oil case of 1911. In the first decision, the Court held the Northern Securities Company's (a holding company) control of the Northern Pacific, Great Northern, Union Pacific, and Burlington railroads to be a violation of the antitrust act and ordered the company dissolved. In 1911 the Court ordered the dissolution of the Standard Oil Company of New Jersey. The antimonopoly program was never prosecuted with full vigor, and it is difficult to assess the real results attained. In the case of Standard Oil, the Supreme Court decision appears to have caused a change in the outward appearance of the organization rather than a basic dissolution of the structure.

The stranglehold that Standard Oil had upon the oil-refining business was broken not by the Supreme Court or Congress but by the march of events. New oil fields were discovered in the Middle West and the plains states, population centers grew rapidly in areas away from the Atlantic Coast, and the automobile provided a market for petroleum products too big to be controlled by one group. It was not that Standard Oil got smaller but rather that the industry increased more rapidly than Standard Oil, so that the relative position of the company declined. The same process of relative decline occurred in other industries as well. In the period 1901–1905 the United States Steel Corporation, the giant of them all, controlled 63 per cent of the steel industry's capacity. By 1930 the company's share of the total industry capacity had declined to 40 per cent, and today they produce only 25 per cent of total steel output.

20–6. *Conclusions*

In the twentieth century new forces were at work that accelerated the decline of many of the old monopolies. In the period of early industrialization the economy was based upon a relatively few technological breakthroughs. The process of industrialization essentially involved the application of this new knowledge to virgin territory. However, the growth of industrial sectors based on this technology could not continue at the same rate indefinitely. At the same time, new technological developments opened up whole new industrial areas competing directly with the old technology or superseding the products of the old technology in the consumer's budget. Thus, the automobile and truck and eventually the airplane destroyed the transportation monopoly of the railroads; and the radio and home-appliance industries drove less desired goods out of the consumer's budget. The force of public opinion should also be included in this list. Since the turn of the century, the government has been encouraged by the public to be more vigorous in its control of monopolies, and businessmen themselves have been persuaded to the view that they have a social responsibility. Basically, however, a rapidly changing economy is the best defense against monopoly.

All this is not meant to imply that the problems raised for society by business consolidation no longer exist. There are always movements toward industrial consolidation in order to effect cost savings, not so much perhaps in production today, but in distribution and selling. Constant vigilance must be maintained to insure that such cost savings are passed on to the consumer. In the case of railroads, we have at present the interesting condition of approved mergers between lines, designed to reduce costs and maintain the railroad's competitive position in the transportation industry. There is, finally, a compelling economic reason to permit the continued existence of "well-behaved" concentrations of economic power. As the process of scientific investigation becomes ever more complex, the existence of these power blocs may be necessary, if sufficient funds are to be made available to support research and development in the new frontiers of science.

Suggested Readings

CLARK, COLIN. *The Conditions of Economic Progress* (3d. ed.). New York: St. Martin's Press, 1957.

HOSELITZ, B. F. (ED.). *Theories of Economic Growth.* Glencoe, Ill.: The Free Press, 1960.

KUZNETS, S. *National Income: A Summary of Findings.* New York: National Bureau of Economic Research, 1946.

MANTOUX, P. J. *The Industrial Revolution in the Eighteenth Century.* Oxford: Clarendon Press, 1928.

MEIER, G. M., AND BALDWIN, R. E. *Economic Development.* New York: John Wiley & Sons, Inc., 1957.

Chapter 21 AGRICULTURE: AN INDUSTRY IN TRANSITION

21–1. *Introduction*

There are several reasons for devoting a chapter to the study of a single industry—agriculture. Throughout most of American history, it was the largest industry in the economy. Although it occupies less than 10 per cent of the labor force today, in 1800 it absorbed about nine out of every ten workers. Moreover, it is an industry that was subject to terrific structural pressures from new lands, new demands, new technologies, and new competitive products, and therefore provides an excellent example of the process of economic change. Finally, it is an industry that has engendered a number of social and political problems—problems that still plague the economy today.

Before we begin to examine the changes that have occurred in the agricultural sector, it is well to note that in the United States agriculture has almost always been a business. Despite anything that one may have read, the typical American farmer has specialized in the production of a relatively narrow range of commodities, he has sold these commodities in a regional or national market, and he has used the proceeds of these sales to purchase the bulk of his requirements. High transport costs, costs that were characteristic of most of the economy before the innovation of the canals and railroads, acted like tariffs and tended to reduce the size of the market and restrict the degree of specialization. Even in this early period, however, farmers depended upon cash crops to buy commodities that could not economically be produced at home. Thus, as early as 1794 the farmers of western Pennsylvania launched the abortive Whiskey Rebellion as a protest against a federal excise on their most important cash crop.

Over the last 150 years the agricultural sector has been subject to a number of pressures. We have already examined some of them, but it might be well to mention them again. The American economy, because of its size and its ability to accumulate and mobilize capital, has historically been characterized by a surplus of land and capital relative to the amount of labor available. The decline in the price of capital relative to wages has made the farmer willing to innovate new techniques that save labor and has tended to place a premium on areas capable of supporting machine agriculture relative to other lands. At the same time, the opening of new western lands (frequently more fertile than their eastern counterparts) tended to undermine the competitive position of eastern farmers and force them to exit from the industry. Advances in science and the mechanical arts that have been translated into a changing agricultural technology have also acted powerfully on the agricultural sector. Together, new lands, new capital, and new technology have underwritten a rapid increase in agricultural output. Since we have already discussed land acquisitions and capital accumulation, we will concentrate here on the nature of technical advance. Then we will examine the impact of all three on the structure of agriculture.

21–2. *Technology and the Addition of New Land to the Market*

We have already sketched in the broad outlines of the development of transportation in the American economy. Let us only briefly mention the impact of these developments on agriculture. Given high transport costs, it follows that only items with a high value relative to their weight may be economically transported (this fact explains the eighteenth-century farmer's concern with the price of whiskey). Although most of the Midwest could have been settled soon after the Revolutionary War, the cost of transport precluded the economic integration of a large portion of the area with the East. As a result, aside from the areas adjoining the Ohio and Mississippi rivers, the land had little economic value. In the South, given the region's natural inland waterways and an all-water route to the east (via the Gulf and Atlantic Ocean), southern agriculture began to move westward at a fairly early date. In the North, however, agriculture remained tied to the eastern seaboard. Farming in New England (certainly among the nation's least fertile areas) remained profitable through the first decade of the nineteenth century) and New Jersey, eastern Pennsylvania, and the great Valley of Virginia could have been called the nation's breadbasket.

With the opening of the Erie Canal, however, the geographic

structure of northern agriculture changed drastically, and within a decade the Old Northwest Territory was satisfying a significant portion of the East's agricultural demands. The center of wheat production, for example, moved from eastern to western Pennsylvania, and then on into Ohio (in 1850 it was located near Columbus). In 1820 Baltimore had been the nation's leading milling center, but by 1840 that city had lost its dominant position to Buffalo (a city with an access to the new western lands). No longer was it possible for farmers in New England to profitably grow corn and hogs. Because of the greater fertility of the lands in Ohio, Indiana, and Illinois costs of production were much lower. As a result, as early as the 1830's Cincinnati became the nation's greatest pork-packing center, but in a few years it was overtaken by cities even farther west (both Alton and Chicago became major packing centers before the Civil War). In the East, farmers faced with western competition were forced to shift production to truck and dairy products (items with great perishability and therefore high transport costs), move to the cities, or migrate west.

By 1860 the Old Northwest Territory was almost completely integrated into the American economy, but across the Mississippi millions of arable acres could not be used because of inadequate transportation. Although it probably would have been possible to open lands as far west as the 100th meridian with canals, by 1860 railroads had proven themselves at least slightly more economical. It was technical change in the transport sector and the expansion of the system across the Mississippi that added these new lands to the economy. By 1880 the names of Gould, Hill, and Jay became synonymous with the transportation of western agriculture to eastern markets. Once again, farm areas farther east were subject to increasing competitive pressure and the center of agricultural production continued to shift westward (by 1900 the center of wheat production was seventy miles west of Des Moines, Iowa).

But it was not only transport that opened new lands. A piece of land can have access to the world's best transportation system, but it is of little value unless it can be used in economic production. In the case of agriculture, certain technical advances were required before some of the nation's land could be farmed.

Chronologically, the first of these developments was the cotton gin. Before Eli Whitney turned out his first crude model, cotton culture had been restricted to the seacoast areas. In these areas the long-stranded sea-island cotton could be grown; and, although the process was expensive, the seeds could be combed out by hand and the cotton sold at a competitive price. Although attempts had been made to grow short-staple upland cotton, no reasonable price could repay the labor needed to remove the seeds by hand. With the invention of the gin (and later with the application of steam and water power) cleaning became much less costly. It was then economically feasible to cultivate upland cotton. Cotton production rose spectacularly. It is estimated that in 1800, 73,000 bales were grown. By 1820 production had risen to 335,000 bales; by 1839 it was 1,976,000; and in 1859 it reached 5,387,000. Moreover, free of its coastal ties, production spilled into the upland areas of the old South and then across into the black belt of Alabama, Mississippi, Louisiana, and east Texas. As production moved west and supply increased, cotton prices fell. As a result, even before the Civil War, cotton farming had largely ceased to be profitable in the older (and less fertile) areas, and, like their counterparts in the Northeast, Atlantic planters were forced into other lines of activity.

Improved transportation played only a minor role in the shift of cotton production into the new South. The same was true after the Civil War. While northern agriculture continued to move westward, the center of cotton production changed but little in the latter half of the nineteenth century (it moved only from Birmingham, Alabama, to Jackson, Mississippi). However, two important technical developments in recent decades have opened up new lands far to the west. In the case of cotton, unlike wheat and corn, despite a flood of patents dating to the 1820's, American inventiveness failed to produce a satisfactory mechanical picker until recently. The first successful prototype of a spindle picker was developed by August Campbell in 1895, but it was only developed by International Harvester in the 1920's, and not introduced until the 1940's (in the meantime, John Deere had begun marketing a successful stripping picker). The pickers were not, however, particularly well suited for the rolling hills of the traditional cotton states; they functioned best in flat areas. With the development in the 1940's of liquid nitrogen fertilizers, it became possible to farm the heretofore largely barren lands of west Texas, Arizona, and California. As a result, within the past decade the grandsons of the farmers in the new South, who in the 1850's had made life difficult for planters in the eastern coastal areas, found themselves subject to similar competition from the far Southwest.

The South, however, was not the only area where new lands

were opened by technical developments not related to transport. The West also benefited from a similar development. The early pattern of western settlement is a puzzling one, in that the lands first brought under cultivation were the forested areas, while the prairies were bypassed. The prairie soil was largely clay and crisscrossed with very tough roots. Early ploughs piled up clay until they couldn't move and still failed to break the roots. Despite the difficulties, it was easier to clear the land of trees than first to break and then annually to plough the prairie soil. The inability to farm the prairies presented relatively few problems as the agricultural frontier swept across the largely forested areas in Ohio, Indiana, and Illinois, but as settlement moved farther west most of the land was inaccessible.

What was needed was a new type of plough. At the beginning of the nineteenth century, ploughs were made of wood, easily broken, and poorly designed. Inefficient even in the best of soils, there was need of improved design (in fact, Thomas Jefferson was one of the first to attempt to apply engineering principles to the design of a plough). In the second decade of the century Jethro Wood designed a satisfactory wood and cast-iron plough. Wood's plough was well designed and the cast-iron parts could be replaced. As a result, it was widely innovated and remained the standard plough in the East until the Civil War. However, because the plough was not self-scouring and was too light to break the tough prairie roots, it was not suited for prairie agriculture. Two decades later a steel plough strong enough to break roots and smooth enough to scour itself was developed. Many such ploughs were designed, but the most famous is associated with the name of John Deere. Once developed, the plough was quickly innovated (in 1856 Deere alone produced 10,000 steel ploughs) and within a few years new corn and wheat areas in northern Indiana, Illinois, and a few years later in Iowa and Nebraska began to compete with the older areas.

Even with the steel plough, the northern plains resisted settlement. Spring came too late to grow corn and winter wheat, and spring wheat, when milled, produced a dirty grey flour that was hard to sell. Moreover, the ravages of rust (a wheat blight) seemed worse in the prairies and the thin margin of water further threatened any crop. If the upper prairies were to be farmed, new techniques had to be developed to mill spring wheat, and the wheat itself had to be made resistant to blight and drought. In the early 1870's the successful innovation of Hungarian reduction-milling made it possible to produce fine flour from spring wheat; and, with the arrival of the

Northern Pacific Railroad at Moorhead, the prairies were opened. Within a few years, however, drought threatened the region's agriculture. In this case, the technical solution was not a new machine but new strains of wheat. In the 1890's Mark Carleton, an agronomist in the Department of Agriculture, proved that the Kharkov strain of durum wheat was rust-resistant and needed considerably less water than the traditional strains. Ten years later, experimentation by the Saunders brothers in Canada produced the Marquis cross, a strain both early ripening and hardy. The new milling techniques, the new wheat strains, and improvements in dry-farming techniques turned the arid northern prairies of Minnesota and North Dakota into the nation's largest wheat-producing region.

21–3. *Technical Improvements and the Rise in Output per Worker*

Because labor has been expensive and represented a major portion of total agricultural costs, there has been a tendency to innovate techniques that saved labor. We have already seen how the invention of the cotton gin made the production of upland cotton profitable, but there have been a myriad of other developments that accomplished the same end (although perhaps not quite so spectacularly). Here we will mention only a few, for purposes of illustration. In the case of corn, for example, the high labor requirements in shelling made the production of shelled corn almost prohibitively expensive. At the same time, transport costs were (and are) too high to permit the shipment of unshelled corn for any great distance. As a result, farmers typically raised both corn and hogs and with few exceptions only corn destined for the distillery moved through the regional markets. The invention of the corn sheller altered this structure. With the new machine, the time required to shell a bushel of corn fell from one hour and forty minutes to about one minute, and it became possible to divorce corn growing from livestock raising. Later the picking operation (the next most labor-intensive) was subject to mechanization. The innovation of the corn picker in the 1890's resulted in a substantial saving of labor, and now, of course, the picking and shelling operations have been combined in the harvester.

Although no single invention resulted in as great a relative saving of labor as did the corn sheller, developments in wheat technology were probably more important in terms of the total amount of labor saved. As in the case of corn, it was the shelling and harvesting operations that were the most labor-intensive; and it was in these activities that the greatest gains were made. In the 1820's and 1830's threshing machines replaced flails in the East, and ten years later they were used almost everywhere in the West. In the late 1840's Cyrus McCormick began to produce reapers on a large scale; and, although he may not have invented the machine, he was certainly the most successful early manufacturer. His machines were widely innovated during the 1850's, and by the end of the Civil War no farm without access to one could hope to compete. (Before the invention of the thresher, it had taken some thirty man-hours to harvest and thresh an acre of wheat; with a Case thresher and a McCormick harvester a farmer could perform both tasks in about one hour.)

The increases in labor productivity continued after the war. The first steam tractors were innovated during the 1860's in California and in the '70's on some of the large bonanza farms of the upper plains. Gasoline tractors replaced a majority of the remaining horses in the 1920's. In the 1880's the first combines appeared in California, and, after the turn of the century, these made their appearance east of the Rockies.

Without these machines, although the eastern areas would have continued to grow wheat, it is unlikely that wheat prices could have supported prairie agriculture where soil and climatic conditions combined to produce low yields. With machines, however, it was these areas that held a comparative advantage in wheat production, and they became the center of the nation's production. In fact, as we have seen, the center of wheat production in 1900 was seventy miles west of Des Moines, Iowa, and by 1960 it had moved several hundred miles farther west.

21–4. *Technical Improvements and the Rise in Per-Acre Yields*

Examination of the history of American agriculture suggests that it has been only in the more recent past that the industry has seen important innovations aimed at increasing per-acre yields. The reason for this delay probably rests in part on the close tie between increasing yields and our knowledge of the science of genetics—a science that has only recently come into its own. More important, however, has probably been the low value of land in a nation with free land still available.

Because of the lag in our understanding of genetics, the first land-saving innovations in the United States (as elsewhere) came in the use of fertilizers. In the 1870's cotton farmers in the older areas of the South began to use rotten cottonseed in an attempt to increase yields to match those in the newer areas of Texas and Oklahoma. Gradually the practice spread, and soon artificial fertilizers had replaced natural ones. By the 1890's farmers both in the South and the North were using phosphates produced in South Carolina (and later in Florida and Texas). In 1876, 60 per cent of South Carolina farms were using fertilizers, but that state was something of an exception. In the North Central states, for example, despite a 350 per cent increase in the use of fertilizer during the previous decade, farmers in 1890 were only fertilizing at the rate of about ten cents an acre. In the same year, the estimates for the prairie states were about one cent. Recently the increases have been more spectacular—as a nation our use of fertilizer has risen 500 per cent since 1935. In general, however, the American farmer continues to use less fertilizer than most of his counterparts in other developed sections of the world.

Improvements in strains have recently produced substantially better yields, but most of these increases have been products of the past few decades. In the case of wheat, the developments of the Kharkov and Marquis strains and their innovation occurred before World War I, but in the case of corn the development came much later. The scientific basis for hybrid corn had been laid as early as the 1870's, but these beginnings were not exploited for almost another half century. It was generally felt that the poor vigor of inbred strains limited the possibility of hybrids. In 1906, G. H. Shull, a geneticist at Cold Spring Harbor, New York, began a new series of fruitful experiments, and in 1918 D. F. Jones at Cornell showed that double-cross hybrids seemed at least a partial answer to the problems of poor vigor in the inbreeds. As a result the first commercial double-cross hybrid, Burr-Leaming, was released in 1921.

Even then adaptation was slow, and commercial innovation on a large scale did not begin until the 1930's. At that time a government buying program, combined with acreage limitations, put a premium on high yields; and within less than a decade innovation was general. Today the economy produces 20 per cent more corn on 25 per cent less land than it did before the widespread innovation of hybrids.

21–5. *The Shifting Structure of American Agriculture*

The past 150 years have witnessed a number of important structural shifts in American agriculture. We have already seen how rapidly increasing technology has resulted in less relative demand for farm labor, and how as a result, the proportion of farmers in the labor force declined from nine out of ten to less than one out of ten. Through most of our history this decline was only a relative one, but since the 1920's it has become an absolute one as well. In 1820, for example, there were over 2 million farmers in a labor force of about

TABLE 21–1

SIX LEADING STATES IN THE PRODUCTION OF MAJOR AGRICULTURAL PRODUCTS

1839	*1859*	*1899*	*1964*
	WHEAT		
Ohio	Illinois	Minnesota	Kansas
Pennsylvania	Indiana	North Dakota	North Dakota
New York	Wisconsin	Ohio	Montana
Virginia	Ohio	South Dakota	Oklahoma
Illinois	Virginia	Kansas	Washington
Indiana	Pennsylvania	California	Nebraska
	CORN		
Tennessee	Illinois	Illinois	Iowa
Kentucky	Ohio	Iowa	Illinois
Ohio	Missouri	Kansas	Indiana
Indiana	Indiana	Nebraska	Nebraska
Illinois	Kentucky	Missouri	Ohio
Missouri	Tennessee	Indiana	Missouri
	COTTON		
1849			
Alabama	Mississippi	Texas	Texas
Georgia	Alabama	Mississippi	California
Mississippi	Louisiana	Georgia	Mississippi
South Carolina	Georgia	Alabama	Arkansas
Tennessee	Texas	South Carolina	Arizona
Louisiana	Arkansas	Arkansas	Alabama

Source: U.S. Census.

2.8 million (70 per cent). By 1920 the number of farmers had risen to almost 11.5 million, but they constituted only about 25 per cent of the labor force. By 1960, their number had fallen to less than 5 million, and they made up less than 10 per cent of the total. On the other hand, over the same period (that is, 1920–60) farm output almost doubled.

We have also seen that important geographical shifts occurred in the location of agriculture. Table 21–1 provides some evidence of the geographic shift in three major commodities: corn, wheat, and cotton. Unfortunately we have no good figures for production before

1839, but even the later data is suggestive. As anyone might guess, there has been a gradual movement westward; but the speed, timing, and distance of that movement has not been uniform. In the case of wheat, the early centers were in the Middle Atlantic states, but with the opening of the Erie Canal the center of production moved into the Old Northwest Territory. Even so, as late as 1839, Pennsylvania, New York, and Virginia still ranked two, three, and four in the production of wheat. The post-bellum period saw a further westward movement as production moved across the Mississippi and into the Great Plains. By the turn of the century Minnesota, North Dakota, Kansas, South Dakota, and California (all unranked in 1859) took over five of the first six places. The westward shift did not, however, stop there. Although California drops from the first five in the most recent list, so does the last of the states on the list in 1859; and the newcomers (Montana, Oklahoma, Washington, and Nebraska) are all on or beyond the 100th meridian.

Geographic movement in corn production began in much the same fashion as that of wheat, but the westward shift appears to have halted about the turn of the century. The census of 1839 showed Tennessee and Kentucky the nation's leading corn producers, but the two quickly surrendered their position to Missouri and the Old Northwest states of Ohio, Indiana, and Illinois. After the Civil War, the westward movement continued, and the fertile plains of Iowa, Kansas, and Nebraska contributed significantly to the nation's total production. During the present century, however, there has been little further shift. In fact, the only change in the first six sees Ohio replacing Kansas.

Cotton, too, displays similar overall characteristics, but differs in significant detail from the other two. If we had the rankings from 1820, it is certain that the center of production would have been in the old South, and even as late as 1849 Georgia and South Carolina still ranked second and fourth. Nor does the pattern change much during the rest of the century. East Texas begins to become important in the decade before the Civil War, and that state becomes the nation's leading producer by 1900. However, with the exception of the replacement of "western" Louisiana by "eastern" South Carolina, the list remains constant over the second half of the century. In fact, the center of production did move west but only from Birmingham, Alabama, to Jackson, Mississippi. In the twentieth century, however (and particularly during the last twenty years), the change has been almost revolutionary. The far western states of California and

Arizona moved into second and fourth position, and although Texas remains first in 1964 it is not the east Texas counties but the far west counties—counties that produced almost no cotton in 1899—that keep Texas in first position.

Changes in costs and demand have altered the product structure of the agricultural sector. Table 21–1 includes corn, wheat, and cotton because they have been among the most important commodities traded interregionally and internationally throughout the nation's history. Although the three are still important, new commodities have risen to challenge their domination, and among the "big three" the order of importance has shown some change. Over the course of the nineteenth century, corn retained its prominence in domestic production, but wheat displaced cotton as the second most important commodity. More recently the position of cotton has been further threatened by truck and soy beans.

Cotton's decline can be traced to a number of factors. In the first place, the Civil War set back cotton production tremendously. Cut off from domestic and foreign markets, southern plantations shifted to the production of foodstuffs. As a result, it was 1879 before the production of 1859 was again achieved. In the second place, mechanization lagged in cotton production much more than it did elsewhere in the agricultural sector. Perhaps because the labor surplus in the area provided less pressure for invention, perhaps because the technical problems were much greater, a successful cotton picker lagged the reaper by almost a hundred years and the corn harvester by fifty. Finally, in the twentieth century, growing competition from synthetic fibers has tended to reduce the demand for cotton. As a result, since the turn of the century, while the nation's output of wheat has risen 50 per cent and the output of corn by a third, cotton production has hardly increased at all.

Other crops, too, have become important in interregional trade. The trend toward urbanization and the widespread innovation of the refrigerator car after the 1880's have made it possible to support national markets in fruit, truck, and dairy products. In the years since 1900 the "big three" commodities have shown increases ranging from nothing to 50 per cent, but in the same period the output of truck and manufactured dairy products rose by two thirds, and the output of fruit and milk by over 100 per cent. Moreover, before 1880 the markets for these perishable commodities were almost entirely local; today there are heavy concentrations of vegetable production in California, dairy products in Wisconsin, and fruit in Virginia, Washington, California, and Florida.

In the same period, the consumer's diet has altered, and, as a result, Americans consume far less wheat and corn and considerably more vegetables and meat than we did before. Moreover, over the same period the consumer has tended to shift his consumption away from pork and toward beef. To a large extent both of these trends have been made possible by the innovation of the refrigerator car that has permitted centralization of production and given the consumer the benefits of certain economies of scale in meat packing and food processing.

21–6. *Farmers and Agrarian Discontent*

This book is not a political history; but politics at times lead to legislation which in turn may have important economic repercussions. Farm legislation has had such impact on the American economy, and it appears useful to examine the background of that legislation.

American farmers have frequently been discontented with their economic lot, and as a group they have never hesitated to express their discontent through political action. The Whiskey Rebellion was followed thirty years later by the sometime violent squatters associations. After the Civil War, discontent was expressed through the Grange in the 1870's and the Populist Party in the '90's. More recently, the same discontent finds its expression through the action of the farm bloc in Congress and through election revolts of the farm areas similar to the one that carried President Truman into office in 1948.

In Chapter 1 we saw that, given competition and freedom of entry, an industry will adjust to changing conditions of supply and demand in a way that leads, in the long run, to normal profits. Agriculture is a fairly competitive industry and one not characterized by any legal barriers to entry or exit. Why then should agricultural problems have plagued the economy for over a century?

In the case of agriculture, although demand has been increasing, supply has been increasing even more rapidly. As a result, even during the nineteenth century the number of farms were increasing less rapidly than the supply of potential farmers (immigrants and sons of farmers), and more recently there has been an actual decline in the number of farmers. Thus, over the past 100 years there has been pressure for some exit from the industry, and in the past 40 years this pressure has been intensified. Similar pressures have been exerted on other industries (shipbuilding, wagon making, iron making, and cotton textile manufacturing, to cite only a few), but seldom have they triggered so much discontent.

The special condition of agriculture flows from several causes. First, the farm sector has been relatively large; therefore the volume of discontent has been large. Moreover, the farmer has lived in relatively concentrated areas and has voiced his discontent in a fairly uniform manner. As a result, given the nation's political structure, he has spoken with a proportionally larger voice. Second, although there are no legal barriers, there are certain economic and social impediments to exit that make the long run a very long time. Unlike the case in many industries, movement out of agriculture involves both geographic and occupational mobility, either of which inhibits outward movement. As a result, the pressure for exit lasts a long time, and the farmer possesses a political voice to express his unhappiness. The result has been a long period of discontent.

The first large-scale movement of farmers into politics to attempt to ease their position occurred in the decades after the Civil War. The farmers, because of their heavy capital requirements, tended to be debtors; and falling prices in this period added to their problems. Although the price fall was world-wide, the monetary policies of the federal government accentuated rather than alleviated it. In addition to blaming federal monetary policy for their plight, the farmers were equally bitter about the growth of monopolies in manufacturing and transportation. With some justification they complained of high storage costs, unscrupulous grading of produce, exorbitant freight rates, high prices of manufactured goods, and high tariffs that not only increased the prices of things they bought but jeopardized their foreign markets as well.

The movement toward specialization in agriculture had increased potential profit, but it also made the farmer dependent upon world and national markets for farm goods and upon the alleged monopolistic markets for the manufactured products and transportation services that he had to buy. Pressure for exit, falling prices and rising debt burdens, and dependence upon little-understood markets all combined to put pressure on the farmer in the decades after 1870. The farmer resisted these pressures with every weapon he could muster.

In the 1870's, acting through their Grange organizations, the farmers entered state politics in an attempt to destroy the power of their "exploiters." With majorities in many of the farm states, they were able to elect legislatures sympathetic to their goals. As a result many farm states passed laws regulating prices charged by railroad and grain storage companies. Their success was, however, short-lived. In the historic Wabash case (1886) the Supreme Court held that the states could not regulate any part of interstate activity.

As a result, further agitation at the local level largely collapsed, and in the next decade the farmers turned toward national politics. In the 1880's farmers in the South joined the Southern Alliance (later the National Farmer's Alliance and Industrial Union) and their western counterparts fed into the National Alliance. In the election of 1890, Alliance candidates scored impressive victories in the farm states. In that year they gained control of seven state legislatures, and, more important, elected three senators and fifty-two federal representatives. Elated with their success they combined into the Peoples (or Populist) Party, and in the elections of 1892 they captured about 10 per cent of the national vote. Two years later, in an off-year election, they increased their total about 50 per cent. Their failure to win the presidency in 1896 (despite their fusion with the Democrats and a very popular candidate) proved that farmers, although vocal, were a minority.

With this failure and an increase in agricultural prices, the farmers once again withdrew from the political scene. Thereafter, with the exception of an abortive attempt to establish a farmer labor party in the 1920's, they have found they can be more effective if they exert their power through the established political parties.

The agricultural picture changed for the better about 1900; and from then until World War I the farmer enjoyed a prosperity all the more impressive because of the contrast with the quarter of a century that had just passed. The prosperity was world-wide. Prices were rising as a result of currency inflation, but agricultural prices were rising faster than the prices of manufactured articles. As population increased in Europe and America and the majority of the increase found employment in cities, the demand for agriculture products finally caught up to the quantity world agriculture was able to supply at prices the farmers considered reasonable.

World War I placed heavy demands on American agriculture to feed the Allies. Agricultural prices rose, but so did the prices of manufactured products. The experience of the Civil War was repeated. Farmers expanded production to levels that could not be maintained when the end of the war came and normal production was restored in Europe. From the end of the war-induced inflation in 1921 through the decades of the 1920's and 1930's, the farmers, finding themselves faced again with problems they could not conquer individually, banded together to demand federal help. After 1932, they found a receptive government at last. Unfortunately, perhaps, there was no turning back; and the story ever since has been one of increasing government regulation and subsidization of major portions of the agricultural industry.

We are not suggesting, of course, that there was first a period when agriculture was unaffected by government action and then another period when government policy directly interfered in and directed agricultural activity. Clearly, government policies concerning the disposal of public lands, internal improvements, tariffs, the money supply, and the regulation of banks have affected agriculture just as much as other sectors of the economy. In addition, before the 1920's there had also been federal legislation relating directly to agriculture. In 1862, along with the Homestead Act, Congress passed the Morrill Act providing for an endowment of public lands in each state to found colleges to teach and do experimental work "in such branches of learning as are related to agriculture and the mechanic arts." Subsequent bills such as the Hatch Act (1887) and the Smith-Lever Act (1914) extended the educational work of the government by providing for county agents and the subsidization of teaching of agricultural subjects in the high schools. In 1862 also, the old Bureau of Agriculture was elevated to the position of Department of Agriculture. In addition to the federal government's interest in agriculture, various state governments provided departments of agriculture in the post–Civil War period.

Beginning in the 1920's, the focus of federal farm legislation shifted from an emphasis upon support for the production of agricultural products to an emphasis upon the problems of marketing agricultural products and of providing farm credit. Tariffs were raised against foreign food imports in 1921, 1922, and 1930, in the vain hope of supporting domestic food prices. Additional legislation designed to extend credits to farmers was passed in the Agricultural Credits Act of 1923 and in the Agricultural Marketing Act of 1929. Finally, direct price supports were included in the McNary-Haugen bills of 1927 and 1928, but both were vetoed by President Coolidge. Such legislation was powerfully supported by national farm lobbies such as the Farm Bureau and a group in Congress known as the farm bloc.

The position of the farmer during the 1920's was desperate; and, in fact, the legislation enacted had little effect. In 1920 the ratio of prices received to prices paid by farmers (1910–14 = 100) stood at 99; by 1928 it had fallen to 92. In 1920 total farm-mortgage debt was roughly $8.4 billion; by 1928 it had risen to $9.8 billion. In 1920 the value of farm land and buildings was $66 billion; by 1928 it had fallen to $47 billion. In 1920 the realized net income of farm operators was $6.9 billion; by 1928 it had fallen to $5.7 billion—all this, remember, at a time when the American economy was supposed to have reached "the permanent plateau of prosperity."

Between 1928 and 1932 American agriculture seriously deteriorated. The ratio of prices received to prices paid by farmers (1910–14 = 100) fell from 92 to 58. Realized net income of farm operators fell from $5.7 billion to $1.9 billion. In 1932, the Roosevelt administration launched an all-out attack upon the farm problem on all fronts.

The first major program was the Agricultural Adjustment Act of 1933. The three major points of the act were (1) a proposal to limit production of cotton, corn, hogs, wheat, tobacco, dairy products, and rice; (2) payments for acreage taken out of production; and (3) the establishment of procedures for efficient marketing of farm products. The cost of the program was met by taxes on food processors. Thus, purchasers of wheat were taxed on the number of bushels they bought, and the tax money distributed the following year to those growers who reduced production in accordance with the recommendations of the Department of Agriculture. This act was declared unconstitutional by the Supreme Court in 1936 on the ground that the power to regulate and control agricultural production resided in the states. That same year, in response to the Supreme Court's action, Congress passed the Soil Conservation and Domestic Allotment Act, providing payments to farmers for taking acreage of basic soil-depleting crops out of production. This measure proved largely ineffective as a means of controlling production, and in 1938 the second Agricultural Adjustment Act was passed. This act has been a basic part of the agricultural program ever since. It provided for payments to farmers taking land out of production, and parity payments to producers of basic crops who conformed to the acreage allotments set by the government. The Commodity Credit Corporation (CCC), created in 1933 by executive order and incorporated in the state of Delaware, was the agency through which prices were supported. The CCC was made part of the Department of Agriculture, and in 1948 it was reincorporated as a federal corporation. At the present time the CCC has a capital stock of $100 million subscribed by the United States and a borrowing power of $14.5 billion. All obligations of the CCC are fully guaranteed as to interest and principal by the government. The act operates in the following manner: a wheat farmer will receive a nonrecourse loan on his wheat crop—for example, at $2 per bushel; thus, if the market price of wheat falls below $2, the farmer defaults on his loan, keeps the full amount of money, but ownership of the wheat is transferred to the CCC. For some other commodities, such as milk for manufacturing, the CCC buys directly on the market to support prices.

To attack the problems of farm credit and farm mortgages the government created the Farm Credit Administration in 1933 to refinance farm mortgages at rates not to exceed 4½ per cent. For farmers whose mortgages had been foreclosed, federal money was made available to permit them to redeem their property. Other acts providing for the electrification of rural areas, the distribution by the government of food to the unemployed, and work projects in rural areas were designed to alleviate the farmer's situation.

How much these programs contributed to helping agriculture can never be accurately determined. The farmer's condition certainly improved, but some part of this improvement is attributable to general economic recovery. What is important is that between 1932 and 1937 the ratio of prices received to prices paid by farmers rose from 58 to 93. The sharp recession in 1938 lowered the ratio to 78 in that year, but by 1940 it was up again to 81.

The demand for food during the war induced Congress to call for high support levels, and these supports were continued in legislation passed in 1948. In the previous section we have already seen how farm productivity had increased. In 1953, output per man-hour of farm labor was 25 per cent greater than in 1945. By 1953 the government, which had not used acreage allotments or marketing quotas since the war years, was faced with a massive accumulation of farm surpluses. The story since then has been one of continually increasing food surpluses, and continually increasing costs for the American taxpayer.

21–7. Government Support of American Agriculture

In terms of the government's aim, a policy of increasing the efficiency of farmers is a desirable one. At the same time one must ask how effective a general program can be in meeting the problems of specific areas. Although general agricultural productivity has increased rapidly since the 1930's, there were still in 1960 large rural areas of extreme poverty. The lower Appalachian region in particular is an area where modern scientific agriculture has made almost no headway. Small inefficient farms frequently isolated in valleys do not produce enough income to provide families with adequate housing, health, or educational facilities. Without these, a source of capital, and contacts with markets, families are bound in a vicious circle of poverty. The agricultural revolution has bypassed such regions. In other areas, where fairly successful commercial farming existed to begin with, the government's agricultural program has been very successful. In the corn belt, for example, production per acre in the decades between 1879 and 1929 fluctuated between roughly 26 and 27 bushels per acre. For the four years between 1949–52, the yield was 38 bushels per acre. In 1960, the United States average is estimated at 51 bushels per acre. The agricultural problem lies with the inefficient farmer, not with the successful one. It may be that in a democracy we must treat all farmers alike, but it is clear from our burgeoning warehouses that the problem of oversupply and low incomes has not been solved by the methods designed to raise the incomes of all who want to farm. Nor does it seem very sensible to pay farmers not to farm by putting their land in a soil bank.

What would have happened to the farmer had the government not intervened? The forces of a free market would have implacably weeded out the inefficient farmer, although it must be admitted that many agricultural inefficiencies do not necessarily reflect personal inefficiency. All those who could not produce and make a decent living at the free-market price would be forced under a rising debt burden to abandon the farm and move to occupations where they could make a living. The increase in productive efficiency would inevitably have accelerated the process. That such a process would be cruel and indifferent to individual hopes may be admitted, but it must also be pointed out that other occupational groups, e.g., glassblowers, blacksmiths, and lamplighters, have been destroyed by progress. If the argument is that farmers as a class are essential to American life, then economics can offer no help; but one is perhaps entitled to ask why farmers alone are selected. Why should the corner grocery not be protected from the price-cutting efficiencies of the supermarket?

Any time the decision is made to interfere with the economic adjustments essential to the process of growth, the efficient allocation of resources is retarded. In some cases interference may be justified on the grounds that the government is able to take a "long-run view" while the market time horizon is too limited. Education, defense, health measures, conservation may be areas where the government can legitimately interfere. On the other hand, the farmers can justly argue that they are not the only ones to be protected. Manufacturers have tariffs and subsidies, labor unions have featherbedding rules, and so on. Agriculture is chosen here only as an example, but because of the extent of the interference it makes a good one.

The economic growth of the United States has involved a continuing diminution of the importance of the agricultural sector of the economy. Clearly, modern industrialism cannot take place in a country whose resources are totally committed to agricultural pursuits. It is also true that today the countries with the lowest incomes per capita are also those with the largest involvement in agricultural pursuits. Those countries with the very lowest incomes per capita are precisely the ones where the vast majority of the population spend their lives in a bitter struggle to wrest a meager living from the soil. Ignorance, poverty, disease, high birth rates, high death rates characterize such populations. In such areas, however, farming methods are often so bad in terms of modern knowledge that it takes relatively little to effect tremendous improvements in productivity. Tractors and combines are not necessary; good seed, natural fertilizers, and simple crop rotation are frequently all that is necessary to substantially improve yields per acre. The question of what the people do with these increased yields is dealt with elsewhere in this book.

It does not follow from this, however, that all economies must reduce the proportion of their total resources devoted to agriculture if they are to achieve high per-capita incomes. Great Britain, with roughly 4 per cent of her total labor force engaged in agriculture, has gone noticeably farther than other countries in the direction of limiting the share of agriculture. Such countries as the Netherlands, Denmark, Canada, and New Zealand, on the other hand, have achieved high per-capita incomes with a labor-force share in agriculture roughly four times as great as that in the United Kingdom. The United States, with approximately 6 per cent of the labor force in agriculture, lies between the United Kingdom and the others.

Why then do we make such a point about the overcommitment of resources to agriculture in the United States? The problem is of course a relative one: the relative efficiencies of labor among the various occupations, given the resources available to a nation. The

Netherlands and Denmark, for example, practice a highly intensive agriculture with heavy applications of resources per acre. Given their limited supply of natural resources, they have found their comparative advantage to lie in a highly commercialized production of agricultural products. With rigid government controls of grading and marketing, these countries trade their products of land and sea around the world for many of the manufactured products and raw materials they desire. Canadian and New Zealand agriculture is extensive by contrast, due to the larger land areas available; but they too find commercial agriculture a useful source of trading power. For the United States, however, given present-day agricultural policies, comparative advantage in trade seems to lie in nonagricultural products and in the provision of manufactured commodities and personal services for the domestic market. Much of the agricultural sector in the United States is as efficient as any in the world and has nothing to fear from free markets, but a large proportion is not efficient enough to compete. If all farms in the United States were made as efficient as the best, then the oversupply would reduce farm incomes far below the incomes of workers in other industries.

It would be clearly impossible to remove all government supports from agriculture. Nor in fact would it be desirable. Even if the government destroyed its accumulated surpluses, the short-run effects would be disastrous for the economy. Even the most efficient farmers would be driven out of business by the fall in farm prices. But is should be possible to move gradually toward a freer market to provide time for the less efficient to find other occupations. At the same time, government-support programs designed to retrain farmers for other occupations and to locate industry in agricultural areas would go a long way toward easing the adjustment process. Whatever the problems, it is clear that supporting workers in agriculture when their product would be greater in some other occupation is an interference with the allocation of resources and retards the growth of American total product.

Suggested Readings

Barger, H., and Landsberg, H. H. *American Agriculture, 1899–1939.* New York: National Bureau of Economic Research, 1942.

Shannon, F. A. *The Farmer's Last Frontier.* New York: Farrar and Rinehart, 1945.

VII
Trends and Fluctuations in American Growth

Chapter 22 MEASURES OF ECONOMIC GROWTH

22–1. *Introduction*

While economists disagree about many things, including the process of economic development, there is general agreement about the way in which to measure economic development. A country is said to be developing economically if its population is growing and if the output of the country is growing more rapidly than the population. If the country's output is growing faster than the population, then the "output per capita" is also growing.

While this definition of economic development is generally accepted, it is clearly a crude measure. By taking a country's output and dividing it by the population, an average is obtained that tells us nothing specifically about any particular economic aspect of the country. The average tells us nothing, for example, of the social structure of the country. Does it have a rigid class structure, such as the caste system of some Asian countries, or are class boundaries weak and easily crossed? The average tells us nothing directly about the health, life expectancy, or literacy of the population. Is the population illiterate with a short life expectancy, or highly literate and long lived? The average does not tell us directly of the availability of raw materials in the country, the products produced, the techniques used in production, or the way the product is distributed among the people taking part in economic activity. Is the country largely agricultural, using primitive techniques of cultivation, with the product being claimed by a small landowning class; or is it a heavily industrialized economy, using the most modern techniques, with a more equal distribution of product? Finally, do the people of the country enjoy a large degree of freedom and political control, or are they the subjects of a totalitarian state?

Why, then, do economists use output per capita as a measure of economic development? The first reason is a very practical one. It is a measure that can be estimated with a tolerable degree of accuracy for almost any country. The second reason, and perhaps the more important one, is that while output per capita says nothing about social conditions, industrialization, and so on, such conditions are nevertheless implied in the measure.

A large number of social, political, and economic conditions may be perfectly compatible with any given level of output per capita. But it is difficult to conceive of a country having a high per-capita income, relative to that in advanced countries, if its people are ignorant, primitive, wracked by disease, living in a poor, barren country under the political control of a feudal despot. Thus, output per capita tells us a great deal more about a country than appears at first.

22–2. *International Comparisons*

Table 22–1 presents figures showing output per capita in selected countries. The countries included in the table were chosen to represent the wide disparity in output per capita existing in the modern world.

Before examining Table 22–1 in more detail, we should emphasize again the comments made in Chapter 2. While output per capita is a convenient and meaningful measure, it is one very difficult to measure with a high degree of accuracy. Thus, the figures of Table 22–1 must be treated with caution and should perhaps be taken as representing an ordinal ranking only. In particular, one should not fall into the fallacy of interpreting them to mean that because they are expressed in terms of U.S. dollars, an output per capita one tenth that of the United States indicates that the people in that country are only one tenth as "well off" as Americans. Or alternatively, that an output per capita of $50 means that the people of that country are as well off as an American with an income of $50 per year.

It is common to distinguish two categories of countries on the basis of their level of economic achievement. One we call the "underdeveloped," and the other the "developed," countries. No attempt is made to draw the line dividing the two categories with great precision, but if we call the United States a "developed" country, it makes sense to call the countries at the lower end of the scale "underdeveloped." The differences in economic achievement are more than just a matter of degree, and they are furthermore indicated only imprecisely by differences in income.

How did it happen that North America and Western Europe

have an output per capita so far ahead of many other countries? The detailed analysis of this question has been discussed in earlier chapters. Here we can suggest that it must have resulted from either of two factors. Either the United States began its development from a level above that of the presently underdeveloped countries, or, beginning at a lower level, the rate of growth of output per capita in the United States far exceeded that of the presently underdeveloped countries. Both hypotheses appear to contain portions of the explanation. Two centuries ago, the countries of Europe were at a higher level of development than the countries of Asia, and in the intervening period the gap between the two groups has widened.

TABLE 22–1

Estimated Income Per Capita in Selected Countries, 1961
(In Terms of American Dollars)

Country	*Income Per Capita*
United States	$2,311
Canada	1,458
New Zealand	1,323
United Kingdom	1,144
Belgium	1,033
Venezuela	565
Italy	558
Greece	366
India	69
Burma	50

Source: United Nations, *Statistical Yearbook, 1962* (New York, 1963), Tables 1, 162, 167. National income per capita was divided by the exchange rate to arrive at the figure in American dollars.

There is no standard definition of an underdeveloped country. Any country is only relatively developed or underdeveloped. In this sense, there will always be underdeveloped countries. It is interesting to note further, following the discussion above, that if we examine a long enough period of history, the ranking of countries by their stage of economic development has changed over the centuries. The countries of Asia and the Mediterranean that we now consider as fit subjects for development programs had wealthy civilizations when Western Europe was roamed by barbaric bands. Some countries rise economically relative to others, as the developed countries are now doing, but the leaders in one epoch may well be the followers of the next. Growth always involves change and nations, like everything else, appear to follow a growth pattern leading eventually to decay.

The concern of this book is with a much less sweeping subject. We deal with a period of less than 200 years so that we are observing only part of the broader changes that affect the relative economic positions of nations. In the short period we are considering, the nations of northwestern Europe and their overseas offshoots have been the economic leaders of the world. This leadership has been a source of pride to many, but in the very recent past there has arisen increasing public concern for the plight of the underdeveloped nations and concerted efforts have been undertaken to narrow the gap between the top and the bottom shown by international comparisons of output per capita. In spite of the efforts made to speed the process of economic development in the underdeveloped areas, the gap appears to be widening so that the underdeveloped countries are falling further behind. This is a problem of serious proportions for all countries of the world.

Again we are encountering questions that can only be fully answered after more extended discussion. However, we can suggest some reasons for the increasing gap between the per-capita incomes of the developed and underdeveloped economies. We are accustomed to think of the recent economic development of the Western world as a revolutionary change. It is true that the world of 1960 was further removed, in many material respects, from the world of 1760 than the world of 1760 was from the world of 1560 or, one is almost tempted to say, from the world of 1360. In this broad sense, the changes of the last 200 years have indeed been revolutionary. But an understanding of the process of development itself is facilitated if we concentrate not so much on the revolutionary aspect of the changes but rather on their evolutionary aspects. The peoples of the Western world had some time to adjust to the changes involved in the process of development. While the process was not a smooth one, the time involved tended to modify the sharpest of the adjustment processes.

The underdeveloped countries of the world, comprising at least two thirds of the world's population, are unwilling to wait for the process of economic development. They want what the developed countries accumulated over so many decades, and they want it fast. Many of the problems of development can be avoided by these countries because they have access to our technical knowledge and they can learn from our experiences. Other problems will be new because of differences in social customs and traditions. The most important problem of all is the lack of resources for development in these countries. By this we mean the lack of a trained labor force and of experienced managers; the lack of raw materials and of the capital, in terms of machines and transportation equipment to exploit them; and finally the lack of what can be called a spirit of capitalism—a desire to work efficiently and accumulate material things. Take, for example, a new nation formed in Africa. If the new country has a source of raw materials that has been opened up by the colonizing power, they must find some means of running the enterprise after the Europeans have gone. Without a commodity to sell abroad they have no source of money to buy things from other nations—the tractors, machines of all kinds, and other supplies they need to grow economically. Such new nations are frequently faced with a tragic shortage of trained personnel in all fields and their efforts to develop are frequently hampered by old tribal systems oriented to the local rather than the national level. The desire for development runs up against practical barriers that the nation cannot scale by itself. It must then turn to the developed nations for the materials and the talent necessary to get the process of development to the point where future progress will sustain itself. Even by remaining uncommitted and playing one power bloc off against another, an inherently dangerous role, such nations usually find outside aid far short of their needs. Private business is unlikely to do much in the face of the uncertainties in the world situation. Thus, the new nation faced with only limited aid tends to spend it where it will produce the most startling results in the shortest period of time. For example, wonder drugs and various sprays are used to achieve drastic reductions in mortality, with no resources available to increase food output at the same time. The result is, therefore, a decline in per-capita income. Or an irrigation-power dam is built to revive hundreds of thousands of acres of parched land and to provide power for industry, but workers are not trained in modern factory methods and the population surges up to devour the increased agricultural production. One is reminded of the chicken and the egg problem. In the case of the underdeveloped countries, a break in the circle must be found if the gap between the developed and underdeveloped economies is to be reduced.

22–3. *Growth Patterns for Selected Countries*

At this point in the discussion we turn to look at some of the data available on the record of economic growth in selected countries. Table 22–2 presents rates of growth, over periods of roughly eighty years, of population, national product, and national product per capita, for eleven countries. It is important to realize the significance of these two dimensions of the table. First, the data only extend for a period of less than a century (except for France). This is not a long period of time relative to the history of these nations or even of the much shorter period of the industrialization of most of them. The figures presented cover only the most recent part of the picture. Second, of the total of over 100 countries existing today, we

TABLE 22–2

RATES OF CHANGE PER DECADE OF POPULATION, NATIONAL PRODUCT, AND PRODUCT PER CAPITA FOR ELEVEN COUNTRIES, FROM THE NINETEENTH INTO THE TWENTIETH CENTURY.

(Product Estimates in Constant Prices)

Country	*Time Interval*	*Percentage Change per Decade*		
		Population (1)	*National Product* (2)	*National Product per Capita* (3)
Ireland and Eire	1860–69 to 1949–53	−3.5	12.8	16.8
France	1841–50 to 1949–53	1.3	15.3	13.8
Sweden	1861–68 to 1950–54	6.6	36.0	27.6
Italy	1862–68 to 1950–54	6.9	18.0	10.4
United Kingdom	1860–69 to 1949–53	8.0	21.5	12.5
Germany	1860–69 to 1950–54	10.1	27.4	15.1
Denmark	1870–78 to 1950–54	11.5	30.1	16.7
Japan	1878–87 to 1950–54	12.7	42.3	26.3
Russia and USSR	1870 to 1954	13.4	31.0	15.4
United States	1869–78 to 1950–54	17.4	41.2	20.3
Canada	1870–79 to 1950–54	18.3	41.3	19.3

Source: Simon Kuznets, "Quantitative Aspects of the Growth of Nations," *Economic Development and Cultural Change,* Vol. V, 1956, Table 2, p. 13.

have information for even this short period for only eleven—and all eleven can be characterized as economically advanced. This is clearly a very small sample of the total. There is a relationship between these two aspects of the table. The data have been reconstructed from census material and other statistical evidence collected in the past (in most cases for quite different purposes) and it is only in the more advanced countries that such information can be found at all.

An understanding of the table requires an understanding of the concept of a rate of change. In the series of numbers, 1, 2, 4, 8, 16, 32, each number is 100 per cent greater than the preceding number. Notice that while the percentage difference between the numbers is constant, the absolute difference between them is increasing. The story is told of the ancient seer who, when asked the reward he desired for inventing the game of chess, told his ruler that he desired nothing more than that two grains of rice be placed on the first square of the board, four on the second, eight on the third, and so on, until the entire 64 squares were covered. The power of percentage increases can be appreciated by the fact—which the king soon realized—that there wasn't enough rice in China to meet the reward.

In Table 22–2, we have time as an integral part of the problem, with growth being expressed as a percentage-change per decade. The problem then becomes one of continuous compound interest. A variable that grows at a compound rate of 10 per cent per decade doubles in size every 6.9 decades; one that grows at a rate of 20 per cent per decade doubles in 3.5 decades; and a variable that grows at 40 per cent per decade doubles in 1.7 decades. As a rough rule of thumb, divide the rate of growth into 70 to find the number of time periods it takes for a variable growing at a given rate to double. In Table 22–2, the rates of change vary from −3.5 per cent (a series growing at a negative rate shows the same characteristics as one growing at a positive rate except that the series approaches zero as a limit) to 42.3 per cent. This is an impressive range of growth rates and indicates that there is no necessary rate at which a country's population or national product has to grow. These figures may not even indicate the limits within which the growth of the variables can be expected to lie. Were it possible to include figures for all the countries of the world, it is quite possible that the range of rates of growth would be even larger.

While the range of the rates is wide, there is an order in the table. The eleven countries have been ranked in ascending order of population growth beginning with Ireland, which shows a negative rate, and ending with Canada, which shows a rate of population growth of 18.3 per cent per decade. The second column, national product, also shows ascending rates of growth, with the conspicuous exception of Sweden and Japan. This indicates that, at least in developed countries, there is a positive correlation between population growth and growth of total product. This may seem like an obvious point; the more people there are in a country, the more they will produce. But the example of the presently underdeveloped countries faced with a "population explosion" is an indication that the point cannot be pushed too far. There is, therefore, some rate of population growth relative to the growth of other factors of production that can prove to be a deterrent to the growth of national product. Clearly there were other factors at work in the eleven countries listed that interacted with the growing (or in the case of Ireland, declining) population, to give growing national product.

Column 3 of Table 22–2 is a further proof of this point. The positive rates of growth of national product per capita show that, for every country listed, national product grew at a faster rate than population, indicating that there is a more than one-to-one relationship between increased population and increased national product. What accounts for this? Many reasons can be given. The most significant factor has been the expanding body of knowledge that lies at the base of modern technology. Any increase in man's understanding of his physical environment will eventually have an economic meaning; for economic activity concerns itself with the extraction of useful products from the environment. The results of the discoveries of the natural sciences are impressive because they intrude so clearly in our everyday life, but man's expanding knowledge in other fields is no less important. Knowledge has been gained about the problems of managing and controlling large-scale business enterprises that gather their raw material and distribute their product across the nation and around the world. The economies of large-scale operations are so great in many industries, and transportation technology has made movement of goods so cheap, that even such bulky commodities as structural steel are sent around the globe. Scientists have discovered new, more powerful sources of energy and have developed the machines to control them. Man himself has become a more efficient tool of production through training and education. Each generation adds to the stock of knowledge it receives so that the process is one of cumulative expansion. As each generation becomes economically more powerful, the resources it can devote to research increase so that the rate of growth of knowledge expands at an increasing rate. There is, of course, no easy relationship between a new scientific discovery and its practical application, but again as an economy grows the resources that can be devoted to making a practical use of a discovery increase and the process becomes more rapid.

There has been a tendency in the study of economic history to break the study into stages of development. For example, the study of the development of a modern industrial economy may begin with a period of self-sufficient agriculture, then the cottage-industry stage, followed by small-scale, regionally oriented manufacturing, with the whole process capped by the emergence of full-scale industrialization. We do not agree with this type of analysis because it has the basic fault of breaking up into segments a process that can only be fully appreciated as a whole. The ever-widening and deepening of the body of knowledge is the basis of the process of development, and the accumulation of knowledge is not something that can meaningfully be broken into stages. The process of growth is not smooth; it is not balanced with all sectors of the economy moving forward together; but this does not mean that it is discontinuous. On the contrary, it is the underlying continuity of the process that is emphasized in this book.

It is now time to turn our attention to the record of American development.

22–4. *Patterns of American Growth*

The growth of the American economy is recorded very impressively in numerous historical series. Records of output of particular commodities such as steel, oil, machinery, automobiles, and food all show truly remarkable progress. We are not going to reproduce such records here. Our interest at this stage of the inquiry is with the more inclusive measures of the progress of the American economy, because the records of achievement of individual sectors of the economy are likely to give a distorted picture of overall development. However, by limiting ourselves in this way, we have also limited the time interval that the study can cover.

In Table 22–3, decade estimates are presented of employed workers, man-hours of work, national income (1950 prices), and estimated energy input used for work by decades from 1850 to 1960.

Again, the most impressive aspect of the table is the growth in the various series shown. The American economy in 1960 was clearly a vastly larger productive machine than it was in 1850. But it is also clear from the table that we were not using all our available resources in 1960 as intensively as we were at the beginning of the period. Between 1850 and 1960, the number of employed workers increased 9.3 times but annual man-hours worked increased only 5.1 times. Clearly, therefore, workers are not devoting as much time to work as they were 110 years ago. The records substantiate this: the average working week in 1850 has been estimated at seventy hours, whereas by 1950 it had fallen to roughly forty hours. The American labor force has made the decision to enjoy leisure time rather than to accumulate goods and services. This conscious substitution of leisure for work has meant that the production of goods and services has not increased as rapidly as it could have. On the other hand, it may well be that people who work only forty hours a week are more contented and therefore more productive workers than those who work seventy hours a week.

In spite of the decline in labor effort, national income (1950 prices) increased 370-fold between 1850 and 1960. The working efficiency of the labor force has therefore increased sufficiently to much more than offset the decline in labor effort. The causes of

TABLE 22–3

MEASURES OF THE GROWTH OF THE AMERICAN ECONOMY, 1850–1960

	(1) *Employed Workers* (Millions)	(2) *Annual Man-Hours of Work* (Billions)	(3) *National Income (1950 Prices)* (Billions)	(4) *Total Horsepower of Prime Movers* (Millions)
1850	7.2	26.1	9.4	8.5
1860	10.1	35.7	14.4	13.8
1870	13.2	44.7	18.6	16.9
1880	17.6	58.4	25.6	26.3
1890	22.5	72.2	44.3	44.1
1900	27.0	84.2	63.3	65.0
1910	34.6	98.7	86.4	114.1
1920	39.2	100.7	94.7	172.6
1930	44.2	105.0	118.5	237.4
1940	47.5	108.0	147.0	247.7
1950	59.7	123.7	241.8	356.6
1960	66.7	133.4	348.0	600.4

Source: Col. (1), 1850–1900, persons engaged, 10 years and over: Stanley Lebergott, *Manpower in Economic Growth* (New York: McGraw-Hill, 1964), Table A1, p. 510. 1900–1960, employment of civilian labor force, 14 years and over: *Ibid.*, Table A3, p. 512.

Col. (2): Col. (1) multiplied by estimated average annual hours of work.

Col. (3), 1850–1940: J. Frederic Dewhurst and Associates, *America's Needs and Resources, A New Survey* (New York: Twentieth Century Fund, 1955), Table 14, p. 40. 1950–60: U.S. Department of Commerce, *Statistical Abstract of the United States, 1963* (Washington, D.C.: U.S. Government Printing Office, 1963), Table 428, p. 321.

Col. (4), 1850–1940 (excludes automotive horsepower): U.S. Department of Commerce, *Historical Statistics of the United States, Colonial Times to 1957* (Washington, D.C.: U.S. Government Printing Office, 1960), Series S-3, p. 506. 1950–60: *Statistical Abstract, 1963,* Table 716, p. 529.

the increased efficiency stem from many things, most of which are unmeasurable. We have already indicated that the decline in the work week itself may be a cause. Additional factors would include skill, training, management ability, attitudes toward work, effects of unions on working ability, increased supplies of capital, more efficient capital, and so on. The series we have included in Table 22–3 is the estimated energy input used for work. Between 1850 and 1960, this series increased 70.6 times. In the service industries, which have grown most rapidly of all sectors of the economy, the energy requirements are very limited. This means then that this increased power input has been concentrated in the primary and secondary industries. Although increased power inputs cannot be a full explanation of the increasing efficiency of the labor force, it is a fundamental part of the explanation. The American labor force has been able to devote a larger proportion of its time to leisure pursuits and still enjoy an increasing material standard of living because each worker has more power at his disposal for the production of goods.

The final thing to notice about the table is that the rate of growth of national income has not been a steady one but rather has fluctuated widely. The range for percentage increase in national income is between 10 per cent for the decade 1910–1920, and 64 per cent for the decade 1940–1950. These figures can be misleading, however, because single-year figures are being compared and comparisons of single-year figures are only meaningful if we can be sure that each of the years lies at the same phase of the business cycle. For example, the figure for 1940 is 12 per cent greater than that for 1930, but the percentage change between 1932 and 1940 would be much greater. An examination of the pattern of American development is only possible if we can compare averages for a sufficient number of years to remove the influence of the business cycle. Unfortunately, this desired increase in detail is only achieved if we further shorten the period of the study.

In Table 22–4, we reproduce percentage changes between overlapping decades that have been calculated for the American economy. The advantage of these rates of change is that they measure differences in averages for ten-year periods, so that the effects of the business cycle have been minimized. It is clear from this table that the unevenness of the growth of the American economy has been a real phenomenon. The rates of growth in all three series show large differences. Two things are observable from the table. First, there appears to be a downward trend in all three rates of increase. As the American economy has become absolutely larger the rates of change of the variables in Table 22–4 have become smaller. The increasing demand for leisure mentioned above is part of the explanation for the decrease in the rates. The rest of the explanation may well lie in the increasingly rigid character of the American economy. Concentrations of economic power have been built up that resist the changes implied by growth and effectively inhibit the efficient allocation of resources.

Second, there appears to be a cycle in the percentage changes and, moreover, the cycle appears to be roughly coincident in all three series. These long swings or "Kuznets cycles," named for Professor Simon Kuznets, are a pervasive element of the American economy and those other economies, such as the British, for which we have sufficient data to observe them. It might be argued that these cycles merely represent the effects of wars and depressions that are not in themselves part of the growth process. Whether they are or not is properly the subject for a book other than this one. We, however, prefer the concept of economic growth as a continuing process, including in the process, if not necessarily part of it, the wars and large-scale depression that are part of American history.

TABLE 22–4

RATES OF CHANGE IN POPULATION, NATIONAL PRODUCT
NATIONAL PRODUCT PER CAPITA, UNITED STATES, 1869–1948

	Percentage Change between One Decade Average and That of the Next		
Decade	*Population*	*National Product*	*National Product per Capita*
1869–78 to 1874–83	12.2	45.7	30.1
1874–83 to 1879–88	12.5	30.7	16.0
1879–88 to 1884–93	11.5	17.3	5.2
1884–93 to 1889–98	10.5	15.2	4.4
1889–98 to 1894–03	9.5	24.4	13.4
1894–03 to 1899–08	9.9	24.6	13.5
1899–08 to 1904–13	10.2	19.5	8.5
1904–13 to 1909–18	8.9	12.3	3.0
1909–18 to 1914–23	7.5	13.7	5.8
1914–23 to 1919–28	7.6	20.6	12.3
1919–28 to 1924–33	6.8	6.2	−0.8
1924–33 to 1929–38	4.5	−1.8	−5.8
1929–38 to 1934–43	3.8	22.1	17.5
1934–43 to 1939–48	5.4	23.9	17.6

Source: Simon Kuznets, "Long-Term Changes in the National Income of the United States of America Since 1870," *Income and Wealth, Series II* (Baltimore: The Johns Hopkins Press, 1952), Table 3, p. 50, and Table 4, p. 55.

The existence of the Kuznets cycle of roughly twenty years in length is one of the more intriguing aspects of Table 22–4. It indicates some underlying pulsing of activity in the economy such that a period of rapid growth is succeeded by a period of more restrained growth. It might be argued, for example, that modern economies can undergo a period of rapid growth and change for only a relatively short time before a period of slowdown and readjustment is required. Or, it could be suggested that a period of rapid growth must inevitably end because the rate at which economic resources can be increased is limited. The most sophisticated analysis of the Kuznets cycle has been put forward by Professor Brinley Thomas. Professor Thomas' studies indicated that the same type of movement found in the American series by Kuznets also existed in the rates of growth of time series of Western European countries and other new countries such as Canada and Australia. However, Professor Thomas found that the cycles in the European countries moved in the opposite direction from those in the new countries. Thus, when the American economy was on the upswing of a Kuznets cycle, Great Britain was on the downswing. At this stage it will be

TABLE 22–5

PEAKS AND TROUGHS IN THE CYCLE OF IMMIGRATION INTO THE UNITED STATES AND IN THE BRITISH AND AMERICAN BUILDING CYCLES, 1838–1920

Immigration		*Building Cycle*			
		British		*American*	
Peak	Trough	Peak	Trough	Peak	Trough
	1838–43				
1849–54			1855	1853	
	1861–62	1863			1864
1869–73			1871	1871	
	1877–78	1877			1878
1882–83			1887	1890	
	1898	1899			1900
1903–07			1912	1909	
		1920			1918

Source: Brinley Thomas, *Migration and Economic Growth* (Study 12 of the N.I.E.S.R.) (Cambridge: University Press, 1954), Table 24, p. 89, and Table 52, p. 175.

sufficient to suggest that when the Atlantic economic community is taken as a whole, the pulsations in any one section, such as America, can be seen to be the result of a free flow of resources from the established economies of Europe to America as opportunities for profit and advancement opened up in America. In the next phase, the resources would stay in Europe as the center of economic growth shifted back across the Atlantic. During the period of free movement of resources among the nations of the Atlantic community in the nineteenth and early twentieth centuries, all nations did not grow evenly. One country would spurt ahead of the others at one time, another country at another time. The flow of resources was an initiating and sustaining factor in these periods of rapid growth for particular nations. But the supply of resources was not unlimited and reacted quite sensitively to relative economic conditions. Thus the pulsation in American economic activity can be related to the international movements of resources during a period of growth of an entire area, when the new nations could only develop successfully with help from others.

Numerous other types of long cycles, as distinct from the short business cycle, have been found and investigated by others. There is, for example, the Juglar cycle of roughly a ten-year duration, and the very long Kondratieff of about sixty years' duration. It is quite likely that as we learn more and more about economies over longer periods of time, cycles of even longer amplitude will be discovered. The interest in cyclical fluctuations stems from an attempt to find an observable pattern of order in the growth of economic units. One is not interested in knowing merely that things go up and down; one wants to know why. Thus the mere proliferation of types of cycles of varying amplitudes adds nothing to knowledge. Nor does it help to say, as some scholars have said, that there is no relationship between the different types of cycles that have been distinguished. What is needed is a model of economic change that either accounts for all types of cycles or disproves the existence of some and establishes the existence of others. So far, no cycle has been disproved, nor has any theory been developed that fits them all into a unified framework. If the various types of cycles do in fact exist then we know there must be some connection between them. Economic events that overlap in time must be connected, with regard to one country or all countries joined in the same trading unit. Unfortunately, the connecting links have not been found.

Suggested Readings

Bauer, B. T., and Yamey, B. S. *The Economics of Underdeveloped Countries.* Chicago: The University of Chicago Press, 1957.

Kindleberger, C. P. *Economic Development.* New York: McGraw-Hill Book Co., Inc., 1958.

Kuznets, S. *Economic Change.* London: William Heineman, 1954.

Lewis, W. A. *The Theory of Economic Growth.* Homewood, Ill.: Richard D. Irwin, Inc., 1955.

Chapter 23 FLUCTUATIONS IN ECONOMIC ACTIVITY

"The history of what we are in the habit of calling the 'state of trade' is an instructive lesson. We find it subject to various conditions which are periodically returning; it revolves apparently in an established cycle. First we find it in a state of quiescence,—next improvement,—growing confidence,—distress,—ending again in quiescence."

Samuel Jones Loyd—*in 1837*[1]

23–1. *The "Business Cycle"*

Economic activity in the United States, as well as in the England of the banker and economist Samuel Jones Loyd, has been subject to considerable variation ever since records have been available. Periods of rapid expansion have been followed by stagnation and depression; rising prices, which have many times produced "inflation," have been time and again succeeded by falling prices; full employment by unemployment; rising wages by falling wages; and expanding output by declining output. To be sure, in the long run (in this country) economic expansion has reasserted itself after even the deepest depression, the level of output in depressions many times being higher than ever before *except* in the immediately preceding expansion. Nevertheless, the recurrence of fluctuations in output and trade has been a disturbing factor in our economic history and, indeed, in our political history. These fluctuations have come to be associated in the public mind as the "business cycle." What precisely is meant by this phrase?

For a long time all succeeding business fluctuations were treated by observers as if they actually represented the same sequences of events as all their predecessors. It was noted that some

[1] *Reflections Suggested by . . . Mr. J. Horsley Palmer's Pamphlet on the Causes and Consequences of the Pressure on the Money Market*, p. 44.

were stronger than others, and that some depressions were more disastrous than others. Later it appeared that there had been "cycles of cycles"; that is, that several shorter cycles combined to make a longer cycle. Moreover, the various sectors of the economy did not always fluctuate in a uniform manner and, when studied separately, tended to show curious and interesting characteristics of their own (for example, house-building seems to have had an eighteen- to twenty-year cycle, compared to the thirty-six- to forty-month cycle of "general business activity"). Careful study of these fluctuations revealed that economic activity seems to be continuously subject to several distinct kinds of fluctuations. The study of these is a special part of economics and is complex. However, in spite of the new information relating to variously and complexly related cycles of different durations, the old notion that there was something unique which could be called *the* business cycle holds on in pretty much its original form in the popular mind. It is important to remember that, even though the name "business cycle" is applied to recurrent fluctuations, we do not mean to say that these fluctuations are all similar in causes and in their effects.

The concept of the business cycle we usually have in mind in this book is the record of fluctuations in the gross national product. For the period before reliable yearly GNP estimates are available (generally before 1919), we rely upon other measures—prices, trade data, production figures, and so forth—to fix the chronology and magnitude of these fluctuations. It is perhaps one of the great curiosities of economics that the "business cycle," about which so much has been written, is so mercurial a phenomenon when it is subjected to close study. It is easy to call fluctuations in such a single aggregative measure as GNP "the business cycle." But in close studies of the myriad statistics of the many branches of our economy, the "business cycle" virtually disappears amid conflicting movements in the data. As A. F. Burns and W. C. Mitchell, perhaps the foremost American students of the subject, put it, business cycles ". . . can be seen through a cloud of witnesses only by the eye of the mind."[2] In an earlier study, Mitchell concluded that what we mean by "business cycle" in ordinary conversation cannot be shown to exist in data. "The more intensively we work, the more we realize that this term is a synthetic product of the imagination—a product whose history is characteristic of our ways of learning. Overtaken

[2] A. F. Burns and W. C. Mitchell, *Measuring Business Cycles* (New York: National Bureau of Economic Research, 1947), p. 12.

by a series of strange experiences, our predecessors leaped to a broad conception, gave it a name, and began to invent explanations, as if they knew what their words meant. But in the process of explaining they demonstrated how inadequate their knowledge was."[3]

Does this mean that the economic fluctuations noted by contemporaries, and later by historians and economists, were just colorless abstractions, a host of recurrent historical mirages? When people spoke of crises, panics, depressions, booms, and the like, were they having hallucinations? Of course not. But as any historian knows, past or present events do not appear the same to all observers. Depressions exist in the minds of the unemployed all right, and might when measured by the number of unemployed, but a millionaire who does not read the papers and whose income is derived from long-term government bonds might not notice depressions. Similarly, periods of great prosperity for some firms or industries might be times of unusual hardship for others.

In the nineteenth century, when cycles were characterized by widespread monetary and banking instability and crises were accompanied by mass sales of securities in short periods of market "panics" or by the runs of depositors on banks in "banking crises," the business cycle was thought to occur every decade or so, since these great financial crises came roughly every ten years. The strength of the expectation was impressive. Consider the case of the London *Times* before the Crisis of 1857. Britain had experienced "crises" in 1825, 1837, and in 1847 (and other fluctuations in between which, not being associated with crises in the monetary sector, had gone by largely unnoticed). On New Year's Day of 1857 the *Times* wrote:

> Eighteen hundred and fifty-seven commences, consequently with numerous signs that it will be a year of animation, but without any extraordinary change. . . . If however, the twelve months should, in a commercial sense, bring forth no strange result of a positive description, they will at least, supposing them to pass over without any excess of wild inflation, be remarkable for a negative one, since it will be the first time in the present generation that a lapse of more than ten years has occurred without symptoms being discernible of the approach of a new reign of recklessness and delusion.

Throughout 1857, the economic difficulties piled up and in November London had a financial crisis (New York had had one in

[3] W. C. Mitchell, *Business Cycles, The Problem and Setting* (New York: National Bureau of Economic Research, 1927), p. 2.

October). In 1866, there was another crisis in London and a year later Karl Marx, one of the founders of modern Communism, noted (doubtless with no little satisfaction) in *Capital*, "It will be remembered that the year 1857 brought one of the great crises with which the industrial cycle periodically ends. The next one was due in 1866."[4]

Careful examination of American statistical records of crises has shown many fluctuations that had gone virtually unnoticed because they had no such spectacular effects in the financial markets. Hence, the notion that cycles were decennial has been abandoned, even though the financial crises did fall in roughly decennial timing in 1873, 1884, 1893, and 1903. (Although, on the basis of decennial repetition such a crisis would not have appeared until 1912 or so, there was a more impressive financial crisis in 1907). It was clear that ups and downs in general business activity, or "the state of trade," were not hallucinations. But it came to be realized that very little was actually known about them. To a large extent the confusion has never been satisfactorily straightened out. We have had fluctuations in business activity in this country since earliest times and, as the recession of 1960–1961 showed, we are still having them. When we talk in this book about business fluctuations, or the "business cycle," usually we will be referring to fluctuations in "general business activity" as defined by W. C. Mitchell as a result of his labors at the National Bureau of Economic Research.

> Business cycles are a type of fluctuations found in the aggregate economic activity of nations that organized their work mainly in business enterprises: a cycle consists of expansions occurring at about the same time in many economic activities, followed by similarly general recessions, contractions, and revivals which merge into the expansion phase of the next cycle; this sequence of changes is recurrent but not periodic; in duration business cycles vary from more than one year to ten or twelve years; they are not divisible into shorter cycles of similar character with amplitudes approximating their own.[5]

There are other widely accepted characterizations of this phenomenon, but, except for the "long cycle" discussed in the last chapter, we will confine our discussion in this book to Professor Mitchell's cycles. The economics student will encounter different concepts and measurements of business fluctuations later in his university career. By concentrating our attentions upon the "business cycle," as de-

[4] Karl Marx, *Capital* (London: Glaisher, 1918), Vol. I, pp. 685–86.
[5] Mitchell, *op. cit.*, p. 468.

fined above, we are generally speaking of a fluctuation in business activity of roughly three to four years on the average, from low point (trough) to low point in the preceding and ensuing depression. The peaks and troughs of business cycles are referred to as "turning points." The main turning points of the cycle in American history from 1834 to the present, as established by the NBER are shown in Table 23–1.

TABLE 23–1
BUSINESS CYCLE TURNING POINTS
1834–1958

Peak	*Trough*	*Years Duration Trough to Trough*	*Peak*	*Trough*	*Years Duration Trough to Trough*	*Peak*	*Trough*	*Years Duration Trough to Trough*
—	1834	–	1882	1885	7	1920	1921	3
1836	1838	4	1887	1888	3	1923	1924	3
1839	1843	5	1890	1891	3	1926	1927	3
1845	1846	3	1892	1894	3	1929	1932	5
1947	1848	2	1895	1896	2	1937	1938	6
1853	1855	7	1899	1900	4	1943	1946	8
1856	1858	3	1903	1904	4	1948	1949	3
1860	1861	3	1907	1908	4	1953	1954	5
1864	1867	6	1910	1911	3	1957	1958	4
1869	1870	3	1913	1914	3	1960	1961	3
1873	1878	8	1918	1919	5			

Source: *Measuring Business Cycles,* p. 78, and NBER since 1946.

Fluctuations of this sort existed before the 1830's (for example, there is evidence of a strong peak in 1818 followed by a severe depression), but the lack of dependable data makes it extremely risky to attempt to date the earlier ones.

23–2. Some Characteristics of the Business Cycle in the United States

As Mitchell noted, the cycles we have had ranged widely in duration. But in spite of that range, fluctuations in the United States have shown a marked tendency to last about three to four years from trough to trough. This, with important exceptions, may be noted in Table 23–1. In spite of the apparent tendency, already noted, for the great financial crises to appear at intervals of ten years or so, there is no evidence of a strong seven-to-ten-year cycle in the United States' experience.

Recent studies indicate that, since 1919, the typical cycle, of three to four years' duration, has been mainly a consequence of periodic changes in inventory holdings of business.[6] Whether this was always the case in the short cycles we cannot be certain. In powerful and relatively sustained expansion—in the period 1896 to 1913, for example—or in the deep depressions like that of the early 1930's, it is clear that changes in fixed investment, plant and equipment, were the more direct sources of changes in the level of general business. Moreover, even the inventory changes were mere reflections of the experiences and expectations of businessmen, so that the underlying "causes" of the fluctuations remain obscure.

The same sorts of observations can be made regarding the whole sequence of known cycles in our economic history. We do not really know what the initiating "causes" of these cycles were. We only know the main characteristics of the cycles as they actually occurred. The expansions before the Civil War usually contained a heavy element of land speculation and related activities (including extensions of roads, canals, and, later, railways) as the agricultural economy spread westward across the Alleghenies and beyond the Mississippi. This was especially true of the "Panic" of 1837. Widespread bank suspensions in that year, and the following depression (which lasted until 1842), were thought somehow to have been due largely to the inability of purchasers and settlers of land in the great expansion of the middle 1830's to meet fixed debt obligations in the face of falling farm prices. In this case, as in later crises, financial difficulties played a considerable role. President Jackson's Specie Circular of 1836 had the initial effect of making a large part of the nation's circulating medium useless for the purchase of land from the government, thus, in effect, killing the land boom.

The difficult times that followed have long perplexed and intrigued economic historians. There were two years of acute financial distress, 1837 and 1839, with a year of depression sandwiched in between. Then, in 1840, 1841, 1842, and 1843 there followed one of the longest periods of sustained contraction in the nation's history, rivaled only by the downswing of 1929–33. A recent study of the explanations that have been offered of the disasters of 1837–43 shows that we really know little about the causal forces at work.[7] We know

[6] In 1921, 1924, 1938, 1949, and 1954, short one-year slumps, reduction of inventories account for 75 per cent of the total fall in investment. R. C. O. Matthews, *The Business Cycle* (Chicago: University of Chicago Press, 1959), p. 94.

[7] J. R. T. Hughes and Nathan Rosenberg, "The United States Business Cycle Before 1860: Some Problems of Interpretation," *Economic History Review*, Second Series, Vol. XV, No. 3, 1963.

that the rate of railroad construction fell sharply in 1838, recovered a bit in 1839, and then remained depressed until the middle 1840's. The aborted land boom, ended abruptly by the Specie Circular, found a sharp expression in government revenues from land sales, which were $24.9 million in 1836, $6.8 million in 1837 and then, except for a slight recovery to $7.1 million in 1839, moved downward to a mere $898,000 in 1843—virtually extinguished. This indicates severe stagnation indeed in an economy so deeply committed to geographical expansion as was the American economy of that period. If imports can be taken as an indicator of domestic consumption, the reduction of two thirds, from $190 million in 1836 to $65 million in 1843, rivaled the great contraction of the 1930's. Exports in 1836–43, indicating foreign earnings, shrunk by only about one third, from $129 million to $84 million, suggesting that foreign trade by itself was scarcely a prime cause of the contraction.

The notion that contractions in economic activity cannot but reflect reductions in the supply of money finds no contradiction in available evidence on bank deposits and bank notes in circulation. Deposits of banks, $190 million in 1837, fell to $78 million in 1843; note circulation declined from $149 million to a mere $59 million, matching the scale of the reduction of imports. During this period the Second Bank of the United States, also a victim of Andrew Jackson's curious beliefs about banking and money, suffered a reduction of its business and went to its final collapse in 1841, eliminating what was by far the largest single bank in the country. Even the number of banks declined—a rare thing before the Civil War—from a high of 901 in 1840 to 691 by 1843.

As business activity declined government revenues and expenditures plummeted, revenues falling from $24.9 million in 1837 to $8.3 million in 1843, expenditures from $37.2 million in 1836 to $16.9 million in 1843. The fact that a deficit was incurred in every year from 1837 to 1843 save 1839 means that the financing of government activity was not as disinflationary as it could have been. But these accidental deficits were of little help in the circumstances. Evidence of prices shows that wholesale price fell steadily from 1837 to 1843, with farm prices falling more sharply than prices of manufactured goods.

Contemporary accounts leave little doubt of the severity of this long depression. Recovery came slowly in 1844 and 1845. The outbreak of war with Mexico, followed by the California goldrush, spelled the end of the troubles of the 1840's. Frustrating as it is to admit, modern scholarship has not yielded a single convincing analysis of the causes of this singular nineteenth-century debacle. Again, in the late summer and fall of 1857, suspensions of payments by the banks in the major cities signaled another "panic," a violent contraction of bank credit and a collapse of prices. Some railroads which had been building in the newly settled regions were unable to meet their fixed obligations, and the agricultural areas, especially in the Ohio Valley, were hard pressed with fixed debt and falling prices of agricultural commodities. The land boom of 1853–55 (moderate compared to 1834–37) had yielded a harvest of new food supplies out of proportion to the market's existing capacity to absorb it at favorable prices to the farmer. Credit contraction swept through the financial system; most banks in the major eastern cities suspended gold payments.

After the Civil War, beginning in the late 1860's, the rise of heavy industry in the United States gave the expansions a distinct industrial cast, until by the turn of the twentieth century the agricultural and transportation sectors were overshadowed by industrial innovation and investment in the expansions. In each of the late nineteenth-century crises—1873, 1884, and 1893—the involvement of banking in railways and industry played a prominent role. The great industrial expansion of 1896–1913 was accompanied by two downturns, in 1903 and 1907. But recovery from each was quick as a renewed surge came from newly developed manufacturing and heavy industry.

The depression of 1873–77 had three interesting characteristics. First, it occurred during a long period of falling prices. Second, it was not a classical depression in that neither natural catastrophe, the agricultural sector, nor the consumer sector appears to have played an important causal role. Third, the recovery that followed was incomplete.

The depression was triggered by a financial panic, but its causes were essentially nonmonetary. However, monetary factors certainly helped intensify its effects. The entire period from 1866 until 1896 was one of falling prices. This price decline was a function both of the reduction of government spending following Appomattox and of certain monetary factors. In particular, it was a function of government monetary policy designed to effect specie resumption and of the decline in gold production.

Despite the decline in the price level, the period from the end of the Civil War to 1873 was a prosperous one for the American economy. The transition from war to peace had been made quite smoothly, and a number of forces acted to increase the level of aggregate demand. First, immigration increased (the number of immigrants rose from 220,000 to 460,000 per year between 1865 and 1873) and their spending increased consumption. Second, certain consumer industries (particularly petroleum) were growing rapidly and increasing their investment demand. Third, the railroads successfully breached the Mississippi barrier and pushed westward, and in the East the rail network was filled out. That industry too increased the total investment demand. Finally, the farmers who moved west in the wake of the railroads demanded still more machinery and construction supplies.

The depression was truly set off by the financial panic of 1873. That crisis was felt first in Europe but its effects moved across the ocean. The western railroads had been building ahead of demand, and even a slight strain was too much for the financial structure. Investors had failed to consider the fact that even the receipt of large government land grants is inadequate to make investment in railroads building into unpopulated territory immediately profitable (although Professor Fogel has shown that, in the case of the Union Pacific, at least, the returns might not be too long deferred). Railroad investment had been based on expectations, and, when these were not realized, the investment stream collapsed. Depression followed and, although the unemployment figures are notoriously unreliable, contemporary authors suggest unemployment may have reached 3 million. Since the total nonagricultural labor force was only slightly over 6 million, the figure, however inflated, suggests a very serious depression. Contemporary accounts record little improvement until the first half of 1878, and even then recovery was slow and incomplete. A sector-by-sector analysis of the period points up some interesting characteristics.

There is little evidence of a major recession in the farm section. Table 23–2 suggests that aggregate real farm income (at least for the major crops) was generally rising. This increase was a function both of rising output and rising relative prices. Moreover (although the evidence is much less reliable), output in other consumer industries appears to have held up reasonably well. In the case of petroleum, for example, the industry suffered a slight setback in 1875, but output increased in each of the other years.

It is the transport and construction sectors that appear to have played the causal role in the downturn. Professor Fishlow has shown

TABLE 23–2

ECONOMIC INDICATORS 1869–79

Year	*Penn. Anthracite Production (1,000 Tons)*	*Railroad Miles Built (1,000 Miles)*	*Imports of Iron and Steel Manufactures ($ Millions)*	*Textile Days Worked*	*Construction Index (1930 = 100)*	*Pig Iron Output (1,000 Short Tons)*	*Wholesale Prices (1910–14 = 100)*	*Corn Output (1,000 Bu.)*	*Corn Price per Bushel*
1869	18.3	4.1		100	20.3	1.9	151	782	.73
1870	20.0	5.7	34	109	17.5	1.9	135	1125	.52
1871	19.4	6.7	53	125	21.5	1.9	130	1142	.46
1872	24.7	7.4	68	130	14.1	2.9	136	1279	.38
1873	25.6	5.2	74	140	12.6	2.9	133	1008	.48
1874	24.3	2.6	47	138	8.4	2.7	128	1058	.64
1875	23.1	1.6	31	134	7.5	2.3	118	1450	.42
1876	22.8	2.6	23	128	6.5	2.1	110	1478	.36
1877	25.7	2.3	19	128	5.5	2.3	106	1516	.36
1878	21.7	2.4	19	132	6.1	2.6	91	1565	.31
1879	30.2	5.0	20	133	8.9	3.0	90	1752	.36

	Wheat		*Cotton*	
	Output (1,000 Bu.)	*Price (per Bu.)*	*Output (1,000 Bales)*	*Price per Lb.*
1869	290	.92	3.011	.17
1870	254	1.04	4.352	.12
1871	272	1.25	2.974	.18
1872	271	1.24	3.933	.17
1873	322	1.17	4.168	.14
1874	356	.95	3.836	.13
1875	314	1.01	4.631	.11
1876	309	1.04	4.474	.10
1877	396	1.09	4.773	.09
1878	449	.77	5.074	.08
1879	459	1.11	5.756	.10

that miles of track are a poor long-run proxy for railroad investment. Since his criticism rests on the gradual increase in the weight of rails, locomotives, and rolling stock, it does not follow that mileage is a poor short-run proxy. Table 23–2 shows an almost 80 per cent decline in new railroad mileage between 1873 and 1876. This decline, as we have seen, can be traced to the unrealized expectations of profits from the western roads, but its effects spread through the markets for rails, timber, and rolling stock to the economy at large. Thereafter, railway investment increased somewhat, and this increase probably underwrote a portion of the recovery.

A fall in construction demand also contributed to the decline in income in the years after 1873. The explanation of this decline is more difficult but there is little doubt about its magnitude. Table 23–2 indicates that construction fell by almost two thirds between 1871 and 1875. Moreover, even the recovery left activity over 50 per cent below the previous peak. The explanation may, in part, be related to the decline in immigration and fall in family formation during the Civil War. More fundamentally, however, it probably reflects the response of business and potential home builders to the falling price level. In periods of falling price, loans must be repaid in more valuable dollars. Nor does payment in cash help, since the builder is buying an asset whose money value is falling faster than depreciation would warrant.

Falling prices appear to have affected economic fluctuations in three ways. First, they seem to have caused people to substitute cash for long-term fixed assets, and, therefore, adversely affected the construction industry. Second, since businessmen with investment in inventories lose out to other groups in periods of price decline, falling prices may well have affected business expectations adversely. Finally, price declines, by increasing the real burden of debt, caused economic problems in the agricultural sector—a sector which on the basis of income alone should have acted to stimulate recovery.

The depression of 1873 represented an intermediate stage in the evolution of business fluctuations. Foreign trade and agriculture were no longer of primal importance, but manufacturing had not yet become important enough to have a decisive role. Instead, it was investment in the large and expanding transport and construction sectors that underlay the downturn of 1872, and it was expansion in transport investments, with some help from investment in the new basic industry (particularly steel), that underwrote the moderate recovery following 1878.

After World War I the pattern seemed to continue. In general, the decade of the 1920's was one in which the underlying forces of expansion, led by such "new" industries as automobiles and related enterprises, electrical and chemical products, dominated the cyclical contractions that did occur in 1924 and 1927. These contractions were relatively minor and short-lived. Also, because of the improved records of the period, we are able to assign their cause, as noted above, to readjustments in business inventories.

As we have already seen from Chapter 2, net additions to inventory represent one component of aggregate demand. When business produces more than it can sell in the current period, the inventory accumulation is part of final product, and the factor payments involved in its production are part of factor incomes. Suppose now that some businessmen feel they accumulated too much inventory in the previous period and so decide to cut back production in the current period. The decision to reduce production will, of course, cause reduced employment and earnings of those engaged in the particular firms involved. But the repercussions of the decision will not end there. The other firms in the economy that supply the firms now producing less will find that the demand for their products has fallen, and so they will tend to lay off workers. The initial decision thus sends ripples through the economy much like the spreading ripples caused by dropping a stone in a pool. Furthermore, the rising unemployment will cause additional effects throughout the economy because consumer expenditure is determined by income, which falls as unemployment increases. As consumers spend less, the firms producing consumer goods will tend to reduce their output and employment.

Whether the spreading effects will lead to a minor or major recession depends basically on the underlying trend in the economy. During the 1920's the effects of the inventory reductions of 1924 and 1927 did not cumulate into major downturns due to the optimism of the business community and the underlying forces of expansion. Quite a different story results in the 1930's when the underlying forces of expansion were absent. The conjunction of events that caused the world-wide depression of the 1930's did not permit an easy exit from the low levels of employment and output that persisted in the United States throughout the decade.

Since 1945 the American economy has shown a great deal of resilience in the minor cyclical downturns of 1949, 1954, 1958, and 1961. The growth of the electronics industry in the 1950's has been a striking example of the development of a new area for economic expansion based upon changes in technology and consumer tastes. At the same time, the economy has not achieved the marked expansions that have characterized earlier periods of growth. It is still not clear what has caused the combination of resilience and successive moderate expansions that characterizes the post–1945 business cycle record, nor the extent to which government policy has contributed to the particular experience.

Although most of the contractions in business activity have been of one year's duration, there have been several long "depressions" which have etched themselves upon the nation's memory. During the nineteenth century these long depressions seem to have occurred more often than they have in this century. From 1836 to 1900, for example, seven out of sixteen slumps, or nearly half, lasted more than a single year, while since 1900, out of fourteen slumps only two lasted more than a single year. There is a powerful temptation here to hypothesize that the American economy has become more resilient since it became predominantly industrial. But the length of time elapsing from peak to trough is not a measure of the severity of the slump. In 1929–39 for example, this country was, so far as employment and investment were concerned, in a continuous depression, in spite of the expansion of physical output in 1933–37. As already noted, long and severe depressions have not been limited to the 1930's. It appears that in the period 1839–42, as well as in 1873–78, 1892–96 (with a slight and temporary recovery in 1895), there were depressions of great severity compared to the usual contraction in the three- to four-year cycle. Some of the short contractions were also very severe in their effects on employment and investment, even though recovery came quickly; 1920–21, 1937–38, and 1957–58 are good examples of this phenomenon.

In addition to the long depressions or periods of stagnation just noted, we have experienced periods of extensive growth within the framework of the business cycle; periods during which growth was typical and the downturns which did occur were short and of slight magnitude. In 1830–37, 1845–55, and 1878–90, the forces of economic expansion prevailed so powerfully as to overcome the depressing effects of minor cyclical downturns. In 1896–1913, 1920–29, and the whole of postwar period 1946–60, the requisite conditions for secular expansion again prevailed, with recessions being of minor importance.

Has there been any net gain to the nation's growth from the

periods of expansion and stagnation? No, say those who argue that a considerable part of our boom-time expenditures represented frivolous, foolish, and extravagant misallocations of resources born of exuberance, instead of the kind of solid long-term additions to the nation's capital plant needed to underpin secular growth. Moreover, some argue, the lost opportunities of depression stagnation can never be regained. The nation permanently suffers from the factories not built, the men not trained, and so forth. To these people, it would be wisdom in government policy to damp down the booms and prevent depressions, allowing for a steady and surer economic growth. But there are opposing answers to our question. Some students of the cycle argue that there are great gains as well as losses from the expansions and contractions, that the gains outweigh the losses, and that the gains could not be achieved without the cycle running its full pattern. The optimism and exuberance of the expansion provide conditions in which new firms can be organized with relative ease, new products launched, and innovations introduced, some of which will be destined to remain as part of the long-term foundation of industrial strength and economic growth. When depression comes the economy is "shaken out"—weak and inefficient firms are driven out of business, leaving the field to the efficient. With efforts all around by producers to reduce unit costs to match the falling prices which characterize a collapse of aggregate demand, the economy works off the "fat" built up in the previous expansion.

When the forces of a new expansion build up, the economy is able to respond with maximum factor mobility, resources being employed where marginal returns are highest. According to this school of thought, the gains from the cycle have clearly offset the losses.

Needless to say, neither position has been very heavily supported by empirical investigation. There is some logic on both sides. Since national policy has been used to treat the disturbances of the cycle, it has mainly favored the first view; that is, in this century we have not as a matter of policy encouraged cyclical swings to facilitate growth; we have, rather, attempted to minimize the effects of such swings. Perhaps we believe that the economy is better off without the extremes of fluctuations; perhaps our ignorance dictates a middle course as the expedient and safe thing; partly, no doubt, it has been shown to be unwise for the political party in power to keep its hands off cyclical swings if that party wishes to continue to win elections. We will return to matters of policy shortly.

23–3. *What Causes Fluctuations?*

The question often arises among economists (especially late at night) as to whether there might not be some general theory of the business cycle which would explain all cycles. There are essentially two problems fundamental to such a business-cycle theory. First, how does income fluctuate? Second, why should there be any regularity (periodicity) in the sequences of such fluctuations? The other major problem, dealing with the sequence of events in fluctuations and the relative size (amplitude) of the fluctuations, could be relatively easily dealt with if the two fundamental questions could be answered satisfactorily. But one must also bear in mind that if one follows the view held by some economists that all such fluctuations are merely the consequences through time of random events whose impact creates fluctuations in output, then the "regularity" of cycles would be spurious.

As we noted earlier (Chapter 4), since the 1930's we have known enough about the components of the national income to collect and study their various movements over all the phases of the cycle. Special studies have been made of saving, consumption, fixed investment, inventories, wages, and so forth, so that we now have a much firmer notion of *how* fluctuations typically develop, once a change in the direction or level of economic activity has been started. Our knowledge of these facts has enabled us in recent years to effectively mitigate some of the most damaging effects of fluctuations, and we have developed policies to actively influence national income without waiting for the next turn of the cycle.

As regards *why* we have, and have had, business cycles, we have not done so well. Here we are in a condition somewhat similar to that of the medical profession and cancer. We can combat it in many ways; we know a great deal about the characteristics which usually occur; but we cannot say what the initial causes are. As we noted earlier, the main problem here is periodicity. Why should alternations in the level of economic activity set up any definite rhythm? Economists have developed a number of ingenious (and sometimes mutually incompatible) theories to explain this. Business-cycle theory is indeed a kind of graveyard of professional renown; few economists have dealt with it and escaped with their reputations for professional competence unblemished.

None of these theories of the business cycle has been satisfactorily tested against the known facts to firmly demonstrate its effectiveness as an explanation of any particular business cycle—not to mention its effectiveness as an explanation of *all* cycles. This is a very unsatisfactory state of affairs, but we see no justification at this time for burdening the reader with a recitation of any of these theories. Suffice it to say that the best hope thus far in developing a satisfactory literature of business-cycle theory has come from special applications of aggregative economics. It must also be noted that our knowledge of the bare facts of the economic history of fluctuations in American business is insufficient to test thoroughly any of the theories already developed. This deplorable situation will doubtless be improved in future years as research in economics and economic history develops. What we know now has been outlined above. We generally know the turning points of cycles in our economic history; a little about the character of the cycles; something of the outstanding features of the economy in the periods in which those cycles occurred; and some outstanding incidents, spectacular business and financial failures, stock market collapses, important changes in government policy, and so forth. This is better than nothing, but it is far from sufficient to convince us that we know with confidence why business cycles occur. Compared with that of fifty years ago, our knowledge of cycles has vastly increased, but we are still only on the threshold of full understanding of this curious set of phenomena which has had such powerful effects upon the American people in their history.

Thus, we cannot hope in this study to understand fully why *all* the cycles in our history have occurred, nor is it our intention to develop a theory in this place. It seems obvious that no single theory could explain why each business cycle in our history occurred, any more than that any one theory could predict all those which might occur in the future. Each cycle to some extent was a unique historical event based partly upon a nonrecurring set of historical incidents. For example, if the crisis and downturn of 1873 were actually related to the reckless activities of railway builders, as many historians have stated, those particular events would not occur again and that part of the overall information relating to 1873 would be of no use in forecasting future cycles. But similar combinations of the components of a cycle might recur under different historical conditions as consequences of different initial expansionary or contractionary forces. For this reason, the development of cycle theories is useful. The best we can do is to plan economic policies to combat the harmful aspects of the cycles on the basis of our incomplete knowledge—derived both from historical and theoretical studies of the sequences of events—once any forces, internal or external, set up the components of economic activity in such a way that we can recognize the cyclical features and can forecast (and therefore influence) their probable courses of development. Wisdom dictates, in these circumstances, that we bear in mind the extent of our ignorance and be prepared to change our policies as our knowledge of economic fluctuations improves. So long as we maintain a free market, economic growth will probably be irregular and the consequences, the various phases of the cycle, will remain as problems to be dealt with by an ameliorating government policy. What have those policies been and what might they be in the future?

23–4. Policy I. The Problem and Its Setting

General acceptance of the notion that society, in the instrument of the federal government, ought to bear responsibility for offsetting and mitigating the more extreme and damaging consequences of the cycle is something relatively new in American history. The general philosophical conflict raised by the rights of private property has been discussed earlier. Here we are concerned with that conflict as it relates to the business cycle; and here, as more generally, the protectors of property have been concerned that government should not encroach upon the individual. To be sure, interested groups have always agitated for specific remedies. Businessmen and industrialists pressed for tariff protection; farmers, as early as the great post–Civil War "Populist Revolt," sought collective action to buoy up the agricultural economy in times of low prices. But there has traditionally been a belief that the national economy, if left to its own adjustment processes, could iron out the short-term maladjustments which resulted from cyclical fluctuations. Moreover, government interference, it was thought, by sidetracking the "natural" adjustments of the economy would do more harm than good. In fact, the government's role was held to be essentially a burdensome potential tyranny which could be eliminated to considerable advantage. President Coolidge once enriched our history with his views on the subject:

> If the Federal Government should go out of existence, the common run of people would not detect the difference in the affairs of their daily life for a considerable length of time.[7]

[7] Arthur M. Schlesinger, Jr., *The Age of Roosevelt* (Boston: Houghton-Mifflin Co., 1957), Vol. I, p. 57.

And certainly there was no role for legislation or governments to play in changing or controlling the level of national income. In 1931, Senator Gore of Oklahoma, in the midst of the great downswing following 1929, argued that a nation could no more improve its economic situation by passing laws

> . . . than you can pass a resolution to prevent disease. This is an economic disease. You might just as well try to prevent the human race from having a disease as to prevent economic grief of this sort.[8]

Moreover, it was thought that somehow the expansion of the government sector necessarily must compress activity in the private sector. Hence, President Hoover was firmly against expanding the federal government's expenditures by raising the national debt through bond issues.

> For the Government to finance by bond issues deprives industry and agriculture of just that much capital for its own use and for employment. Prosperity cannot be restored by raids on the public treasury.[9]

It followed that the government must always stay within its revenues to promote economic expansion. Indeed, President Coolidge had earlier held that "economy" in government operations comprised the most important contribution government could make.

> . . . the Government can do more to remedy the economic ills of the people by a system of rigid economy in public expenditure than can be accomplished through any other action.[10]

President Hoover, in the midst of depression in 1930, was and remained in fundamental agreement with that philosophy. To balance the annual federal budget was ". . . the primary duty of Government. . . ."[11] He also felt that federal help to the unemployed was an evil to be avoided, that relief would undermine the character of labor, and that, if implemented, federal relief measures would have ". . . struck at the roots of self-government."[12]

These views were not the property of a single political party. Franklin D. Roosevelt ran for the presidency in 1932 on a platform promising, among other things, a reduction in federal expenditures and an annually balanced budget. In the summer of 1932, Roosevelt had expressed his opinions about federal deficits.

[8] *Ibid.*, p. 226.
[9] *Ibid.*, p. 232.
[10] *Ibid.*, p. 232.
[11] *Ibid.*, p. 120.
[12] *Ibid.*

> Stop the deficits. . . . Any Government, like any family, can for a year spend a little more than it earns. But you and I know that a continuation of that habit means the poorhouse.[13]

Such views, of course, had a long and respectable tradition in American politics. That they were fallacious logically, and errant nonsense economically, was not widely appreciated. There were economists and politicians, of course, who knew better. But it took years of bitter experience for their views to finally win out over those who insisted that federal finance was simply personal finance on a gigantic scale, who insisted that the fallacy of composition was an engine of eternal verities. It took a revolution in theoretical economics, a decade of the appalling economic waste of mass unemployment, and the soaring federal deficits of World War II ($55.9 billion in 1943, the peak—compared to $4.5 billion in 1936, the highest New Deal deficit) to teach both scholars and "practical men" the elementary fact that national income is measured by expenditure on output.

During World War II, the lessons of the 1930's, embodied in the famous social and economic institutions of the first two Roosevelt administrations, "The New Deal" (1932–40), as well as those of the war, were digested in both theory and practice. By 1945, the postwar world witnessed the assumption of government responsibility in the national economy for prices, output, employment, and economic growth to an extent which must have seemed revolutionary indeed to the survivors of the 1920's and 1930's (of course, not all Americans by any means have accepted such responsibility as either wise or necessary).

During the 1930's, the United States, like many other industrial countries, launched fairly extensive programs of government expenditure, based upon new debt and money creation. In the war years, experience developed with central government control of an expanding economy. The war economies presented opportunities to apply the lessons of, and see the solutions to, many of the problems which perplexed economists in the depressed 1930's. The development of aggregative economics, together with centralization of power in the wartime economy, gave us knowledge of the economy and its working on both the theoretical and practical planes. Among the European nations, this combination of experience contributed to the development of planned economies in the early postwar years. As early as the British government's budget of 1941 (largely the product of Lord Keynes' influence upon fiscal thinking), a complete

[13] *Ibid.*, p. 420.

blueprint of a "national budget" as a device for planning and control in a national economy was adopted in a nontotalitarian country. These "national budgets" became fixtures in much of Western European fiscal planning and control.

Planning was not carried so far in the United States. But we had been sufficiently impressed by the lessons of 1929–45 that in the Employment Act of 1946 the federal government was given broad (if somewhat vague) responsibility for the maintenance of a wide degree of national well-being in economic affairs.

> The Congress hereby declares that it is the continuing policy and responsibility of the Federal Government to use all practicable means consistent with its needs and obligations and other essential considerations of national policy with the assistance and cooperation of industry, agricultural, labor and State and local governments to coordinate and utilize all its plans, functions, and resources for the purposes of erecting and maintaining in a manner calculated to foster and promote free competitive enterprise and the general welfare, conditions under which these will be afforded useful employment for those able, willing, and seeking to work, and to promote maximum exployment, production, and purchasing power.

Among fiscal experts, so far as the impact of the business cycle was concerned, it came to be widely accepted that this responsibility ought to be interpreted as involving two goals: "full employment" and "price stability." Of course, by "full employment" it was not meant that there should be *no* unemployment but that unemployment should mainly be held at a "frictional" level (voluntary resignations from jobs). Hence, "full" employment meant unemployment in the neighborhood of 2.5 to 3 per cent of the labor force. Similarly, "price stability" did not mean *no* changes in prices, but rather the absence of trends toward inflation or deflation. Relative prices should change with easy flexibility as technological progress and other supply conditions, as well as consumers' taste, might dictate.

The emphasis on these twin objects for federal responsibility in the national economy reflected the wisdom of experience. General devices of government policy (and therefore relatively efficient ones and inexpensive to administer) could be developed to influence prices and employment. We will examine some of these shortly. An examination of available data on fluctuations in prices and employment in previous cycles shows the evils our policy makers were (and are) attempting to avoid.

Prices have generally fluctuated during the business cycle within the longer swings of prices noted earlier. In the deep depressions—from 1819 to 1822, the early 1840's, the decade after the crisis of 1873, the early 1890's and the depression of the 1930's—the price level remained down for periods as long as a decade. The economy has never experienced the kind of hyperinflation that other countries have experienced (except in the Confederacy toward the end of the Civil War). In our periods of major wars, strong inflationary forces were loosed; but, for the most part, increases in output partly countered those forces. As far as price indexes can be trusted to indicate long-period trends, the whole twentieth century has been one in which prices have tended to rise, overcoming the temporary price declines of the depressions. Even in the 1930's, prices in general did not fall back to pre-1914 levels. Since 1940, consumer prices have doubled. This increase is an extraordinary one in American history (only the increases in prices in the Civil War and in World War I were as powerful) since the customary postwar price decline did not come after 1945. Partly this indicates the impact of the backlog of demand from the depression of the 1930's as well as from World War II, and partly the inflationary impact of government expenditures in the cold-war era, but it also is in keeping with the general movement of prices since about 1896. The question, then, naturally arises as to what general forces could account for such a long upward movement? Our price data show no other movement of equal magnitude and duration in American history.

The short-period fluctuations, however, have been serious and their consequences widely felt. In the twentieth century, in terms of fluctuations relative to the nearest peaks or troughs before World War II, price movements have been as wide as in the nineteenth century. And since production, investment, and employment have fluctuated closely with these price movements, the focus of attention upon prices by policy makers is at least upon a significant indicator of movements in business activity. Whether or not control of prices alone would suffice to significantly influence general activity in the desired direction is something of an open question. For example, anti-inflationary policies may hold down prices, but if they hold down output too, such policies would have perverse effects. When prices continually rise, on the other hand, real incomes of persons with fixed money incomes tend to melt away. Hence, equity seems to demand that public policy should not encourage inflation, except possibly in drastic recessions. In the 1930's, the New Deal aimed to raise prices in the hope both of restoring money incomes and of encouraging producers to expand their own operations and reduce unemployment. Such policies did not prove fruitful. Since that time, public policy has only rarely been concerned with raising prices.

Moreover, while we have thus far been mainly concerned with prices in general, it is important to understand that relative prices do not always move in the same way. Some prices fluctuate more violently than do others, and some can run counter to the movement of general prices. Changes in industrial structure find expression in changes of relative prices. Wholesale prices generally have fluc-

CHART 23–1

PERCENTAGE OF THE LABOR FORCE UNEMPLOYED, 1900–1960
(Annual Averages)

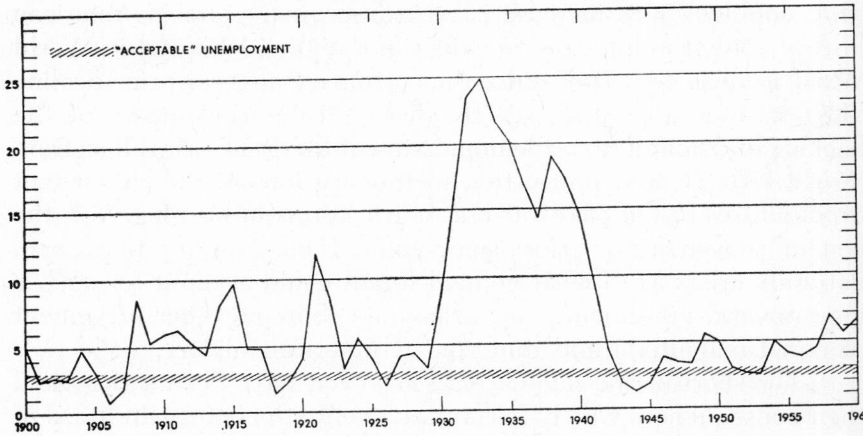

SOURCES: 1900–1957, *Historical Statistics;* 1958–1960, *Bureau of Labor Statistics.*

tuated much more widely than retail prices, and prices of producers' goods more than those of consumers' goods; in the 1957–58 recession, general prices actually rose, both on the consumer and wholesale levels.

The attention of policy makers upon unemployment is concerned with something less mercurial than prices. In the diagram (Chart 23–1), the percentage of the civilian labor force unemployed is shown. These data are dangerously easy to misinterpret because of the different definitions of both "labor force" and "unemployment." However, we will use them in a very rough way and will not depend upon fine differences to reach our conclusions. As we noted earlier, economists have come to agree that "acceptable unemployment" might be in the neighborhood of 2.5 to 3 per cent. Since 1900, as can be seen in the chart, the figures have fluctuated a great deal around that range. Before 1900, we cannot even make respectable guesses about this. Data are lacking for this purpose, and even if we did have them, in an economy which was largely agricultural—such as the U.S. in most of the nineteenth century—such data would be especially difficult to interpret.

It is clear in the chart that since 1900, the figure for unemployment has been above the desired 2.5 to 3 per cent range in the recessions. The Great Depression of 1929–32 especially stands out in that regard. It is also noticeable that, except for the period of the Korean War, the post–World War II American economy has conspicuously failed to keep the percentage of unemployed down, even in the best years, such as 1955–57. Compared to the pre-1929 era, this would seem to be a most lamentable performance. From 1953 to mid-1964 unemployment has only rarely been less than 5 per cent of the labor force; much of the time a level above 6 per cent has been the rule. Unemployed men are a tragic waste of productive resources and a potential source of political difficulties; and the experience of prolonged unemployment often creates a permanent psychic scar on those concerned. When, then, should such unemployment exist?

The depression unemployment is perhaps easiest to comprehend. In times when business is poor and factories are on short time or are entirely closed down, jobs requiring the skills of the displaced workers are simply not available in the right number in the right locations. In times of expansion, such as we had in 1946–48, in 1955–57, in 1959–60, and in 1961–64, our relatively high level of unemployment is more difficult to comprehend. "Traditionally" (that is, before 1929), the expansion of economic activity in the upswing of the cycle tended to absorb unemployment. Perhaps the answer lies simply in the rate of increase of the civilian labor force relative to the needs of modern industry and trade to absorb them. Increasing "automation" and laborsaving methods developed since 1945 relative to advances in the training of relatively unskilled, or narrowly trained personnel, could be at the root of the problem here; and if so, the solution would seem to lie in greater width as well as in depth of training, and better education of workers to increase their job mobility in a world of rapidly changing technology where a single skill may not suffice to carry a man through a normal working career. Finally, of course, there is the specter of "secular stagnation." It may be that perhaps due to our unequal distribution of income, expenditures in peacetime years since the 1920's have been simply too low to fully employ an expanding labor force. The recent expansion from the depression low in the rate of growth of the labor force has not eased any problems here.

Let us consider the secular growth of our labor force for a moment. Our data (Table 23–2) are not strictly homogeneous and care must be taken of their uses. We see the enormous growth of the "civilian labor force"—variously defined—since 1820. We can note that it has grown much more rapidly in the past than it has grown in this century. But the problems of absorbing rapid increases in the

TABLE 23–2
American Civilian Labor Force
1820–1960

	Civilian Labor Force (Millions)	*Mean Annual Percentage Increase*
1820	2.9	—
1830	3.9	3.4
1840	5.4	3.9
1850	7.7	4.2
1860	10.5	3.6
1870	12.9	2.3
1880	17.4	3.4
1890	23.3	3.4
1900	29.1	2.4
1910	37.4	2.9
1920	42.4	1.3
1930	48.8	1.5
1940	51.7	0.6
1950	59.0	1.4
1960	70.7	1.9
1964 (May)	76.5	2.0

Sources: *Historical Statistics, U.S. Statistical Abstract* and *Economic Indicators,* May, 1960 (Prepared for the Joint Economic Committee by the Council of Economic Advisers).

labor force were different in the nineteenth century and were perhaps more easily met when we had an empty continent to fill. It is possible that labor mobility between trades, professions, and industrial occupations has become more difficult, so that cyclical fluctuations have taken a higher toll in percentage unemployed than in earlier years. Increased job protection (unionization), together with the gradual decline in demand for unskilled workmen, might contribute to this phenomenon. Also, it is possible that the relatively high level of unemployment since 1945 (if the data can be trusted) is linked to the upturn of growth of the labor force which has occurred since 1940. Here, it would seem, policies of "full employment" might need to be considered as more than just a cyclical problem. We seem now to have greater resilience in the economy with which to avoid deep depression than in the past, but, paradoxically, we seem to have a more continuously high level of unemployment than at any time in this century, except for a couple of years during World War I and in the catastrophic 1930's.

23–5. *Policy II. A Brief History of American Contracyclical Measures*

Since, as we have already noted, it has become a matter of public policy to restrain the violence of the business cycle, we must ask which methods are used and why? If full employment and price stability are the goals of public policy, it follows that such policy must be firmly rooted in fact and theory.

There is a long history, in Europe and in America, of such contracyclical policy. However, the precise goals of this policy have not always been firmly established. In Britain, for example, the central bank, the Bank of England (founded in 1694), has long followed practices designed to offset certain phenomena associated with the cycle. By control of the terms and cost of borrowing, the Bank sought also to control movements of prices and movements in and out of the country of precious metals. The policy was long practiced, and it was long condemned by its opponents: they said such a policy was blind to the effects of such controls upon employment. In the United States, such central-bank policy ("monetary policy") existed far back in our history, as policies exercised by the First and Second Banks of the United States (see Chapter 12 on banking). In the long interregnum from Jackson's veto of the Second Bank's charter in 1832 to the establishment of the Federal Reserve System in 1914, the United States Treasury performed rudimentary central-banking functions, such as the movement of specie (gold and silver) into the nation's financial centers in times of crisis and monetary disorders associated with the cycle. Since 1914, the Federal Reserve System has practiced monetary policy measures which have been partly designed to counteract the cycle. These have not always been successful and have been subjected to much criticism. We will return to this subject in more detail shortly.

Direct government actions specifically designed to counteract cyclical fluctuations also have a long history. These actions ("fiscal policy") were long associated with direct efforts to mitigate the impact of the cycle upon production and employment, taking the form of public works and other forms of subsidized output. Manipulation of the tariff (a typically American procedure up to 1931) to protect domestic markets for national industry, and local poor-relief measures, are other typical fiscal measures. Since most of the expenditure policies had to be financed by the creation and control of money through the issue of government debt, fiscal policy has always been linked up with monetary policy. Although the two kinds of policies are often treated separately, it is important to bear in mind that they are not, in fact, completely separate and unrelated phenomena.

Although both fiscal and monetary policies have a long history in this country as well as abroad, it was mainly after the catastrophe of the depression of the 1930's and the subsequent development of national income theory that economists began systematically to study the potentials of monetary and fiscal policies for control of the level of output and employment.

Except for direct public financial assistance to industry—such as the Reconstruction Finance Corporation, inaugurated at the beginning of the Great Depression by the Hoover administration; the meager industrial loans of the Federal Reserve System authorized in 1934; and the public relief spending in 1933 under Harry Hopkins—early efforts to stop the Great Depression were centered in a kind of federal intervention already developed: direct controls over business methods. This tradition of control came from the early antimonopoly legislation. The Interstate Commerce Act of 1887, the Sherman Antitrust Act of 1890, and the Clayton Antitrust Act of 1914 were all measures designed to restrict those business practices which were in restraint of trade. This opening wedge of federal intercession in the business community was widened, for roughly the opposite purposes, in the Webb-Pomerene Act of 1918, which authorized U.S. business engaged in foreign trade to combine and act monopolistically where their overseas markets were threatened by foreign competitors who practiced such monopolistic policies as regional price discrimination. Among the first New Deal measures to combat the depression was a similar kind of government action, the National Industrial Recovery Act (1933), which encouraged industry-wide collusion regarding prices, wages, output, and the like, to attempt to stabilize and "rationalize" American business and thus to prop up business confidence. In 1935, the NIRA was declared by the Supreme Court to be unconstitutional. The Robinson-Patman Act of 1936 was an effort to stabilize prices by controlling price discrimination and dumping by manufacturers, as was the Miller-Tydings Act of 1937, an amendment to the Sherman Act which made price fixing mandatory between manufacturers and dealers of branded items in some states where such activity was permitted (the Miller-Tydings Act was overruled by the Supreme Court in 1951).

These were desperation attempts to encourage a recovery of prices, and they were (and are, where they still exist) in direct opposition to the system of "competitive markets" as understood by most Americans.

Federal government expenditures in the economy in the 1930's, while not an entirely new thing in our history, had a long-run impact upon fiscal thinking which far overshadowed the system of direct intervention in the business community which we have just considered. During the 1930's, both of these systems operated side by side. While the policy of intervention-in-detail in business practices was begun early and vigorously, commencing with the NIRA followed by the Agricultural Adjustment Act (1933), the method of building a separate government sector by debt-creating expenditures on federal public works and grants-in-aid to state and local administrations gained prominence by the end of the 1930's as the best method of dealing with a general deficiency of aggregate demand. The full-employment experience of World War II was abundant verification, if any were needed, that government could directly change the level of national income by its own expenditure programs.

This point had been made by many, long before it "caught on" after the collapse of the recovery in 1937. Governments from time immemorial had used public works (the pyramids of Egypt?) to create employment. But in modern times, in the nations influenced by the laissez faire doctrines of Adam Smith and his successors, direct government expenditure in peacetime had been traditionally viewed as a movement away from reason; only in wars had it seemed justified, and even then it seemed slightly deplorable. The tradition died hard. As early as December, 1933, J. M. Keynes, in an open letter to President Roosevelt published in *The New York Times*, emphasized that the agenda of business reform in the NIRA could not achieve the direct-income effects which were needed and which might be achieved by a system of public works. Perhaps the point was considered "too radical" at the time. In any case, the famous New Deal largely failed to solve the problems of unemployment because its attempts to raise output by trying to inflate prices were accompanied by a train of opposing contractionary actions (including a decline in expenditures of state and local government). With the advantage of hindsight, and the experiences of World War II we can now see that the fiscal policies of the later 1930's were on the right track, although of insufficient magnitude to solve the problems at hand. In the postwar era, we have not faced the problem of mass unemployment again, but from the experience of the past it is clear that appropriate policies could now be available, should the occasion arise. We will deal with these policies in general shortly. Such stabilization policies are now called "discretionary" stabilizers, since their implementation depends upon specific, purposeful government action.

Since the Great Depression we have experienced several "recessions," or depressions which were small compared to the 1930's. Fiscal policy in these recessions has succeeded in helping to stabilize income after a short initial decline. But these fiscal policies have not been of the nature of public works. They have been more or less "automatic" stabilizers which have been brought into play quickly and with a minimum of policy decision. These automatic stabilizers are also mainly the fruits of the depression of the 1930's, but their origin was different from both the business reformism of the NIRA and Patman Act, and the fiscal programs of public works. The origin of a large part of our system of automatic stabilization was, curiously enough, social reform.

One of the most glaring tragedies of the factory system since its inception has been the tendency for cyclical recessions to produce mass unemployment as the system of interrelated factories closed down or cut production in response to a reduction of market demand. The resulting suffering not only was a waste of human resources but was held to be "unjust," since the sufferers had little or nothing to do with the causes of their dismissals. Moreover, their unemployment constituted a further reduction of aggregate demand because of wages (and hence comsumption) lost; and their daily needs were an added burden upon limited public relief funds which were already under pressure from the mounting tide of nonindustrial unemployment. Accordingly, in the Social Security Act of 1935, the states were induced to organize unemployment relief funds. Since expenditures of these funds are "contracyclical"—they decline in expansions and rise in contractions—they add a stabilizing element in the cyclical fluctuations. Unemployment compensation helped to put a "floor" under national income and, thus, to halt the contraction of consumption expenditures at a point higher than would be the case without such expenditures.

Because no separate government policy decisions are needed for the national economy to feel the impact of the unemployment compensation funds, they are referred to as "automatic" or "built-in" stabilizers. We now have several such devices at work whose net effect is to limit the amplitude of fluctuations. The "progressive" income tax structure shaves off an increasing proportion of income as national income rises, while taxes are reduced more than proportionately as income declines, thus contributing either to a surplus in expansions or to a deficit in recessions—other things being equal. Many other forms of government activity, corporation taxes, federal relief measures, and so forth, produce similar effects.

In the area of monetary policy, the experience of the 1930's produced little which has changed our views of the banking system as a stabilizing force, except possibly that our awareness was sharpened concerning the limitations of the main instruments of monetary control. In this area, there was already an established tradition in the United States from our own past, but especially from the Bank of England's long experience, which was considered, at the time of the National Monetary Commission in 1907 (see Chapter 12), to be part of our "Anglo-Saxon heritage." This tradition, derived from the pre-1914 Gold Standard, consisted primarily of central-bank action, through the interest it charged on loans and changes in the conditions of lending, to mitigate against extreme swings in economic activity. The policy—recently described by the chairman of the Board of Governors of the Federal Reserve System as "leaning against the wind," and usually characterized by such phrases as "discretionary control" over credit—remains essentially unchanged from the period before the 1930's, except that some new measures of control, such as flexible commercial-bank reserve requirements, are now used. In the 1920's, the Federal Reserve System's policies were largely ineffective, when not indeed wrong (such as cheap credit in 1927 and high interest rates in 1931–32). In the 1930's, the existence of ultra-low interest rates and massive idle balances in the commercial banks left central-bank policy primarily a dead letter in the United States. From 1941 to 1945, the Federal Reserve System was simply an arm of the U.S. Treasury's war effort, of course; and from 1945 to 1951 the policy of supporting the prices of government securities (hence keeping interest rates low and stable) mitigated against an effective monetary policy to combat the inflation of that period. Since 1951, the central bank has returned to its traditional policies, attempting to moderate both expansions and contractions, and contributing to price stability, and perhaps, if not always, to full employment.

There is thus an element of "preventive medicine" in our policy measures for controlling the business cycle. These measures are the result of long and painful experience. Have they any general underlying logic? In 1950, a committee of distinguished American economists, in a survey of "the problem of economic stability," stated that our policies should have two strategic principles:

1. Government tax revenue should be higher relative to government expenditure in periods of high employment than in periods of substantial unemployment.
2. Money and credit should be relatively tight in periods of high employment and relatively easy in periods of substantial unemployment.[14]

These principles are meant to deal with the specific problems of controlling the "business cycle." They clearly are not meant to eliminate the cycle, and the problem of the "long cycle" discussed in the previous chapter is not within the scope of present policy thinking. That might well call for a degree of economic planning and control which is beyond the reach of a free-enterprise economy. Certainly it is clear that cycles, short and long, have been characteristic of our country's economic history and a part of our economic development. They may well be part of the price of the degree of economic freedom we enjoy.

Suggested Readings

BURNS, A. F., AND MITCHELL, W. C. *Measuring Business Cycles.* New York: National Bureau of Economic Research, 1947.

FELS, RENDIGS. *American Business Cycles, 1865–1897.* Chapel Hill: University of North Carolina Press, 1959.

MATTHEWS, R. C. O. *The Business Cycle.* Chicago: University of Chicago Press, 1959.

MITCHELL, W. C. *Business Cycles, the Problem and Setting.* New York: National Bureau of Economic Research, 1927.

SMITH, W. B., AND COLE, A. H. *Fluctuations in American Business, 1790–1860.* Cambridge: Harvard University Press, 1935.

[14] A. E. A., *Readings in Fiscal Policy* (Homewood, Illinois: Richard D. Irwin, Inc., 1955), p. 419.

Chapter 24 THE BIRD'S-EYE VIEW

In spite of the danger of some repetition it will be useful here to consider changes in some of the broadest measures of economic activity at various critical junctures in the nation's economic development. We do this in order to get a bird's-eye view of the basic structural changes that have been produced over time by the growth and development of the national economy. The discussion will be confined to a minimal number of aggregative indicators.

Basically, the development of the American economy has been the story of a small population's growing large, occupying, until the end of the nineteenth century, an expanding, economically viable geographical region, and moving toward an ever-increasing proliferation of specialization and division of labor. The latter has been solidly based upon continued increases in productivity from the application of scientific and mechanical principles in all areas of economic life—from agriculture and mining to the uses of products and services in consumption and investment. The effects of this process have been felt in basic structural changes: (1) the population has become increasingly more widely distributed across a continental economy; (2) the proportion of the labor force engaged in agriculture has declined, as has the actual number of workers in this sector in recent decades; (3) the proportion in manufacturing first increased as that in agriculture fell, and then declined as productivity increases "released" an ever-increasing proportion of the population from the necessity to engage in basic production. In fact, each developing sector seems to show this pattern, first rising as a proportion of the total labor force, and then leveling off and even declining as new uses of labor develop; transportation and public utilities are two further examples of this phenomenon. As a result of this pattern there is a steady growth of specialization and division of labor. Accordingly (4), there has been a rise in the more "sophisticated" uses of human resources in education, professions, and services. Accompanying this has been a dramatic rise in the penetration of secondary and higher education among the population. (5) Our foreign trade, representing our successes in production (exports) and our additional needs as the character of the economy changed (imports), makes an interesting mirror of these basic developments. We moved from an agricultural-products to a manufactured-goods exporter, and then, after World War II, crude and manufactured foodstuffs rose again as a proportion of our total exports. Similarly, we moved from a basic importer of finished manufactured goods toward a food and raw materials importer, but we have apparently begun a reversal of this process as the proportion of our imports of finished and semifinished goods grows. The latter, representing changes in the tastes of the American consumer, gives evidence of a much more sophisticated consumer than existed a generation or two ago.

It will be useful to reduce these conclusions to a schematic framework which can be usefully employed. Arbitrarily, and as a method of simplifying the discussion, we can divide American economic development into three chronological phases based on the fundamental characteristics of the economy since 1790. *Phase I, high point somewhere about 1860:* We were from the first primarily an agricultural nation, with minor manufacturing and other activities comprising a very small part of the total national economic effort. We traded our raw materials and food products to the world for manufactured goods. *Phase II, high point in late 1930's to the opening years of the 1940's:* The accelerated development of manufacturing and transportation from the 1870's onward, partly made possible by increasing farm output, was accompanied by a marked decline in the proportion of labor and income in the agricultural sector. The structure of our foreign trade shifted. We imported proportionally less manufactured goods and more food and raw materials. At the same time, the *sum* of the proportions of the labor force in agriculture and industry fell sharply as more manpower was freed for trade, services, and professions. *Phase III, characteristics strongly visible since the 1940's:* The continuing rise in productivity and per-capita income raised the proportion of the labor force in education, professions (including finance, insurance, etc.), and services. The vastly enriched national economy began to rely upon a greater variety of manufactured and semimanufactured goods than before (Phase II). As a result the proportion of imports of finished and semifinished goods rose again, and by the mid-1960's we used as great a proportion of imported manufactures as we did in the 1880's. At the same time, the combination of world food needs, American governmental policies, and American agricultural proficiency brought a recrudescence of American exports of food. Throughout all this the steadily growing population filled up formerly empty parts of the continent, shifting the population westward.

These three phases, substantially inclusive as far as they go, are a drastic simplification of a complex reality. The reader should use these as a thinking tool, but should not let them stand in the way of a comprehensive view of the whole span of our economic history. We are talking about continuous change, and merely labeling the economy, for the sake of convenience, where the labels fit easiest. We shall now "look in" on the American economy at six specific points in time, 1820, 1860, 1880, 1920, 1940, and 1960 and later. We will try to make substantially the same comparisons, so far as the available data allow, as we go along.

In 1820, about thirty years after the Constitution was promulgated fixing the basic governmental institutions, the American population was about 9,600,000. Of these, something like 693,000, or a mere 7 per cent, lived in what can be classified as urban areas. Of the land area at that time there were only 5.6 persons per square mile. The median age was around seventeen years, and fewer than 2 million lived away from states that bordered the Atlantic. Of workers gainfully employed, about 72 per cent worked in agriculture, 12 per cent in manufacturing and trades, and the remaining 16 per cent was distributed among the services and professions. Except that it involved a small population, this distribution of labor was not too different from that in a typical underdeveloped Asian nation today. Of our exports over 60 per cent was crude materials, 25 per cent was crude and processed food, 9 per cent was semimanufactures and less than 6 per cent was finished manufactures. Imports consisted of about 57 per cent finished manufactures, and crude foodstuffs and crude materials together amounted to only about 15 per cent. In Phase I these ratios are slowly reversing themselves for the most part, in Phase II they *are* reversed, and in Phase III some are reversed again.

By 1860 the features which dominate our Phase II are beginning to appear, even though the characteristics of Phase I are, in some areas, most strongly reflected in the data. The population had grown to 31.5 millions. Of these, 9.7 millions, or nearly a third, now lived in the middle western states (6.9 millions in Ohio, Indiana, Illinois, Michigan, and Wisconsin), and the Pacific Coast and Mountain states—although the latter two divisions had only about half a million people between them. The middle western frontier was being occupied in depth and the far West was opening up. More than 6 millions, or about 20 per cent of the total, now lived in urban areas. There were more than ten persons per square mile, and the median age was nearly twenty years. Agriculture now employed about 59 per cent of those gainfully employed, industrial employment had risen to 18 per cent, and nearly 23 per cent of the population was now freed from agriculture and manufacturing to follow other pursuits. Cotton was still king in our exports. Crude materials (mostly cotton) occupied 61.7 per cent of total exports. But exports of finished manufactures had more than doubled in proportion and stood at 12.3 per cent of the total. Food exports had actually fallen somewhat as a proportion of the total. A fairly dramatic change was apparent in imports, where the proportion of finished manufactures had fallen to about 40 per cent of the total.

At our next viewing point, 1880, the characteristics of Phase II have become prominent. Also, we have more aggregative data to look at, as scholars have been able to construct national income estimates as far back as the late 1860's. In 1880 the population had risen to 50 million, nearly 17 per square mile, and 28 per cent lived in urban areas. Only about 49 per cent of those gainfully employed were in agriculture, and they received about 20 per cent of income earned by market activities. Just over 18 per cent of those gainfully employed were in industry and trades, earning roughly 14 per cent of income. By then, nearly one third of those gainfully employed were in nonfarm, nonmanufacturing employment and received more than 50 per cent of earned income. Foreign trade reflected these changes. Farm exports, representing a more productive agriculture, showed crude food at 18 per cent of the total, manufactured food at a quarter of the total. Finished manufactures, about 15 per cent of the total, had now tripled their proportion since 1820, a gain exceeded only by food exports. Crude materials had fallen to about 36 per cent of total exports. On the other hand, imports of crude materials now reached some 21 per cent of total imports and imports of finished manufactures had declined to just over 30 per cent of the total. The economy was now turning sharply away from that kind of national economic life which had characterized Phase I, and the succeeding decades would change it even more.

The rise of "sophisticated" uses of manpower, which by 1880 occupied a third of all those employed, was a singular phenomenon and one which we now know, to be characteristic of an advanced technology. Consider what has happened since to sophisticated labor. By the mid-1960's more than 65 per cent of the employed population worked at jobs other than those directly concerned with making the essentials of food, clothing, and shelter—agriculture and manufacturing industry. In 1820, as we noted earlier, only 16 per cent of the nation's workers were thus employed. This vast, radical change in the distribution of employed labor represented two characteristics of American development: (1) the steady rise of productivity in agriculture and industry which made possible a vast "liberation" of labor from basic production, and (2) the proliferation of education and the consequent increasing pervasiveness of technical knowledge and ever-widening demands for variety in production and consumption. These characteristics fed each other; they were largely mutually determined, and by our own time, the 1960's, made possible a society whose uses of applied technology had created a labor force sophisticated beyond the wildest dreams of our nineteenth-century forebears. This process was part of the general movement away from rural and into urban life.

This continuing process of change, evident in Phase II and ubiquitous in Phase III, is clearly seen in data for public education. There has been a giant increase in the extent of formal education in the labor force, and this, in Phase III, is continuing and perhaps accelerating at the higher levels. By 1870 about 57 per cent of the population between 5 and 17 years of age was in public day schools. In earlier years the proportion had been smaller. By 1920 the number was 78 per cent and by the late 1950's about 85 per cent. As the struggle against high-school dropouts continues the number can probably be pushed higher. But a far more dramatic change has come in the extent of education per capita. In 1870 the average length of the school term was 132 days, and about 2 per cent of those 17 years of age graduated from high school. By 1920 the term length was 162 days and 17 per cent of those in the 17-year age group graduated. The next three decades saw a radical change. By 1940 the term was 175 school days, and about 51 per cent of the 17-year-olds graduated. By 1960, with a school term of 178 days, about two thirds of the 17-year-olds graduated—roughly 65 per cent against the 2 per cent of 1870. There was an educational revolution indeed! In 1870 the average student only attended 78 days of his 132-day term. In 1960 he attended 160 days of his 178-day term.

As might be expected, such an educational "tooling up" extended upward into the colleges and universities. Accordingly, in 1870, of those between 18 and 21 years of age, only about 1.7 per cent were enrolled in institutions of higher learning. By 1920 the number was over 8 per cent, and by the early 1960's over 30 per cent. Here was a population in which high-school graduation was almost a natural condition of life, and college graduation a commonplace. Even the attainment of the Ph.D. increasingly has become a requirement for research employment, college teaching, and in certain areas even employment in secondary education. These facts measure a change in the "quality" of the labor force which has been both a cause and a consequence of our economic development. As we obtain our bird's-eye view of the twentieth-century American economy, the end of Phase II and the development of Phase III, bear in mind the change in the labor force's grasp of sophisticated knowledge implied by the data on education.

In 1920, after World War I and near the peak of our Phase II, the population numbered more than 106 millions. By 1940 it was more than 132 millions. By 1940 there were 44 persons per square mile of territory (recall the 5.6 persons per square mile in 1820). By 1920 over half of the population lived in urban areas, and by 1940 only about 23 per cent of the population actually lived on farms. In 1920 only about 27 per cent of those gainfully employed were in agriculture, and by 1940 this number was down to 17 per cent. By 1920 manufacturing industry employed 26 per cent of the workers, and that proportion was down to 22 per cent by 1940. As a result, the population released from direct production of commodities and goods rose from 47 per cent in 1920 to 61 per cent by 1940. The average age of the typical American was 29.5 years in 1940, nearly middle-aged compared to the advanced juveniles of 1820, and in 1940 as we noted, the average worker was vastly better educated than his forebear. By 1940, 77.8 millions, or nearly 60 per cent of the population, lived away from the Atlantic Coast states. The nation had become truly continental. About 12 per cent of income in the 1920's went to agriculture, but only about 9 per cent did so in the 1930's. Manufacturing industry received 22 per cent of income in the 1920's and (reflecting the Great Depression) about 19 per cent in the 1930's. By 1940 then, roughly 72 per cent of income received was outside direct production of commodities and manufactured goods. The proportion has not changed markedly since (but with the steady reduction of numbers employed in agriculture and manufacturing industry, more income per head is available in those sectors). In 1920 and 1940 we see the completion of Phase II in the foreign trade figures. Exports of crude materials fell to about 25 per cent of the total by the end of the 1930's and exports of finished manufactures reached 49.5 per cent. Finished and semi-finished manufactures together equaled 64 per cent of the total, and crude food exports, reflecting the dissolution of the world food market, were down to a mere 4 per cent of the total, manufactured foodstuffs down to 7 per cent (compared to 18 and 25 per cent, respectively, in the 1880's!). By the end of the 1930's only about 20 per cent of our imports were finished manufactures, while semi-manufactures had risen to nearly the same level.

The forces of change seemed to be accelerated by the upheavals of World War II and its aftermath. The characteristics of our Phase III, including a considerable turnabout in certain aspects of our foreign trade, became dominant. By 1960 our highly educated population totaled over 180 million, over 50 per square mile; the average age was 30.3 years, and 70 per cent lived in urban areas. Of the 30 per cent still classified as rural, only 7.4 per cent were actually in farm families. Since 1820 the population balance had reversed itself, as between urban and rural life. Sixty per cent of the population by 1960 lived away from the Atlantic Coast states, and the West Coast had double New England's population. By 1963 a mere 5.8 per cent of the civilian labor force engaged in agricultural production. By 1960 three fourths of the 94 per cent of the labor force not employed in agriculture were not employed in either manufacturing or in transportation. The revolution in the uses of labor force had gone far. Productivity was making the society vastly more complex and specialized than it had been a century earlier. By 1963 there were well over twice as many (11.3 million to 4.3 million) persons employed in retail and wholesale trade as there were in farming. By 1961, with 4.1 per cent of the national income going to agriculture and 28.4 per cent going to manufacturing industry, more than two thirds of the national income was received by those *not* making food and manufactured goods, and a full 12 per cent of the national income went for professional services not related to government, transportation, public utilities, or communications. This proliferation of specialization and division of labor was the "payoff" of a century and a half of technological, scientific, social, and economic change. If Phase I could be called "the age of agriculture," Phase II "the age of industry," Phase III could almost be called "the age of sophisticated labor." Moreover, the process seems to be speeding up as the era of computers and automation is upon us. This conclusion is of course a commonplace one, but viewed against this historical background it can be seen as a dramatic illustration of one of the main themes of this book, the revolutionary and ubiquitous consequences of technological change.

One cannot forecast the future with confidence. The characteristics of our Phase III may seem a logical outcome of Phase II, but could they have been forecast during Phase II? Consider the changes in the structure of our foreign trade in Phase III. Predictably, the rise in the proportion of finished manufactures in total exports has continued, being in the neighborhood of 60 per cent since the 1950's (compared to 12 per cent a century earlier). There has been a further increase in the proportion of semimanufactures (14 per cent in 1963) and a further decline in exports of crude materials (10.5 per cent of the total in 1963). But the rise in food exports in the twenty years since World War II might not have been foreseen, even though American agriculture may well be our most efficient industry compared to parallel foreign industries. Exports of crude foodstuffs, below 4 per cent of the total at the end of the 1930's, now stands at 9.4 per cent of the total, rising strongly since the early 1950's. Manufactured foodstuffs have also risen. Imports are more surprising. The historical pattern of a falling proportion of finished manufactures, a major characteristic of Phase II, has apparently been reversed and in 1962 finished manufactures stood at 36.6 per cent of total imports—the highest since the 1880's. Semimanufactures are now higher than at any time before the 1950's. Paradoxically then, the world's largest manufacturer, the United States, is now the largest importer of manufactured goods. On the other hand, the long-period increase of the proportion of crude materials in our imports has been sharply reversed, so that it was 21 per cent of the total in 1962 compared to 37 per cent in the 1920's. The proportion of crude and manufactured foods has also declined since World War II.

Sumner Slichter,[1] studying American productivity, found that the transformation of the structure of economic growth in the United States could be divided into three phases which roughly approximate, and slightly overlap, those we have been discussing. (1) Up to 1880–1900 principal reliance for growth was placed upon capital expansion, the growth of capital stock was faster than the growth of income, and the capital-output ratio expanded (from 1.63:1 in 1850 to 2.86:1 in 1900, industrial capital to national income). (2) From 1880–1900 to about 1929, changes in energy sources, primarily electric power and internal combustion engines, underpinned economic growth. (3) Since 1929 ". . . revolutionary changes in the art of management and a sensational growth of technological research" have been prime movers in economic growth. Since 1929 increasingly greater productivity of investment has caused the capital/output ratio to decline (2.53:1 in 1953). The modern economy, using efficient energy sources, applied science, and a more systematically skilled management now produced more income for every dollar of investment than was the case six decades ago. This of course is one reason the economy can afford to free such a large portion of its labor force from direct work on the production of food and goods.

These changes are obviously a result of changes in the basic components of economic activity, the technology, the quality of the labor force, consumer tastes, and even in the demographic structure, as we have noted. Of course the whole story is not so simple as we have made it here, but our bird's-eye view will serve as a brief summary of the more completely worked-out analysis and descriptions of economic change in the preceding chapters. We have purposely avoided the complications here of the internal structure of industry, of finance, and so forth. But even so brief a summary underscores the point made again and again in the preceding chapters, that economic growth and technological change are by themselves thoroughly revolutionary forces in their impact upon the social organism.

[1] Sumner Slichter, *Economic Growth in the United States, Its History, Problems and Prospects* (Baton Rouge: Louisiana State University Press, 1961).

VIII
Concluding Remarks

Chapter 25 THE AMERICAN EXPERIENCE AND THE PROBLEMS OF ECONOMIC UNDERDEVELOPMENT

25–1. *The Study of History*

Is a nation's history of any consequence? Henry Ford is reputed to have defined history as "bunk," and there are many today who agree with him. There are two overriding reasons for this Draconian verdict. Let us consider them in turn. First, it is plain enough that human history, the sum total of man's experience, is not reproduced in the writings of any historian. Each historian chooses his "facts" on the basis of some preconceived viewpoint—he is biased. Hence each history book is only a biased and partial account of what in fact happened. Much more might be written about any event or sequence of events. Therefore, if only the "whole truth" and nothing else is acceptable as "history," clearly the partial and biased accounts of the historians might be classified as "bunk."

Second, why study history—any history—anyway? It can be argued that nations and peoples make their own destiny by their day-to-day actions. Such actions and the reactions to them do not, however, follow any logical sequence. Therefore, the study of history, while a diverting academic exercise, is of no use as a guide to the future. One cannot foretell events. Nor can one successfully handle today's problems with the solutions to yesterday's problems. So run the arguments. The successors of Ford rest their case.

Now it is clear that we do not align ourselves with the "bunk" tradition. Let us deal with our opponents point by point. First, we not only *admit* that the historian "selects" his data from the infinity of facts that comprise the whole body of "history," we *insist* that this is the only method whereby past events can be rendered coherent to the student of them. Moreover, we insist not only upon bias in the selection, but upon *systematic* bias. The more systematic the bias—that is, the better the logical structure used as a basis for selection—the more likely are the selected events to be understood satisfactorily.

In this book we have used economic theory as a basis for selecting from the whole kaleidoscope of human experience those patterns that combine to make an intelligent picture of American economic development. Our analysis purports to study and explain only those events within our chosen province.

What about the second complaint that history is worthless as a guide to the future? We do not claim that history repeats itself. But neither do we agree that experience is useless. The history of our economic development is our experience in this vital area of human endeavor. Since we are, to date, the most affluent economy in history, our experience ought to be of some use to ourselves and to others. We do not necessarily expect to experience again the problems that faced the American economy in the past. Nor do we expect that other economies will face, in the process of development, the same problems we faced. But so long as economic scarcity exists, we expect that the solutions found in the past will be relevant information to those seeking to solve the problems of the future. Even our knowledge of errors in the past will hopefully aid us, and others, in avoiding similar ones in the future. We think there are lessons, if only negative ones, in history. One need only to know how to find them.

25–2. *American Economic Development*

Let us now briefly recapitulate, in very broad and general terms, the main features of our own experience in economic development. Then we will ask what these experiences might suggest about our own future and our relations with the rest of the world—both the developed and underdeveloped parts.

Perhaps the single most outstanding feature in our economic development has been the thoroughgoing revolutionary impact of technological change and the willingness of the people to adjust to the change. American society has been one that has aggressively initiated change of all sorts, but especially technological change, and has then been willing to make the sometimes painful adjustments required by the change. In this way the balance of our economic life has been constantly shifting. The great growth of our population and labor force has not been based upon any straightforward growth of occupations or even of economic areas. The occupational and income distribution of the working population has changed ceaselessly. Similarly, new centers of industrial power have grown up, some at the expense of areas which had earlier been in the vanguard of economic growth.

All of this change, except for the demands of government, has of course been intimately associated with changes in consumer tastes over time. Consumption of goods and services by our growing population has determined profitability in economic activity, and hence the flow of resources. This fact explains many of the paradoxes in our economic growth; i.e., what isn't profitable isn't done, or at least not by private enterprise. For this reason, most of our "social-overhead" investments—roads, schools, libraries, and so forth—have not been developed primarily as private undertakings. That they exist at all in an economy like ours is a tribute to the balanced judgment of our people. These investments had to be undertaken, one by one, as conscious acts of will by the population as a whole in the general interest—the private economy makes no provisions for nonprofit investment. In both cases it is clear that "progress" has been produced by a people fortunate enough to be progressive in science, the arts, and in political and social organization. Economic progress was not automatically associated with the state of science; it had to be initiated and made into a way of life.

A further example of our good fortune in having a mature people accustomed to acting upon long-run judgments by orderly means can be found in the nondogmatic role of government in the history of our economic development. Despite wild claims and assertions by extremists of every variety, we have in fact generally used the collective power of the state where it has seemed to be expedient and, for the most part, in the interests of growth. In the development of judicial and regulatory powers we have been a moderate people, just as we have been in the balance between the consumption and social-overhead sectors of the economy.

Now it is obvious that our methods of dealing with future economic problems may differ, even quite radically, from those of our history. But there will doubtless be many similarities, too. Men only rarely strike out in altogether new directions, and our history gives us many precedents. We have a tradition that provides us with bench marks and indicates for us the broad limits of policies that are not inimical to our accepted constitutional practices.

Not only does history give us information for domestic policy making, but to some extent we learn from it important lessons about the world economy. Our long experience of economic relations with the industrial nations is another source of guidance for us in the future. We know from our experience that economic growth has been even more rapid when developing countries have been willing to specialize and trade with each other. Such trade has been one of the main vehicles of progress. In this connection, we have seen how, for a century and a half, the American economy has used the world marketplace to sell its surplus and to buy what it did not supply. We know that the future can be one of expanding markets if productivity continues to rise in the economically developed countries and if we continue to take advantage of this through relatively unrestricted trade. There is every reason to suppose that such a future is a realistic expectation. Our history has shown us the clear advantages of specialization and trade on the basis of comparative advantage, and, as we noted earlier, in recent years there has been a lively realization of these advantages among American industrialists.

25–3. *Underdeveloped Economies*

One problem looming large in America's economic (as well as political) future is that of economic underdevelopment. Here our own history is of use to us, but not in the same way as it is in connection with industrial countries. As much as two thirds of the earth's population, living in Asia, Africa, and Latin America, exist in a state of dire poverty. Some believe the future of mankind will be decided by the fate of these peoples. Our relations with these peoples pose very difficult problems. We can probably learn more from American history about what *cannot* be done in the underdeveloped countries than we can about what can be done to solve their problems. But, as we will see, even this indirect use of our own experience can be worthwhile.

On the basis of American experience we might make some straightforward recommendations. We might recommend, for instance, that the Indian economy should plan to emphasize the following things to achieve development: building a large-scale internal-transportation network, establishing a set of national financial institutions, consolidating agricultural production, moving resources out of agriculture into manufacturing, and constructing large-scale basic manufacturing complexes. The difficulty with such a prescription is primarily twofold. First, we are not sure how necessary for *all* economic development the ingredients are. Second, the economies that are presently developed are not a random sample of all economies. What has been good for them may not necessarily be good for others. It is important to recall that Britain and her North American colonies, France, and other industrial Western countries were not as economically underdeveloped 200 years ago as are India, Indonesia, China, and the other underdeveloped countries today.

Moreover the other ingredients, cultural and social, that existed in Western Europe and North America are not present in the underdeveloped countries. We do not know that, once started, development toward an American-style economy in India (for example) would lead in the end to the desired result. Latin America, to cite a case in point, is strewn with long-established but unsuccessful efforts to reach an American-style economy by the same methods used in American development.

Requirements for development differ according to the cultural and social heritage of a nation as well as to its resources and the state of science. We can certainly see how unplanned development might not succeed in backward countries elsewhere in the same fashion that it did in the United States. Also, the laissez faire approach that existed in the developing countries of Western Europe during the nineteenth century may not be appropriate in development programs for underdeveloped countries today. In the nineteenth century there were resources to waste and vast markets to satisfy, and mistakes did not bring disastrous consequences. In fact, our understanding of the uniqueness of the conditions surrounding American and European economic development in the nineteenth century is one of the most important contributions made by a study of our own development. We can see the great freedom those rich resource endowments, liberal governments, burgeoning markets, and technological advances gave us.

An underdeveloped economy today, especially one overburdened with population, has no such freedom. Some form of overall design, assigning priorities to projects and carefully husbanding the nation's available resources, is in most cases a necessity. The economy that fritters away its limited resources and productive effort on projects with no lasting benefit will find itself severely handicapped in the race for development. We do not mean by this that the underdeveloped economy necessarily should move wholeheartedly in the direction of a centralized economy. We have too much faith in the efficiency of a privately operated economic system. But it is apparent that for many economically backward countries there will need to be some central planning to avoid an excessive flow of resources into purely short-run speculative ventures. The general requirements of social-overhead investment doubtless will need to be met by the political authority.

The degree of government supervision required in an underdeveloped economy will depend partly upon the number of people in the economy with managerial abilities. In some countries, colonial powers have left behind the nucleus of a managerial group capable of running national economic organizations. In other countries, no such nucleus exists and the problems of transforming a tribal economy to a national economic system can only be undertaken with extensive use of government power. It is essential that the use of government power have the support of the population. The changes that will be required of the population are tremendous and will increase, say exponentially, with the speed with which the development process is undertaken. In the absence of widespread public support, and such is perhaps too much to ask of backward peoples, many new countries find the ex-colonial powers convenient "whipping-boys" in cementing a national feeling and orienting the population toward the goal of economic reform.

As we have emphasized before, a nation's people is its most vital economic resource. To drag a people unwillingly into modern economic life can only lead to turmoil and tremendous waste. However, even the most willing people are of little use unless they are trained in the new methods of production associated with an industrial society. For this reason, the economic plan by which development is to proceed must contain provisions for education and training. With education and training the people can be permitted wider areas of economic and political freedom; they can be trusted to manage their own destiny.

Along with the improvement of the human resource must come the improvement of the natural resource base. The government should do all in its power to make an accurate inventory of the raw materials available and to encourage the use of such resources. Some resources may be found that command a ready market (such as oil) and the exploitation of such resources should be facilitated either by inviting foreign companies to invest in the country or by diverting domestic resources to the task. Government financing of transportation and harbor facilities may do a great deal to invite private capital, domestic or foreign, into a region. Agricultural resources are equally important. In some cases it takes relatively little research to find more efficient ways of farming that lead to spectacular increases in farm productivity. Scientific animal breeding, development of new crops, simple fertilization, and different methods of cultivation can lead to large-scale increases in farm output.

If the development scheme operates successfully, output per capita will begin to rise and more problems will emerge. People accustomed to existing with but a tenuous hold on life find themselves possessed of something "extra." How will they react to their changed circumstances? If the reaction is to increase the number of children to meet the increased output, the whole painful process must be begun again. Some countries have found that development programs have led, at least in the short run, merely to an increased population and no change in living standards. The same result may occur if health measures are introduced that make the population more productive and longer-lived, but not sufficiently more productive to lead to any increase in per-capita output.

Assume, however, that a maintained increase in output per capita is achieved. If growth is to continue, and foreign governments express no willingness to continue aid indefinitely, then the population must be willing to save part of its output to devote to capital formation. The introduction of trustworthy financial institutions will go some way toward encouraging such thrift. Some countries have experimented with direct expropriation, taxation, or currency inflation as a means of financing capital formation. Such methods, however put the job of investment directly in government hands, and there are circumstances in which such activity can better be handled by the private sector.

At some point the development process, if it continues, will become self-sustaining. The people will accept the changes required of them; they will willingly work to achieve high per-capita outputs; they will save and invest to develop their resources; and they will acquire the scientific knowledge that will open up further vistas for development. Economic development is a desirable end and we should be willing and eager to do all we can to encourage it throughout the world. At the same time, we should not be too surprised if peoples of different cultures develop in different patterns than we did. In fact, if we could look forward to a time when all people are members of a uniform economic and political system, one wonders if the process would be worthwhile. Rather than insist that people do as we did, we might well encourage them to develop in their own way, taking from us or borrowing from others that which is valuable to them and adapting the rest to their own environment. This, after all, is what we did with our European heritage and with the native American culture.

Finally, two factors that stand out in our study of American development are worth emphasizing once more in connection with our discussion of underdevelopment. First, economic development is an exceedingly complex phenomenon; and second, it takes time to come to fruition. Development thrives best the more pervasive its effects within the economy, preferably when it embraces everything from basic agriculture to the most sophisticated scientific research programs. Success tends to be contagious, but it is not instantaneous. The one indisputable lesson the history of American development has for the world is that, in spite of the difficulty, successful economic development rewards the population involved with the physical means to a better life.

Index

INDEX

G

H

I

V

W

This book has been set on the Linotype in 11 point Caledonia, leaded 2 points, and 10 point Caledonia, leaded 1 point. Part and chapter numbers and titles are in 18 point Spartan Medium. The size of the type page is 27 by 46½ picas.